Fifth Edition

100

B E S T

Romantic Resorts
of the World

KATHARINE D. DYSON

The
Globe
Pequot
Press

GUILFORD, CONNECTICUT

To buy books in quantity for corporate use
or incentives, call **(800) 962–0973, ext. 4551,**
or e-mail **premiums@GlobePequot.com.**

Text design: Mary Ballachino
Photo layout: Sue Preneta

ISSN 1540-6822
ISBN 0-7627-3435-3

Manufactured in the United States of America
Fifth Edition/First Printing

The prices, rates, and general information listed in this guidebook were confirmed at press time but under no circumstances are they guaranteed. We recommend that you call establishments before making firm travel plans to obtain current information. This recommendation especially applies to resorts in the Caribbean, the Bahamas, and Cancun, where recent hurricanes have left a wide swath of damage in their wake.

Fifth Edition

100
B E S T
Romantic Resorts
of the World

a photo essay

Post Ranch Inn  Amanpuri

Bora Bora Lagoon
Resort & Spa   Château de
la Chèvre d'Or

Cap Juluca   Windjammer Landing
Villa Beach Resort
& Spa

Inn of the Anasazi   Amanwana

Cambridge Beaches   The Fairmont Chateau
Lake Louise

Amangani  The Boulders

MalaMala  Hotel Hana-Maui
and Honua Spa

AUTHOR'S THANKS

Because the quality of a resort can change dramatically in a short time, I have ensured that each place comes with a first-person, recent recommendation, preferably (and in most cases) mine. However, because of the time constraints involved in researching and writing such a book, it would have been physically impossible for me to personally revisit each of the one hundred resorts within the allotted time frame and still get the material to the publisher on deadline. Thus I am indebted to many fellow travel writers and others who have generously helped me put together an accurate, up-to-date account of these one hundred most romantic resorts around the globe.

My deepest appreciation to the following people who helped me update this fifth edition: Anamary Pelayo, for her profiles of Amangani and Snake River Lodge & Spa in Wyoming; Risa Weinreb, for her contributions in Hawaii and Tahiti; Christopher Pinckney and Cathy, for Sandals St. Lucia; and Merrie Murray, for Four Seasons Maui. Thanks also to Virginia Haynes-Montgomery, of BCA Commmunications; Marilyn Marx, of Marilyn Marx PR; Ellin Ginsburg; Frank "Poncho" Shiell, for help in Zihuatanejo; Richard Kahn, of Kahn Travel Communications; Norman Pieters, of Karell's African Dream Vacations; Karen Hoffman, for her Africa expertise; Kristin Wherry, of PPR; Rosann Valentini, of Relais & Châteaux; Karen Preston, of Leading Hotels of the World; Alice Marshall, Christa Guidi, and Gillian Garfinkle of Alice Marshall Public Relations; Mara Begley of MMG Mardiks; Brooke Lawer of Virgin Atlantic Airways; Virginia M. Sheridan of M. Silver Associates; Martin Armes of Greater Raleigh CVB; and Holly Wood, of Fairmont Hotels. Also thanks to Elizabeth Taylor, managing editor, Mimi Egan, senior editor, and Sue Preneta, photo editor, at Globe Pequot Press for their patience and hard work. Thanks also to avid travelers who took time to share their resort experiences with me, including Jack and Jeanne Klinge, Bill and Terry Delavan, Doug and Georgina Pinckney, Michael Pinckney, Bill Giering, and Dave Cornwell.

CONTENTS

INTRODUCTION

In preparing the material for the fifth edition of *100 Best Romantic Resorts of the World,* I have noticed a couple of new trends: an increasing number of smaller, boutique-style resorts, the growth of in-house spa facilities, and the addition of Wi-Fi services.

Since the last edition, I have continued to travel widely, discovering many wonderful resorts to tell you about, places that extend a heartwarming welcome without overpowering you by being intrusive. When I check into a hotel, I am not looking to find a "new best friend." I don't need someone knocking on my door every ten minutes to replace towels or do a turndown when I've just stepped into the shower. With the really cool resorts, your needs are taken care of, your bed is made, and the dirty glasses replaced but you haven't a clue when it happened.

Really comfortable beds, linens, and pillows are so important. No matter how great the room looks, if the bed is lumpy, the linens coarse or worn, or the pillow a Flintstone throwback, your beauty rest may be hard to come by. Frette linens are nice, but there are others that work just as well; a good hotelier knows what they are. Down duvets, white goose down pillows, and quality options for those who are allergic are important, too. Some resorts even offer a pillow menu.

Another of my pet peeves (now that I'm on a roll) is a pretentious staff. A satisfying resort experience has nothing to do with glitz or pretension. And little things count. I like good lights on either side of the bed, a full-length mirror, plenty of light in the bathroom, hooks on the back of the bathroom door, and hangers that do not require Houdini to get them off the rod.

Above all, a smile goes a long way.

Each of the "100 Best Romantic Resorts of the World" has unique, special qualities—some may even be a bit quirky. In my travels and research, I came across some marvelous places that perhaps didn't quite fit the definition of a full-service resort. Nonetheless, because they are especially romantic and may be just what you're looking for, I've included them in the book.

Each of the 100 Best is characterized by the following:

1. Has a romantic setting
2. Rates best in category/region for overall quality
3. Caters primarily to vacationers seeking recreation, entertainment, and escape from the "real world"
4. Is easy to reach
5. Is in a safe location
6. Provides excellent, friendly service
7. Has one or more restaurants on or within walking distance of the property
8. Is spiffy clean and superbly maintained
9. Appeals to couples in love
10. Offers good value

Romantic setting. This is highly subjective. What will it be? A cabin in the woods, a castle on a hilltop, an over-the-water bungalow, a thatched beachfront cottage? I invite you to browse through these profiles and decide for yourself.

Best in category. It might have made my job easier had I simply selected the most expensive and exclusive places in each region. Expense doesn't necessarily add up to value, though, and since many honeymooners are just starting out, I've included a number of reasonably priced resorts as well as the pricier hotels to give you a range of choices— all which represent the best in their price category for ambience and quality.

Recreation, entertainment, and escape. These resorts are more than just a place to spend the night. Most have pools and/or beaches for swimming, tennis courts, and fitness facilities. Recreation covers a wide spectrum—it might be skiing, hiking, horseback riding, sailboarding, or croquet—and entertainment could be anything from soft piano music to disco. The bottom line is that these resorts cater to travelers who are on vacation, rather than on a business trip. The 100 Best exist for fun and romance.

Easy to reach. The majority of the resorts in this book are within reasonable traveling distance of North America. This is particularly important for honeymooners. After all the excitement of the wedding festivities, you could very well be exhausted. It would help if your trip to your destination is a quick and easy one. I have, however, included some properties in exotic faraway places for those who feel adventurous and have the time.

Safe location. You want to feel safe and secure. Going to an iffy area with a history of turbulence is not a good idea if you want to relax and simply enjoy each other. The 100 Best are located in what are considered (at press time) safe, stable areas. If you have any questions, you can check the U.S. Travel Advisories available on the internet. Remember that no matter where you go, you should always take necessary precautions, such as putting your money in traveler's checks, stowing cash in two or three different places, and bringing along an ATM card, often the best way to get additional cash abroad. Carry all the "must have" items with you on the plane (don't

check them with your luggage) and put your valuable items in the hotel safe. Better yet, leave expensive jewelry at home, and you won't have to worry about it.

Excellent, friendly service. When you order room service at 3:00 A.M., you'd like to get your order before the sun rises. When your waiter greets you at the table, it would be nice to see a smile. All these things help to enhance your resort experience.

Choice of restaurants. It's good to have two or more places to eat, ranging from gourmet/formal to casual. A range of prices, ambience, and kinds of cuisine is also important. The most important element, however, is good food, whether the resort has one restaurant or several, or is located in an area where there are several good restaurants.

Clean and superbly maintained. There's nothing like a leaky faucet dripping in the middle of the night or a dust ball behind a chair to turn the romance level down a notch or two. The 100 Best get high ratings in the cleanliness and maintenance departments.

Appeals to couples in love. Now here's where it gets tricky. I discovered some great resorts that met all my other criteria except this one. Perhaps the kids took over the pool most of the day. Or the resort was just too exclusive, geared to the hopelessly well-off and out of reach to all but 2 percent of our readers (who probably already know where they are jetting off to and don't need anyone to tell them where to go). Resorts like these didn't make it.

Good value. Very important. I tried to eliminate any place that was unreasonable or doing the "big rip-off." If prices are steep to begin with and you know it, you can budget for it. If rates at first sound reasonable and then the cash register starts ringing up every time you go waterskiing, play an hour of tennis, or walk into the nightclub, your good deal starts to drift into the sunset. Whenever possible, I have listed romance packages and other plans that give you the biggest bang for your buck. And remember: Even if a package is not listed in the book, ask the resort if it offers any special plans, such as ones for tennis, scuba diving, or golf. Many do; they just may not promote them.

One of the best bets for some budget-minded travelers is the all-inclusive resort, where one price pays for everything, including drinks, meals, and sports activities. No surprises here at checkout time.

HELPFUL TIPS FOR USING THIS BOOK

Each resort profile in this guide begins with a complete description of the resort, including its special features, ambience, décor, cuisine, and activities offered. Following the description is a section of at-a-glance information about the resort—types of accommodations, rates, sports and facilities available, and so on. Most of this information is self-explanatory, but the following clarification of a few items should help you utilize this book to the fullest as you plan your romantic holiday.

Rates: Each resort has its own unique way of putting together its rate schedule. Although I have tried to give you the rates in as consistent a manner as possible, you will see several variations on such details as seasons—some offer special rates, some do not. In some cases package rates are quoted. I have given you my best shot in describing these rates so that you can understand what is and is not offered.

Following are terms used throughout the book in reference to rates.

Rack Rates: Published rates—usually the top retail price without any discounts

MAP: Modified American Plan; includes accommodations, breakfast, and dinner

AP: American Plan; includes accommodations, breakfast, lunch, and dinner

EP: European Plan; includes no meals

Package Rates: Promotional packages geared in some cases to specific-interest groups such as honeymooners. Most include a number of extra features such as champagne and room upgrade.

All-Inclusive: Usually this means that the rate includes accommodations, all meals, sports, and other activities. A truly all-inclusive rate will include all beverages, including name-brand liquors; some even include the wedding ceremony. Occasionally resorts advertise an all-inclusive rate but still make you pay for your beverages. Read the fine print and make sure you know what you're buying.

Room Upgrade: This means getting a better room than you paid for. It is dependent on whether one is available and is usually not guaranteed. If you are on your honeymoon, tell the resort manager. Upgrades are often given to newlyweds.

Seasonal Rates: Prices are geared to the time of year and can vary widely from hotel to hotel. The high season is the most expensive and is the time when the resort is the busiest. In the Caribbean this means the colder months; in Europe it's usually spring, summer, and fall; in New England it is usually foliage season; and in Bermuda, it's summer. Christmastime is also considered high season by many places. Low-season rates are the least expensive and are available when the resort is not in such great demand. Some resorts do not use season designations but instead give you a schedule of periods during the year with corresponding rates. Some offer just one year-round rate. ("Shoulder" season rates are those between high and low.)

Deposit: Deposit and refund policies vary greatly with each hotel. Some require only a guarantee with a credit card. Typically you get your money back if you cancel within a particular period. Check with the hotel and be sure you understand their policy.

Exchange Rates: You'll find that some of the rates in this book are in U.S. dollars, others in local currency. Often when the hotel has a U.S. representative, you'll find rates quoted in U.S. dollars. Some hotels, however, quote only in their local money. For these we have provided an approximate rate in U.S. dollars. To convert to U.S. dollars, look up the exchange rate in the daily paper (usually in the business section) or on the Internet.

Arrival/Departure: Transfers mentioned under this item refer to the resort's arrangements from getting you from and to the airport—by bus, boat, van, private car, or otherwise.

Weddings: If you want to get married at your honeymoon destination, make sure you inquire well ahead of time as to residency requirements, documents required, etc. Your travel agent, resort, and/or country tourism office representative in the United States can help you with this. Many resorts offer the services of an in-house wedding planner.

A Note about Electricity: Dual-voltage appliances such as hair dryers often have a special switch that allows you to convert to either 110 or 220 volts. You will also, however, need a special plug for your appliances when traveling to many places out of the country. Hardware stores usually sell these plugs in sets.

TIPS FOR THOSE PLANNING A HONEYMOON

Attention to the following details can make the difference between having an OK honeymoon and a great one.

1. Book a late flight the morning after the wedding, when possible.

2. Know what your budget is and work within these limits. If money is tight, look into an all-inclusive resort, where you know ahead of time what you'll spend. Many resorts sound reasonably priced until you add up all the extra charges. Checkout time can be a mind-blower.

3. Book the best room you can afford. Complaints from returning honeymooners tend to focus on the quality of their accommodations.

4. Ask about bed size. In some parts of the world, double beds may be smaller than what you'd expect. In Europe you'll find a lot of twin-bedded rooms, so if you're Europe-bound, you might want to ask for a "matrimonial bed."

5. Both the bride and the groom should take part in deciding where to go and how much to spend.

6. Unless you want to keep your honeymoon a secret, let the hotel know ahead of time that you are newly married (your travel agent can do this for you). Honeymooners often enjoy special perks, such as champagne and breakfast in bed.

7. It is often helpful to be in the travel agent's office while your room is being booked so that you can answer any questions the hotel might have.

8. If being directly on the beach overlooking the water is very important to you, make sure the room you book is just that. Sometimes properties advertised as "beachfront hotels" are in reality not right on the beach, but close by. Rooms may also have a view of the garden instead of the water.

9. Ask about the best way to get from the airport to your resort. Are you being met? Do you need to look for someone

in particular? How much is a taxi or van service?

10. If you are renting a car, find out ahead of time about insurance requirements. Check with your credit card company to see if you are covered by collision damage waiver.

11. Check what travel documentation you will need and get everything in order. Carry two forms of photo identification in two separate places. If you lose one, you'll still be able to get on the plane with the other. Remember a valid photo ID is required to board. No ID, no flight.

12. On international travel it is good to fax hotels a few days before your arrival date to reconfirm your arrangements. This is particularly important when the booking was made well in advance. This is one vacation you want to make sure runs like clockwork. Your travel agent should do this for you, but be sure to request that it be done.

13. I highly recommend purchasing trip cancellation insurance. If you have to cancel for any reason (heaven forbid), you'll get your deposit back. Ask your travel agent about this.

14. If you are traveling to a place such as Africa or the South Pacific, check with your doctor or local health authority to find out if you need any special inoculations or medicines to take either prior to or during your trip. In some areas you must show proof that you are up to date on certain disease-preventing immunizations (e.g., yellow fever and malaria) in order to enter the country.

15. If you are not leaving for your vacation destination until a day or two after your wedding, you may want to stay at a relaxing, romantic inn on your first night. Most couples find they are quite exhausted after the festivities and need some time to unwind.

16. Book your airline seats at the same time you make plane reservations. This is also the time to order special meals if you have any dietary restrictions.

HONEYMOON COUNTDOWN

Don't wait until the last minute to plan your honeymoon. Good groundwork can really pay off when it comes to lining up the perfect romantic holiday. Here are some guidelines.

- Five months before your wedding: Select a travel agent, read up on destinations, and nail down your budget. Be sure to include spending money in your calculations.

- Four months: Decide where you're going and book your reservations with your travel agent.

- Three months: Get your travel documents together. Allow up to six weeks to process the paperwork for a new passport. Applications are available at the main branch of your local post office and at U.S. government passport agencies.

- Two months: Get your confirmation numbers for hotel, airlines, rental cars, and so forth.

- One month to one week: Purchase film for your camera. Check to make sure your camera batteries are working. Get out the converter plugs for your hair dryer, and so on, or purchase them from a hardware store. Confirm your reservations and get your traveler's checks.

This book offers a wide range of resorts to choose from. You and your partner should look through it individually and select a few establishments that appeal to each of your tastes. Then compare notes and narrow down the list to the ones that sound wonderful to both of you. The next step is to contact your travel agent for brochures and more information.

TIPS FOR PACKING

1. Plan ahead. Think layers. Temperatures in many areas can soar one day, plunge the next.

2. Limit your color choices to basics. Grey, white, black, and beige work. Add color with silk scarves, belts and jewelry.

3. Take costume jewelry. Take nothing you couldn't bear losing unless you wear it all the time.

4. Bring no more than three pairs of shoes unless you want to squeeze in a pair of sandals.

5. Pack mix-and-match outfits—shirts, slacks, etc.—that can be worn two or more times in different combinations.

6. Wear your bulkiest (and most comfortable) things on the plane.

7. Think silk, tencel, and anything that is thin and will not wrinkle easily.

8. Pack or wear a basic all-purpose jacket. Black works great.

9. Don't carry large bottles of anything. Use small bottles, containers, and plastic bags. Film cartridge canisters are handy for things like pills and pins.

10. Put together a mini-medicine kit (just in case), and carry it in a small sandwich-size baggie.

11. Before you pack, lay out on your bed everything you want to take. Put aside all those things that you absolutely can't live without. Pack them. Put everything else back in the closet.

12. Take a midsize wheely bag and a small carry-on. Bring nothing you cannot easily move yourself and preferably carry on the plane. Movability is flexibility. And remember that cars in Europe are smaller than most of those in the United States.

13. Check out special travel collections featuring clothes and other items available by catalogue and on the Net from companies such as Travel Smith and L.L. Bean Travel.

My hope is that your holiday will be far more romantic than you ever dreamed; that you'll have the opportunity to get off the beaten track and create memories that will last a lifetime as you discover what is unique and special about a place, its people, and its traditions.

If you have any suggestions for how this guide could be improved, please feel free to e-mail your comments to editorial@globe pequot.com (please put the book title in the subject line of your e-mail message). Or you can send them to The Globe Pequot Press, Reader Response, P.O. Box 480, Guilford, Connecticut 06437.

UNITED STATES

THE BOULDERS
Arizona

As you approach the resort, you see just ahead some huge, reddish boulders. At first you don't see the resort itself—it blends so well into its environment. Individual casitas are molded into the terrain; colors blend perfectly. Here and there you catch a view of the golf courses with their green tees and greens looking very much like neat toupees sitting on the red-tan desert ground. This is the Boulders, one of the country's most romantic resorts.

You know you are in the desert. The air is hot yet dry. The days are sunny and warm, the nights cool. The sky goes on forever. Giant fingers of the saguaros, several times as tall as you are and much older, stick up out of the desert scrub, silhouetted against the brilliant sunset skies and morning sunrises.

Granite boulders, their edges rounded and smoothed by millions of years of wear, sit one atop another in a bit of a hodge-podge, just as they have lain for centuries, like silent sentries watching over the desert. Tucked in the crevices and cracks and rooted in the land are the flowers and plants of this rich desert environment.

The 160 casitas, made of earth-tone adobe, were hand-molded and rubbed to follow the contours of the rocks, and, like the ancient boulders themselves.

Each individual casita has a sitting area and fireplace, private patio or deck, a mini-bar, a large tiled bath with a vanity, and comfortable leather chairs, ottomans, and sofas upholstered in flame stitch and earthy fabrics reflecting the rich colors and patterns of the desert. Stone floors, hand-hewn beamed ceilings, area rugs, baskets, clay pots, and regional art objects and paintings add to the Southwestern ambience. Lights are perfectly placed for reading or for romance. And many of the Indian weavings and paintings hanging on the walls are for sale—just ask.

Life at the Boulders revolves around the main lodge, the pool, and the two superb golf courses. A trail nearby leads up a steep, rocky hill; at the top you get sweeping views of the beautiful Sonoran Desert with its armies of erect saguaro cactus and low-growing bushes and flowers.

In the main lounge a lofty ceiling has been installed using the latilla and viga method of construction: Spokes of wood radiate from a center "pole" much like a giant umbrella. Adobe walls are brightened by original artwork, such as an 1890s chief's blanket and antique tapestries.

Every evening as the sun goes down and things get cooler, the giant fireplace inside the lodge and the one just outside the entrance are lit, sending the sweet spicy odor of shaggy juniper into the air. The aroma lingers the next day, buoyed by additional fires in the restaurants and casitas.

The five restaurants at the Boulders place a strong emphasis on healthful eating. You can enjoy food such as mesquite-grilled meats and fish, roast range chicken, anchiote-basted veal chop with sun-dried tomato orzo, grilled salmon and quesadilla with Anaheim chiles. The chef seeks out local farmers who produce organically grown fruits and vegetables, finds sources for fresh meat and special seafood items like "diver scallops," and harvests such things as cactus fruits right from the desert.

You really don't have to leave the grounds to find both a variety of restaurants and a change in moods. Through its large windows the Latilla restaurant affords marvelous views of the Sonoran landscape and a softy lit waterfall. The Palo Verde restaurant, with its colorful exhibition kitchen, features Southwestern cuisine.

The informal Rusty's at the Club, located in the golf course clubhouse, is a popular choice for lunch and dinner, and you can eat in the main dining room. You also can stay "home" and enjoy a private breakfast or dinner on your balcony or patio or get cozy in front of your fireplace while the wood fire blazes away.

The Boulders' two excellent golf courses have been carefully integrated into the landscape. One ancient cactus sits smack in the center of a rather formidable sand-trap. These are true desert courses: No plants are growing here that are not indigenous to the area, and local grasses are used that require much less water than the type normally associated with golf courses. Named by *Golf* magazine as a Gold Medal Golf Resort 1988–2004, The Boulders treats its players to stunning vistas from elevated tees—on one hole you actually tee off from the top of a boulder.

In addition to the two golf courses, the Boulders Club, a private country club reserved exclusively for resort guests and club members, includes a tennis center with eight tennis courts, including three classic clay courts and five premier cushion courts, a pro shop, and another pool. Clinics and private lessons are offered daily.

The Boulders is home to the Golden Door Spa, a 33,000-square-foot facility. A sibling to the original Golden Door in Escondido, California, this luxury spa blends eastern and western influences in its architectural design, healing methods, treatments, and philosophies. Here you'll find a labyrinth for reflection, fitness center, movement studio, and classroom for wellness lectures.

For the ultimate romantic indulgence, book the spa's couples' suite with views of the desert garden. Share a relaxing Golden Door aromatherapy or reflexology massage and, to enhance the treatment, enjoy your own private pool.

You can explore the area on horseback or hike on the Apache Trail, which passes by lakes, volcanic rock formations, and awesome buttes. You can take a sunset jeep tour or a moonlight horseback ride. Or tackle the desert trails on foot or bike; ask for a special hike and gourmet picnic lunch designed just for the two of you. You can spend hours in the colorful market area, El Pedregal, which contains more than thirty-five boutiques, restaurants, and art galleries, plus an amphitheater.

Just as any great resort cannot stand on its physical beauty and facilities alone, the Boulders goes to the top of the class for its personal people skills. You are greeted warmly on your arrival, and if you come back for more visits (and you will), you are remembered and catered to.

The Boulders

Location: Nestled in the high Sonoran Desert northeast of Phoenix and Scottsdale, Arizona, on 1,300 acres

Romantic Highlights: Vast beauty of the desert setting; fireplaces in your private casita; hikes on the magnificent grounds; balloon rides over the desert

Address/Phone: P.O. Box 2090, 34631 North Tom Darlington Drive, Carefree, AZ 85377; (480) 488–9009; fax (480) 488–4118

Web Site: www.wyndham.com

U.S. Reservations: (800) 553–1717

Owner/Manager: Gary Gutierrez, general manager

Arrival/Departure: Pickup at either the Scottsdale or the Phoenix Airport can be arranged.

Distance from Scottsdale Airport: 13 miles (30 minutes); 33 miles from Phoenix Sky Harbor Airport

Distance from Phoenix: 16 miles

Accommodations: 160 adobe-style guest casitas; 55 one-, two-, and three-bedroom Pueblo Villas

Most Romantic Room/Suite: If you like water views, try one of the casitas near the end, overlooking the pond

Amenities: Air-conditioning, ceiling fans, wood-burning fireplace, minibar, large dressing area, TV, toiletries, padded hangers, umbrella, room service, telephone, robes

Electricity: 110 volts

Sports and Facilities: 2 championship 18-hole golf courses; tennis park, featuring 8 tennis courts (3 classic clay) and pro shop; fitness center with aerobic studio, weight room, heated outdoor lap pool, hiking pro-

gram; desert jeep tours, hot air ballooning, rock climbing, horseback riding; Golden Door Spa

Dress Code: Casually smart

Weddings: Can be arranged

Rates/Packages: $279–$649 per room for casitas; $435–$799 for a one-bedroom/den pueblo villa. Golden Door Romance, $970–$1,490, including 2 nights' casita accommodations, breakfasts, dinner, couples' massage in the Golden Door couples' suite, and a butler-drawn bath

Payment/Credit Cards: Most major

Deposit: 2-night deposit or half the package rate to be applied to first and last night's stay. Cancel 3 weeks in advance of arrival date for full refund.

Government Taxes: 11.92 percent room tax; 7.95 percent sales tax

Service Charges: $27 per night in lieu of cash gratuities for all resort personnel, excluding food and beverage, and daily entrance to the Golden Door Spa.

CAMELBACK INN
Arizona

We drove up to the inn when the sun was just setting, lending a bronze burnish to the desert landscape with Camelback Mountain black against the sky. The silhouette of tall cacti and palms lined the walkways leading to adobe-style casitas, the spa, and gardens that spread out over 125 acres.

With 330 days of sunshine each year, is it any wonder that this area is called the Valley of the Sun? Certainly a perfect place for a resort. And that's exactly what young entrepreneur Jack Stewart thought as he set to work in the early 1930s to put together

financing for his new resort. When Stewart first opened Camelback Inn in 1936, there were just seventy-five rooms at rates ranging from $10 to $25 a night. In the inn's Spanish cantina, you could buy margaritas for 30 cents, beer for 25 cents, and afternoon tea for 75 cents. The resort was an immediate success, becoming a favorite with celebrities like Mrs. Dwight D. Eisenhower, Clark Gable, Jimmy Stewart, and Bette Davis. In 1967 Stewart sold his resort to J.W. Marriott.

Today with 453 rooms, the resort continues to be a popular getaway spot for stars and celebs, as well as others who appreciate the privacy and quiet elegance of the surroundings. Casitas have private entrances, garden patios or balconies, and some come with private swimming pools, sundecks, and fireplaces. Rooms and suites are extremely spacious.

In our suite, a floor-to-ceiling double door separated the bedroom from the dressing area and bathroom, which featured a shower big enough to hold a party. Distinctive features included a corner fireplace and wet bar, dining and sitting areas. Native American artwork including pottery, sculpture, and woven tapestries, as well as carved wood beds and fabrics detailed with Native American designs in rich rusts, browns, and natural colors enhanced the desert ambience.

Although you may be tempted to stay in your room or suite and have a romantic dinner by the fireplace or on the patio, be sure to book a table one night at the Chaparral Supper Club. (Come early and you'll be rewarded with stunning sunset views of Camelback Mountain.) In addition to superb steak dishes, the menu features fresh seafood and chef-baked pastries. The wine cellar is stocked with more than 12,000 bottles, and you can order from a selection of more than forty wines by the glass. On the night we were there, we enjoyed the piano music of a local entertainer.

For more casual Southwestern fare, The Navajo serves breakfast, lunch, and dinner and prime rib and shrimp are big sellers at the nightly buffet. Lighter spa-style fare is served at Sprouts, located in the spa. The breakfast pita, a toasted wheat pita stuffed with a sauté of egg whites, turkey bacon, bell peppers, red onions, Roma tomatoes, spinach, and fresh organic herbs is delicious; the multi-grain waffles with fresh berries are also winners.

Other places to eat and drink include Kokopelli Cafe for great coffee, lattés, warm muffins, bagels, and yes, Krispy Kremes (eat outside at one of the tables on the patio); Rita's Taqueria & Bar serving margaritas, sangrias, and other cool drinks along with fresh tortillas and salads; and Hoppin' Jack's by the pool where you can get burgers, sandwiches, salads, and drinks.

On the property you can find plenty to do: Swim in three pools, play tennis, golf, hike, bike, and use the facilities of the 32,000-square-foot spa, which recently completed an $8 million renovation. This is a serious spa with thirty-two treatment rooms, spa boutique, wellness/fitness center, plunge pools, locker rooms, spa pool, and its own restaurant. The spa menu offers a full range of treatments and services, such as the hot stone massage, reflexology, shiatsu massage, facials, wraps, and adobe clay purification.

Nearby the resort's Club Course provides a challenging and fun round of golf without beating you up. Laid out in links style, it's easy to walk but carts are available. After a $16 million renovation Camelback Golf Club facilities now include the newly designed Resort Course by Arthur Hills, an attractive new Clubhouse, golf shop, and grill, as well as a practice range. The John Jacobs Practical Golf School is also located here.

If you feel adventurous, there are many things to do in the area including guided nature walks, hiking, horseback riding, jeep adventures, hot air ballooning over the desert, and river rafting. I suggest you take a day trip to Sedona, where the bright colors of layered red cliffs will blow you away. On the way stop at Montezuma's Castle, a number of caves carved into the rock face once used as homes by the Native Americans. A five-hour drive away is the seventh "Wonder of the World," the magnificent Grand Canyon, where you can go on nature hikes, mule rides down the canyon, scenic rim drives, and rafting on the Colorado River.

Camelback Inn

Location: Hunkers at the base of Mummy Mountain overlooking Camelback Mountain in the Sonoran Desert

Romantic Highlights: Fireplaces, huge showers for two, private bungalows, magic of the Sonoran Desert, on-site chapel

Address/Phone: 5402 East Lincoln Drive, Scottsdale, AZ 85253; (480) 948–1700; fax (480) 951–8469

Web Site: www.camelbackinn.com

U.S. Reservations: (800) 24–CAMEL

Owner/Manager: Wynn Tyner, general manager

Arrival/Departure: Most rent a car at the airport or just off the airport (which can be considerably cheaper) and drive to the resort.

Distance from Phoenix Sky Harbor International Airport: 10 miles

Accommodations: 453 rooms and suites in adobe-style casitas

Most Romantic Room/Suite: Suites with private patios and a view of Camelback Mountain

Amenities: Air-conditioning, hair dryer, telephones, cable TV with on-demand movies and video games, radio, CD player, alarm clock, ironing facilities, robes and slippers, designer toiletries, in-room dining, computer/fax hook-up, high-speed Internet access, in-room safe, kitchenettes, refrigerator/minibar, coffeemaker

Electricity: 110 volts

Sports and Facilities: 3 outdoor heated pools and whirlpools, tennis pavilion (6 all-weather courts, 5 lit for night play and 1 screened for private play), 2 18-hole golf courses, 9-hole pitch-and-putt course, full-service spa, hiking, biking, fitness club, shuffleboard, Ping Pong, basketball, sand volleyball, horseback riding, and skiing nearby

Dress Code: Casual; smart casual for the Chaparral Supper Club

Weddings: be arranged

Rates/Packages: $139–$489 for rooms; from $335 for suites; packages available

Payment/Credit Cards: Most major

Deposit: By credit card

Government Taxes: 11.92 percent room tax; 7.95 percent sales tax

Service Charges: None

HYATT REGENCY SCOTTSDALE RESORT
Arizona

For a hotel with 500 rooms, the Hyatt Regency Scottsdale Resort has an amazing feeling of intimacy, accomplished through superb design of space both in and out. With waterways winding through the landscape, a two-and-one-half-acre "Water Playground" featuring ten separate pools (including four cold plunge pools), twenty-eight fountains, and forty-seven waterfalls along with hundreds of palms, fir trees, hanging plants, and flowers, this is indeed a lush desert oasis.

The epicenter of the resort, the Fountain Court, is punctuated by giant saguaros, groves of palms, and huge ceramic containers filled with desert plants and flowers. At night glass columns light the way in the stunning "Water Playground." In the lobby two movable glass walls open to a three-story atrium with views of the pool, lake, golf course, and mountains.

Most of the rooms are located in the H-shaped four-story building, where individual sections center around five different garden courtyards, giving a sense of privacy and character. The incredibly romantic casitas are perched on the shore of the lagoon. Furnishings draw from a color palette of copper, eggplant, and sand, echoing the desert mood, along with granite, maple, stone, and wrought iron. Live cacti stand in pots, ceramic bowls and plates sit in niches, and original artwork, including tapestries, paintings, and sculpture, enhance guest rooms.

You will find art throughout the public areas as well—a rare feather mask from South America, a pair of handmade puppets from Thailand, hand-carved jade pieces. As you walk through the entrance to the pool, you'll pass through twelve-foot-wide sculptural gates, an original design by Christopher Sproat.

Stroll through the atriums and hallways and you'll find each area evokes the Southwestern environment and cultures. Among them Lagoons, the Heavens, the Sonoran Desert, Indian Peoples of the Southwest, the Plains Horse Culture, and A Tale of Hispania.

There are a variety of places to eat and drink, ranging from Vu to the casual Waterfall Juice Bar. At Vu, Hyatt's award-winning signature restaurant overlooking the lagoon, the menu features contemporary steak and seafood. Entrees include such items as veal tenderloin with lentils, roque-fort, and bacon; dry aged New York steak with cherries, swiss chard, and mustard; and black bass with eggplant, arugula, and chermoula.

Savor Venetian-inspired dishes at Ristorante Sandolo, eating indoors or out by the water (in fact you are nearly in the water) where you are entertained by singing servers and after dinner treated to a complimentary gondola ride through the resort's waterways. For casual fare try Squash Blossom, open for breakfast, lunch, and dinner. The Regency Club Lounge is open for a European-style breakfast, light refreshments in the afternoon, and evening hors d'oeuvres; there is an honor bar for those with Regency Club access.

Winding through the residential areas, the resort's three nine-hole golf courses—Lakes, Dunes, and Arroyo—are lush parkland layouts beautifully maintained and punctuated with gardens, wide wash areas, plenty of bunkers, and ponds. There are also tennis courts, bicycles, and the Spa Avania offering several treatments.

But this resort is more than just about lounging by the pool, getting massages, and playing golf or tennis. There is a spirit about the place that ties it to the land and the Native Americans who first lived here. Just off the lobby, in a cross-cultural effort between the resort and the Hopi tribe (and eventually with other tribes), the Learning Center lifts the lid on the rich cultural heritage of the native people. Here you can hear about the life and arts of the Hopis from cultural interpreters like Lance Polingyouma and Rod "Tsongomoki" Davis and you can visit the Native Heritage Seed Garden featuring about twenty-five plants that were grown in the Southwest centuries ago.

Dressed simply in green slacks and a crisp cream shirt, his shiny black hair pulled back into a ponytail, Lance Polingyouma, a

Hopi from Second Mesa and caretaker of the garden, proudly showed us the corn, cotton, St. John's Wort, sunflowers, chili peppers, and other crops. "Here it's all about touching, feeling, tasting, smelling," he said.

Hyatt is dedicated to similar programs. "We try to be careful to preserve and protect what people come here for in the first place," said Polingyouma. On Fridays guests are entertained by Native American dancers in the Fountain Court; flora and fauna tours of the Sonoran Desert are offered weekly; and other activities include native beadworking, weaving, clay whistle–making, whiskey tasting, and cooking demonstrations.

Hyatt Regency Scottsdale Resort

Location: Set against the McDowell Mountains on 27 acres, part of the 560-acre Gainey Ranch Resort development, in the Sonoran Desert

Romantic Highlights: Private lakeside casitas; fireplaces; rooftop lounging area; gondola rides on the lake; couples' massage in your room

Address/Phone: 7500 East Doubletree Ranch Road, Scottsdale, AZ 85258; (480) 444–1234

Web Site: www.hyatt.com

U.S. Reservations: (800) 55–HYATT or (800) 123–1234

Owner/Manager: David R. Phillips, general manager

Arrival/Departure: Most rent a car at the airport or just off the airport (which can be considerably cheaper) and drive to the resort; there is a Hertz rental car company located in the resort. There is also a scheduled Valley bus, shuttle, limo, and taxi service.

Distance from Phoenix Sky Harbor International Airport: 10 miles (25 minutes)

Distance from Phoenix: 10 minutes

Accommodations: 490 rooms and suites

Most Romantic Room/Suite: Waterfront casitas with living rooms, fireplaces, rooftop sitting area, and patios on the lagoon

Amenities: Air-conditioning, hair dryer, robes, in-room safes, two-speaker two-line telephones, data-port, high-speed Internet access, minibar, designer toiletries, 24-hour room service, gift shop; high-speed wireless network in the lobby, pool area, and Regency Club.

Electricity: 110 volts

Sports and Facilities: 2½ acres of swimming pools with sand beach, 3 9-hole golf courses, 8 tennis courts, Spa Avania, fitness center, bicycles, and Venetian-style gondola boats. Horseback riding, mountain biking, hot air ballooning, nature walks, desert four-wheel adventures, cultural activities, and guided day trips to places like Sedona can be arranged.

Dress Code: Casual; resort casual in Vu

Weddings: Can be arranged

Rates/Packages: Winter season, from $365 per room, per night; summer season, from $189 per room, per night

Payment/Credit Cards: Most major

Deposit: Guarantee with credit card

Government Taxes: 11.92 percent room tax, 7.95 percent sales tax

Service Charges: Gratuity service charges are 22 percent (taxable)

THE AHWAHNEE
California

Sounds of birds, the rustle of grasses and trees, glimpses of coyotes, badgers, or even bears along with awesome views of rock cliffs, redwoods, rivers, and lakes await those who visit the Ahwahnee, located in Yosemite National Park. The main attraction here is nature, which provides the perfect getaway destination for those who love the outdoors.

The Ahwahnee is nestled in the heart of Yosemite Valley, an ideal location since just getting in and out of the center of the park can take an hour or more. Yosemite is huge! Since 1993, the Ahwahnee has been operated by the Delaware North Companies Parks & Resorts at Yosemite, an authorized concessioner of the National Park Service. This hospitality company is dedicated to balancing environmental stewardship and customer service at the park. So if you are looking for luxury and a candlelit dinner at the end of a day of exploring the more than 350 miles of marked trails, climbing a mountain, or taking a horseback ride through the hills, then the Ahwahnee is the place to be.

When Lady Astor, England's first female member of Parliament, came to Yosemite in the early 1920s she thumbed her nose at her unheated room and bathroom, which was down the hall. She checked out and returned to the gentler comforts of the city. This prompted Stephen T. Mather, director of the National Park Service, to order that a new luxury hotel be built to attract more people to his beloved park.

Since the seven-story granite-and-timber structure and cottages were built, the Ahwahnee has welcomed such important guests as Queen Elizabeth II, President John F. Kennedy, Judy Garland, Winston Churchill, Ronald Reagan, and First Lady Laura Bush.

From the beginning the theme of the furnishings and decor was derived from Native American culture. The public rooms are massive with soaring ceilings that replicate the park's towering pines and giant sequoias. Large windows as well as the long outdoor terrace are oriented toward Glacier Point and Sentinel Dome. Pull out your binoculars and look carefully; you may be able to spot someone climbing the sheer rock faces.

Although it was used as a Navy hospital for three years during World War II, it has primarily served as a gracious place to stay in the woods. Over the years it has been refurbished and redecorated, but some things have stayed the same. The original big oak tables, wrought-iron chandeliers in the Great Lounge, the beautiful Native American carpets hanging on the walls, and the intricate rubber mosaic tiles in the entrance lobby are still here.

Accommodations are located in the main lodge and in nearby cottages that are strung along paths leading from the hotel. Beautifully decorated in Native American prints and rusts, browns, black, greens, and blues, the rooms have all necessary amenities, including cable television and mini-fridges.

For privacy the cottages are great and come with stone patios furnished with a wrought-iron table and chairs. You won't see much beyond the trees that surround the cottages, and the decor is a bit more rustic; still you have basically the same amenities as the rooms in the main lodge along with a small dressing room, separate vanity area, and a sitting area. Most cottages are furnished with king-size beds with wood headboards edged by a twig border. A few cottages are furnished with double beds.

Inside the lodge, the Great Lounge is huge (77 feet long, 55 feet wide, and 24 feet high), and the fireplace is large enough to roast a cow. The dining room is equally impressive, especially at night when the chandeliers and candles set a romantic mood. For casual dining and drinks you can order such items as turkey quesadillas, salads, and sandwiches in the bar.

You will probably run out of time before you run out of things to do in Yosemite. In addition to the obvious—hiking, biking, riding, climbing—have the hotel pack a lunch basket or stop at the convenience store for some wine, bread, and cheese. Then drive up to Tuolumne Meadows, stopping at Tenaya Lake for a picnic by the shore. The lake is surrounded by tall pines and the north side is blessed by a lovely sand beach. The lake is sparkling clean and swimmable if you like your water briskly cool.

Keep in mind that the drive up to Tuolumne is about 50 miles and takes about one and one-half hours. You can visit the giant sequoias on the way or head to Mariposa for a guided tour of the massive trees with trunks so large that you could drive a truck through the middle.

For an overview of the valley, sign on for a two-hour valley floor tour, a 26-mile journey in an open-air tram. (If you are driving a convertible, you can use a map and do it yourself.) If you like to paint, join one of the art classes that are offered every day April through November.

If you want a break head to the Ahwahnee pool for a soothing swim and soak up the dramatic views from your lounge chair.

The Ahwahnee

Location: Inside Yosemite National Park

Romantic Highlights: Spectacular vistas of forests, waterfalls, and mountains; miles of trails to explore on foot and horseback; private cottages in the woods

Address/Phone: Yosemite National Park, Yosemite, CA 95389; (559) 252–4848; fax (209) 372–1463

Web Site: www.yosemitepark.com

U.S. Reservations: (559) 252–4848

Owner/Manager: Roger Young, general manager

Arrival/Departure: Car rentals available at San Francisco and Oakland Airports

Distance from San Francisco Airport: 214 miles (4 to 5 hours); Fresno Airport, 105 miles (2½ hours)

Distance from Yosemite: Right in the park

Accommodations: 123 rooms and cottages

Most Romantic Room/Suite: Mary Tresidder Room (605), a minisuite with balcony and huge bath; The Duke's Suite (602), a spacious suite with a king-size bed, library, fireplace; cottages for those who want rustic privacy

Amenities: Hair dryer, mini-refrigerator, TV, coffeemaker (cottages), toiletries, robes, ice service, concierge service, valet parking, turndown service, complimentary morning coffee, *USA Today* delivered to your door, Wi-Fi in hotel

Electricity: 110 volts

Sports and Facilities: Pool, walking, hiking, fishing, horseback riding, mountain climbing, Alpine and cross-country skiing, ice skating, art classes, river rafting; golf at Wawona outside the valley

Dress Code: Resort casual (no jeans)

Weddings: Can be arranged

Rates/Packages: $379–$936 per couple, per night for rooms; two-night Romance Package $949 midweek, $1,061 weekend, including accommodations, in-room candlelight dinner, one breakfast in bed, picnic lunch, champagne, rose, and gifts

Payment/Credit Cards: Most major

Deposit: By credit card

Government Taxes: 10 percent

Service Charges: Not included

AUBERGE DU SOLEIL
California

Location, location, location is yours to savor at this luxury resort in the heart of Napa Valley wine country. Snuggled in an olive grove in the eastern foothills, Auberge du Soleil overlooks a tapestry of vineyards, stone wineries, and the rugged ridge of the Mayacamas Mountains. A Relais & Châteaux property, it's the perfect hideaway for couples wanting to sample the best of the wine country lifestyle—tasting rooms and fine restaurants, smart boutiques and antiques stores, hot air ballooning and bicycling.

Auberge surrounds guests in tranquil beauty from the moment they enter the lobby, with its oversize floral display placed on a massive wood and stone table. The grounds are spectacular, with gardens and courtyards hidden in nooks and crannies and accented by pergolas, fountains, and gigantic pots overflowing with ivy geraniums.

A four-acre olive grove provides a unique venue for appreciating alfresco works in the inn's sculpture garden. The collection of sixty works by well-known local and national artists are fun and unique. A shapely pair of stone legs sprawl under a tree; cheerful metal flowers "grow" in the gardens; a dancer turns on her toe in the wind; giant nails are hammered in the ground; colorful rings frolic on the hillside.

Accommodations are tucked into two-story cottages that are staggered up the hillside. Stuccoed in warm earth tones, each cottage has a patio or terrace. Inside, the decor is class, not flash. Cream matelasse bed coverings are accented with striking persimmon-colored coverlets and bolsters. The fabric, custom-dyed and woven in France for Auberge, is a copy of a vintage Pierre Frey design. Ceruse hand-stained oak and wheat-colored limestone counters create a stylish, updated look that still manages to evoke a secluded Côte d'Azur retreat.

The two cottages are a whopping 1,800 square feet and come with nonstop views and every imaginable amenity.

Everything encourages you to relax, from the two chaise lounges poised on the terrace with the comfortable padded cushions, chairs for two, and sofas with huge overstuffed pillows. Music is piped from a CD/stereo player, logs are laid in your fireplace, and candles and amber bath salts wait by the side of the tub (some units have Jacuzzis for two). The king-size bed is primped with a medley of colorful pillows; live orchids and flowers are everywhere.

Original artwork, such as large canvasses and three-dimensional pieces, reflects the sunny warmth of the Napa Valley.

If perfection lies in details, Auberge has it all figured out. Light switches are marked for location, including one to spotlight the art . . . even the extra roll of toilet paper comes "gift wrapped" with a bow. Both drawer and closet spaces are ample, and the wet bar includes a refrigerator stocked with drinks and snacks.

In fine weather (almost a certainty in Northern California), you'll enjoy basking by the lovely swimming pool, heated to a comfy 85 degrees year-round. Broad wooden decks provide plenty of space for sunning, while a flotilla of market umbrellas seems to mirror the contours of distant mountain peaks. You can play tennis or work out in the well-equipped gym.

The new Spa du Soléil, tucked into an olive garden near the entrance, occupies a 7,000-square foot stucco building where windows open to superb views of the valley. The centerpiece of the spa, a courtyard punctuated by fountains and hundred-year-old olive trees, reflects a French-country spirit.

Six treatment rooms with French doors are arranged around the courtyard and there is a private guest patio, with an outdoor shower and tub, and a Tranquility Room with a fireplace. Massages, facials, exfoliations, masques, wraps, foot therapies, and hair and scalp treatments make use of things from the outdoors: The Valley (mud and minerals), The Grove (olive oil), The Garden (herbs and flowers), and The Vineyard (grapes).

If you want to relax in total privacy, book a two-hour spa package at the spa's Melisse Suite. This spacious spa suite, designed for couples, has a fireplace, private tanning deck, and exclusive use of the resort's spectacular soaking tub for the duration of your treatments. Sip a pre-treatment elixir while gazing out over the Napa Valley, then indulge in side-by-side massages and a private soak in the hot tub. A glass of sparkling wine and a specially prepared plate of food are included in the package.

You will certainly want to explore several of Napa's more than 220 vineyards. Ask Auberge to prepare a picnic basket for your day in the valley, and pick up a special wine along the way.

For wining and dining there's the Auberge du Soleil Restaurant, with meals served either indoors in a country-French dining room or outdoors on a trellis-covered wooden deck with awesome views of the valley. No need to worry about a chilly evening while savoring the sunset—overhead heaters keep you cozy. Service is friendly, not intrusive. Advice on wine and cuisine choices is delivered by the maître d' and highly knowledgeable waiters.

Executive Chef Robert Curry welcomes guests to the Restaurant at Auberge du Soleil, offering exquisitely prepared wine country dishes. Chef Curry has worked with Wolfgang Puck at Ma Cuisine and Michel Richard and Alain Giraud at Citrus, and he trained with several world-renowned chefs. Now as Auberge's chef, he has quickly gained a reputation for his superb cuisine. He continues to enhance Auberge's reputation as an elite dining venue with his fusion of French-Mediterranean-California cuisine. Paired with Auberge's expansive selection of rare and fine wines, meals here are indeed a memorable experience. To complement the Spa du Soleil, new menu item are being created incorporating freshly harvested ingredients indigenous to the Napa Valley.

Time your reservation so that you catch the last glow of the sun going down, flaming behind the mountains. By dessert, the stars will be twinkling out *good night.*

Auberge du Soleil

Location: Thirty-three–acre olive grove in the Rutherford foothills of northern California

Romantic Highlights: Knockout views of Napa Valley's most illustrious vineyards (each room has a private deck and fireplace); half-mile nature trail studded with more than sixty sculptures

Address/Phone: P.O. Drawer B, 180 Rutherford Hill Road, Rutherford, CA 94573; (707) 963–1211; fax (707) 963–8764

E-mail: reserve@aubergedusoleil.com

Web Site: www.aubergedusoleil.com

U.S. Reservations: (800) 348–5406; Relais & Châteaux, (800) RELAIS–8

Owner/Manager: Bradley Reynolds, general manager

Arrival/Departure: Car rentals available at airports; limousine service available from San Francisco at $225 each way

Distance from San Francisco Airport: 65 miles north (1½ hours)

Distance from Rutherford: 5 minutes

Accommodations: 50 rooms, one- and two-room suites, each with valley views and fireplaces

Most Romantic Room/Suite: The 2 private cottages are the most spectacular, with a bedroom, living room, den, and huge patio with stainless Jacuzzi outdoor tub.

Amenities: Air-conditioning, fireplace, refrigerator stocked with drinks and snacks, TV, VCR, coffeemaker, toiletries, skylights in bath, double sinks, some rooms with Jacuzzis, hair dryer, valet, 24-hour room service, down comforter, bathrobes, slippers, twice-daily maid service, full-service spa and beauty salon, voice mail, and business center

Electricity: 110 volts

Sports and Facilities: Swimming pool and large sundeck; whirlpool, massage, and steam rooms; gym/Spa du Soleil; tennis court (instruction available); golf, horseback riding, bicycling, hot air ballooning, and jogging nearby

Dress Code: Casually smart

Weddings: Can be arranged

Rates/Packages: $450–$875 per couple, per night for rooms; $675–$1,400 for suites; $2,500–$3,500 for private cottages

Payment/Credit Cards: Most major

Deposit: Prepayment is required at time of booking to secure your reservation. Your reservation will be confirmed in writing upon receipt of full payment. Reservations must be canceled 14 days prior to scheduled arrival date to receive a refund.

Government Taxes: 12 percent

Service Charges: Not included

CHATEAU DU SUREAU

California

This red-roofed palace with its stone tower, balustrades, gardens, and wrought-iron balconies beckons to all the Romeos and Juliets in the world. There may be plenty to explore in nearby Yosemite, but Chateau du Sureau, a member of the Relais & Château group, seduces you to linger inside. Discover unusual treasures—one-of-a-kind pieces of furniture, accessories, and artwork, all carefully collected by Erna Kubin-Clanin, Chateau du Sureau's owner, whose inspiration and superb taste is revealed throughout the property, which consists of the Erna's Elderberry House Restaurant, the Chateau, and the exquisite new two-bedroom Villa Sureau.

Picture hand-painted ceilings and alcoves; 1780s tapestry; Oriental carpets; period prints, urns, and china; beamed ceilings; tall arched windows; period light fixtures; a 1,000-year-old floor obtained from a chateau in Paris; gardens; and a herringbone pattern brick fireplace in the Grand Salon.

Growing up in Vienna, Austria, castles and romance were woven into Erna's dreams from an early age. In 1962 Erna came to New York, found her way to Yosemite, and was responsible for turning the rather lackluster Redwood Inn into one of the finest restaurants around.

When it came time for her to renew the lease, the government clamped down on the use of parkland, sending Erna hunting for a new challenge. She found it: nine wooded hillside acres full of pines, black oak, manzanita, and elderberry bushes reminding her of her native land. First she built her restaurant, Elderberry House, named for the elderberries she found on the property.

Over the door she placed a sign quoting Oscar Wilde: I HAVE THE SIMPLEST OF TASTES: I WANT ONLY THE BEST. That's what she demanded and that's what her customers got. The restaurant's reputation for superb cuisine and meticulous service brought diners from San Francisco and beyond, people like Robert DeNiro and Kevin Bacon. One day Craig Claibourne stopped in. His glowing article in the *New York Times* that followed brought "foodies" from everywhere to Erna's restaurant. Reservations were hard to get. Erna's success with the restaurant served as a springboard for the fulfillment of Erna's second dream: to build a place where people could stay overnight in complete comfort.

With her new husband, Rene, Erna built the ten-room Chateau du Sureau and, most recently, the two-bedroom Villa Sureau. She has used her creative talents and boundless energy to fill the rooms with authentic antiques and other unique pieces gathered from around the world.

Each room is different and named after Provençal herbs and flowers: elderberry, thyme, rosehip, sweet geranium, mint, lavender, chamomile, rosemary, and saffron. The Saffron Room is decorated in bold golds and yellows and boasts a handsome 1834 Napoleonic ebony armoire and bed inlaid with ivory; the Lavender Room features delicate lavender-and-white fabrics and wall coverings and the Elderberry Room has a canopy bed with blue-and-white flowered drapes. Baths are trimmed in hand-painted French tile and beds are dressed with down duvets and Italian linens. There are massive four-poster beds, sleigh beds, canopies with flowing side draperies, fireplaces, and oversize tubs. Fresh flowers are everywhere.

An ornate gazebo overlooks a pond, a nice place to sip a cup of tea or a cocktail; nearby, a giant chess game is tucked into its own garden setting.

Four full-time gardeners keep flowers and shrubs looking their best and supply fresh blooms for arrangements and herbs and vegetables for the kitchen. Staff is always on hand to see that your every wish is granted. Chambermaids dressed in crisp black uniforms with ruffled white aprons deliver room service orders, make the beds, resupply fluffy fresh towels, and keep everything spotless.

Chef James Overbaugh presides over the award-winning kitchen, creating a California-French cuisine with fresh fruits, vegetables, and meats. A six-course prix-fixe dinner in the red-toned candlelit dining room costs $85.00; Sunday Brunch $38.00 plus dessert for $9.00. The menu changes each night and might include grilled foie gras with apples, braised turnips and elderberry grappa emulsion, vegetable couscous, brochette of rib eye and shiitake mushrooms with boudin noir mashed potatoes and celery root and black trumpet sauce—topped off by semolina flummery, a white and dark chocolate pâté plum sorbet. The wine list offer more than 700 choices; be sure to stop at the wine cellar bar for a drink.

The newest addition to Erna's kingdom, Villa Sureau, goes over the top in elegance and amenities and is furnished with turn-of-the-century pieces from France: original art, stained-glass windows, massive carved wood doors, fireplaces, highly polished marble-topped tables, full-length gold-gilt mirrors, Oriental carpets, crystal chandeliers, a king-size bed swathed from floor to ceiling with filmy turquoise-and-gold organdy, hand-painted trompe l'oeil detailing, a grand piano, library of leather-bound books, and an opulent black-marble bath with columns—Nero would love it. There is

a private gate, a garden with a fountain, and another beautiful bedroom. And let's not forget the butler and the outdoor Roman spa.

At Chateau du Sureau, fairy tales do come true.

Chateau du Sureau

Location: Poised in the foothills of the Sierras on 9 wooded acres south of Yosemite National Park

Romantic Highlights: Balconies and fireplaces, canopy beds, intimate dining in Erna's Elderberry House Restaurant

Address/Phone: 48688 Victoria Lane, Oakhurst, CA 93644; (559) 683–6800; fax (559) 683–0800

E-mail: chateau@chateausureau.com

Web Site: www.chateaudusureau.com

U.S. Reservations: (559) 683–6860; Relais & Châteaux, (800) RELAIS–8

Owner/Manager: Erna Kubin-Clanin; Lucy Royse, director

Arrival/Departure: Car rentals available at San Francisco, Oakland, and Fresno/Yosemite airports

Distance from San Francisco Airport: 210 miles (3 hours); Fresno airport, 35 miles (45 minutes)

Distance from Yosemite: 17 miles

Accommodations: 10 rooms and suites plus the two-bedroom Villa Sureau

Most Romantic Room/Suite: It's a tough call. The Lavender Room's balcony overlooks the pool; the Rosehip Room features Empire-period furniture and a tub-for-two with a view out a large window; Mint has a wonderful wide canopy; Elderberry, a corner room, is decorated in blue and yellow and has a high, vaulted ceiling. If you really want to splurge, take the Villa Sureau. All rooms are no-smoking.

Amenities: Hair dryer, CD/VCR stereo system, toiletries, robes, TV on request

Electricity: 110 volts

Sports and Facilities: Pool, chess, walking, hiking, bocce ball; Yosemite about 17 miles away

Dress Code: Jackets requested in main dining room

Weddings: Can be arranged for guests staying in the Chateau. In addition to the gazebo and gardens, there is a mini-chapel in the Chateau with just 3 pews.

Rates/Packages: $350–$550 per room per couple, including full European breakfast and complimentary bar in the Grand Salon; $2,800 for Villa Sureau with a private butler

Payment/Credit Cards: Most major

Deposit: 50 percent at time of booking; cancel 14 days prior to arrival for refund less 10 percent service fee

Government Taxes: 9 percent

Service Charges: 12 percent

FOUR SEASONS BILTMORE
California

Celebrating its eightieth anniversary in 2007, the Four Seasons Biltmore reigns as the red-tile–roofed queen of Santa Barbara. You can't beat the vintage 1920s style or the California dream setting, with the deep-blue Pacific glimmering just across the way.

The resort glows with the burnished patina of a classic. It opened in 1927 as part of the original Biltmore chain; the property became a Four Seasons resort in 1987. Over the years the clientele has included everyone from Douglas Fairbanks to Michael Douglas and President Ronald Reagan. (The Reagan ranch is located in the nearby Santa Ynez foothills.)

Set on twenty-two acres, the Spanish-Mediterranean resort is composed of a main building plus separate wings and cottages. Public areas resemble the castle of a Spanish grandee, with high, coffered ceilings; thick, red-tile floors; and hand-painted tiles adorning the corridors and stairways. Red-tile and artfully laid brick walkways illuminated with gas lanterns ramble past bright green lawns and impeccable flower borders. Giant blue gum trees, broad Monterey cypress, and spreading camphor trees shade the grounds.

The restored accommodations all differ in layout and view; there are also separate cottages poised along the back ridge of the property amidst the resorts seventy-eight-year-old specimen gardens. Furnishings reflect the Biltmore's 1927 heritage with a mix of Mission-style furniture, antiques, and custom iron work, combined with modern technology, forty-two-inch plasma screen televisions, and wireless high-speed Internet access. The redesigned bathrooms feature deep soaking tubs and rain showerheads; some have radiant floor heating and private steam showers. Several of the rooms have fireplaces, balconies, or private patios.

The executive chef, Martin Frost, who had garnered top notices while at the Four Seasons Nevis in the Caribbean, presides over the Biltmore's three superb restaurants.

Dining in the Patio is like eating in a country garden—there's even a glass roof with retractable panels to open or close to fit the weather's moods. The themed dinner buffets earn raves, and Sunday brunch is a Santa Barbara tradition, with huge platters of seafood, a caviar station, stir-fry table, omelet and Belgian waffle stations, chocolate fountains, and lots more.

Afternoon tea is served in the Sala Lounge, an elegant drawing room beautified with a high, open-beamed ceiling and a fireplace. La Marina is known for romantic dining, with flowers, candlelight, and arched windows framing the seaward view. In addition to a la carte selections, Chef Frost presents a four-course tasting menu, where choices might include squab with scallion polenta and mission figs, followed by roast tenderloin of veal. Heading to a polo match or into Santa Barbara wine country? The hotel can customize a picnic basket for you.

Guests enjoy preferred tee-times privileges at the oceanside Sandpiper Golf Course, one of the top-rated public golf layouts in the country, and at Rancho San Marcos, designed by Robert Trent Jones Jr. On the property there is also an eighteen-hole putting green, as well as three lighted tennis courts, croquet, and complimentary bicycles. The concierge can set up sports fishing, wine country tours, and sailing.

With ten treatment rooms (including four oceanview suites with deep-soaking tubs and fireplaces), a state-of-the-art fitness center, and an Olympic-size swimming pool on the edge of the Pacific, the resort's 10,000-square-foot spa helps make life luxuriously wonderful.

Another perk for guests includes privileges at the Art Deco–era Coral Casino, a private club that has been the center of Santa Barbara social life for over half a century.

Four Seasons Biltmore

Location: Across the street from Butterfly Beach, in the exclusive Montecito enclave

Romantic Highlights: Beachfront setting, Roaring Twenties panache (the hotel opened in 1927), glamorous public areas

Address/Phone: 1260 Channel Drive, Santa Barbara, CA 93108; (805) 969–2261; fax (805) 565–8323

Web Site: www.fourseasons.com/santabarbara

U.S. Reservations: (800) 332–3442

Owner/Manager: Managed by the Four Seasons Hotels & Resorts

Arrival/Departure: Transfers can be arranged; car rentals available at airport

Distance from Santa Barbara Airport: 12 miles

Distance from downtown Santa Barbara: 2 miles (5 minutes)

Accommodations: 207 rooms, suites, and cottages, many with balconies or private patios and fireplaces

Most Romantic Room/Suite: Cottage suites; Odell Cottage suite is top of the heap.

Amenities: Ceiling fan, hair dryer, 3 phones, VCR, 42-inch plasma screen TV, high-speed Internet, deep soaking tubs, air-conditioning, 24-hour business services, 24-hour in-room dining, complimentary shoeshine, twice-daily maid service, on-site dry cleaning, one-hour pressing, in-room safe, minibar, bathrobes, AM/FM clock radio, toiletries; in-room spa treatments

Electricity: 110 volts

Sports and Facilities: 3 tennis courts, full-service luxury spa, 2 fitness centers, 2 swimming pools, bicycles; golf, sailing, shuffleboard, wine tasting, and whale-watching expeditions nearby (February to mid-April).

Dress Code: Casually elegant

Weddings: Can be arranged; popular sites include outdoor courtyards and the ocean-view ballroom

Rates/Packages: $550–$840 per room, per night single or double occupancy; $1,025 and up for a suite. Spa Package: $778 per night (includes tax) for Superior Guestroom, single or double occupancy, and includes

(2) 50-minute spa treatments per night. Two-night minimum on weekends.

Payment/Credit Cards: Most major

Deposit: Deposits are required within 14 days of making reservation. Cancellations are accepted with a full refund up to 72 hours prior to the expected arrival date.

Government Taxes: 10 percent

Service Charges: Not included

LA VALENCIA
California

Since it was built in 1926, La Valencia, the legendary "Pink Lady of La Jolla," has been a San Diego tradition attracting the rich and notable such as Groucho Marx, Lillian Gish, and Mary Pickford. More recent famous guests have included Pearl Jam, Madonna, Rush Limbaugh, and Ellen DeGeneres.

Reigning over La Jolla Cove, this elegant pink palace is planted in the heart of the trendy seaside town of La Jolla, within walking distance of many great little boutiques and restaurants. Fifteen new villa suites have been added that just about knock your socks off. These accommodations, which came with a $10 million price tag, have been tucked into the terraced hillside without changing the overall ambience one little bit. In fact, I had a hard time trying to remember just what it had looked like before the change.

Villas, which range from 400 to 1,200 square feet, come with separate sitting room, patio or balcony, dining area, and huge bath. Most have fireplaces and are designed so that from your king-size bed you can look through the living room out to the patio, gardens, and sea. Room features include hand-painted Mexican tiles; a

Lyceum digital audio system; bathroom with steam shower; down duvets; Italian marble floors, sinks, and bath; Jacuzzi tub; and a private butler service. The television in the living room rises by remote control out of a handsome wood cabinet—very cool. The shower has two oversized rain showerheads that give you the feeling you are standing under Victoria Falls. (Even if you don't need a shower, take one. So sensual.)

Most of the 115 guestrooms have terraces or patios with views of the sea and gardens. Each room is different, each with its own charm. I especially like the rooms with French doors opening onto balconies where flowers tumble down terraces below and the sea glistens beyond. All rooms have windows that open, allowing you to enjoy the fresh sea air and fragrant tropical flowers.

La Valencia has a decidedly Mediterranean flavor with elegant appointments such as Oriental carpets, grand potted plants, antique furniture and accessories, Spanish mosaics, and hand-painted murals and ceilings. The hand-painted coffered ceiling in the elegant La Sala lounge is magnificent. What better place to sip a cocktail while listening to piano music and gazing out to sea.

Dining options include French cuisine in the Sky Room Restaurant on the tenth floor where there are but twelve tables offering 180-degree views of the Pacific; the more casual Whaling Bar & Grill; the Mediterranean Room overlooking the Pacific; or alfresco dining at the Tropical Patio, poolside cafe, or Ocean View Terrace. A variety of picnic baskets can be prepared for a special day excursion with that someone special.

On the ocean side there is a park and a coastal walk leads to a small cove, a popular hangout for seals. With an average year-round temperature of 70 degrees, you can almost be guaranteed springlike weather whenever you come.

La Valencia

Location: Terraced up a flower-filled hillside overlooking the Pacific in the seaside community of La Jolla, California

Romantic Highlights: French doors opening onto balconies looking out to the sea; tiered gardens, a riot of color; fireplaces; private butler service

Address/Phone: 1132 Prospect Street, La Jolla, CA 92037; (800) 451–0772, (858) 454–0771; fax (858) 456–1664

E-mail: info@lavalencia.com

Web Site: www.lavalencia.com

U.S. Reservations: (800) 451–0772

Owner/Manager: Michael J. Ullman, managing director

Arrival/Departure: Private limousine service can be arranged from the San Diego Airport. If you drive, there is valet service at the door.

Distance from San Diego Airport: 12 miles

Distance from San Diego: 12 miles

Accommodations: 115 rooms, suites, and villas

Most Romantic Room/Suite: Ultraprivate La Valencia suite

Amenities: Air-conditioning, fans, cable TV and VCR, custom toiletries, terry robes, hair dryer, complimentary shoeshine, morning newspaper, 24-hour room service, valet parking, in-room safe, iron/ironing board, minibar

Electricity: 110 volts

Sports and Facilities: Pool, Jacuzzi, fitness center, sauna; golf and tennis can be arranged

Dress Code: Casually elegant

Weddings: Can be arranged

Rates/Packages: Per night from $300–$1,400, rooms; $699–$3,500, suites and villas

Payment/Credit Cards: Most major

Deposit: By credit card

Government Taxes: Included

Service Charges: Included

POST RANCH INN
California

They sometimes have problems with deer grazing on the roofs. That challenge reflects the uniqueness of Post Ranch Inn, a magnificent resort located in one of the most majestic spots on earth—Big Sur. Opened in 1992, Post Ranch was the first new hotel in nearly twenty years to debut along this untamed, almost mythological coastline, which over the decades has attracted avant-garde writers and actors such as Henry Miller, Jack Kerouac, and Orson Welles. Big Sur was one of America's last frontiers, a place where roads did not arrive until the 1930s, electricity until the 1950s.

To win the approval of development-abhorring locals and legislators, the resort had to meet stringent environmental standards. In part, the property was planned by Bill Post III, whose great-grandfather had homesteaded the land (he paid $4.00 an acre for 160 acres) some 130 years previously. The resultant enclave manages to feel both rustic and futuristic—*Star Wars* meets the Old West.

Planked with redwood, the accommodations seem more like private houses than hotel rooms. Although rooms vary in layout and view, all offer the same amenities and square footage and make extensive use of gold-gray rajah slate, quarried by hand in India, for the floors. Railings and doors in Cor-Ten steel weather to the same brown-red tone of the neighboring oaks and madrone trees. Furnishings are comfortable, with features such as curvilinear sofas or window seats. Color schemes of blue, green, and earth tones soothe the spirit. Bathrooms are embellished with slate and granite; many have tubs next to windows positioned so that no one can see you but

you can enjoy a 100-mile view. Bath towels are thick, the down comforters plump.

Tree Houses live up to their name, built on stilts so as not to disturb the adjoining redwoods. Walls are angled to maximize views and privacy. Personal favorites are the Ocean Houses, which hunker into the ridge-line—the terrain rising from the back to form the sod-covered roofs, the aforementioned salad bar for perambulating deer. Out front, views of the Pacific surge to the horizon. The fireplace is arranged so that you can view it from both the living room and the bathroom.

Because Post Ranch's creators wanted to spotlight the splendor of nature rather than the playthings of man, distractions are kept to a minimum. Rooms are television-free (though they do come with pretty nifty stereo/CD systems), and there are no tennis courts or golf courses. What you have are miles of big-country hiking trails through redwood forests into the valleys snaking hillward behind Highway 1. Some guided hikes are offered, including nature treks and off-property hikes; herb garden talks are also available. The lap pool awaits, a warm 80 degrees year-round. A fitness room offers a step machine, free weights, and exercise machines; yoga classes are held poolside in the morning. Dramatic seascapes can be enjoyed at Pfeiffer and Andrew Molera Beaches, both less than 5 miles to the north.

Rates include an elaborate continental breakfast, served in your room or in the restaurant. Choices generally include fresh fruits, home-baked breads, granola, and quiche. Floor-to-ceiling glass windows (each of which took nine people to carry into position during construction) of the Sierra Mar restaurant afford cliff-hanging views of the water. So as not to compete with the vistas, decor is simple, with slate floors and a big fireplace.

Superintended by executive chef Craig von Forester, the Californian menu dallies with flavors from around the world. Entrees might feature a grilled venison chop with fermented black beans or John Dory (a fish that is like sole) with lemongrass, papaya, chili, and roasted peanuts. Prices run $78 per person for the four-course, prix-fixe dinner. The wine list is phenomenal, encompassing 2,000 different wines.

Not much is known about the Ohlone Indians, the original inhabitants of the Northern California coast. From their celebrations only a line from a song remains, "dancing on the brink of the world." From your cliffside perch at Post Ranch Inn, you'll probably experience a similar feeling of joy.

Post Ranch Inn

Location: On 98 acres amid the seaside cliffs of Big Sur in northern California

Romantic Highlights: Endless views of the Pacific from the villas' ridge-top perches; a large, night-lighted outdoor hot tub on the edge of a cliff; guided nature hikes; on-staff tarot reader and astrologer; stargazing through a 10-inch Meade electronic tracking telescope

Address/Phone: P.O. Box 219, Highway 1, Big Sur, CA 93920; (831) 667–2200; fax (831) 667–2824

U.S. Reservations: (800) 527–2200

Owner/Manager: Dan Priano, general manager

Arrival/Departure: Easily accessible by car

Distance from Monterey Airport: 35 miles south; 90 miles south of San Jose Airport; 150 miles south of San Francisco International Airport

Distance from Carmel: Approximately 30 miles south; 150 miles south of San Francisco

Accommodations: 30 villas, each with ocean or mountain views, in four styles: 5 Ocean Houses recessed into ridge with sod roofs, 7 Tree Houses on stilts, 10 Coast Houses, 2 Mountain Houses, and 6 guest accommodations in three-level Butterfly House

Most Romantic Room/Suite: Top-of-the-line Ocean Houses hang on the brink of the cliff and feature private, slate-floored terraces. These often book up way in advance.

Amenities: Wood-burning fireplace, bathtub/Jacuzzi, satellite stereo/CD music system, in-room massage table, coffeemaker, minibar, toiletries, terry-cloth robes, hair dryer

Electricity: 110 volts

Sports and Facilities: A "basking pool" (a giant hot tub); fitness center and spa; hiking and walking trails

Dress Code: Casually elegant

Weddings: Can be arranged

Rates/Packages: $495–$1,085 per couple, per night

Payment/Credit Cards: Most major

Deposit: Reservations require guarantee or deposit in advance. Cancellations must be made 14 days in advance.

Government Taxes: 10 to 15 percent

Service Charges: Not included

RANCHO VALENCIA
California

Rancho Valencia, a Relais & Châteaux all-suite property, sits atop a forty-acre plateau in the rolling hills of Rancho Santa Fe. The twenty-six casitas and forty-nine one- and two-room suites, in Southwestern style, feature red-tile roofs, mountains of bougainvillea, and red clay pots brimming over with hot pink flowers—creating a virtual garden of Eden. Walkways wind through the grounds, which are liberally planted with vibrantly blooming flowers and shrubs: Impatiens, agapanthus, hibiscus, geraniums, palms, and wildflowers burst in great exuberance in the gardens and on the hillsides. Trumpet flower vines in red, orange, and pink surround the tennis courts and cover trellises and casita walls, and fragrant honeysuckle wafts through the air.

Built in 1989, Rancho Valencia has welcomed guests such as Bill Gates, President Clinton, Michael Jordan, Regis Philbin, and Rene Russo. These elite guests might occupy the Hacienda, a luxurious three-suite adobe brick home built in the 1940s, but perchance if the Hacienda is taken, they should be quite happy, thank you, in the suites which are spacious and private.

It's a tough call as to which suite style to recommend. The 1,150-square-foot Rancho Santa Fe suite comes with a separate bedroom and sitting room; the Del Mar suite occupies 850 square feet of open space, with a low, tile-topped divider that contains a desk, built-in bureau, and bar separating the sleeping area and sitting area. The new Grove suites are spacious and offer private patios with outdoor Jacuzzis, huge steam showers with large rainhead sprays, and large whirlpool tubs.

All configurations reflect a combination of California chic and traditional hacienda with whitewashed, beamed cathedral ceilings, earth-toned stucco walls, French doors, and a mix of white carpets and red-tile floors. Suites feature walk-in closets, separate vanities, wet bar, gas fireplaces, patios or balconies, wonderful red clay and glazed pots planted with live orchids and tropical plants. There are wicker baskets, plantation shutters, and a color palette that reflects nature. Bathrooms are so large that you don't fog up the mirror after a hot, steamy shower.

Furnishings combine Southwestern antiques and antique reproductions. King-size beds are dressed in creamy white and, if high-quality linens are important to you, you'll love the Italian duvet cover and sheets that are dreamy high-thread-count Fili D'Oro Egyptian cotton. Pillows are fine goose down. (Synthetic-filled pillows are available for those who have allergy problems.)

Each suite has a CD player and a collection of CDs. (In my room I had *Romancing the Guitar* by Ron Freshman, *Dream Melodies,* and selections by Mozart and Tchaikovsky.)

The pool is surrounded by gardens, palms, and plenty of chaise lounges. There is a fitness center, croquet lawn, and a golf course nearby. Once the John Gardener Tennis Center, Rancho Valencia has an impressive array of tennis facilities with eighteen tennis courts, eight pros, and a program of clinics and private lessons available to guests. It's no wonder that Rancho Valencia has been consistently rated as one of the Top Ten Tennis Resorts in the country by *Tennis Magazine.*

When you get up in the morning, you'll find glasses of fresh-squeezed orange juice, the daily newspaper, and a flower just outside your door on a tiled ledge. Although you might be tempted to linger on your patio sipping your juice and reading the paper, you'll be rewarded with a sumptuous breakfast in the Sunrise Room where cobalt blue, white, and yellow tiles cover the walls. Eat inside or just outside where the French doors open onto flower-filled patios overlooking lines of lemon trees and the tennis courts.

Breakfast might be Belgian waffles surrounded by fresh raspberries, blackberries, blueberries, and currants or Valencia Eggs Benedict. For those wishing lighter fare, there are always choices from the alternative spa menu such as Rancho Frittata made with egg whites and oat bran waffles served with berries and fresh fruit.

The Main Dining Room is casually elegant with white-linen–topped tables, crystal, and superb vistas of the countryside. There is also the open-air Fountain Courtyard where a kiva fire casts a romantic glow in the evening and large mazeta pots filled with clouds of bougainvillea fill the space with color.

California-Mediterranean cuisine features the freshest of local produce. The resort's chef uses fresh herbs grown on the property, and guests enjoy fresh oranges, grapefruit, limes, lemons, and tangerines from Rancho Valencia's orchards.

Lunch choices include items such as Spicy Sautéed Crabcake on a bed of shiitake mushrooms or mesculin salad with champagne vinaigrette and pear tomatoes. Dinner may start with chilled white asparagus salad with Chino's baby greens or lobster bisque with Armagnac. Entrees are equally tempting: pan-roasted veal chop with Valencia garden herb gnocchi or sautéed duck breast served with roasted

tricolor potatoes and a black-cherry balsamic bigarade sauce and mushrooms and a Madeira demi-cream sauce. Then if you have room for dessert, you can try the flourless chocolate soufflé served with roasted espresso sauce and vanilla bean cheesecake. And of course you have a choice of some excellent wines from California and France as well as from all over the world.

Rancho Valencia

Location: 30 miles north of San Diego, California

Romantic Highlights: Flower-studded hilltop setting; private courtyards; fireplaces; luxuriously dressed king-size beds

Address/Phone: P.O Box 9126, Rancho Santa Fe, CA 92067-4126; (800) 548–3664, (858) 756–1123; fax (858) 756–0165

E-mail: reservations@ranchovalencia.com

Web Site: www.ranchovalencia.com

U.S. Reservations: (800) 548–3664

Owner/Manager: Michael J. Ullman, general manager

Arrival/Departure: Most arrive by car; pickup can be arranged.

Distance from San Diego Airport: 30 minutes

Distance from San Diego: 30 minutes

Accommodations: 49 suites

Most Romantic Room/Suite: The Grove suites, with private patios and Jacuzzis, fireplaces, and large baths; Room #100, a Rancho Santa Fe suite that is close to the pool and the dining rooms; and the Del Mar open-plan suites

Amenities: Walk-in closets, separate vanities, gas fireplace, 2 cable TVs and a VCR, CD player, terry robes, turndown service, wet bar and mini-fridge, coffee/tea maker, clock radio, safe, full-length mirror, hair dryer, 24-hour room service, fine toiletries, valet parking. The Grove suites feature Jacuzzi tubs on patios, whirlpool tubs, and steam showers with rainheads.

Electricity: 110 volts

Sports and Facilities: Pool, 18 Deco-Turf tennis courts, croquet lawn, boutique, pro shop, biking, hiking, fitness center; golf and hot air ballooning nearby

Dress Code: Resort casual

Weddings: Can be arranged

Rates/Packages: Daily rates per suite range from $470 to $1,420 per night. A 2-night "Romantic Getaway" including accommodations, champagne, dinner for two, breakfasts on your patio or in the dining room, 1 aromatherapy massage or European Facial per person, use of tennis courts and fitness center, all taxes, and restaurant and spa gratuities is $1,425 to $1,705 per couple. Tennis packages are also available.

Payment/Credit Cards: Most major

Deposit: By credit card

Government Taxes: Included in package

Service Charges: Not included

SONNENALP RESORT OF VAIL
Colorado

You don't have to go all the way to Austria to find the archetypal European ski and mountain resort. Just grab your skis and head to Vail, where the Fässler family has created a resort that fairly sings with charms of the Old World. The Sonnenalp Resort of Vail is a year-round destination offering plenty to do.

The resort features eighty-eight luxurious suites ranging from the 490-square-foot Lodgepole Suites to the 795-square-foot Bald Mountain suites. They are decorated with handcrafted woodwork, original artwork of Native American scenes, gas fireplaces, cozy sitting areas, European fixtures, and warm, natural wood furniture. Bathrooms have heated marble floors, double sinks, and large tubs just right for soaking out kinks acquired on the ski slopes.

Sonnenalp has five places to eat and drink, as well as a full-service spa. There is the elegant Ludwig's Restaurant, the more casual Bully Ranch Restaurant, and the

King's Club Lounge, with a piano bar and library, where food ranges from burgers to caviar. At the golf course, you can enjoy a meal at Balata Restaurant, and the spa offers light fare by the pool.

The light, airy, 5,000-square-foot spa features a 1,200-square-foot indoor/outdoor pool, indoor and outdoor Jacuzzis, ten treatment rooms, a sauna, steam rooms, and an exercise room with the latest in exercise and weight-lifting equipment. You can also pamper yourself with various massages, seaweed wraps, and other soothing treatments. The spa has lots of windows affording great views of the beautiful mountain world just outside. Pevonia and Jurlique products, as well as yoga wear and other clothing products, are available in the spa.

With its white exterior trimmed with wooden balconies and stone arches and a roofline that swoops over towers and gables, Sonnenalp Resort of Vail is reminiscent of a lovely palace chalet. Covered with snow, it's a picture postcard. Send this one to your friends, and they won't believe it's not somewhere in the Alps.

During the summer months Sonnenalp is a wonderful base for those who love hiking, biking, swimming, horseback riding, tennis, and exploring this lovely mountain area. The Sonnenalp Golf Club features an eighteen-hole, links-style course.

If you've got Europe on your mind but want to leave your passports at home, Sonnenalp Resort is highly recommended.

The Sonnenalp Resort is in the midst of its Refining Luxury project, which includes putting all parking underground in a heated parking garage (valet service), as well as the addition of forty new rooms and suites and some retail space. Completion is scheduled for the end of 2005.

Sonnenalp Resort of Vail

Location: Set in the center of the mountain town of Vail, Colorado

Romantic Highlights: Sitting by a blazing fire in your suite while the snow falls softly outside; sleeping under fluffy down duvets; moonlight sleigh ride; European ambience

Address/Phone: 20 Vail Road, Vail, CO 81657; (970) 476–5656; fax (970) 476–1639

E-mail: info@sonnenalp.com

Web Site: www.sonnenalp.com

U.S. Reservations: (800) 654–8312; fax (970) 476–1639

Owner/Manager: Johannes Fässler, owner/general manager

Arrival/Departure: Colorado Mountain Express shuttle service available from Denver International Airport and from Eagle.

Distance from Denver International Airport: 2 hours. Eagle County Airport is only a 45-minute drive.

Distance from Denver: 100 miles west

Accommodations: 88 suites (one- and two-bedroom)

Most Romantic Room/Suite: Bald Mountain Suites overlook a creek and come with a separate bedroom. Lodgepole Suites are also roomy and luxurious, with views of Vail Village or Gore Creek.

Amenities: Hair dryer, bathrobes, iron and ironing board, toiletries, telephone, high-speed Internet access in rooms, TV, VCR, Wi-Fi, down duvet, minibar, air-conditioning, in-room safe. Suites have fireplace, minibar, double vanity, soaking tub, balcony, separate living room, and loft.

Electricity: 110 volts

Sports and Facilities: Vail Mountain has 4,000 skiable acres serviced by 25 lifts; in addition to Alpine and cross-country skiing, you can go snowboarding, snowshoeing, bobsledding, paragliding, dogsledding, snowmobiling, and ice skating. There is also an 18-hole golf course with pro shop, pool, and clubhouse; outdoor Jacuzzi, indoor and outdoor heated pools; 2 European spas; 4 tennis courts.

Dress Code: Casual; for Ludwig's, neat casual attire

Weddings: Can be arranged

Rates/Packages: Romance Package, $185–$250 per person, double occupancy, including suite accommodations, flowers, champagne, chocolate-covered strawberries, breakfast, and dinner, as well as your choice of gondola tickets or bike rentals (rates higher in winter season).

Payment/Credit Cards: Most major

Deposit: 1-night deposit due within 10 days of booking

Government Taxes: 8.4 percent

Service Charges: Not included

THE BILTMORE
Florida

The Biltmore Hotel in Coral Gables, a creamy Spanish-style 1920s grand dame, which recently completed a 10-year $40-million refurbishment program, is characterized by a 93-foot bell tower and the largest hotel pool in the country—so large it appears to be more like a lake than a pool. Designated a National Historic Landmark in 1996, this imposing hotel rises several stories and is topped by a red roof.

The soaring vaulted-ceiling lobby is grand indeed and furnishings are appropriately elegant and posh. Tall gold leaf mirrors, oriental carpets, carved wooden tables, travertine marble floors and columns, interior patios, terraces, gardens, intricate · leaded-glass fixtures, ornately painted ceilings, chandeliers, period artwork, and wood paneling evoke the opulent twenties.

Guest rooms, which look out over the golf course, pool, or city of Coral Gables, are spacious and decorated with beautiful soft-colored fabrics, coral and off-white ceramic tile floors, European feather beds, writing desks, sofas, easy chairs, armoires, Egyptian cotton duvet covers, artwork, and plants. Furniture is upholstered in rich tapestry fabrics and beds are made up with high thread-count linens and fluffy pillows. Scalloped wood headboards are painted in leafy green and gold patterns. Many of the rooms open out to views of the pool. Each room has a desk and the deluxe rooms come with sitting areas. Baths are large and come with a full array of toiletries and thick plush towels.

Of course, for over-the-top luxury book the two-story Everglades or "Al Capone" suite, where luminaries like President Calvin Coolidge, Douglas Fairbanks, Cor-nelius Vanderbilt Jr., the Duke and Duchess of Windsor, President Bill Clinton, Robert Redford, Lauren Bacall, and many other rich and famous have slept for a few nights. Distinctive features include hand-painted high-domed ceilings, antique Spanish woodwork, and a magnificent coral rock fireplace. The marble floored bathroom has a Roman Jacuzzi tub and large walk-in shower with two showerheads.

Lounge around the pool on one of the chaises or share one of the tables that line the sculpture arcade along one side of the pool. Get totally pampered in the brand-new Biltmore Spa, where a variety of treatments are offered, including massages, facials, and beauty services.

Have cocktails in the wood-paneled Biltmore bar or sip a frosty drink under a cascading 23-foot waterfall in the Boule Bar set next to the petanque court (pronounced pay-*tonk*, petanque is an outdoor bowling game similar to both horseshoes and bocce). Dine in the chic Palme d'Or Restaurant overlooking the pool, where executive chef Philippe Ruiz creates delicious French cuisine served on elegantly appointed tables set with fine china, crystal, and linens. Or book a table near the fountain in the 1200 Courtyard Grill, where you enjoy Mediterranean-inspired appetizers and pastas prepared with local ingredients. At 1200, you can eat outdoors in a romantic garden courtyard or, if you prefer, inside at one of the tables along a colonnade-lined loggia. Cascade, yet another restaurant, which runs along the pool, is a good place to enjoy casual fare and daily spa cuisine specials. Sandwiches and light fare are available at the 19th Hole. After dinner, head to the hotel's Cellar Club, a perfect place for those who love wine and cigars, which are offered in the adjacent Cigar Salon. (Yes, women smoke them too.)

The Biltmore is a destination in itself with a spa, fitness center, a legendary golf course, and ten tennis courts. For golfing couples, a big plus here is the John Pallot Golf School, where John and the other teaching pros are masters at analyzing what you need to do to improve your game. The Biltmore course is considered a classic and was designed by the legendary Donald Ross. Once played by Gene Sarazen and Walter Hagen, and more recently by former President Bill Clinton and actor Will Smith, it is a pretty course with a ribbon of water winding through it and its share of well-placed fairway bunkers.

At the end of the day, or the beginning of the morning, however you want to look at it, you've got to do the South Beach scene at least once. Get some rest because nothing really gets going until after 11:00 P.M., when the hip and restless of Miami start lining up in front of nightclubs like State and Mynt. Start with dinner at one of the trendy restaurants like chef-owned Pacific Time or Touch. At Touch, both a restaurant and a nightclub, you can really swing into action—a huge swing on ropes greets you as you enter.

The D.J.s pound out the music, which hits you right in the heart as you walk onto the tiny "dance" floor. There is so little space, you really can't get too clever with your moves. But no one will notice. With all the smoke drifting into the rafters, you can't see much anyway.

Bring bundles of money. A glass of gut-wretching wine in these places can cost around $15. Still the whole thing is great theater, and afterwards you can either go to bed or go to breakfast.

The Biltmore

Location: Set in gardens and along a historic golf course in Coral Gables, Florida

Romantic Highlights: Huge pool with private quiet places all around; old-world elegance; dining outdoors under the palms by candlelight in the 1200 Courtyard Grill.

Address/Phone: 1200 Anastasia Avenue, Coral Gables, FL 33134; (800) 727–1926 or (305) 445–1926 or (305) 913–3159

Web Site: www.biltmorehotel.com

U.S. Reservations: (800) 727–1926

Owner/Manager: Dennis Doucette, general manager

Arrival/Departure: Most arrive by car or taxi from the airport.

Distance from Miami International Airport: 5 miles (10–15 minutes)

Distance to downtown Coral Gables: 1 mile

Distance to Miami Beach: 11 miles

Accommodations: 276 rooms, including 133 suites

Most Romantic Room/Suite: Junior suite overlooking the pool

Amenities: Television (flat screen plasma TVs in suites), TV Internet, Sony Playstation, digital on-demand movies, minibar, air-conditioning, signature slippers and robes, turndown service, hair dryer, fine toiletries, in-room safe, high-speed Internet (Ethernet connection), dual phone lines for cordless telephones with voice mail and data port, iron and ironing board

Electricity: 110 volts

Sports/Recreation: 10 tennis courts, boules, adjacent golf course, pro shop, the John Pallot Golf School, spa, fitness center, gift shops, business center

Dress Code: Smart casual for lunch; coat

and tie appreciated for dinner in the Palme d'Or restaurant

Weddings: Yes

Rates/Packages: Romance Package includes deluxe accommodations, champagne and strawberries, his and her spa treatments, and daily continental breakfast in bed from $129 per person. A more extensive package from $229 per person

includes carriage ride, junior suite accommodations, dinner for two, and other gifts.

Payment/Credit Cards: Most major

Deposit: By credit card (rooms are guaranteed until 6:00 P.M. unless a deposit has been paid to hold the reservation)

Government Taxes: 13 percent

Daily Incidental Fee: $9.00

Service Charges: Included

DISNEY'S GRAND FLORIDIAN RESORT & SPA
Florida

If you thought Walt Disney World was just for kids, think again. This area, with all its various attractions, is one of the top honeymoon destinations in the world. And within this complex of fun and games, the Grand Floridian Resort & Spa is just about the most romantic place you can stay. Special Concierge honeymoon rooms overlook the lagoon, with views of Cinderella's Castle in the Magic Kingdom or of the palm-studded pool. This Victorian-style hotel rests like an oasis right in the heart of all the action just beyond its entrance.

Designed in the grand manner of the Victorian era and reminiscent of the setting for *The Great Gatsby,* the Grand Floridian, with its sprawling white facade accented by gabled roofs, intricate latticework, and ornate balustrades, is set amid gardens and lawns planted with canary palms, magnolias, hibiscus, and other lush tropical flora. This grand hotel boasts wide verandas with wicker rockers, more than 120 miles of decorative scrollwork, white towers, and a red-shingle roof.

A curious touch in the lofty, five-story atrium lobby is an open-cage elevator that whisks guests up and down. Look up and admire the lobby's ceiling, with its three illuminated stained-glass domes, ornate chandeliers, and metal scrolls.

Rooms, which are located in a 225,000-square-foot main building and in five lodge buildings, carry out the early 1920s mood, though the colors used are softer and lighter. Applied with flair are printed wall coverings coordinated with fabrics, light woods, marble-topped sinks (but with old fashioned–looking fittings), and Victorian woodwork. Most rooms have two queen-size beds; some have kings. Suites include a parlor plus one or more bedrooms.

The mood may hark back to the turn of the century and the days of John D. Rockefeller and Thomas Edison, but the amenities are pure twenty-first century modern, with monorail service and air-conditioning—the monorail stops right beside the Grand Lobby. The resort has five restaurants, four lounges, two snack bars, five shops, a 9,000-square-foot spa and health club, a marina, and children's facilities. One of the two pools overlooks the Seven

Seas Lagoon and has a waterfall that drops from a 27-foot-high stone mountain. A water slide carries you on a thrilling ride through the mountain, past trees, and under a waterbridge.

The opportunities for fun and romance are seemingly unlimited. At the resort's spa you can unwind with a soothing massage, a native Floridian floral bath, or a hydrating paraffin body wrap. Or rent a boat from the marina and explore the lagoon. At Epcot Center you can visit the cultures and entertainment worlds of many countries as well as thrill at the sharks and tropical fish at The Living Seas. You can ride the spine-tingling Thunder Mountain at the Magic Kingdom; whiz down the 120-foot-high Summit Plummet from the top of Mt. Gushmore at the sixty-six-acre Blizzard Beach water park; go on "safari" at the new Disney Animal Kingdom Park; and dodge (imaginary) flying objects at the 3-D exhibit, "Honey, I Shrunk the Audience." Later, back in the Grand Floridian, you can dine by candlelight in the privacy of your room and enjoy a moonlit walk on the white-sand beach.

You can go nightclub hopping at Pleasure Island (yes, that man's eyes in the portrait at the Adventurers Club really do follow you), where you will most likely laugh at the comedians at the Comedy Warehouse, and dance up a storm at the Mannequins Dance Palace. See how films are made and special effects created at Disney's MGM Studios and shop at the many, many stores.

Restaurants at the Grand Floridian range from the formal fare served in Victoria & Albert's to the hamburgers and hot dogs of Gasparilla Grill and Games. At V&A's the menu changes daily, and what you get depends on what is available in the local market that day. Selections include fresh seafood and meat. A nice touch is the red rose you are given at the end of your meal.

For a market-fresh blend of Florida and Mediterranean cooking, try Citricos, and for Southern specialties head for the Grand Floridian Cafe. The 1900 Park Fare serves a Disney-character breakfast and dinner buffet; Narcoosee's features a variety of seafood. All serve baked goods prepared in the hotel bakery.

At the close of the evening, the night sky lights up at Epcot with a spectacular display of fireworks during IllumiNations, a laser and water spectacular. It's guaranteed you'll see stars!

Disney's Grand Floridian Resort & Spa

Location: On 40 acres in the heart of Walt Disney World Resort on the west side of Seven Seas Lagoon

Romantic Highlights: Walt Disney World at your doorstep; luxurious spa; champagne cruise; couples' massages

Address/Phone: P.O. Box 10,000, Lake Buena Vista, FL 32830-1000; (407) 824–3000; fax (407) 824–2968

U.S. Reservations: (407) W–DISNEY

Owner/Manager: Kent Mitchell, general manager

Arrival/Departure: Transfers can be arranged at an additional cost for the Disney Fairy Tale Honeymoon Package.

Distance from Orlando International Airport: 26 miles

Distance from Orlando: 25 miles southwest

Accommodations: 867 rooms and suites

Most Romantic Room/Suite: Honeymoon rooms have king beds and amenities included in the Concierge rooms, with a few differences. Some are octagonal; some have balconies; some Jacuzzis. Lodge suites, located in a separate building, enjoy such special amenities as afternoon tea, complimentary continental breakfast, and hors d'oeuvres and wine.

Amenities: Air-conditioning, ceiling fans, hair dryer, telephone, minibar, in-room safe, bathrobes, turndown service, room service, iron and ironing board, and toiletries. Main building Concierge rooms also include special shampoos and lotions, slippers, VCR, continental breakfast, tea, hors d'oeuvres, and late-night dessert and cordials.

Electricity: 110 volts

Sports and Facilities: A 275,000-gallon swimming pool and a second pool overlooking the Seven Seas Lagoon with a waterfall and slide; beach, marina, water sports; health club, exercise room, saunas, massage room. Also in the Disney complex are 5 championship golf courses, tennis courts, jogging paths, horseback riding, ponds, and pools.

Dress Code: Casual; dressier at Victoria & Albert's

Weddings: The glass-enclosed Fairy Tale Wedding Pavilion, on an island in the Seven Seas Lagoon, offers a magical site for the ceremony. You can also arrange for a wedding and Cinderella reception at the Grand Floridian or a Sunset Beach wedding. Call (407) 828–3400 for details.

Rates/Packages: Rates range from $349 to $2,000 per couple, per night. A fee of $63.64 covers admission to one of the four theme parks, one day only, which can be combined with the room rates at time of booking. More expansive "Magic Your Way" packages are available for multiple days.

Payment/Credit Cards: Most major

Deposit: 1-night deposit at time of booking to cover first and last nights' accommodations

Government Taxes: 11.5 percent sales tax on rooms; 6 percent on food

Service Charges: Some gratuities included in honeymoon packages

LITTLE PALM ISLAND
Florida

It used to be a rustic fishing retreat for America's presidents and high-profile stars. It still attracts people like Mario Andretti, Robert Wagner, Jill St. John, and Ivana Trump, but Little Palm Island is no longer rustic. The South Seas–style thatched bungalows, which stand on stilts amid the more than 250 coconut palm trees, tropical foliage, and gardens of this idyllic island Shangri-la, just 3 miles offshore in the Lower Florida Keys, come with air-conditioning, whirlpool baths, king-size beds, and fully stocked minibars. Little Palm Island, which opened as a public resort in 1988, succeeds in combining the best of both worlds.

Once your boat pulls into the pier—and that's the only way you get here—you leave behind things like TVs, cars, alarm clocks, and telephones. There's one public phone located in a former outhouse (used by President Truman, they say), but that's it. So look around, stroll along the gravel paths that link the cottages to the pool area and beach, find a hammock, settle in, and relax. Since young children are not allowed here, you'll have the pool and the beach all to yourself.

You share the island, maintained as a nature preserve, with a variety of species of birds and animals, including herons, parrots, manatees, Key deer, and loggerhead turtles, which lay their eggs each year on the beach. A recently completed $2 million landscape program includes a Zen garden.

The sugar-white sand beach runs in a thin strip around the five-acre island and broadens out at one end, where you'll find a vast tidal flat, home to a fascinating number of birds and other creatures, which are best seen in the early morning or evening. During the day, from your lounge on the beach you need only plant your pink flag in the sand to summon a member of the ever-watchful staff, who will be quick to take your drink or snack order.

Sunsets are special here. Look carefully and you can see the green flash just as the sun drops below the horizon. Walk completely around the island in the early evening and watch the colors brighten and mellow.

Your suite has a soaring pitched ceiling of thatch and bamboo, a ceiling fan, a king-size bed draped with a filmy white net canopy, a sitting area furnished in traditional British colonial style, wraparound sundecks, a dressing area, and a bathroom decorated with Mexican tile.

Although each bathroom comes with a whirlpool tub, the most popular way to freshen up is to use your outdoor shower, which is enclosed by bamboo walls and is totally private. On Little Palm's list of ways to conserve natural resources is the suggestion to "shower with a friend."

Louvered wood walls (with screens) open to let the sea breezes in—you rarely need to turn on your air-conditioning; some never do.

Of course you'll have to make major decisions, like whether to go snorkeling or try out one of the canoes, whether to loll at the lagoonlike pool or head to the spa for a massage. Since the water off the beach is usually too shallow to swim in, you'll need the pool for your lap work.

Nearby are superb dive sites for scuba enthusiasts. Just 3 miles away, Looe Key, a long reef protected by the National Park Service, stretches for miles and is home to myriad multicolored fish and other sea creatures.

There is a small library with a good selection of books to borrow, and nearby are hammocks strung in the trees. At Little Palm, hammocks are in. And if you really can't stand all this serenity and good living, you can sneak down to the Quarter Deck, which is located on the dock, and rent a TV/VCR.

You can dine indoors in the main restaurant or outside on the terrace. You can also dine at the casual, literally on-the-beach restaurant, where your dining chairs and table sit on wood "island" platforms set right on the sand. And the food prepared by executive chef Adam Votaw is as good as it looks—using mostly fresh local ingredients.

Especially tasty are the fresh dolphin-fish, grouper, tuna, grilled salmon, rack of lamb, and homemade soups and pastas. Fresh herbs and seasonings are just right, sauces splendid, desserts impossible to resist. On Sunday it's brunch time. Everything can be accompanied by a bottle of red or white from Little Palm's impressive wine cellar.

Physically, Little Palm Island is fifteen minutes from shore; psychologically, it's another world, where cares wash away and romance blooms.

Little Palm Island

Location: Off the tip of Little Torch Key, 120 miles southwest of Miami and 28 miles east of Key West, Florida

Romantic Highlights: Your own thatched cottage—it's like being in the South

Pacific, only you don't have to knock your-self out getting there.

Address/Phone: 28500 Overseas Highway, Little Torch Key, FL 33042; (305) 872–2524; fax (305) 872–4843

E-mail: getlost@littlepalmisland.com

Web Site: www.littlepalmisland.com

U.S. Reservations: (800) 3–GET–LOST; Relais & Châteaux, (800) RELAIS–8

Owner/Manager: Emanuel Gardinier, general manager

Arrival/Departure: Transfer and van service to the Little Torch Key Shore Station (mile marker 28.5) is available from both Key West and Marathon Airports. Little Palm's shuttle service will meet you and take you to their shore station, where you will board a boat for the 3-mile, 15-minute ride to the island. Limousine service can also be arranged from Miami International.

Distance from Miami International Airport: 120 miles; Key West International Airport, 28 miles

Distance from Key West: 28 miles

Accommodations: 30 one-bedroom suites located in 15 thatched-cottage bungalows, 28 bungalow suites, and 2 Island Grand suites

Most Romantic Room/Suite: Although all rooms have a view of the sea, the Island Grand suites are the most coveted.

Amenities: Air-conditioning, minibar, wet bar, coffee bar, whirlpool bath, outdoor shower, ceiling fans, bathrobes. (TVs, tele-phones, and alarm clocks are "banned" from the island. There is one public phone, located in the former outhouse, and it takes credit cards only.)

Electricity: 110 volts

Sports and Facilities: Pool, beach, full-service spa, exercise room; sailing, kayaking, canoeing, fishing, snorkeling; pontoon boats and Sun-Kat motorized lounge chairs can be rented; deep-sea fishing, scuba diving, guided nature tours can be arranged.

Dress Code: Casually elegant

Weddings: Can be arranged

Rates/Packages: $745–$2,395 per suite per night; dinner plans available at additional cost. Honeymoon package $7,595–$10,075 includes 6 nights bungalow accommodations, Key West airport transfers, Dom Perignon champagne, all meals, snorkel trip, $480 spa credit per person, boat excursion, and bathrobes, plus taxes and gratuities.

Payment/Credit Cards: Most major

Deposit: First and last nights' lodging at time of booking, refundable if canceled no later than 30 days prior to arrival date; $50 service charge applies. Deposit will be forfeited if canceled 30 days or less prior to arrival date.

Government Taxes: 11.5 percent

Service Charges: 10 percent

BARNSLEY GARDENS RESORT
Georgia

Barnsley Gardens has a real-life Fairy God-mother, Denise Webb, whose job it is to make guests happy whatever it takes: per-haps you'd like a "Fiesta No Siesta"—a pitcher of frozen margaritas, chips, salsa, and sombreros displayed on a candlelit tray with special "instructions." Then there's the surprise Bathroom Blessing: a rose petal path to the bathroom, candles, bubble bath, champagne, and a bathroom filled from floor to ceiling with balloons. There are paths to wander, ponds to sit by, and a friendly ghost or two to encounter at Barns-ley Gardens.

Barnsley Gardens is no ordinary resort. It's a place with a past of love, tragedy, and myths. To fully appreciate a stay in this beautiful place, it is important that you know its history.

In the 1840s when Godfrey Barnsley, a young handsome Englishman from a privi-leged background, came to Savannah, he met Julia Scarborough, the daughter of a rich cotton shipper. Despite opposition from her mother, Julia married Godfrey and, as a cotton baron, the Englishman became one of the most affluent men in the south. The Barnsleys had eight children (although three died) and were very happy, but sadly Julia's health began to decline.

Wishing to take his wife to a place where the air was fresher and cooler, he purchased 10,000 acres in Bartow County in upcoun-try Georgia and started building a stunning Italianate brick mansion on the crest of a hill on land that once belonged to the Cherokees. "Woodlands" was only partially completed when Julia died of consumption at thirty-four years of age. Devastated, God-frey didn't have the heart to continue the construction of the grand house that was to have been his present to his cherished Julia—that was until he felt her spirit dur-ing his walks in the gardens and understood that she wanted him to finish the mansion.

Godfrey did go on to finish the house and gardens, following the principles of renowned nineteenth-century landscape architect Andrew Jackson Downing. Bricks to build the mansion were made on the property from clay dug out of the hills, tiles came from Italy, and the place was fur-nished with many valuable pieces from Godfrey's travels abroad, including items from Napoleon's Palace.

With the advent of the Civil War, the Barnsley family fortunes began to change. The mansion was ransacked by Union sol-diers, and Godfrey left for New Orleans to try to rebuild his wealth, leaving his chil-dren on the estate. His daughter Julia stayed behind, and with grit and courage she tried to hold the family together. Julia is believed to have written in a letter to a friend, "With God as my witness, I will never go hungry again," which is also the infamous line spoken by Scarlett O'Hara in the movie *Gone with the Wind*. In fact it is believed that Julia was the inspiration for Margaret Mitchell's 1936 classic novel, *Gone with the Wind*.

In 1906 a tornado blew the roof off the mansion, and members of the Barnsley family still living there moved into the kitchen wing. In 1942 the descendents of Godfrey and Julia sold the property at auc-tion, but the property continued to fall into disrepair. Great trees and vines filled the ruins of the mansion and the gardens grew into a tangle.

In 1988 Prince Hubertus Fugger and his wife, Princess Alexandra of Bavaria, came to the rescue. They bought the property, spending more than $3.5 million to restore the gardens and the rare pine arboretum, which contains the largest collection of private conifers in the Southeast (there are eighty-eight species dating to the 1850s). It took eight years to revive the original boxwood, clear trees and vines out of the ruins, and restore the plant life around the property.

In 1992 the Fugger family opened the gardens to the public. A few years later the Fuggers decided to build a resort in the style of an English village and in keeping with the vision and design principles of the original mansion and gardens. The resort opened in 1999, and then in 2004, a company of private investors, BGAC, LLC, purchased the resort from the Fugger family. Today Barnsley Gardens continues to grow and flourish, mindful of the story of its past.

Imaginative design using gables, fretwork, and shingles along with roof peaks and cupolas, porches, and shutters creates a fanciful village of thirty-three guest cottages housing seventy suites, along with a club house, a spa with eleven treatment rooms, and other buildings. Buildings are sided with dark-stained vertical wood and shingles accented by deep blues and greens.

Laid neatly along roadways of pebbles (used for golf cart transportation) and sidewalks, each of the fifty-plus buildings is different, yet designed to fit into the overall design scheme. Everything from the dark wicker chairs on the Woodside Grill patio to the bridges over the brooks complements the mood of unspoiled nature. Even the practice putting green blends into the whole. It has no red- or white-flagged holes; in fact there are no holes at all. You simply roll out a ball and start putting to get a feel for the surface.

Cottages are spacious, more like homes, with sitting rooms, fireplaces (wood for fireplaces is stacked on the porch during the colder months), twelve-foot tray ceilings, beadboard paneling, and French doors leading to porches with rocking chairs and private gardens. Creamy walls are accented by soft muted blues, browns, burgundys, pinks, and greens; artwork includes paintings of the region by area artists and original prints by Princess Alexandra, a noted botanical expert and former *National Geographic* photographer.

Oriental-style carpets cover dark wood floors and the accessories in the built-in hutch and on the mantels include homey things like books, old luggage pieces stacked on top of a shelf, crystal decanters, small leather boxes, model cars, photos in frames, and pieces of china. The king-size beds are extremely comfortable, with duvets, piles of pillows, Egyptian cotton linens, and thick mattresses. Bathrooms are large and tiled. Showers are big enough for two, and there is a claw-footed tub and enclosed toilet room.

Executive Chef Charles Vosburgh presides over the resort's restaurants, while Alistair Glen, who most recently came from Cape Grace in South Africa, one of the top hotels in the world, oversees the entire food and beverage operation. The food and service are excellent.

You can dine in the Rice House, where specialties might include grilled shiitake salad; roast Carolina quail stuffed with cornbread, apples, and Georgia pecans over butternut squash; dried fig risotto with cabernet sauce; and a deliciously decadent chocolate bread pudding. The Rice House is particularly interesting as it dates back to the mid-nineteenth century and was brought to the property in 1994 from its original site 30 miles away.

The Bavarian Beer Garden, sitting under a canopy of trees, is also fun for casual fare and sometimes music. For general dining and drinks, there is also the Woodlands Grill and patio.

A favorite dining venue for couples is in the historic Manor House Ruins, but you can have your own private dinner in any number of places—on the end of a pier, in a bamboo stand, by a lily pond, or on your porch.

The extensive grounds offer a variety of sports and activities, including golf on a Jim Fazio–designed course, tennis, horseback riding, clay pigeon shooting, walking, and billiards in a formal billiards room. There is an outdoor Grecian-style pool and a full-service spa, and arrangements can be made for fly fishing, mountain biking, canoeing, and several other activities.

The former kitchen wing houses the Museum at Barnsley Gardens, a thirty-year collection that tells the story of the Barnsley family and includes artifacts from the Civil War. The museum contains many of the original pieces of furniture, letters, books, photographs, and other items.

This is a relaxing place with many choices, including just doing nothing. It's a place to connect with those you love and reconnect and fall in love all over again. And it's a place that casts a spell—if you let it.

Barnsley Gardens Resort

Location: In the foothills of the Blue Ridge Mountains, set on 1,300 acres of beautiful woodlands, 160-year-old gardens, and rolling meadows about 75 minutes north of Atlanta, Georgia

Romantic Highlights: Your own private cottage with a fireplace overlooking a pond; dinner in the Ruins; a "Love Potion Spell" from the resort's Fairy Godmother; deep red rose petals, red wine, dark chocolates, and a candlelit bedroom to greet you on your return from dinner; a starlit tête-à-tête on a secluded pier; sharing a drink in a garden

alcove under a canopy of muscadine grape vines hung with candles; picnic lunches

Address/Phone: 597 Barnsley Gardens Road, Adairsville, GA 30103; (877) 773–2447; fax (770) 773–1779

E-mail: info@barnsleyinn.com

Web Site: www.barnsleyresort.com

U.S. Reservations: (877) 773–2447; Small Luxury Hotels of the World (800) 525–4800

Owner/Manager: Scott Mahr, general manager

Arrival/Departure: Many rent cars at Atlanta's Hartsfield Jackson Airport or Chattanooga Airport and drive. Private car transfers can also be arranged through the resort.

Distance from Hartsfield Jackson Airport: 50 miles (1 hour 15 minutes); Chattanooga: 52 miles (about .1 hour)

Accommodations: 33 guest cottages that house 70 individual, private suites

Most Romantic Room/Suite: Honeymoon Cottage with an oversize bathroom; cottages in the 1900 row which run along the woods and are more private; 1500, a separate cottage near the pond

Amenities: Air-conditioning, hair dryer, two-line data-port telephones, cable TV, CD players, hi-speed Internet access, radio/alarm clock, king beds, ironing facilities, robes, Molton Brown toiletries, wood-burning fireplaces, porches, minifridges, complimentary soft drinks and water, wet bar, coffee/tea facilities, umbrellas, twice-daily maid service

Electricity: 110 volts

Sports and Facilities: 18-hole championship golf course, spa, Jacuzzi, sauna, steam room, fitness room, swimming pool, clay pigeon shooting, horseback riding, hiking, fishing, mountain biking

Dress Code: Casual

Weddings: Can be arranged for up to 400 people. Popular venues include the gardens, the Ruins, and the Meeting House. Many weddings as well as vow renewals have taken place on the Barnsley Gardens grounds. Only problem you'll have is deciding where to tie the knot. The historic Manor House Ruins, with its brick arches, clematis twining up the walls, and views of the gardens and lily pond are ideal. You can also say your vows in the charming Town Hall with its large windows looking out into the rose arbor, or under a flowered arbor in the gardens. Barnsley's Wedding Planner will help you arrange the wedding you want. Here it's not preconceived . . . rather you will be asked what you want; with all the facilities on site, they can make it happen.

Rates/Packages: From $390 including breakfast; Godfrey and Julia's Romantic Escape priced at $1,475 includes two-night accommodations in a Cottage Suite, champagne, keepsake flutes, flowers, breakfast on your private porch or in the Woodlands Grill Restaurant, picnic lunch for two, romantic candlelit dinner, and couples' massage. Other packages available including a golf and spa package.

Payment/Credit Cards: Most major

Deposit: 1 night deposit (plus tax)

Government Taxes: 7 percent sales tax; 5 percent hotel tax; included in packages

Service Charges: 15 percent; included in packages

FOUR SEASONS RESORT MAUI AT WAILEA

Hawaii

Everything about the Four Seasons Resort Maui at Wailea since the resort opened in 1990 is as it should be—geared for the pleasure of its guests. Most would agree that chilled towels, ice water, and Evian mist brought to your poolside cabana throughout the day are not necessities. But boy are they appreciated! The Four Seasons' propensity for pampering and attention to detail has helped it earn the distinction of ranking consistently among the top hotels in the world.

The young, energetic staff look more like winners from central casting for a new California surfing movie than their real-life roles as dispensers of goodwill, frosty drinks, and fluffy towels. Four Seasons in

Maui has managed to put together a great package, combining exquisite facilities with superb personnel.

A study of elegance and style, the property has the look and feel of a plantation home settled in perfect harmony with its seaside surroundings. The lofty, open design integrates the vibrant blues of the Pacific with pastel-colored walls, floor-to-ceiling wooden shutters, ceiling fans, and plump-cushioned rattan couches. Gentle trade winds keep a profusion of white orchids in constant motion. Scattered throughout the lobby and other (un)common areas are pieces of art and period furniture.

Measuring a generous 600 square feet, the guest rooms are both elegant and comfortable and are decorated in a decidedly tropical mode. The in-room safe is simple to use; the light in the closet, a welcome touch; and sitting on your bedside table is a reading light.

Catering to the diversity of its many guests, the Four Seasons maintains the delicate balance between too much activity and not enough, and successfully separates activities geared for children and adults. With two pools, water sports galore, a health club/spa, a jogging trail, aerobics, and more, there is no lack of things to do. Sea kayaks and water scooters are available nearby.

A special surprise (priced at $215) awaits the unsuspecting: A trail of flower petals is laid from your bedroom door to a drawn bubble bath. Candles, CD music, roses, and champagne set the mood. At the heart of the resort, royal palms define the borders of a large swimming pool, which boasts an adjacent computer-controlled fountain; it's programmed to react to the whims of the trade winds so that its spray keeps within defined boundaries. Two Jacuzzis spill into the pool; one is for adults only. Hundreds of flowers follow a sweeping stairway from the upper lobby to the pool area and beyond. Beneath the stairway two tropical birds greet visitors as they pass. A manicured lawn between the pool and Wailea Beach provides an additional lounging area, and even the sand is water-cooled, making it easygoing on bare feet when the sun is hot.

Nearby, a waterfall cools guests as they swim in the smaller, second pool, effectively hidden by tropical plants. The resort also has two tennis courts; cold, wet towels are provided.

Dining options abound and range from casual to elegant haute cuisine. Wolfgang Puck's new Spago restaurant is a treat for even the most assiduous gourmet. The offerings are varied and exceptional, with the Pacific Rim menu featuring fresh island fish and local ingredients. All are presented with pride in a pleasing, open setting with wonderful ocean views.

Soft breezes and a breathtaking view also factor in at the Pacific Grill, where guests can enjoy a sumptuous buffet breakfast, lunch, or dinner. For more casual dining Ferraro's Bar e Ristorante serves informal fare during the day. At night try authentic Italian cuisine and watch the sunset while enjoying seductive Italian music.

A car isn't necessary, as other dining options, shops, and golf are just a short walk away along Wailea's 2-mile ocean pathway. A complimentary shuttle is also available within the Wailea Resort. However, if you want to go off on your own and go exploring, you will probably want to rent a car for a couple of days. There is a lot to see and do on Maui. You can get up early in the morning, be driven up to the top of the volcano, and then ride back down the mountain on a bike, and you can visit some of the small nearby villages and browse in the shops. Or you can stay just where you are on your lounge and wait for someone to come by and refresh you with a light mist of cool Evian water.

Four Seasons Resort Maui at Wailea

Location: On 15 waterfront acres between the slopes of the Haleakala Crater and the Pacific shore in Wailea, along Maui's southwestern coast

Romantic Highlights: Breathtaking views of the rugged volcanic coast and moonlit surf; huge marble bath; the ultimate romantic dinner for two on a grassy knoll, high above the sea; limo picnic lunch with champagne; outdoor massages along the ocean

Address/Phone: 3900 Wailea Alanui, Wailea, Maui, HI 96753; (800) 334–6284 or (808) 874–8000; fax (808) 874–2222

Web Site: www.fourseasons.com

U.S. Reservations: (800) 332–3442 or (800) 334–6284

Owner/Manager: MSD Capital L.P., owner; Thomas Steinhauer, general manager

Arrival/Departure: Airport limousine transfers; Budget rental cars; motor-coach minibus and van service can be arranged

Distance from Kahului Airport: 17 miles

Distance from Kihei: 4 miles

Accommodations: 380 spacious rooms and suites, all with one or more lanais (porches); 85 percent have ocean views

Most Romantic Room/Suite: Ocean-view or executive suite

Amenities: Air-conditioning, ceiling fans, hair dryer, bathrobes, room safe, double vanity as well as separate vanity, built-in refrigerator bar, separate soaking tub, TV, cosmetic mirror, toiletries, complimentary morning coffee

Electricity: 110 volts

Sports and Facilities: 2 pools, 2 whirlpools, beach, use of 3 golf courses at Wailea Golf Club, tennis at the 14-court Wailea Tennis Center (including 3 grass courts), complimentary use of 2 on-site tennis courts lighted for night play, health club with exercise machines and steam room; full-service spa; running paths, snorkeling, scuba diving, sailing instruction, aerobics, aqua exercise, power walking

Dress Code: Casually elegant

Weddings: Packages range from $3,800 for the Ku'uipo Wedding, with ceremony, leis, solo musician, and a bottle of champagne, to $14,000 for the more elaborate Lokelani Wedding.

Rates/Packages: Rooms $365–$815 per couple, per night; suites $660–$4,650. Ask about the romantic "amenity," including private dinner and in-room massages.

Payment/Credit Cards: Most major

Deposit: 1-night deposit plus tax

Government Taxes: 11.42 percent

Service Charges: Included except for extras like room service special delivery charges.

HALEKULANI
Hawaii

Originally a private oceanfront estate, the quietly posh Halekulani, on the middle of Waikiki Beach, has been welcoming guests since 1917. Over the years ownership has changed and buildings have been built and demolished and built again. What remains of the original hotel is a 1930s building (now called the "main building") that has been incorporated into the overall design, consisting of five interconnected structures. Throughout the resort you'll find lots of marble, Italian terrazzo, and fine woods in creating this Hawaiian oasis.

From your languorous lanai you'll see the exquisite oval pool and, beyond that, the beach and sea. Halekulani, which means "house befitting heaven," has everything you'll require to make it your own personal paradise.

Wraparound lanais with nonstop views of the sunsets, the sea, and Diamond Head are only the beginning. Decorated in soft whites and neutrals enlivened by the color of orchids and flowers so perfect you'll wonder if they're real, rooms are furnished with rattan and upholstered furniture, glass-top tables, king-size beds, louvered-window walls, and plush carpets. Everything is quietly elegant. You'll not find any Hawaiian clichés lurking in the decorating schemes of these rooms.

Baths have marble vanities, ceramic tiles with outrigger motifs, and mirrored doors opening into a closet. Open the louvered doors on the other (bedroom) side of the closet and you can watch the surfers ride the waves while you relax in your tub. You'll also have a desk, plenty of drawers, extra shelves in the closet, padded hangers, an in-room safe, a minibar, and a TV that slides into a wall cabinet. The Halekulani gets my vote for the best-designed room I've ever seen: not necessarily the largest or the poshest, but a space perfectly crafted for its size in visual beauty and ease of use. Even the toiletries, which are in small, sleek containers, fit into your hand or cosmetic bag just right.

Your room comes with all the amenities you'd expect, such as hair dryers and state-of-the-art phones, but there is more. A phone in the enclosed toilet area, spa-type bottled water, and lovely little pillow gifts each night—ranging from shells to orchids, all attached to a soft sweet message—pamper guests. Even your laundry rates special treatment: It comes back carefully wrapped in tissue in a wicker basket. And they really go over the top with honeymooners and deliver champagne to help celebrate the happy occasion.

A new over-the-top accommodation, the Vera Wang Suite at Halekulani, with 2,135 square feet, is pure luxury at $4,000 a night. Along with the designer room comes round-trip airport transfers by limousine, butler service, plasma screen television, color bath therapies, and more.

Your opportunities for dining are no less impressive. Orchids, an oceanside indoor/outdoor restaurant open for all meals, specializes in international seafood cuisine along with Hawaiian items created by chef Jean-Pierre Maharibatcha. Living up to its name, this three-tiered restaurant has live orchids placed throughout it.

House Without A Key, another indoor/outdoor restaurant, serves breakfast, lunch, and sunset cocktails with Hawaiian entertainment and dancing under the stars each night. Arrive in time to watch the sun go down—it's one of the best seats in town for this nightly spectacle.

French-style meals are served at La Mer, an elegant indoor restaurant in the main building, with great ocean views and high accolades from those who rate. You'll find several Hawaiian-produced products on the menu, such as yellowfin tuna, Kula tomatoes, and Big Island lobster. Plates appear at your elbow like a series of gifts. Even the names of your dishes, like fine wines, need to be rolled across the tongue: Tartares of Hamachi, Ahi, and Salmon with Three Caviars and Three Coulis, and Baked Moano Fillets with Opakapaka Mousse and Lobster Medallions.

Tea is served every afternoon in the living room in the main building, and cocktails hold center stage in Lewers Lounge each evening.

I took a tour of "the back of the house," those places tourists don't normally see. Very impressive. I saw the yogurt and ice-cream machines at work, chocolates being dipped, and exotic flowers being artfully arranged. In the bakery the wonderful aromas of freshly baked rolls and breads and the miniature muffins reminded me it was getting time for yet another meal.

Halekulani offers a full range of water sports as well as a fitness room, the Spa-Halekulani, and sight-seeing programs. And I loved the pool. A simple, elegant large oval, it has no diving boards, slides, or waterfalls—just a huge orchid "painted" in mosaic glass tiles on the bottom. It really takes your breath away and only gets more beautiful as night falls.

Even when the hotel is full, there is never a need for you to do the early-morning scramble to stake out your territory on a favorite chaise with your towel. There are more than enough chairs, tables, and lounges.

You may never want to leave the grounds, but if you do there's a whole other world out there filled with fun and excitement. If you want action like an outrigger canoe ride, party time every Sunday at Duke's just down the beach, or shopping at the countless upscale stores, you'll find that almost everything is within a five- to ten-minute walk. Discos, nightclubs, streetcars—all close by. Catch the latest exhibit at the Contemporary Museum; picnic in the park and lie back on a blanket while the Hawaiian Royal Band plays the "Kamehameha Waltz." Try some rainbow-flavored shaved ice from the Waiola Store; shop for wild-looking veggies in Chinatown; pick up a yummy *malasada* (fluffy Portuguese doughnut) at Leonard's Bakery; and eat some great Thai food at Singha. Cap off the evening in the Hard Rock Cafe.

If you really feel adventurous, hop on a bus and go to Hanauma Bay for some snorkeling, hike up to the top of Diamond Head for a fabulous view of Honolulu, or explore Waimea Bay on the North Shore, where you can sit on a rock overlooking the beach and watch the sailboarders.

At sunset on Halekulani's terrace of the House Without A Key, sip a cool Chardonnay or Mai Tai as Kanoe Miller, elegantly dressed in a long brown velvet skirt and white Victorian-style blouse, dances gracefully under an aged Kiawe tree to lilting Hawaiian music played by the trio just behind her. With a backdrop of palms and the sea and the sun sinking slowly, turning the sky a rich pink, you'll find it hard to believe you are but a few yards from Waikiki Beach. Here, it would seem, you can have it all.

Staying at Halekulani may not be at the low end of the budget scale, but for your vacation of a lifetime, it's worth going the extra mile.

Halekulani

Location: On 5 oceanfront acres on Waikiki Beach, Oahu

Romantic Highlights: At twilight sounds of Hawaiian music floating up to your balcony overlooking the sea; candlelight dinner on your own private lanai

Address/Phone: 2199 Kalia Road, Honolulu, HI 96815-1988; (808) 923–2311; fax (808) 926–8004

Web Site: www.halekulani.com

U.S. Reservations: (800) 367–2343

Owner/Manager: Fred Honda, general manager

Arrival/Departure: Taxis available at airport; one-way is approximately $25; limousine service is $80

Distance from Honolulu Airport: 10 miles (25 minutes)

Distance from Honolulu: You're in the center of the Waikiki action; downtown Honolulu is 4 miles (15 minutes) away.

Accommodations: 455 rooms and suites, located in 5 low-density buildings ranging in height from 2 to 17 stories; 90 percent have ocean views.

Most Romantic Room/Suite: Vera Wang Suite and corner ocean-view suites have a separate bedroom, bathroom, powder room, living room, wet bar, and dining area. Club ocean-view suites come with two lanais, bedroom/sitting area, bathroom, wet bar, and cozy bay window.

Amenities: Air-conditioning, hair dryer, remote color cable TV, mini-refrigerator, 3 telephones, in-room safe, separate glassed-in shower with thermostatic control, bathrobes, chocolates, fruit bowl

Electricity: 110 volts

Sports and Facilities: Large 46-by-82-foot pool; new SpaHalekulani; outrigger canoes, surfing, snorkeling, deep-sea fishing, sail-boarding, and golf and tennis lessons can be arranged

Dress Code: Evening, resort attire in restaurants; LaMer, long-sleeved collared shirt or jacket for gentlemen

Weddings: The Halekulani does a lot of weddings, each one personalized.

Rates/Packages: Rates per couple $385–$535 per night; $850–$5,000 for suites. Romance Package, 3 nights from $1,500 for room; from $2,800 for suites including round-trip limousine service, champagne, strawberries, and exotic flowers; daily breakfast, chef's special dinner in Orchids, and Halekulani champagne flutes

Payment/Credit Cards: Most major

Deposit: Guarantee with credit card

Government Taxes: 11.42 percent

Service Charges: Not included

HOTEL HANA-MAUI
AND HONUA SPA
Hawaii

Geography has played a key role in making Hotel Hana-Maui and Honua Spa one of the most romantic resorts in Hawaii. Located on the eastern end of Maui, Hana is isolated from the more developed touristy areas by deep valleys and ravines dividing this part of the island from areas around Kahana and Kaanapali. In order to reach Hana, you embark on a breathtaking 50-mile journey along the Hana Highway, called one of the most beautiful roads in the world.

Around many of the 617 bends of the road, which twists and wiggles along the rugged coastline, waterfalls bubble and gush, falling into deep pools of clear mountain water—bring your bathing suit and take a dip in these clean, cool mountain "Jacuzzis." Jungle vegetation, lush and

dense, cloaks the hills in a rich, dark green blanket damp with moisture and glistening in the sun, which filters through during the fickle mood shifts in the weather.

Finally, after crossing about fifty-four bridges along the Hana Highway (from Kahului), you come to the small town of Hana. There's not much here except for a couple of small stores, a bank, a post office, a gas station, and a restaurant. And Hotel Hana Maui. Sitting prettily on the very end of the island, below the rainy slopes of Haleakala, this hideaway resort is located on sixty-six acres of rolling, landscaped grounds.

This land was once devoted to the production of sugarcane and later to raising cattle. In the late forties Hotel Hana Ranch was created by Paul Fagan, the owner of the

14,000-acre Puu O Hoku cattle ranch, specifically to accommodate Fagan's wealthy friends. There are still several thousand head of cattle on the property, but the hub of activity for most who find their way here is the hotel itself.

Once you check in and stroll around the gardens and lawns, richly planted with heliconias, exotic palms, and a wide variety of flowering shrubs, and walk to the top of the hill overlooking the coast, where waves crash against jagged black rocks, the spell of Hana will soon captivate. Whether you stay in one of the Bay cottages or in the traditionally styled Sea Ranch cottages, you'll appreciate the appointments and details that make this place so special. Live orchids growing out of ceramic containers and baskets, original Hawaiian arts and crafts, teak furniture, and beautiful tiled baths designed so that you don't need a curtain or door lend an air of low-key elegance.

Bleached hardwood floors, stone countertops, and carpets of Lauhala, along with rich, muted natural colors of soft browns and greens, appeal to those who love things that are warm and welcoming, not overdone. Bathrobes are yakuta-style, towels are thick and thirsty.

Your view from your trellised patio or deck could be a fragrant garden or the sea. The one-story Bay Cottage Junior Suites are quite different from the Sea Ranch accommodations. Bay Cottage suites are nestled into the gardens, and the views from the patios are of flowers and palms and towering trees. You'll find it hard to resist scooping up the petals from the plumeria trees, which drop their fragrant blossoms along the walkways.

The Sea Ranch cottages have spacious, private decks, and some come with private hot tubs that overlook the sea. Louvered-window walls allow the sea breezes to cool the rooms, which are comfortable, quiet, and secluded.

Hana has a number of recreational facilities on the grounds or nearby. A 1932 Packard sedan takes you on a five-minute ride to a silver-black sand volcanic beach right down the road, a beach author James Michener called the most perfect crescent beach in the Pacific. The beach is public but never crowded, and the hotel has its own changing and refreshment house.

Early risers may want to join the morning walk. You can also go horseback riding along the sea or follow the trails up the lower slopes of Haleakala volcano. An excursion to Ulaino brings you to beautiful Kahanu Garden.

You can also go bicycle riding, play tennis and croquet, or practice your golf on the three-hole pitch and putt, where tees are marked by coconuts. Take a nature hike into the forest, or head to the Wellness Center, located near the pool at the top of a grassy hill above the sea, where you'll find the latest in fitness equipment. Aquacise and yoga classes are offered daily. The award-winning Honua Spa offers a full complement of wellness treatments. The Couples Retreat combines a massage and spa treatment for the ultimate in romantic bliss.

The dining room, with its beautiful garden view and dramatic 35-foot open-beamed ceiling, overlooks the gardens and Hana Bay and features a range of Hawaiian specialties along with Polynesian, American, and Oriental cuisine. The chef uses lots of local produce, such as herbs, vegetables, taro, coconut, mango, and bananas. The Paniolo Bar, on the covered lanai overlooking the bay, is the place to go for those who want to relax after dinner. The more casual Hana Ranch Restaurant is open daily for lunch and on Friday and Saturday for dinner.

The marvelous Hana Coast Gallery features the finest in genuine Hawaiian art and master crafts, including paintings, pottery, sculpture, wooden bowls, and rare antique floral prints.

You'll find the staff extremely friendly and helpful. Most live in the village and walk to work. Some have been employed at the hotel since its opening in 1946!

The Hotel Hana-Maui casts its spell with exquisite subtlety. Serene and lovely, it's a resort romantics must discover at some point in their lifetime. A honeymoon is a good place to start.

Hotel Hana-Maui and Honua Spa

Location: Eastern end of the island, in Maui's back pocket

Romantic Highlights: Quiet, secluded area recalling Old Hawaii; private hot tubs on bungalow decks overlooking Pacific; secluded spa suites for couples

Address/Phone: P.O. Box 9, Hana, Maui, HI 96713-9989; (808) 248–8211; fax (808) 248–7202

U.S. Reservations: (800) 321–4262

Owner/Manager: Douglas Chang, general manager

Arrival/Departure: By car from Kahului Airport: a 55-mile drive along the scenic (and winding) Hana Highway. If you're going to rent a car, make arrangements in advance, and rent the car in Kahului. You'll pay more if you rent in Hana, and only Dollar has an office there. By air: a 15-minute flight to Hana from Kahului Airport by Pacific Wings. You can also fly from Honolulu to Hana via Pacific Wings (60 minutes) or take a private charter or private helicopter. The hotel's open jitney picks up guests at all flights coming into Hana Airport and transports them to the property, a 10-minute ride.

Distance from Kahului Airport: 55 miles

Distance from Hana: In town; 50 miles from Kahului

Accommodations: 70 rooms and suites, including Garden View Bay cottages and Sea Ranch cottages on the ground sloping to the seacoast on the Pacific side

Most Romantic Room/Suite: Sea Ranch cottages with private hot tubs

Amenities: Coffee bar with coffeemaker, grinder, and selection of Maui coffee beans; hair dryer, toiletries; ceiling fans and refrigerator with ice maker; minibar with complimentary snacks and refreshments

Electricity: 110 volts

Sports and Facilities: Beach, tennis court, pool, 3-hole pitch-and-putt course, hiking, horseback riding, snorkeling, croquet, new spa

Dress Code: Casual by day; dressier during evening

Weddings: The wide veranda of the Plantation House and the beautiful lawn and gardens are popular sites.

Rates/Packages: $395–$895 per couple, per day, including tennis, bicycles, snorkeling, and beach equipment; $95 per person, per day for breakfast, lunch, and dinner; $75 for breakfast and dinner. The Honeymoon Package offers a discount of 10 percent off rack rates as well as dinner 1 evening, champagne, and a massage for two with minimum four-night stay.

Payment/Credit Cards: Most major

Deposit: 1-night deposit, guaranteed with credit card

Government Taxes: 11.42 percent

Service Charges: 15 percent

KONA VILLAGE RESORT

Hawaii

Native grass shacks were never like the luxurious hales that loll along the crystal-blue bay at Kona Village Resort, a hideaway strung around peaceful lagoons and blessed by a natural black-and-white speckled beach. The setting is something of a miracle—a small oasis of coco palms and beach that was left untouched by a fiery lava flow in 1801. Today Kona Village remains a lush, eighty-two-acre paradise of emerald lawns and mirror-still ponds. It's a quiet retreat for simple pleasures: watching a coconut drift in with the tide or stopping to watch the nightly "water ballet" by the resident manta rays, which softly swirl near shore.

Located at the site of an ancient Hawaiian fishing community, the resort resembles an old Hawaiian village. Its paths are edged by fragrant pikake and plumeria blossoms, and bungalows are thatched with coconut fronds and planted on stilts beside the ocean and lagoons or on lava fields. The resort is, in fact, the largest group of thatched buildings in the state of Hawaii. Local materials, such as coral, stone, and koa and ohia woods, are used extensively.

Inside, however, twenty-first century accoutrements include king-size beds in most accommodations, a refrigerator stocked with juices and soft drinks, and modern bathrooms. The designs of the *hales* reflect nine different Polynesian cultures. The Hawaiian accommodations, for example, have steeply pitched thatched roofs, while the Maori feature boldly patterned fronts and carved figures on the rooflines. Interiors are paneled with wood, and ceilings are lined with lauhala matting. Furnishings might include rattan chairs and tropical-print spreads. The *hales* are also notable for what they don't have—in-room telephones, radios, or television. Instead of air-conditioners, ceiling fans enhance nature's cooling trade winds. A coconut placed in front of your door alerts the staff to leave you alone.

Every mealtime is special, from the macadamia-nut pancakes with coconut syrup at breakfast to duck breast with taro leaves and mango coulis at dinner. Friday night the resort hosts a traditional luau, one of the most authentic in the islands—many Big Island residents drop by to enjoy the feast. Kalua pig is roasted in the imu (underground oven), accompanied by other delicacies, such as lau lau (pork and fish in taro leaves) and lomi salmon.

Afterward a Polynesian revue showcases Pacific Island dances, including the Samoan fire dance and hip-quivering Tahitian tamure. Another favorite is the paniolo steak cookout, with ukulele music to accompany the kiawe-grilled steaks.

A bevy of water sports and activities are available for guests, including outrigger canoeing and glass-bottom boat excursions. In addition to the crescent-shaped swimming beach, the property offers two freshwater pools and whirlpools. The resort has three lighted outdoor Premier court tennis courts; you can take advantage of the complimentary adult clinic or sign on for the round-robin series for practice and fun.

At the Oceanside Massage Hale, a variety of massages from lomi lomi to Thai and cranial-sacral therapy soothe weary travelers.

The grounds also include many Hawaiian archaeological sites, including fishponds, house sites, and shelter caves. You can learn more about Hawaiian culture on several different excursions, including historical walks, tide-pool explorations, and petroglyph tours highlighting the powerful depictions of turtles, fish, dogs, and humans.

About half of the guests at Kona Village have stayed at the resort previously. You'll probably want to add your names to the roster of returnees soon.

Kona Village Resort

Location: On 82 acres amid palms, gardens, and historic fishponds along a natural black-and-white beach on Kahuwai Bay, the Big Island

Romantic Highlights: Luxury *hales* (cottages), each designed in a different Polynesian style, such as Tahitian, Fijian, and Samoan; privacy protected when you place coconut at door; private massage for two in garden setting; private Jacuzzis

Address/Phone: P.O. Box 1299, Kailua-Kona, HI 96745; (808) 325–5555; fax (808) 325–5124

E-mail: info@konavillage.com

Web Site: www.konavillage.com; www.konavillagehoneymoon.com

U.S. Reservations: (800) 367–5290 or (800) 423–5450 (in Hawaii)

Manager: Ulrich Krauer, general manager

Arrival/Departure: Transfers included in honeymoon package

Distance from Keahole-Kona Airport: 6 miles

Distance from Kailua-Kona: 15 miles

Accommodations: 125 thatched *hales* (cottages) in 9 architectural styles

Most Romantic Room/Suite: The luxurious Lava Tahitians are set out on the lava rock along the ocean, away from other *hales*. The Sand Marquesans are also very luxurious and are located on the water, with lots of greenery to provide privacy.

Amenities: Ceiling fans, hair dryer, toiletries, king-size bed, dressing room, refrigerator stocked with juices and soft drinks, coffeemaker, coffee grinder, and in-room safe

Electricity: 110 volts

Sports and Facilities: Sunfish sailboats, outrigger canoes, snorkeling, new Oceanside spa, 3 lighted tennis courts all available on premises; nearby activities include 5 18-hole championship golf courses, horseback riding, fishing

Dress Code: Tropically casual

Weddings: Can be arranged

Rates/Packages: $590–$960 per couple, per night, including breakfast, lunch, and dinner daily. Prices also cover most resort activities, including tennis, kayaking, Sunfish sailing, historical and petroglyph tours, and more. The Honeymoon Hideaway package costs $1,590– $2,820 per couple for 3 nights; $4,035–$6,965 for 7 nights. It includes all meals, accommodations, and a line-art reproduction of your honeymoon *hale.*

Payment/Credit Cards: Most major (except Discover)

Deposit: 2-night deposit, guarantee with credit card

Government Taxes: 11.42 percent

Service Charges: Not included

THE MANELE BAY HOTEL
Hawaii

A dozen years ago the island of Lanai was about a twenty-five–minute flight from— and about fifty years behind—Honolulu. With 98 percent of the land owned by Castle & Cooke, Lanai was called the Pineapple Island, a laid-back world with one funky hotel and a one-room airport.

All that changed in the early 1990s with the debut of two elegant new sister resorts, among the most luxurious in Hawaii. In the short time they have been open, the hotels have wowed rich and famous guests such as Kevin Costner and Billy Crystal and hosted major sporting events such as the Merrill Lynch Senior Shoot-Out on the PGA tour.

Playful spinner dolphins often visit Hulopoe Bay, Lanai's best beach and the setting for the Manele Bay Hotel, which opened in May 1991. Architecturally, the resort combines both Hawaiian and Mediterranean detailing, with arcaded loggias and sloping roofs. White walls and a sea-green tile roof harmonize with plush lawns and ochre pathways. To maintain an intimate feeling, individual wings surround garden courtyards, each with a different theme, such as Hawaiian, Japanese, or bromeliad.

In the lobby, murals by John Wullbrandt depict the legend of Kaululaau, said to have chased evil spirits from the island. Honoring Lanai's pineapple-plantation heritage, bronze chandeliers incorporate leaves and fruit in their design; vintage Hawaiian prints line the corridors.

As you stroll through the lush grounds, you'll encounter staff members diligently pursuing perfection—perhaps a wizened gardener raking imaginary leaves from an immaculate lawn, or a housekeeper polishing a bronze urn until it's mirror bright.

Rooms are very large and decorated in chinoiserie chic, with bamboo-framed chairs, porcelains poised on the armoire, and a four-poster bed. Spacious bathrooms sparkle with marble floors and counters and a separate glass stall shower. In addition to the usual shampoos and soaps, the lavish toiletries basket also includes hair spray, a miniloofah, and prethreaded needles. The lanai (terrace) is designed to be enjoyed and is furnished with a plump-cushioned chaise lounge and two comfy armchairs. About half of the rooms have ocean views.

A diamond-bright crescent, Hulopoe is one of the loveliest beaches in the islands. When conditions are calm, there's good snorkeling along the rocks at the left (as you face the ocean).

Through the hotel, guests can arrange various excursions, including a snorkel cruise aboard the *Trilogy* trimaran. They can also sign on for an ocean rafting trip along Lanai's coast, which is lined by 1,000-foot cliffs and secret coves.

For dining-with-a-view, you can't top the outside terrace of the Ihilani, with sound effects courtesy of the rustling palm fronds and wash of surf. Accented by crystal chandeliers and murals, the Ihilani formal dining room re-creates the splendor of the Hawaiian monarchy and serves a French Mediterranean cuisine.

The Lodge at Koele, Manele Bay's sister property, is also extremely Hawaiian—but in a way mainlanders rarely imagine Hawaii to be. The upland setting—a cool 1,700-foot elevation where hills often wear clouds like misty halos—resembles a scene more from *The Sound of Music* than *South Pacific*.

Styled after a turn-of-the-twentieth-century plantation estate, the resort features 35-foot beamed ceilings, twin natural stone fireplaces in the Great Hall, and spacious verandas arranged with wicker armchairs.

Although Koele feels as though it has purred along in Grand Hotel perfection for at least a century or two, it only opened in April 1990. Connoisseurs can happily browse among rarities, ranging from a Burmese elephant howdah in the foyer to the eighth-century Persian painting in the music room. At the same time, the ambience is friendly, thanks to interior designer Joszi Meskan's sprightly touches, such as monkeys cavorting among the 8-foot-tall chandeliers.

Coddling remains the byword here, from the butter-soft suede armchairs in the library to the real down pillows on your bed. Rooms encourage relaxing, with a lavishly cushioned window seat, two wicker armchairs, and a four-poster bed crowned with pineapples. Bathrooms feature exotic blue-marble countertops paired with Italian tile floors and hand-painted cups from Portugal. Look carefully at the walls—they're painstakingly hand-painted, not papered.

Lanai is golfers' heaven, with two spectacular eighteen-hole layouts. Designed by Jack Nicklaus, the championship Challenge at Manele opened in December 1993 to immediate acclaim. Every hole on the course offers an unobstructed ocean vista. Upland, the Experience at Koele, designed by Greg Norman and Ted Robinson, boasts panoramic views and several dramatic elevation drops from tees to greens. The newly renovated Spa at Manele is reminiscent of an old-style plantation home with bamboo, stone, wood, and water features.

It all adds up to the perfect choice for couples who love outdoor adventures by day and sumptuous accommodations at night.

The Manele Bay Hotel

Location: Southeastern coast of Lanai

Romantic Highlights: White-sand Hulopoe Beach; serene courtyard gardens; two hotels for the price of one—stay at Mahele Bay and enjoy facilities at the upcountry Lodge at Koele.

Address/Phone: P.O. Box 630310, Lanai City, HI 96763; (808) 565–7700; fax (808) 565–2483

E-mail: reservations@lanai-resorts.com

Web Site: www.islandoflanai.com

U.S. Reservations: (800) 321–4666 or (808) 565–3800

Owner/Manager: Castle & Cooke Resorts, LLC

Arrival/Departure: Shuttle service between both hotels, golf courses, and Lanai airport is provided.

Distance from Lanai Airport: 12 miles (35 minutes)

Distance from Koele: 7 miles (20 minutes)

Accommodations: 250 rooms and suites

Most Romantic Room/Suite: If you want to splurge, ask for one of the suites that includes butler service (e.g., the midpriced Mauka Mini Suite); deluxe oceanfront rooms are also very romantic.

Amenities: Air-conditioning, ceiling fans, hair dryer, minibar, toiletries, TV, radio, clock; coffee/tea service; room service. Some suites have butler service.

Electricity: 110 volts

Sports and Facilities: 36 holes of championship golf, 6 tennis courts, sporting clays, archery range, croquet, lawn bowling, swimming pool, snorkeling, sea kayaking, scuba diving. The hotel can arrange scuba diving and snorkel sails.

Dress Code: Casually elegant

Weddings: Can be arranged

Rates/Packages: $400–$800 per couple, per night for a room; $795–$3,500 for a suite. Honeymoon & Romance Package: from $1,996 for 4 nights; accommodations, limousine airport transfers, aromatic bath salts and oils, champagne and chocolates, nightly turndown, couples' massage, 4-wheel-drive vehicle for 1 day with picnic lunch, breakfast in bed, and 1 dinner for two.

Payment/Credit Cards: Most major

Deposit: Two-night deposit required within 14 days of the reservation request. Deposits will be refunded in full when cancellations are received at least 14 days prior to arrival.

Government Taxes: 11.42 percent

Service Charges: Not included

MAUNA LANI BAY HOTEL & BUNGALOWS
Hawaii

Its name means "mountain reaching to the heaven"—a perfect visual for honeymooners, who will feel as though they've come close to finding paradise at the Mauna Lani Bay Resort. Located on the sunny, dry (only 7 inches of rain annually) Kohala Coast, this six-story hotel presents a bold, contemporary design. Shaped like an arrowhead thrust seaward toward Makaiwa Bay, Mauna Lani Bay is a true-blue haven fringed by pearl-white beaches. The lobby reflects a spare elegance, with koi ponds and banks of orchids, torch ginger, and birds of paradise flanking the atrium. Jet-weary travelers are immediately soothed by the whoosh of waterfalls, view of the sapphire-blue Pacific, and friendly ministrations of the concierge, who checks you in.

The resort is built around fifteen acres of ancient fishponds, once *kapu* (forbidden) to all but Hawaiian royalty. They're stocked with mullet, awa, and lemon butterflies, whose brilliant colors swirl like an aquatic kaleidoscope. Paths encourage peaceful wanderings.

Decorated in serene tones of white and sand, each of the accommodations measures more than 550 square feet and has a private lanai. Ceiling fans, polished teak furnishings, and live orchids complement the tropical oasis decor. Top-of-the-line accommodations are the five bungalows— private houses, really, encompassing more than 4,000 square feet. Each has a private swimming pool and whirlpool spa and is served by a butler who can handle everything from unpacking your bags to grilling mahimahi on the barbecue. Steven Spielberg and Roseanne are among the celebrities who have roosted amid the sumptuous decor, accented by koa wood, marble, and crystal.

The signature restaurant is the celebrated CanoeHouse, which has won accolades in magazines such as *Bon Appétit*. Poised on the brink of the ocean, it offers diners ringside views of the polychromatic Kohala Coast sunsets and a menu reflecting cuisine from the Pacific Rim. For example, you might start with Ani Poke and avocado, move to Hilo corn and lemongrass soup followed by grilled mahimahi with pineapple relish and coconut ginger broth. The Honu Bar is open for late-night music and dancing. In all, Mauna Lani has five restaurants.

Carved from a sixteenth-century lava flow, the two championship golf courses (home to the 1999–2000 Senior Skins golf tournament) present dramatic juxtapositions between stark black lava rock, smooth emerald turf, and an ever-changing sea. Meanwhile *Tennis Magazine* has included the ten Plexi-pave tennis courts on its list of top U.S. resort facilities. The roster of activities also includes aerobics classes, hula and lei-making lessons, beach picnics, and more. In July 2001, Mauna Lani debuted its indoor/outdoor spa. Options range from private yoga classes at water's edge to lomi lomi, an ancient Hawaiian-style massage choreographed to Hawaiian music.

For relaxing and sunning Mauna Lani's two beaches are regarded as some of the finest on the Big Island. Try to snare one of the private cabanas, and lie back on the two-person lounge chairs shaded by a cabriolet roof. One of Hawaii's best scuba-diving locales, the waters off the Kohala Coast are stippled with lava tubes, archways, caves, canyons, and coral heads. Favorite sites include Turtles Reef, a cleaning station for Hawaiian green sea turtles. Dive packages are available.

According to Hawaiians, Mauna Lani Bay is set on sacred ground. Perhaps that explains the tremendous feeling of mana (spiritual power) that the resort exerts over all those who visit.

Mauna Lani Bay Hotel & Bungalows

Location: On 29 oceanfront acres at Kalahuipua'a, on the Big Island's Kohala Coast

Romantic Highlights: 2 white-sand beaches; 15 acres of ancient, spring-fed Hawaiian fishponds plus pools teeming with tropical fish; award-winning oceanfront restaurant

Address/Phone: 68–1400 Mauna Lani Drive, Kohala Coast, HI 96743; (808) 885–6622, fax (808) 885–1484

E-mail: maunalani@maunalani.com

Web Site: www.maunalani.com

U.S. Reservations: (800) 367–2323; (808) 885–6622 (in Hawaii)

Owner/Manager: Mauna Lani Resort (operation), Inc., owner; Kurt Matsumoto, managing director

Arrival/Departure: Taxis available at airport; transfers can be arranged

Distance from Keahole-Kona Airport: 23 miles north

Distance from Kona: 34 miles north

Accommodations: 342 guest rooms; 5 bungalows with private swimming pools and 24-hour butler service; 29 ocean villas. More than 92 percent of the accommodations have ocean views.

Most Romantic Room/Suite: Bungalows with pools; ocean villas

Amenities: Oversize TV (with cable) and on-command movies, VCR, honor bar, electronic safe, clock radio, umbrella, refrigerator, makeup mirror, toiletries, his and hers marble basins, robes and slippers, hair dryer, concierge service, 24-hour room service

Electricity: 110 volts

Sports and Facilities: 36 holes of golf, 10 tennis courts, heated swimming pool, full-service spa, fitness center with outdoor lap pool, sailing, snorkeling, sailboarding, boogie boarding, and surfing. Scuba diving and deep-sea fishing can be arranged.

Dress Code: Casually elegant

Weddings: Can be arranged

Rates/Packages: $395–$850 per couple, per night for a room; $950–$1,650 for a suite; $575 for a one-bedroom villa; $4,600–$5,300 per night for a bungalow. Romantic Interludes Package from $3,075 includes 5 nights accommodations, champagne, breakfasts, snorkel or sunset sail or CanoeHouse for 2, 2 50-minute spa treatments, helicopter tour.

Payment/Credit Cards: Most major

Deposit: 2-night deposit to guarantee reservation

Government Taxes: 11.42 percent

Service Charges: None

THE WHITE BARN INN
Maine

The White Barn Inn, a cozy enclave consisting of cottages, an 1850s homestead, and two 170-year-old barns, has been carefully crafted by owner Laurence Bongiorno to meet the expectations of guests who come to Kennebunkport looking for privacy, luxury, and over-the-top dining. They are not disappointed.

Bongiorno has raised the bar when it comes to setting standards for country inns. Hand-painted furniture, CD stereo systems, steam showers, fireplaces, a heated infinity granite-and-stone pool, and an award-winning restaurant where the cuisine and service live up to the highly romantic ambience, all score points in the "above and beyond column."

There are contrasts here and they all seem to work. Rustic beams and formally attired waiters; primitive farm implements and white linen table cloths; elaborate international cuisine and simply grilled local fish; 40-foot ceilings and intimate cottages; primitive antiques and contemporary art.

In the main house, once a Boothbay boarding house, there are twelve rooms featuring whimsically painted beds and original art. The four garden rooms have queen-size sleigh beds, fireplaces, and whirlpool baths; a stylish new color palette brings in restful greens and yellows. The seven junior suites are furnished with four-poster king-size beds and come with sitting areas, fireplaces, and spacious marble baths with whirlpool.

May's Cottage, one of the most romantic places to stay, is located by the pool and has a king-size bed, double-sided fireplace, living room, whirlpool bath, and steam shower. The new loft suite features a private deck, cathedral ceilings, and a private entrance as well as a king-size bed, oversize marble bath, steam shower, and whirlpool bath.

The Wharf Cottages and Marina, a new gated compound located ⅕ of a mile from the main inn and just a stone's throw from the Kennebunk River, offers three separate cottages and a large clubhouse. Available year-round, Tern Cottage and Gull Cottage each feature one queen-size down-topped bed, a stylish bathroom, a wood-burning fireplace, plasma cable TV, and a private waterfront patio overlooking the river. Loon Cottage features two bedrooms, each with one queen-size bed and private bath, plasma cable TV, a wood-burning fireplace, and a waterfront patio.

In the compound's clubhouse, called "Friendship Cottage," there is a spacious great room with water views on three sides and a large fireplace. The cottage is furnished with comfortable leather and upholstered sofas and armchairs, and there is a self-serve bar and three-quarter bath. Friendship Cottage is for the use of guests staying at the compound.

All rooms and suites are decorated with a mix of traditional furnishings and contemporary accents with coordinated fabrics and wallcoverings that are stylish and handsome, not cutesy Americana. Furniture is mostly nineteenth-century polished traditional pieces such as carved mahogany four-poster beds and Chippendale chairs. Mantels frame wood-burning fireplaces. Suites were recently renovated.

Bedspreads are creamy white matelasse; towels are thick and luxurious. On your bedside table, you'll find a bottle of water and you may decide to delve into one of the current novels left for you to read.

Breakfast—including fresh-squeezed juices, eggs, cheeses, cereals, and breads— is served in the main house dining room each morning; tea is served in the parlor in the afternoon during the cooler months around a roaring fire. Port is offered as a fitting nightcap, perhaps after a brisk walk around town.

The White Barn Inn restaurant is adjacent to the cottages. As you walk into the lofty candlelit room, you'll see at once the huge window wall framing a changing tableau each season: in the spring, brilliant displays of flowers and greenery; at Christmas, close to twenty trees all silvery with balls, bows, and white lights dusted with snow. A pianist plays soft dinner music and service is attentive, not intrusive. If ever you were looking for a place to pop the question, this is it.

Table-to-floor white linen cloths topped by fanciful silver sculptures (of New England wildlife creatures such as lobsters and pheasants crafted by French artist Gerard Bouvier from silver spoons, forks, knives,

and other flatware) along with elegant brocade upholstered chairs are juxtaposed against the rustic barn-siding backdrop of highly varnished wide board floors, soaring ceilings, and displays of oldtime farm equipment and antique signs. A bar with a highly polished brass top is tucked into a corner.

And if the setting isn't enough to ooh and ahh you, the highly acclaimed and artfully presented cuisine prepared by executive chef Jonathan Cartwright will tip the scales (and probably yours). Paying homage to Maine produce and seafood, Chef Cartwright combines regional fish, seafood, game, and poultry with unusual ingredients such as truffles, wild mushrooms, and quail eggs. The prix-fixe menu at $89 changes weekly and features items such as steamed lobster on fettucine with a cognac butter sauce, chargrilled native salmon, roasted lamb rack, and Grand Marnier custard. Meals start with an *amuse-bouche* from the chef, perhaps a bit of chicken liver mousse with truffles.

Small dinner parties of fifteen or less can enjoy private dining in the Wine Room, which is decorated with a mural of Tuscany by local artist Judith Harden and an Italian chiaro marble floor. More than 7,000 bottles of fine wine are stored here.

During the summer, a light bistro menu is offered poolside from 12:30 to 2:00 P.M. It consists of baguette sandwiches, salads, and brick oven pizza. And of course frosty drinks and champagne trolley.

The White Barn Inn celebrates all seasons. In the summer lawns, flowers, and shrubs invite you to linger; in the winter the courtyard is alive with tiny white lights that glow against the snow and purple light of night creating a beautiful fairyland. Spring is light and lacy with new flowering shrubs and trees; fall is bold and colorful.

There's not much nightlife in Kennebunkport, but then, who needs it?

The White Barn Inn

Location: In historic Kennebunkport

Romantic Highlights: Elegant candlelight dining in a rustic barn; wood-burning fireplaces; whirlpool baths for two; poolside cottage

Address/Phone: P.O. Box 560C, Beach Street, Kennebunkport, ME 04046; (207) 967–2321; fax (207) 967–1100

E-mail: innkeeper@whitebarninn.com

Web Site: www.whitebarninn.com

U.S. Reservations: Contact the hotel directly.

Owner/Manager: Laurence Bongiorno, proprietor; Roderick Anderson, hotel manager

Arrival/Departure: Rental cars available at Portland (35 minutes driving time) or Logan International Airports (Boston, 1½ hours driving time)

Distance from Portland Airport: 25 miles

Distance from Logan International Airport: 80 miles

Distance from downtown Kennebunkport: In town

Accommodations: 28 rooms, suites, and waterfront cottages

Most Romantic Room/Suite: May's Cottage, with a double-sided fireplace, living room, whirlpool bath, and steam shower. Newly renovated Loft Suite features a private deck, cathedral ceilings, private entrance, king-size bed, oversize marble bath, steam shower, and whirlpool bath.

Amenities: Air-conditioning, plasma flat-screen TV with DVD player, Wi-Fi access, hair dryer, terry robes, CD stereo system, toiletries, telephone, complimentary tea and port, turndown service. Some have fireplaces, whirlpool tubs, steam showers, and decks.

Electricity: 110 volts

Sports and Facilities: Heated "brimming" pool, canoeing, tennis, and biking. Horseback riding, whale watching, and picnics can be arranged.

Dress Code: Informal; jackets required at dinner

Weddings: Can be arranged

Rates/Packages: $320–$785, including breakfast; packages available

Payment/Credit Cards: Most major

Deposit: Required (depends on length of stay); cancel 30 days prior to arrival during summer (high season) for full refund; 14 days in low season.

Government Taxes: 7 percent

Service Charges: None

CHATHAM BARS INN
Massachusetts

When you walk into this weathered, gray-shingled Cape Cod landmark, which sits on a bluff above the Atlantic Ocean and Pleasant Bay, it is easy to imagine what life was like at the beginning of the last century. A spacious porch filled with comfy wicker furniture, a huge lounge with overstuffed chairs, vases of fresh flowers, marble-topped tables, comfortable sofas, blue-and-white striped beach cabanas, and a wood paneled library set the tone.

The inn has been welcoming guests since 1914 when it opened as a hunting lodge. At that time you could sit on the porch and sip a frosty glass of lemonade while watching the world go by on land and sea. You still can.

Accommodations are spread throughout the property. You can stay in the main inn itself, in one of the cottages or houses on the water, or in one of the spacious new master suites featuring hand-painted furniture, fireplaces, upholstered window seats, and sliding doors that open onto decks. The intent of the designers who orchestrated a recent $35 million restoration was to create accommodations that felt more like a classic Cape Cod home than a hotel room. Comfort was key. Some rooms are themed, for example, fishing, sailing, horseback riding, hunting lodge, and English country cottage.

Fabrics are keyed to the room style, some light and cheerful chintz, perhaps flowers or plaids; others feature natural hickory furniture and rich colors and textures. Fireplaces are bordered by decorative ceramic tile and there are many interesting appointments throughout the rooms: ship models, wood carvings, baskets, and books.

The Main Dining Room, where expansive, panoramic windows offer superb views of the water, is the venue for a grand dining experience. Executive chef Juho Lee blends classic French cuisine with a Pan-Asian influence such as in poelle of Chatham lobster with mango, avocado, beets, and a cilantro-ginger sauce. More casual fare is available at the nautically appointed Tavern, and one of the best seats in the summertime is at the oceanfront Beach House Grill, where you can eat breakfast, lunch, and dinner. The grill is also the scene of clambakes, barbecues, and festive beach parties.

The inn has a private beach, large pool on the edge of the beach, and tennis courts. Spa treatments, including Swedish, sports, deep-tissue, and aromatherapy massages

and sea-salt scrubs, are offered at the Health & Wellness Centre. You can work out on Stairmasters and other state-of-the-art equipment in the fitness center.

The daily calendar of activities is impressive. There are fitness walks, harbor tours, clam and lobster bakes, pool Scrabble, croquet lessons, tennis clinics, and nature walks as well as bike tours, gardening walks, and water aerobics.

It's an easy walk into town where you can spend several hours browsing through Chatham's boutiques, gift shops, and art galleries. Although summer is the busiest time, when you can unwind on the beach, perhaps under one of the canvas cabanas that dot the seafront, other seasons hold special delights. In the spring, the gardens that are located along pathways and throughout the property come alive; in fall the sea air is crisp and fresh, a wonderful time to play golf and tennis and take long walks. In winter you can sip a mug of mulled wine in front of a blazing fireplace either in the privacy of your room or in the lounge.

The nine-hole Chatham Seaside Links (which is not owned by the inn) is just out the back door. It's good for a quick warm-up to get you ready for some of the better courses. The hilly layout has potential, but in its present state is not for serious golfers. The artificial turf on some of the tee boxes presented a real challenge when it came to putting in your tees. Still there are some superb courses within a half-hour drive, including Ocean Edge, the two Captains Golf Courses in Brewster, and the New Seabury course in Mashpee, all highly rated.

Chatham Bars Inn

Location: Hugging the elbow of Cape Cod within walking distance of Chatham on 25 acres facing the Atlantic Ocean

Romantic Highlights: Walks along the salty sea; fireplace in your suite; dinner by the sea

Address/Phone: 297 Shore Road, Chatham, MA 02633; (508) 945–0096 or (800) 527–4884; fax (508) 945–6785

E-mail: welcome@chathambarsinn.com

Web Site: www.chathambarsinn.com

U.S. Reservations: (800) 527–4884

Owner/Manager: Christopher Diego, managing director

Arrival/Departure: Guests arrive by car or taxi. Rental cars are available at Providence and Boston airports.

Distance from Logan International Airport: 90 miles (closest airport, Hyannis, 25 miles)

Distance from Boston: 90 miles

Accommodations: 205 rooms, including 41 suites, 28 cottages, and 11 master suites

Most Romantic Room/Suite: Master suites with balconies, wet bars, fireplaces; #110 rose-covered cottage, very private and overlooking the golf course

Amenities: Air-conditioning, hair dryer, toiletries, safe, TV, clock radio, telephone, dataport, iron, some fireplaces, fans, balcony or patio, nightly turndown service

Electricity: 110 volts

Sports and Facilities: Beach, outdoor heated pool, 3 clay tennis courts, croquet; Health & Wellness Centre; putting green, beach volleyball, summer launch service to Outer Bar Beach, bikes, adjacent 9-hole golf course.

Dress Code: Resort casual except for dinner in the Main Dining Room, which is dressier and where gentlemen are expected to wear jackets and ties

Weddings: Can be arranged; sites include the Main Dining Room and The Beach House

Rates/Packages: From $330 per room (summer season); from $260 (late spring and early fall); from $205 (early spring and late fall); and from $150 (value season, Jan. 1 to end of March; end of November to end of December). Master Suites range from $460 to $1,600 depending on the season.

Payment/Credit Cards: Most major

Deposit: 1-night deposit at time of reservation is required.

Government Taxes: 9.7 percent

Service Charges: Not included

THE WAUWINET
Massachusetts

Situated 30 miles out to sea south of Cape Cod, Nantucket is a 50-square-mile island, town, and county of incredible natural beauty as well as a National Historic Landmark. Beach roads are lined with rugosa roses, beach plum, and blackberry bushes; cranberry bogs spread out over several acres; hundreds of deer roam the island; and ring-necked pheasant, piping plovers, terns, osprey, ducks, and geese make Nantucket a popular venue for birdwatchers.

Because of its proximity to the Gulf Stream, Nantucket is 10 percent cooler than the mainland in the summer and 10 percent warmer in the winter, making possible year-round golf, biking, and hiking as well as a plethora of water sports.

The weathered clapboard houses and tucked-away gardens brimming over with hollyhocks, black-eyed Susans, blue-and-purple hydrangeas, and cascades of roses tumbling over white picket fences are all part of Nantucket's inescapable charm. At the heart of it all is one of the oldest inns on the island, the Wauwinet. Located just about as far away as you can get from the noise and complexities of everyday life, the Wauwinet stands firmly planted on its grassy carpet, a bastion of peace and tranquility.

Its traditions reach back to the mid-1800s, when the inn was a restaurant, known as Wauwinet House, that served shore dinners to guests arriving by boat. In 1876 it became an inn and soon emerged as not only a Nantucket social center but a hot spot for Northeasterners to head for their vacation. It went through a period of decline until 1986, when Bostonians Stephen and Jill Karp purchased the property, restoring it with great care. Recent facelifts have resulted in new wall treatments, upholstery, furniture, and artwork.

On one side of the inn, a buff-colored ribbon of sand stretches for miles along the Atlantic providing a wonderful walking venue. In front of the inn, another beach runs along Nantucket Bay, reached by sandy paths and boardwalks from the Wauwinet's lawns. Both sides have private beaches for guests. Next door is a wildlife sanctuary.

Wicker chaises and white lawn chairs with superthick cushions entice you to settle back and relax while gazing out at the magnificent, endless ocean views, gentle grass-topped dunes, and wispy gardens of wildflowers and roses.

Rooms are individually decorated, many with an eclectic mix of English-style period pieces and pine country antiques. Chintz and stenciling add to the warmth of the decor, headboards are custom wood or upholstered. Around the rooms you'll find special touches such as baskets, hatboxes, books, and woodcarvings.

You have all the amenities you could wish for to ensure that you will be sublimely comfortable—extra things like Egyptian cotton bathrobes; armoires with soft, scented hangers; eyelet-trimmed linens; bottled water beside your bed; and fresh flowers. Windows are large, letting in lots of fresh air and light; ceilings are high.

Wauwinet's Topper's continues to garner rave reviews for its award-winning cuisine and wines. You can dine alfresco on the umbrella-shaded Bayview Terrace or eat inside in two indoor dining rooms. The executive chef, Chris Freeman, uses local produce, such as bushberries and cranberries, as well as fresh fish and seafood to prepare his American cuisine with a light touch. Lobster and fish caught from just offshore are prepared and served in a variety of flavorful dishes. Food is enhanced by fresh herbs from the Wauwinet's own herb gardens. A tasting menu featuring a delicious lobster course is served with appropriate wines. I found the staff very well trained. They knew how to serve and how to handle special guest requests and were well versed in what dishes and wines were being offered. And they were pleasant, not pretentious.

The inn's jitney is available to take you into Nantucket Town, always an interesting excursion. (You can also bicycle in.) Once one of the largest whaling centers in the world, Nantucket has a fascinating museum that details the history of the whaling industry. The town's streets are lined by more than 800 homes built between 1740 and 1840, many owned by whaling captains. You can spend hours browsing through the countless small shops, cozy restaurants, and art galleries. And take time to check out the harbor, where there are many lovely yachts riding at anchor or tied to the wharfs.

For a more intimate outing, ask the staff to prepare a gourmet basket lunch and take the *Topper, Too* launch to a secluded beach for a lazy afternoon of sunning and swimming.

Activities and sports at the Wauwinet are centered on Nantucket's natural assets. You can swim; go out in the inn's many boats and sailing craft; hike and jog through the trails that wind through the area; or play tennis or croquet. Golf can be arranged nearby.

Fishing is fabulous both from the beach and in the waters that surround the island, and biking is not only a favorite sport but a mode of transportation, especially during the summer when tourism swells the population from 10,000 to about 50,000. Paved bike paths link major areas of the island making it easy to get around even when the roads are teeming with traffic. The Wauwinet's fleet of bikes is available to guests.

But the Wauwinet is more than just a romantic place to stay. Its special hands-on programs give guests a chance to discover what the island and its people are all about. I can heartily recommend the lobster outing or shellfishing with Captain Rob McMullen, a native of Nantucket who truly "knows the ropes." Quite likely your catch of the day will be incorporated into the evening's meal by Chef Freeman.

Jeep safaris take you to Great Point or Coatue and through nature preserve lands. Your guide is an expert in wildlife and the history of the island. Other pleasures include cruising aboard the Wauwinet's two boats, whale-watching cruises, deep-sea fishing, surf fishing, sailing, yachting, golf, and biking.

During the crisper months, which some feel are the very best, after a walk through the dunes you can head to the cozy library, sit before the fire, and sip sherry or port.

Once you've stayed there, when you define the word *bliss,* you'll naturally think Wauwinet.

The Wauwinet

Location: On the northeastern end of the island of Nantucket

Romantic Features: Walks on windswept beaches; bike rides; picnics in a secluded cove; watching sunsets from the lawn chairs

Address/Phone: P.O. Box 2580, 120 Wauwinet Road, Nantucket, MA 02584; (508) 228–0145; fax (508) 228–6712

E-mail: email@wauwinet.com

Web Site: www.wauwinet.com

U.S. Reservations: (800) 426–8718

Owner/Manager: Stephen and Jill Karp, owners; Betina Landt, innkeeper

Arrival/Departure: Nantucket is accessible by ferry from Hyannis via 3 services: The Steamship Authority (508–477–8600 or 508–495–3278), Hy-Line Cruises (508–778–2600), and Freedom Cruise Line (508–432–8999). Air services are provided to the small Nantucket airport from Boston and other major gateways.

Distance from Nantucket Airport: 9 miles

Distance from Nantucket Town: 9 miles

Accommodations: 30 rooms; 25 located in the inn, 5 in private guest cottages

Most Romantic Room/Suite: Guest cottages are more private; deluxe rooms have king-size beds. French doors from corner room #101 open onto a generous covered porch with wonderful water views and lead directly to the lawn and beaches. Room #302 has huge views of the bay, and the cottage suite, Idlewild, has a fireplace, living room, and separate bedroom.

Amenities: Air-conditioning, ceiling fans, hair dryer, TV, Wi-Fi, VCR, cotton bathrobes, irons and ironing boards, telephone, evening turndown service

Electricity: 110 volts

Sports and Facilities: 2 Har-Tru clay tennis courts; jogging, hiking, and walking trails; swimming at 2 private beaches, sailing; jeep safaris, croquet, mountain bikes, fishing; golf (spring and fall)

Dress Code: Casually smart; jackets with or without ties or dress sweaters and slacks are requested for gentlemen dining at Topper's after 6:00 P.M.

Weddings: Can be arranged

Rates/Packages: Rates per couple, per night include room, breakfast, cheese, port and wine, tennis, use of bikes, boating, natural history excursions, jitney service into town: $260–$1,025 (one-bedroom cottage).

Payment/Credit Cards: Most major

Deposit: Prepayment required

Government Taxes: 9.75 percent room tax

Service Charges: Not included

Closed: November–late April

THE WINNETU INN & RESORT
Massachusetts

From the moment you step from the ferry onto the weathered wooden pier in Edgartown on Martha's Vineyard, it won't take long for you to shift into a hair-down, tie-off mode. You don't need much in the way of luggage, either: Boat shoes, jeans, a pair of khakis, and sweaters, as well as a bathing suit for summertime, will take you just about anywhere on the island, from the Black Dog Tavern and the Ice House (a local hot spot) to places such as The Winnetu's Lure Restaurant.

Anyone who has been here before knows that on Martha's Vineyard, it's all about shaking off stress. Relaxing. Chilling out. A perfect place to unwind after your wedding. The Vineyard, quieter and less fancy than its sibling island to the east (Nantucket), is a place where big doings include the annual Fishing Derby, the Edgartown Regatta, and the Catboat Clambake. Even at the height of the summer months on Martha's Vineyard, when the population of 15,000 swells to more than 100,000, there is room to bike, breathe, spread out.

The Winnetu Inn & Resort on South Beach is located just outside of Edgartown, once a thriving nineteenth-century whaling port. Winnetu is a Native American Wampanoag word meaning "beautiful," and the shingle-style Winnetu settles well into the beauty of its surroundings—spreading over the dunes to the beach, just a 250-yard walk away. The Winnetu resembles a large, three-story cruise ship with its rows of windows and balconies rising from a sea of waving grasses. A winding shell path just off the grounds leads to the 21-mile-wide beach washed by the serious waves of the Atlantic.

Although it looks classic New England, like it's been here forever, the inn actually opened in 2000, when owners Mark and Gwenn Snider bought the property, demolished the wreck of a place that stood on the grounds, and built the grand new hotel on the site. Each of the fifty accommodations including studios, one-, two-, three-, and four-bedroom suites, which face the dunes, pool, or ocean, is decorated in soft off-whites, yellows, and blues, reflecting the colors just outside.

Suites come with spacious living and dining areas, deck or patio, and kitchenette, which in the larger suites feature full-size appliances including a stove, dishwasher, refrigerator, washer, and dryer. Some suites have sofa beds, two televisions, and king beds. Furnishings include a mix of oak and wicker, chairs with deep cushions, chaises, a selection of books, and even high-speed Internet service.

For a romantic evening head to the Resort's Lure Restaurant where you can dine accompanied by a magnificent ocean view. Muted colors and smart decor establish a sophisticated, yet comfortable ambience. Lure features casually elegant dining in a comfortable and relaxed environment and specializes in contemporary, regional seafood—as well as a few of the classics. Lure is managed by Executive Chef Ed Gannon and Michelle Gannon. Ed was the former executive chef at the Four Seasons Hotel Boston where he received acclaim for achieving five-diamond status in the restaurant, Aujourd'Hui. Michelle is the former director of event operations for The Catered Affair in Boston where she organized many weddings. On the menu are favorite dishes like lobster bisque "en cassoulet"; seared Angus tenderloin with a garlic potato tower, cassis onions, and a fig and balsamic glaze; and a coconut crème brûlée "croustillant."

Take-out items for a more casual breakfast, lunch, and dinner are available in the General Store and Cafe, and Mel's Diner located less than a mile from the Winnetu, serves breakfast and lunch in season. You can also ask the resort to prepare a picnic meal for you or a take-out dinner to enjoy on your deck—or sign up in advance for the grocery delivery service amenity and have your favorite foods delivered directly to your suite.

On the property's eleven acres you'll find a heated outdoor pool, ten tennis courts, barbecue grills, putting green, pond, fitness room, library, General Store, complimentary yoga classes, massage and spa services, outdoor life-size chess, and sunset water taxi service into Edgartown for shopping, dining, and sightseeing opportunities (in-season). Direct shuttle service is provided to and from the Winnetu and Edgartown ferry, as well as into town on a regular basis. Bikes are also available for rental.

If you decide to go exploring, be sure to stop at Oak Bluffs, a colorful neighborhood of gingerbread Victorian cottages painted in fanciful combinations of blues, yellows, pinks, and other upbeat hues. Clustered around a park and a covered tabernacle topped by a steeple, these houses, which replaced the original tents that were used in the mid-1800s for Methodist summer gatherings, are today highly prized. Nearby try to grab the brass ring on the Flying Horses Carousel, the oldest working carousel in the country.

Take the ferry shuttle to Chappaquiddick, a ride that lasts about a nanosecond and lands you on a 650-acre wildlife preserve where you can meet up with a staffer from the Trustees of Reservations for a safari jeep tour of the island. Other options on the island: Climb up to the top of the Cape Pogue lighthouse; kayak on the reed-lined salt water ponds and waterways; drive out to Gay Head and Aquinnah, a Native American community on the western tip of the island where the view atop the towering ruddy clay cliffs is magnificent; and stop at Menemsha, a quaint fishing village.

Come here to enjoy the beaches, fish, hike, bike, and soak up the peace and natural beauty, which can capture your soul, and before you leave—be sure to take one last walk along the beach and watch the sun going down, raking the sky with streaks of orange, red, and yellow.

The Winnetu Inn & Resort

Location: On Martha's Vineyard near Edgartown, 7 miles from the coast of Cape Cod in Massachusetts

Romantic Highlights: Moonlit walks along a 21-mile beach; toasting the sunset from your private balcony overlooking dunes and sea. Private cottage also available with its own hot tub and roof-top deck

Address/Phone: 31 Dunes Road, Edgartown, MA 02539; (508) 627–4747, (508) 627–4749

E-mail: reservations@winnetu.com

Web Site: www.winnetu.com

U.S. Reservations: (978) 443–1733

Owner/Managers: Mark and Gwenn Snider, owners; Ed and Michelle Gannon, general managers

Arrival/Departure: Arrive by boat or plane. Ferries leave from Falmouth, Woods Hole, New Bedford, Hyannis, Nantucket, and Rhode Island for Edgartown, Vineyard Haven, and Oak Bluffs. Direct ferry-to-resort service with mainland valet parking and luggage check-in is available through pre-arrangement with The Winnetu.

It's important to make ferry reservations in advance, particularly in the high summer season, especially if you want to bring your car (for cars use the Woods Hole ferry). New high-speed passenger ferry service is also available from Rhode Island and New Bedford—in addition to Woods Hole. Air service is available from New York, Boston, Hyannis, Nantucket, New Bedford, Providence, Pennsylvania, and Washington, D.C.

Distance from Logan International Airport: 2–3 hours, depending on season

Accommodations: 50 suites and studios, all with deck or patio, living room, dining room, and kitchen area

Most Romantic Room/Suite: Ocean-facing suites

Amenities: Air-conditioning, hair dryer, telephones, cable TV/VCR, kitchens/kitchenettes, ironing facilities, toiletries, high-speed Internet service

Electricity: 110 volts

Sports and Facilities: Beach, heated outdoor pool, 10 tennis courts, putting green, bikes, bike paths, barbecue grills, Ping Pong, fitness room, library, life-size outdoor chess, complimentary yoga classes, massage and spa services, fine-dining at Lure Restaurant, General Store, fishing excursions, beach/dune tour to Cape Pogue Lighthouse

Dress Code: Casual

Weddings: Can be arranged

Rates/Packages: Peak Season: From $270 per night; three-night packages in summer begin at $960; save 30 percent in the fall and spring

Payment/Credit Cards: Most major

Deposit: Full payment is due in advance

Government Taxes: 5 percent state tax plus 4.7 percent local room tax

Service Charges: Not included

THE RITZ-CARLTON
LAKE LAS VEGAS
Nevada

The lights of the Las Vegas strip glimmer in the distance beckoning with the promise of outrageous entertainment and the jingle of slots. Yet here in the desert, just 17 miles away at the Ritz-Carlton's Lake Las Vegas Resort, gondolas glide across a 320-acre lake while you sip champagne and nibble Godiva chocolates.

It's hard to believe that only eighteen years ago, this oasis of upscale luxury was just a 3,592-acre plot of barren desert land. Today is another story. You find lush greenery and exuberant flowers, the largest privately owned lake in Southern Nevada, golf courses, a 40,000-square-foot casino, multi-million dollar homes, and a cobblestone Tuscan-inspired pedestrian village, MonteLago. Stroll hand-in-hand through the streets, browse in the shops, sip a coffee in one of the sidewalk cafes, or kayak on the lake.

The Ritz-Carlton Lake Las Vegas, which opened in 2003, reflects the mood of the other buildings in MonteLago, with red-clay tile roofs, arched doorways, balustrades, flower courtyards, and sunny interiors. Rooms are decorated in soft colors—sand, peach, yellow, sage green—while furnishings are imported and stylish. The spacious granite and marble bathrooms feature a separate tub and shower.

Many of the rooms have private balconies with views of trellises, shaded loggias, water, mountains, or gardens. Reminiscent of Venice, an arched bridge topped by three stories contains guest rooms and public rooms. On the second and third levels of the bridge, sixty-four rooms and suites occupy the exclusive Ritz-Carlton Club, which has upgraded amenities and a private lounge that offers food and beverages throughout the day. (The club section is accessed with a private key.)

The resort has five places to eat and drink, including the casual Firenze Lobby Lounge, serving Afternoon Florentine Tea, and the Medici Cafe and Terrace, featuring a Chef's Market Menu dinner with optional wine pairings. Dine by candlelight under glittering chandeliers in a room rich with gold wall brocades, deep-cut moldings, coffered ceilings, and European botanical and Italian Renaissance art. Menu items in the Medici include seafood, poultry, fine meats, and meatless items (New American cuisine), with simple dishes as well as more varied choices. For example try the sautéed diver scallops with parmesan risotto, confit of cherry tomatoes, and sautéed baby squash, or the eighteen-ounce blackened dry-aged ribeye steak with french fries, baby lettuce salad, and béarnaise.

A light spa menu and specialty health drinks are available at the Spa Vita di Lago and at the pool; the Galileo Bar offers cocktails, desserts, and hors d'oeuvres.

The 30,000-square-foot Spa Vita di Lago focuses on New Age methods inspired by water and desert yet rooted in the traditions of Italy. There are twenty-four treatment rooms, a fitness center, a meditation garden, and a line-up of stimulating classes including stretching, yoga, and spinning.

Try the Hydrating Blue Flowers treatment, where aromatic botanicals are applied in a silken veil-like wrap that smoothes away desert dryness and nourishes the skin, or book a couple's massage in a deluxe treatment room for two. The Fours Hands full body massage performed by two therapists is divine, and the Hot Stone massage is one of the best treatments for re-energizing your muscles.

There are two golf courses adjacent to MonteLago Village: The Falls Golf Club, featuring a Tom Weiskopf-designed course with waterfalls, canyons, arroyos, and views of the Las Vegas Strip in the distance from several holes, and the Reflection Bay Golf Club, a highly ranked course with a dramatic desert layout designed by Jack Nicklaus.

A network of hiking, biking, and walking trails winds through the area, and horseback riding can be arranged. The hotel has a small white sand beach, which could seem a bit redundant since you are, after all, in a desert. Sure, the sand's been brought in, but you won't really care as you doze in a lounge chair on the beach, the lake glistening in front of you. It's a wonderful way to spend an afternoon together.

A perfect setting for a destination wedding, the most popular places to say "I do" on the property include the ballroom, the Florentine garden, and the lakeside bridal gazebo in Pontevecchio Park.

Looking for excitement? Head into the strip and watch the amazing laser display and the glittering shows, browse through the enticing shops, try your luck at the slots or tables—even take a roller coaster ride. Here in "Sin City," where the mantra is "anything goes," possibilities are over the moon.

Then no matter what the hour, return to your private Lake Las Vegas oasis, put on some music and dance on your balcony under a starlit sky or check out the stars for real: The Ritz has a bank of state-of-the-art GPS telescopes.

The Ritz-Carlton Lake Las Vegas

Location: A deluxe desert retreat located 17 miles from Las Vegas strip on the shores of the largest privately owned lake in the United States

Romantic Highlights: Gondola rides on the lake; massage treatments; star-gazing

Address/Phone: 1610 Lake Las Vegas Parkway, Henderson, Nevada 89011; (702) 567–4700; fax (702) 567–4777

E-mail: lasrz.leads@ritzcarlton.com

Web Site: www.ritzcarlton.com

U.S. Reservations: (800) 241–3333

Owner/Manager: Mark Stevenson

Arrival/Departure: Most rent a car at the Las Vegas Airport.

Distance from Las Vegas Airport: 16 miles (20 minutes)

Distance from Las Vegas: 17 miles (20 minutes)

Accommodations: 349 rooms, including 35 suites

Most Romantic Room/Suite: 64 Ritz-Carlton Club level suites on the Pontevecchio Bridge

Amenities: Air-conditioning, hair dryer, two-line telephones, data-ports, cable TV, high-speed Internet access, radio, alarm clock, plush terry robes and slippers, designer toiletries, luxury linens, 24-hour room service.

Electricity: 110 volts

Sports and Facilities: Full-service spa, fitness center, pool, hiking and biking trails, fly fishing, kayaking, canoeing, pedal boating, sailing, swimming, pool, and small white sand beach

Dress Code: Casual

Weddings: Can be arranged

Rates/Packages: $199–$5,000 per room

Payment/Credit Cards: Most major

Deposit: Call or e-mail for details.

Government Taxes: 10 percent

Service Charges: $20 daily resort fee includes $20 shopping and spa discount on $100 purchase, in-room high-speed Internet access, bottled water, morning coffee, spa and fitness center access, free use of Reflection Bay driving range, intra-resort transportation, one complimentary Ritz Kids session per stay, 24-hour computer access in Business Center.

THE MANOR ON GOLDEN POND
New Hampshire

The regal yellow stucco-and-shingle Manor on Golden Pond is just far enough up a hill to give you stunning views of New Hampshire's Squam Lake and the surrounding White Mountains. You can savor this view from your patio or from the white Adirondack chairs that march along the crest of the hill, a perfect perch from which to sit and watch the sun set on the water below.

Built as a summer residence in 1903 by Mr. and Mrs. Van Horn, a prominent Boston couple, the original manor was the scene of many fine parties and social events. In the mid-1940s *Life* magazine editor Harold Fowler converted the mansion into the Holderness Photographic Colony, then, beginning in the early 1950s, the property passed through several more owners until Brian and Mary Ellen Shields purchased the estate in 1999. After extensive refurbishment, they opened it as a year-round inn and restaurant.

The majestic mountains, pristine lakes, and old-growth forests provide endless outdoor activities, from kayaking and hiking to swimming and boating. From your luxurious nest, you can wake to the plaintive sounds of loons who live along the shores of Squam Lake—very peaceful, seductive. And you can explore the lake's 7,700 acres, which are home to more than sixty-seven islands, including Church (Chocorua) Island, where a birch cross near the water's edge marks the site of many wedding ceremonies.

You can't beat the Manor's location or the inn's owners, Mary Ellen and Brian, who oversee *every* detail—from the wonderful room amenities, like rain showerheads, CD players (with CDs, including one with recorded loon calls!), soaking tubs, and woodburning fireplaces (eighteen in all) to impeccable service in the dining room.

Each of the twenty-five rooms in the main house and cottages has been exquisitely decorated by Mary Ellen, who was an interior designer prior to becoming innkeeper. With names like Savoy, Churchill, and Buckingham, the guest rooms evoke an English country estate; each room is different, with enough styles to please all kinds of tastes. For example, Avon on the third floor is reached by a private staircase and features a king bed, in-room Jacuzzi for two, and skylights where you can literally sleep under the stars.

The burgundy-hued Savoy Court, one of the largest rooms, has a huge outdoor terrace overlooking the lake, a fireplace, a walk-in shower, a claw-foot tub, and a majestic baronial mahogany king bed. Stratford, at the end of a wing off the main building, has a private entrance and is designed to bring out the animal in you, with safari-printed fabrics, weathered barn siding for the walls, a four-poster bed, a fireplace, and wildlife accents, including a bear skin rug and wildlife trophies and prints.

The Yorkshire and Sandwich one-bedroom suites evoke a feeling of luxury and elegance and provide a perfect home away from home, but one with deluxe amenities—everything from steam showers and Kohler "air baths" (think whirlpool only quieter and gentler for a more relaxing soak) to private decks and breathtaking, panoramic views of the lake and mountains.

The main lounge is furnished with comfortable upholstered chairs parked near a fireplace. If you're into games, there are puzzles as well as a fabulous chess set made of various shapes and sizes of salt and pepper shakers, filled with black pepper for the black pieces and salt for the white. An adjacent smaller sitting room can be used for quiet reading.

Tea is served each afternoon and you can usually find lemonade and cookies or other snacks in the lounge to munch on between meals. Copper-topped tables and a decor of deep reds and navy create a cozy intimate atmosphere in the Three Cocks Pub piano bar.

The fifteen-acre property is enhanced by gardens, brick walkways bordered by flowers, an outdoor pool, clay tennis court, croquet court, and a sandy beach with pedal boats and canoes. All around, the area is a paradise for those who love to hike, canoe, kayak, ski, and play golf (the new Owl's Nest course is close by).

Natural and unspoiled, Squam Lake is the reason the area was chosen as the site for the movie *On Golden Pond*. You can canoe by the camp that was used in the film, a private rustic retreat on one of the islands.

Breakfast is lavish, perhaps Belgian waffles served with cream and fresh raspberries or an egg soufflé. Dinner served in the Van Horne Dining Room draws from fresh local produce and meats prepared by Executive Chef Jeff Woolley. On the menu you might find appetizers like wild mushrooms and sesame crepes or escargot gratin and entrees like Atlantic salmon with citrus butter or roasted breast of Maine duck in a port wine sauce. To accompany your meal, choose a fine bottle of wine from the Manor's extensive wine cellar.

If you have a big appetite, try the Chef's Tasting Menu priced at $65 but go slowly—leave some of the zucchini and eggplant bisque in the bowl or you may never get to the apple-oat bake with vanilla soy ice cream. And that would be a pity.

The Manor on Golden Pond

Location: Surrounded by New Hampshire's White Mountains, the Manor is nestled on the pine-clad slopes of Shepard Hill above Squam Lake

Romantic Highlights: Woodburning fireplaces, antique four-poster beds, views of the lake, candlelight dining, waterfront playground of kayaks and paddle boats

Address/Phone: Route 3, P.O. Box T, Holderness, NH 03245; (603) 968–3348; fax (603) 968–2116

E-mail: Info@manorongoldenpond.com

Web Site: www.manorongoldenpond.com

U.S. Reservations: (800) 545–2141

Owner/Manager: Brian and Mary Ellen Shields

Arrival/Departure: Most rent a car and drive. The entrance is 4.7 miles from exit 24 off Interstate 93.

Distance from Logan International Airport: 2 hours

Distance from Manchester Airport: 1 hour

Accommodations: 21 luxury chambers, 2 suites, 2 cottages

Most Romantic Room/Suite: Yorkshire and Sandwich suites; Avon on the 3rd floor; Savoy with a large patio

Amenities: Air-conditioning, hair dryer, telephones, cable TV/VCR, Wi-Fi, radio, CD player, alarm clock, personal climate control, ironing facilities, robes and slippers, Aveda toiletries, wood-burning fireplaces, whirlpool tubs, air baths, steam showers

Electricity: 110 volts

Sports and Facilities: Sandy beach, outdoor pool, canoeing, kayaking, paddle boats, hiking, golf, tennis, horseback riding, fly fishing, skiing, badminton, tennis, spa treatment room

Dress Code: Casual

Weddings: Can be arranged

Rates/Packages: On Golden Pond Package from $700 includes accommodations for two nights, gourmet dinner, breakfasts, afternoon tea, boat tour, DVD copy of *On Golden Pond,* and a tote bag.

Payment/Credit Cards: Most major

Deposit: 50 percent at time of reservation on multiple-night reservations; 100 percent on single night. 14–30 day cancellation depending on season

Government Taxes: 8 percent sales tax

Service Charges: Not included

HYATT REGENCY TAMAYA
RESORT AND SPA
New Mexico

The Sandia Mountains paint the horizon stretching out beyond desert, wildflowers, and the Bosque (native cottonwood forest). An unlikely place to find a chain hotel? You bet. But then the Hyatt Regency Tamaya Resort and Spa is no ordinary hotel. Built along the Rio Grande on sacred lands belonging to the Tamayame, the Native Americans of the Santa Ana Pueblo, everything about this hotel respects the spirit of this peaceful and industrious Pueblo nation—starting with the architecture.

As you drive towards the resort, you see the red-adobe buildings spreading out over the desert, blending into the surroundings. Approaching the porte-cochère, you are greeted by a huge piece of sculpture, a Santa Ana Pueblo woman nearly seven feet tall, reaching her arms out to welcome guests. Flower-filled courtyards, Native American art, the stunning circular Kiva pool, and desert colors like maize, sand, and pumpkin create an oasis of serenity.

Most of the adobe-style rooms open to a private patio or balcony overlooking the mountains and cottonwood forest, the Grand Courtyard, or the Twin Warriors Golf Club. Pottery, blankets, and other Native American artwork are used throughout the decor, as are natural materials like stone and wood, reinforcing the strong southwestern flavor.

One of the most unique aspects of this resort are the hands-on activities that are offered, all designed to give you a sense of place and the rich cultural heritage of the Tamayame. Start your journey at the Tamaya Cultural Center, a museum dedicated to the history, culture, and art of the Santa Ana Pueblo. Then check out some of the wonderful cultural programs. For example, learn the time-honored way the Tamayame bake bread. Mix it, knead it, and bake it in a traditional pueblo oven (and take the bread home with you, perhaps in the shape of a heart).

Learn the history and culture of the Pueblo by taking part in a nature walk led by a tribal member of the Santa Ana Pueblo; make your own adobe bricks (once it's dry, you may take it home); hear legends and timeless tales told by skilled Native American storytellers under the blanket of a starry sky, or float over the desert in a hot air balloon. Let the music of Native Americans, the drums and flutes, get into your soul.

One of the best ways of really getting to know the area around here is on horseback, so take a ride through the cottonwoods and follow the trails that are laced throughout the region. At Tamaya finding a horse and a guide/instructor is easy: Trail rides are offered at least twice daily, beginning with a horse-drawn vehicle ride up to the stables.

Old-fashioned hayrides can also be arranged. At the end of the Sunset Margarita Trail Ride, you are rewarded with the opportunity to enjoy the beautiful New Mexico sunset with a margarita.

At the higher altitude, you get more flight for your buck at the Twin Warriors Championship Golf Club. Built with great sensitivity around twenty historic sites—places of previous tribal activity, some sacred to the Tamayame—this is a spectacular course. As you play you'll pass an ancient cave and an 800-year-old abandoned horse corral. With a backdrop of the blue-tinged mountains, the course, designed by Gary Parks, is studded with juniper and piñon pine. You'll hit over *arroyos* (dry washes) and navigate around wide bunkers, many of which can be quite unforgiving. There are several elevated greens and on hole number four, five waterfalls cascade into a lake.

The Santa Ana Golf Course running along the Rio Grande, the sister course to Twin Warriors, gives you a choice of twenty-seven holes and five sets of tees. This course is more forgiving for the average golfer than Twin Warriors and is open to the public.

On the less rugged side, head to the Tamaya Mist Spa, where treatments range from massages, herbal treatments, and aromatherapy to wraps, facials, and scrubs. The colors of the spa are earthy in tone; live plants and flowers abound. Native American artwork, such as handmade rugs, hang on the walls. There is also a well-equipped fitness center and a yoga/aerobic wellness theater. Separate areas are set aside for women and men's meditation, sauna and steam rooms, and changing areas. For a very special experience, book a couple's massage in your own room.

You will never go hungry here. The Corn Maiden, the signature restaurant, features "foods on fire," meaning foods that are slow-cooked, like skewered spit-fired meats, poultry, and fish accompanied by marinated, grilled, and roasted vegetables. Samples of regional specialties are served in small portions, tapa style. An especially innovative dish inspired by traditional cooking methods is the terra-cotta–baked veal. Delicious.

Other restaurant choices include the Santa Ana Cafe, just off the pool patio, for breakfast, lunch, or a casual dinner, and the Rio Grande Lounge and the poolside bar and grill for light fare and beverages.

If you decide to have your wedding here, say "I do" on the patio with the cottonwood forest and mountains as a backdrop, or take your vows by the Kiva circular pool under an arbor, or in the gardens. Have your wedding dinner in the Corn Maiden Restaurant or hold a reception in the ballroom or in a pavilion under the cottonwoods.

The Hyatt's wedding planner can help you with all the details from your ceremony to your reception. If the idea of riding off into the sunset in a horse and buggy or a chuck-wagon breakfast for your wedding guests the morning after sounds fun, just ask.

Here where vistas go on forever, shifting sand, desert flowers, cacti, and the sunrises and sunsets can blow you away. Whether you are coming for a romantic getaway, your wedding, or a honeymoon, you'll find a kaleidoscope of feasts for the senses.

Hyatt Regency Tamaya Resort and Spa

Location: On 500 acres of the Santa Ana Pueblo, with spectacular views of the Sandia Mountains and the Rio Grande

Romantic Highlights: Carriage rides in the Cottonwood forest; dinner in the Corn Maiden Restaurant; sunset trail rides

Address/Phone: 1300 Tuyuna Trail, Santa Ana Pueblo, NM 87004; (505) 867–1400, (505) 867–1234; fax (505) 867–1400

E-mail: cjburns@hyatt.com

Web Site: www.tamaya.hyatt.com

U.S. Reservations: (800) 55–HYATT

Owner/Manager: Steve Dewire, manager

Arrival/Departure: Most rent cars at the Albuquerque Airport or take a cab. Transfers can be arranged.

Distance from Albuquerque Airport: 30 minutes

Distance from Santa Fe: 40 minutes

Accommodations: 350 rooms and suites

Most Romantic Room/Suite: Presidential Suite connects to a king room, and can connect to a double room as well. Suite is 1,218 square feet, located on first floor with mountain view.

Amenities: Air-conditioning, hair dryer, two-line telephone, data-port, high-speed Internet access, cable TV, coffeemaker, radio, alarm clock, iron and ironing board, robe, designer toiletries, refrigerator, room service, gift shop.

Electricity: 110 volts

Sports and Facilities: Kiva pool, plaza pool with waterslide, Oxbow pool with waterfall and beach setting, golf course, golf school, horseback riding, spa, fitness room, hot air balloon rides, tennis, nature walks, cultural activities, and guided day trips

Dress Code: Casual

Weddings: Can be arranged

Rates/Packages: From $155 per room; from $500 per suite; special romance packages available

Payment/Credit Cards: Most major

Deposit: Guaranteed by credit card

Government Taxes: 11.5 percent room tax; 6 percent sales tax

Service Charges: $12 daily resort fee per room, per night

THE INN ON THE ALAMEDA

New Mexico

In the desert around Santa Fe, bright bursts of tiny cactus flowers color the desert. All around are brilliant blue skies, the blue Sangre de Cristo Mountains, the cooling ribbon of the Rio Grande where white-water rafters plunge through water chutes. At dusk you hear coyotes cry in the distance. Food is spicy, hot; art is everywhere—in the sky, in the rolling hills, the worn patina of old mining towns, the thick adobe walls, and the rocks where layers of lava over thousands of years have settled into ribbons of weird and wonderful formations. High desert magic.

Santa Fe is justifiably a popular place for tourists and it is for this reason that the location of the Inn on the Alameda is just about perfect: close to everything, yet a quiet oasis from the general hubbub.

The inn's two-story golden adobe buildings are arranged around garden courtyards. The feeling is intimate and private. There are seventy-one rooms, each decorated to evoke the flavor of the Southwest with light wood cupboards and handmade armoires, hand-woven rugs, Spanish tile and wrought iron pieces, subtly hued fabrics, and Native American motifs. Straight pine and aspen timbers are used throughout, a nice contrast to the curves of adobe arches and wonderful pieces of pottery and hand-tooled metal mirrors that provide additional interest.

Rooms come with a balcony or patio, and luxuries like Egyptian cotton linens and thick terry robes make you feel special. Flowers are everywhere: spilling over walls, lining the paths, decorating each room. And for those with a suite, what better way to relax after a day of touring then to fire up the kiva fireplace in your room?

Steal some private moments on your balcony or in front of a blazing fireplace while sipping margaritas, or stroll through the flowered courtyards hand in hand. The scent of the flowers will seduce you.

Breakfast is included in the rate. Each morning when you arrive at the tiled serving bar, you are greeted by the "Breakfast of Enchantment," a colorful array of more than twenty-five gourmet items. Fill your plate with things like homemade rolls and pastries, fruit pies and flans, quiches, spinach-cheese croissants, and fresh fruits. Enjoy juices plus flavorful coffees and teas in the Agoyo Room or outdoor terrace.

In the Agoyo Room white adobe walls and dark wood floors provide a perfect backdrop for fine pieces of Southwestern art. It's an ideal place to sit by the fire, read a book, and sip a margarita. Each afternoon wine, cheese, and margaritas, including the house specialty, a turquoise margarita, are offered. There is no restaurant at the inn, but steps away are a number of fine places to eat.

The inn has a small fitness room, two open-air hot tubs, and massages can be arranged as well as a number of excursions in and around Santa Fe. Whatever you want to do, you'll find the staff very eager to help, whether it be to arrange an outing or to give you directions to the golf course.

In Santa Fe you can spends hours just browsing through the galleries and shops. Here nature has inspired an incredible variety of artwork from silver and turquoise jewelry to fine pottery, leather work, paintings, and the carved stone animal fetishes of the Zuni Native Americans. In addition to shops like Eagle Dancer, where the homemade jewelry is exquisite; Keshi, a little gem containing a fantastic collection of authentic handcarved Zuni fetishes; and the Hopalong Boot Company, crafts of Native American artisans are displayed on blankets spread out along the long covered arcade that runs down one side of the plaza.

Just outside the city there is much to discover. Start with an archaeological tour of the Kasha-Katuwe Tent Rocks in the mining district of Cerrillos Hills, where cone-shaped products of volcanic eruptions 6 to 7 million years ago stand like giant tees holding golf balls atop limestone cliffs. Rise early for a spectacular balloon ride over the desert; visit Native American pueblos; play golf; get a hot rock massage; and head out to Broken Saddle Riding Company in Cerrillos for a sunset horseback ride into the hills on smooth-riding Tennessee Walkers. Visit the Georgia O'Keeffe Museum and explore the museums on Museum Hill, especially the whimsical Museum of International Folk Art.

Often referred to as "that enchanting small hotel in old Santa Fe," the Inn on the Alameda is a place you will savor coming home to.

The Inn on the Alameda

Location: In the midst of one of Santa Fe's most historic and artistic areas, just 3 blocks from the Plaza and 1 block from Canyon Road, home to a number of art galleries

Romantic Highlights: Kiva fireplaces, turquoise margaritas, secluded courtyards

Address/Phone: 303 East Alameda, Santa Fe, NM 87501; (505) 984–2121; fax (505) 986–8325

E-mail: info@inn.alameda.com

Web Site: www.inn-alameda.com

U.S. Reservations: (888) 984–2122

Owner/Manager: Joe and Kathy Schepps, owners; Debbie Allmann, manager

Arrival/Departure: Car rentals and shuttle service are available at the airport; Amtrak leaves passengers at Lamy, 17 miles from Santa Fe, where shuttle service is available into town by calling (505) 982–8829. Mesa Airlines operates a daily schedule of flights between Albuquerque and Santa Fe Municipal Airport. Taxis are available and transportation can be arranged through the hotel.

Distance from Albuquerque International Airport: 60 miles

Accommodations: 71 rooms and suites

Most Romantic Room/Suite: Fireplace suites in the 140s

Amenities: Air-conditioning, hair dryer, telephones, cable TV, data-port, radio/alarm clock, Egyptian cotton bedding, ironing facilities, robes, designer toiletries. Many rooms have kiva fireplaces, patios or balconies, safes, and refrigerators. Lap blankets also available on request. Free parking.

Sports and Facilities: Fitness room, 2 open-air hot tubs; golf, horseback riding, hiking, archaeological excursions, boating, fishing, skiing, hot air ballooning, and white-water rafting can be arranged.

Dress Code: Casual

Weddings: Can be arranged

Rates/Packages: From $129 per room, including breakfast and afternoon wine and cheese reception

Credit Cards: Most major

Deposit: 1-night deposit, plus tax

Government Taxes: 13.7 percent

Service Charges: Not included

INN OF THE ANASAZI
New Mexico

Although the Inn of the Anasazi has only been open since 1991, its spirit stretches back over 700 years ago to a time when the creative Anasazi Indians lived in cliffs in the Southwest. The Indians, who were artistic and in tune with their surroundings, left a heritage of beautiful geometric designs that were found in everyday items such as pottery and weavings.

When the Inn of the Anasazi was built, the creators successfully captured the essence of the culture of this ancient people throughout the inn without imposing any of the clichés often found in such tourism-related endeavors. This place feels as if it has sat here in the heart of historic Santa Fe for many, many years.

Its romantic appeal is in both the low-key, classy way the inn has been designed and the warmth of the people who run it. Each room has its own private kiva fireplace, king-size bed (most rooms) with a fluffy duvet, fine, 100 percent cotton sheets, down pillows, and colors that carry you out to the desert.

Lie back on your bed and look up at the ceiling, which is made of authentic *vigas* and *latillas*, a traditional wooden beam and pole construction. Really interesting and indicative of the kind of thought that went into the inn's design.

The decor is pure Southwestern: massive hand-hewn furniture, Indian blankets, mellow brown leather chairs, stone-top tables; terra-cotta pots filled with cactus, original artwork and crafts by Native American artists, and antique Indian rugs. Baskets woven in Anasazi-style patterns, unpainted sandstone and adobe walls (hand-plastered), wide plank floors, a palette of desert earth tones, and handmade tile baths all add to a mood that is soft and seductive.

The Anasazi Restaurant focuses on foods of the American Southwest; for example, on the menu you might find grilled corn tortilla and lime soup, chayote-sweet potato hash, or Montana buffalo *osso buco* with a red wine reduction and ancho-basil polenta.

The ninety-two-seat restaurant serves a lot of fresh, organically grown food purchased from local farmers. The menu, which changes twice a year, is contemporary Southwestern fare and might include grilled corn tortilla soup with ginger pork; peanut-and-coconut–grilled prawns with watermelon salsa; Anasazi flatbread with fire-roasted sweet peppers; and fresh herb-and-lime marinated rack of lamb.

Santa Fe has a lot going for it, and you're just steps away from it all. Right outside Anasazi's bold timbered entrance, you can stroll to the market stands of the Pueblo Indians who sell turquoise and silver jewelry and belts, and you can visit the many art galleries that feature wonderful, handcrafted pots, baskets, and paintings. The inn can arrange for you to visit the ancient Anasazi ruins of Chaco Canyon and see some of the northern pueblos that are in the area. You can also go hiking, whitewater rafting, and fishing. In the winter months you can head to the ski slopes not too far away.

Steeped in the earthy world of the Southwest, the Inn of the Anasazi will enchant those romantics who love the culture and spirit of the West. This place is really well done.

Inn of the Anasazi

Location: In the center of Santa Fe

Romantic Highlights: Seductive desert colors; private kiva fireplace; four-poster bed

Address/Phone: 113 Washington Avenue, Santa Fe, NM 87501; (505) 988–3030; fax (505) 988–3277

E-mail: reservations@innoftheanasazi.com

Web Site: www.innoftheanasazi.com

U.S. Reservations: (800) 688–8100

Owner/Manager: Jeff Mahan, general manager

Arrival/Departure: By rail: Amtrak leaves passengers at Lamy, 17 miles from Santa Fe. Shuttle service is available into town by calling (505) 982–8829. By air: Shuttle service to downtown Santa Fe available at Albuquerque International Airport. Mesa Airlines operates a daily schedule of flights between Albuquerque and Santa Fe Municipal Airport. Transportation can be arranged to hotel. Taxis also available.

Distance from Albuquerque International Airport: 60 miles

Distance from Santa Fe: In the center of town

Accommodations: 57 rooms. Traditional rooms are fairly small; Superior rooms are larger, and Deluxe rooms, the largest, have small sitting areas. 52 rooms have king-size beds; 5 have 2 twins.

Most Romantic Room/Suite: Deluxe or superior rooms

Amenities: Hair dryer, air-conditioning; toiletries with organic bath oils, shampoo and soaps; minibar, bathrobe, TV, VCR, Wi-Fi, coffeemaker, safe, two-line telephone, 100 percent cotton sheets, duvet, down pillows, stationary bike for use in room on request; room service 6:00 A.M. to 11:00 P.M.; some rooms have stereos.

Electricity: 110 volts

Sports and Facilities: Massage therapist; white-water rafting and horseback riding can be arranged

Dress Code: Southwestern casual

Weddings: Can be arranged

Rates/Packages: Per couple, per night rates: $199–$409 (low season, January 6–February 28; December 2–19); $259–$409 (high season, March 1–June 27); $299–$479 (peak season, June 28–November 20; December 20–January 4). Romance packages available. $10 parking fee.

Payment/Credit Cards: Most major

Deposit: 1-night deposit; cancel 14 days prior to arrival for full refund

Government Taxes: 14.3125 percent

Service Charges: Not included

MIRBEAU INN & SPA

New York

Mirbeau Inn & Spa easily recalls a French country chateau with its deep ochre stuccoed walls and blue trim and shutters, high pitched tile-like roofs, arched windows, and massive 300-year-old timbers that have been designed into the buildings. The inn's lodge along with the spa facility and four villa-cottages are arranged around a Monet-like water garden and pond in a twelve-acre setting studded with tall spruce trees. (Mirbeau loosely defined means "reflected beauty.")

A perfect base for exploring spectacular gorges, vineyards, and glacier lakes, Mirbeau's location in Skaneateles, one of the nation's loveliest little towns, is a big asset. Nestled around the northern end of the pristine 16-mile-long lake of the same name, Skaneateles (pronounced skinny-AT-liss), with less than 3,000 people, reigns as the prima donna of the Finger Lakes region. Its streets are lined with pristine vintage homes dating from the eighteenth and nineteenth centuries, including several from the Victorian period. The lake's waters, which are known to be extremely pure, often change dramatically from swirls of deep cobalt to brilliant turquoise.

Mirbeau is a small inn with big services. When you arrive you are appointed a personal valet who escorts you to your room and helps you with whatever you might need, golf tee times, wine tasting information, or dinner reservations.

Guest rooms are spacious, superbly designed and appointed. Each is different. Fabrics were designed for Mirbeau in France; linens, including Frette, come from Italy; and duvets are filled with Canadian down. Furnishings include custom-made armoires and other furniture hand-crafted by a cabinetmaker from Italy and antiques with fine inlays. Many rooms have beamed ceilings and are painted in deep red or gold. Each room has a fireplace and those on the first floor have a patio with wrought-iron tables and chairs. The large bathrooms come with deep, French soaking tubs on feet, walk-in showers, and double vanities. The sound system is Bose with a CD player (music is chosen just for you), and televisions are equipped with DVD players.

Walls of the public rooms are faux-painted by hand in deep ochre; one has a border of grape vines tastefully rendered along the top of the room. Tile floors are accented by oriental carpets; lighting is subtle. The art and colors of Provence enhance the mood.

Even the fencing that defines the property is special, made of interwoven willow branches and arched iron trellises with climbing roses and wisteria to create romantic entries to the cottages.

Mirbeau's 10,000 square-foot full-service spa has ten treatment rooms, most with fireplaces and personal sound systems. A new concept for the region, the spa offers a wide variety of classic European body and facial treatments, classes, and on-site peaceful places that invite lingering, such as the "spruce cathedral," a grove of tall trees and wildflowers that is conducive to meditation.

Try a massage, wrap, seaweed bath, or facial. And while you wait for your treatment (or after it), relax in the elegant resting area modeled after a Roman bath, with a subterranean foot-massage pool, soft lighting, columns, lovely wall frescos, teak chaises with soft, comfortable cushions, and radiantly heated floors. A new water feature—a waterfall tumbling into a large open-air Jacuzzi located just off the spa's rest and relaxation lounge—is set to open in the fall of 2005.

Two treatments are designed just for couples, both in front of a glowing fireplace. The Art of Living (100 minutes, $365) invites you to first relax with a warm herbal soak in an oversized French tub for two, followed by side-by-side massages with massage therapists. It Takes Two (50 minutes, $215), a couples' massage, takes place in Mirbeau's signature couples' treatment room.

Other spa facilities include an aerobic workout and weight room, a motion studio, men's and women's locker rooms, herbal-infused steam, saunas, and a nail salon. Classes in aerobics, body sculpting, yoga, and meditation along with additional programs designed to treat body and mind are offered. Runners and walkers will find sidewalks just outside the property that lead to town and the lakeside parks, a ten-minute walk at the most.

The dining room, which leads out to a terrace, overlooks the pond with its arched bridge, water iris, and many other flowers and shrubs. Although this is one of the pricier dining venues in the area, most who have eaten here feel the cuisine is worth it.

Executive Chef Edward Moro, whose credits include the Hotel Hershey and the Little Nell Hotel in Aspen, has created "Mirbeau Estate Cuisine," which can be defined as fresh, light American with French country accents. Moro's choices include butter-roasted Maine lobster tail with melted leeks and carrot-ginger sauce, Fallow Hollow Farm venison with apple conserve, rosemary fingerling potatoes,

and sour cherry sauce and wild berry soufflé. Lunch and breakfast choices are equally tempting, the lemon soufflé pancakes with glazed blackberries and toasted almonds and the caramelized onion and white bean soup with Gruyère toast and mushroom salad, for example. Moro draws on herbs from Mirbeau's own gardens and local produce from the region's many farms.

In spite of its small size of less than 3,000 residents, no matter what time of year you come to Skaneateles, you will always find something going on. In the summer there are sight-seeing and dinner cruises on Skaneateles Lake on the *Judge Ben Wiles,* a two-decker replica of a lake steamer; free band concerts in a lakeside park Friday nights; the Musical Festival showcasing a feast of music under the stars; the Antique & Classic Boat Show; and polo matches on Sundays. Fall brings wine tastings in the Finger Lakes vineyards; and winter showcases a bevy of Dickens characters who stroll village streets during the holidays, and there is ice fishing, cross-country skiing, and ice skating.

Shoppers any time of year can enjoy browsing through the antiques shops, boutiques, bakeries, food shops, and specialty stores that open onto brick sidewalks lined with period lighting.

If you decide to go exploring, the Finger Lakes area has a lot to offer. There are more than seventy vineyards within an hour's drive, fifty public golf courses, several great parks with waterfalls and deep gorges, shopping galore, and museums such as Corning Glass Museum, the Erie Canal Museum, and Ste. Maria of the Iroquois, a fascinating indoor-outdoor exhibit featuring costumed period personalities who relive the interaction of Native Americans and French soldiers during an early period of the area's history.

The sun may not shine quite as much here as in most other places and winters can be rugged with lots of snow, but most folks don't seem to notice. For when the sun does come out, sparkling on the lake, burnishing the fall leaves, or glistening on the snow, there is no place prettier on earth.

Mirbeau Inn & Spa

Location: Tucked into a hillside within walking distance of Skaneateles, a pampered and prosperous town in the Finger Lakes region of middle New York State; vineyards and spectacular gorges of the Finger Lakes within easy driving distance

Romantic Highlights: Roman bath-style spa; flower-rimmed water garden; dinner on the terrace alongside the pond; side-by-side massages by the fireplace

Address/Phone: 851 West Genesee Street, Skaneateles, NY 13152; (877) MIRBEAU, (315) 685–5006; fax (315) 685–5150

E-mail: reservations@mirbeau.com

Web Site: www.mirbeau.com

U.S. Reservations: (877) MIRBEAU or (315) 685–1927

Owner/Manager: Gary and Linda Dower; Yoachim Ohlin, general manager

Arrival/Departure: Most drive here or fly into Syracuse and rent a car.

Distance from Hancock International Airport, Syracuse: 20 miles (35–40 minutes)

Distance from Syracuse: 20 miles

Accommodations: 34 rooms

Most Romantic Room/Suite: Rooms that face gardens and pond

Amenities: Air-conditioning, oversize bath, French soaking tubs, double sinks, Bose radio/CD and DVD player, TV, fireplace, hair dryer, iron/ironing board

Electricity: 110 volts

Sports and Facilities: 10,000-square-foot spa, aerobic workout and weight room, motion studio, library, sauna, nail salon

Dress Code: Resort casual

Weddings: Can be arranged

Rates/Packages: From $175 including use of spa facilities; Romance and Spa packages available

Payment/Credit Cards: Most major

Deposit: 1 night required at time of booking via credit card

Government Taxes: 12 percent

Service Charges: Not included

THE WAWBEEK ON UPPER SARANAC LAKE

New York

Imagine loons gliding on the water, log cabins with private decks, pines so tall they hide in the early morning mist, miles of trails, and balsam-scented fresh air, and you get the picture. God's country. Who wouldn't find romance at the Wawbeek, a turn-of-the-century Adirondack Great Camp. Sprawled on more than forty wooded acres on Upper Saranac Lake, this is the great outdoors at its best—but with such comforts as heated cabins, warm blankets, and a superb restaurant.

The Wawbeek (*Wawbeek* is the Native American word for "big rock") is just one of a handful of Great Camps located in Adirondack State Park, the nation's largest state park. Constructed in the style we now call "Adirondack," these camps were built with dark wood exteriors, often logs, porches with railings made of thick branches, and large central great rooms with stone fireplaces.

The Wawbeek, my choice for a place that combines a rustic ambience with private cabins and candlelight dining, is managed by co-owners Nancy and Norman Howard, refugees from the corporate world in Connecticut, who preside over this special resort set on the shores of Upper Saranac Lake, whose calm, sparkling waters are dotted with small islands.

The Wawbeek has its own fleet of canoes, paddleboats, and Sunfish, promising days of water-oriented fun. Land-based amusements include two tennis courts, croquet, and a game house where you can challenge your mate to Ping-Pong, pool, darts, or a board game. Some evenings there may even be a campfire with a storyteller or guitar player.

Of the Wawbeek's twenty-nine rooms, six are located in Mountain House, a two-story building and one of the original houses built on the property. Some rooms open onto porches where you can look out to the shimmering lake and islands. There are eight rooms and suites with decks and firelaces in Lake House Lodge, which has a lofty two-story great room with a massive stone fireplace. Hannah's Lounge on the second floor is exclusively for Lake House Lodge guests.

Five rustic, traditional, log-cabin–style cottages come with sitting rooms, efficiency kitchens, pull-out sofas (for emergency snoring relief), and a spacious deck with glimpses of the water. Each cabin comes with a small kitchen; some have sitting rooms, fireplaces, screened porches or decks, and eating areas. Some are tucked into the hillside and are very private. Most have queen- or king-size comfortable beds with good quality linens, blankets, and quilts. All have updated fresh decor in pine green, tan, and brown and are squeaky clean. Books and knitted afghans lend a homey touch.

Other rooms are in the Carriage House, including a spacious corner suite with a private entrance, king-size bed, and deck.

Bathrooms are modern, with a tub and shower combo, and the new Lake House rooms have waterjet tubs. Wawbeek's rooms do not have telephones, TVs, or air-conditioning; however, if this creates any sense of panic, these contrivances can be arranged.

Nature trails fan out from the main reception area, leading to the lakefront and dock, to the restaurant, and to a secluded spot at water's edge where you can settle back in one of the Adirondack chairs, read, or simply savor the moment. The Adirondack Park's many hiking trails are right at your doorstep. You might follow the Bloomingdale Bog Trail, only 1.8 miles, or bike along the 7-mile Deer Pond Loop across the way or the 18-mile Paul Smith Loop up the road. Then cool off with a swim. The lake is clean and refreshing.

Nearby there are plenty of places to explore. The Adirondack Museum in Blue Mountain Lake is crammed with a day's worth or more of things to see, such as antique boats, trains, historical exhibits, survival tools, art exhibits, and more. There are miles of canoe routes and mountains to climb.

Spring, fall, and winter are lovely here, too. In the fall brilliant red, orange, and yellow leaves drift down, carpeting the trails, and the air is brisk—perfect for long hikes. In the winter pristine snow blankets the ground in great drifts, catching the sunlight and making it sparkle. There are 100 miles of snowmobiling trails, endless cross-country ski trails, and snowshoeing and Alpine skiing down Big Tupper and Whiteface Mountains. There is ice skating on the lake and dinner and cocktails in the Wawbeek restaurant in front of a blazing fire. Early in February everyone in town turns out for Saranac Lake's Winter Carnival, renowned for its ice castle, and later for the annual Woodchuck Shuffle snowshoe event.

And Spring. Budding flowers poke up through the melting snow; energy levels turn up a notch or two. Things are waking up. It's a great time for brisk hikes, golf, and other outdoor pursuits—perhaps the Ice Breaker 5-mile canoe race on Saranac River.

All year long in the town of nearby Saranac Lake, there are stores to poke through, concerts, performances at the Pendragon Theatre, and sports events galore from canoe races to ski-jumping contests.

Once back at the Wawbeek, you can look forward to a really fine meal. The Wawbeek restaurant, which sits high on a rocky promontory overlooking the lake, delivers both romantic ambience and exceptional cuisine. Executive Chef Eric Rottner spins his magic, creating dishes such as Maple Chicken Dijon, Veal Wawbeek sautéed and topped with raisin chutney, and Duck Island Sauté (medallions of venison with forest mushrooms, roasted garlic, and fresh tarragon in a bourbon *demi-glace*). For dessert try Fried Ice Cream or Diane's Apple Torte. Chef Rottner prides himself on using as many fresh ingredients as he can find, including herbs and berries from the grounds, locally grown vegetables, fresh trout, and regional meats.

It is very quiet here at the Wawbeek—indeed so quiet that the scampering of a squirrel or two across your roof or the hoot of an owl in the night can put you into a momentary state of panic. "Just who is that?" No one. Go back to sleep. Listen to the rustle of the pines. You're in a good place where even the thought of locking your door may seem a bit silly. And when you must finally leave, listen carefully for the sounds of a pileated woodpecker tapping out "good-bye."

The Wawbeek on Upper Saranac Lake

Location: Adirondack Great Camp on 1,400 feet of shoreline on Upper Saranac Lake in Tupper Lake, NY

Romantic Highlights: Canoeing on a pine-fringed glassy lake; hikes in the forest; dining on the porches overlooking the water; your own private cabin

Address/Phone: Panther Mountain Road, Tupper Lake, NY 12986; (800) 953–2656; (518) 359–2656; fax (518) 359–2475

E-mail: wawbeek@capital.net

Web Site: www.wawbeek.com

U.S. Reservations: (800) 953–2656

Owner/Manager: Nancy and Norman Howard

Arrival/Departure: Rental cars available at Adirondack Airport just 9 miles from Saranac Lake and Albany Airport

Distance from Albany Airport: 150 miles (2½ hours)

Distance from Tupper Lake: 10 minutes to village; 15 miles to Saranac Lake

Accommodations: 29 rooms in several buildings, including rustic cottages

Most Romantic Room/Suite: Partridgeberry, a secluded cabin with a fireplace, vaulted ceiling, and screened porch; Tamarack, a cottage close to the boat dock with a good view of the water from the corner deck; Lake House Lodge rooms with king beds, whirlpool tubs, and decks overlooking the water: Hemlock Cabin, a secluded, redecorated cottage with a king bed and a porch

Amenities: Ceiling fans, coffee and tea making facilities, toiletries, grill, kitchen, laundry facilities. Some have fireplaces, fold-out queen-size sofas, daily housekeeping services.

Electricity: 110 volts

Sports and Facilities: Canoes, paddleboats, Sunfish, sloop; 2 tennis courts; swimming, walking, hiking, biking, skiing, snowshoeing, cross-country skiing, Alpine skiing, ice fishing; golf and horseback riding nearby

Dress Code: Informal

Weddings: Can be arranged

Rates/Packages: $195–$395 per couple, per night (summer); $195–$340 (fall and holidays); $100–$260 (winter/ spring), including full breakfast and use of boats, bikes, and snowshoes. Weekly rates start at $1,290–$2,600

Payment/Credit Cards: Most major

Deposit: 50 percent deposit required to hold booking. Balance due on arrival. Cancel 30 days or more before arrival date for refund less 10 percent (60 days if booking more than one sleeping room).

Government Taxes: 7 percent

Service Charges: 10 percent recommended

THE GROVE PARK INN RESORT & SPA

North Carolina

With the dramatic backdrop of the Blue Ridge Mountains and a stunning hilltop setting, The Grove Park Inn Resort & Spa promises a grand romantic experience. Just driving up the road leading to this massive, stone building impresses. Then once you walk through the huge Great Hall lobby to the terraces in the back, the views can take your breath away.

This is one of the country's most majestic hotels, the equivalent in this country of a feudal castle. Built in 1913 using boulders from nearby Sunset Mountain and capped by an orange-red tiled roof, the Grove Park Inn dominates its hilltop setting, swooping down to a scenic golf course below. Listed on the National Register of Historic Places, the Grove Park Inn has hosted many famous guests, including eight presidents.

Guest rooms, all recently refurbished, are furnished in the original Arts and Crafts style—simple, yet clean and elegant. (If you look at the lamps closely you can see the hammer blows dealt by the artisans of the Roycrofters workshop.) Yet you have a choice. Stay in the more contemporary Vanderbilt and Sammons Wings, which still evoke the inn's historic style and are furnished with Arts and Crafts reproduction furniture, or stay in the older part of the original Main Inn. Rooms are not overly large and would probably not be called "elegant," but comfort is a given here with pillow-top mattresses, stereos with radios and CD players, and mini-refrigerators.

One of the great on-site perks of the inn is the 40,000-square-foot, $42 million spa that was unveiled in 2001. Considered one of the best in the country, it has a grotto pool framed by two waterfalls and a lap pool where you can float and look up to more than 2,000 fiberoptic stars twinkling in the rock ceiling overhead. There is also a mineral pool, twenty-four treatment rooms, and five fireplaces.

If you love massages, try a couples' massage in one of the two open-air pagodas or spring for the ultimate, a Couples' Retreat, where the treatment room is sprinkled with rose petals and you and your love receive in tandem candlelit massages followed by an aromatic bath and an offering of chilled champagne and chocolate-covered strawberries. Other special treatments are as good as they sound; for example, there is the Sanctuary of the Senses body treatment, which combines exfoliation, a body wrap, and a full body massage using rose essential oils; the Fire, Rock, Water, and Light treatment includes a full body exfoliation, body wrap, buttermilk and honey whirlpool bath, and a waterfall massage with a Vichy shower.

If you're a golfer, you've got to love this course. Designed in 1924 by Donald Ross, the famed Scottish course architect, the 6,720-yard layout recently received a $2.5 million restoration and is now better than ever. The park-style track, with strategically located bunkers and rolling greens, is lined by mature trees and features some elevations. (Hint: Don't trust your eyes; everything breaks away from the mountains.) Tennis players will also find a love match with three indoor and three outdoor courts.

You have a choice of eating in the Blue Ridge Dining Room known for its extensive breakfast buffet, Sunday Brunch Buffet, superb views, and contemporary cuisine; Chops at Sunset Terrace, a traditional steakhouse where you can take in sweeping views of the city and mountains and dine on the veranda in good weather (if you crave Angus beef, this is the place); the Spa Cafe, featuring light cuisine; or Horizons, for gourmet dining, great views, and live music nightly. For pool-side dining during the summer, there is also a Pool Cabana. If you prefer an intimate dinner in your room, you can order room service. For drinks and nightly entertainment, there is the Great Hall Bar, a favorite watering hole since the place opened.

Although there is plenty to do on the property, you will want to check out the area, for Asheville is one of the country's hippest cities. Many artists call it home, inspired by the region's natural beauty. The energized downtown is home to sidewalk cafes, trolleys, galleries, and a wonderful group of Art Deco buildings.

In the 1,000-acre Chimney Park, a short drive outside Asheville, you can walk up the steps of the 32-foot Chimney Rock and catch the awesome view of the valley and the mountains that spread out all around. In fact, if you want to marry here, that can be arranged too.

While in Asheville, take time to visit the vast Biltmore Estate and Winery. Set on 8,000-acres, once the expansive country retreat of the George Vanderbilt family, you can tour the 250-room Biltmore House, gardens, and winery. Take a self-guided tour of the winery production areas and cellars from the crushing dock to fermentation bay, sample the wines, and fuel up at the Bistro, European-style countryside eatery.

The Grove Park Inn Resort & Spa

Location: On 161 acres in the Blue Ridge Mountains just 2 miles from downtown Asheville, North Carolina

Romantic Highlights: Awesome views of the mountains; cocktails on the terraces as the sun goes down; side-by-side massages in an open-air pagoda at the spa

Address/Phone: 290 Macon Avenue, Asheville, NC 28804; (828) 252–2711; fax (828) 252–6040

Web Site: www.groveparkinn.com

U.S. Reservations: (800) 438–5800

Owner/Manager: William Kelley

Arrival/Departure: Most arrive by car; rentals available at airport

Distance from Asheville Regional Airport: 17 miles (20 minutes)

Accommodations: 510 rooms and suites

Most Romantic Room/Suite: New themed rooms and suites located on the exclusive Club Floor level and in the Vanderbilt Wing including The Spa, Swingin' 60s, The Gatsby, and The Donald Ross. Main inn rooms are also very nostalgic and romantic

Amenities: Air-conditioning, hair dryer, telephones, cable TV/VCR, Wi-Fi, stereos with radio and CD players, data-ports, coffeemakers, microwave ovens, refrigerators, alarm clock, ironing facilities, robes, designer toiletries; some rooms have 6-foot whirlpool bathtubs and 10-jet waterfall showers.

Electricity: 110 volts

Sports and Facilities: A 40,000-square-foot spa, indoor and outdoor pools located at the Sports Complex or Country Club, golf course, fitness center, 6 tennis courts, racquet ball; hiking trails, horseback riding, mountain biking, fishing and white-water rafting nearby.

Dress Code: Casual; dinner jacket required if dining at Horizons

Weddings: Can be arranged via Convention Services

Rates/Packages: From $115–$385 per room; Romance package available

Payment/Credit Cards: Most major

Deposit: By major credit card

Government Taxes: 5 percent room tax; 7 percent local tax

Service Charges: Included

THE EQUINOX RESORT & SPA
Vermont

The allure of Vermont's Green Mountains beckons to those who love the outdoors. From your base at the Equinox, a charming country inn resort that holds center stage in the small village of Manchester, you can hike; go horseback riding in the surrounding hills; play golf on a picturesque, par 71, 6,423-yard championship course; swim, fish, and ski. You can even learn off-road driving or falconry.

Close to the ski areas of Bromley and Stratton Mountains, the stately Equinox has a long history of welcoming guests. It started life in the 1700s as the Marsh Tavern (now one of the hotel's restaurants), and by the mid-1800s the hotel had put Manchester Village on the map as one of America's finest year-round destinations. In 1972 the resort was added to the National Register of Historic Places, and in 1991 the Equinox underwent an ambitious renovation program, including the restoration of all public areas and guest rooms as well as the golf course.

Anyone driving through the center of Manchester Village could not possibly miss it. The Equinox, which faces the village green, is simply the most impressive structure in town. It boasts an imposing, white-pillared facade with a long porch set up with green rocking chairs and two wings

that create an interior garden courtyard. Just across the street from the front entrance are a number of classy clothing and gift shops—fun to browse through, but bring lots of cash if you intend to buy. Also located here are a number of 200-year-old buildings, including the Congregational Church and Bennington County Courthouse.

You'll find the rooms at the Equinox very comfortable. Furnished in a traditional style in muted New England colors, some of these rooms include king-size beds, washed-pine armoires, desks, wing chairs, rich drapes and bedspreads, and marble-tiled baths.

Next door is the newest Equinox addition, the Charles Orvis Inn. Dating back to 1833, this house was originally used to accommodate guests during the winter months, when the main hotel was closed. Today it has been totally rebuilt and houses nine one- and two-bedroom deluxe suites, each with its own working fireplace, living room, dining room, full kitchen, and super appointments. Check in here and you'll have your own private en-suite Jacuzzi and the use of an intimate bar and billiard room.

If you're into golf, perhaps one of the best parts of staying here is that you can easily walk from the hotel to the first tee of one of the loveliest golf courses in New England. The Gleneagles course, originally designed by the legendary Walter Travis, has been improved and updated by the well-known golf course designer Rees Jones. The course's ups and downs will very likely do the same to your score card. It's hilly, challenging, and breathtaking in its beauty. As you hit your ball from the tee on the eighth hole, your ball will soar into the sky against a backdrop of dense green mountains and deep blue skies. Straight ahead is the white spire of a quintessential New England church, nestled at the base of a mountain. On the fifth hole you'll have to wait for those ahead of you to ring a bell before hitting over the blind hill. This is one course you can play again and again without getting bored—there are new challenges around every bend.

The Equinox has a 13,000-square-foot full-service Avanyu spa with eleven treatment rooms, indoor lap pool, hot tub, fitness facilities, steam room, sauna, and image studio. There are three Har-Tru tennis courts for year-round play, a 75-foot heated swimming pool outdoors, and a 47-foot heated indoor pool. You can rent bikes and cycle out to the many trails in the area and play croquet. Hikers have a good selection of wooded mountain trails to explore.

Canoeing trips on the Battenkill River can be arranged, and if you ever wanted to try your hand at fly-fishing or shooting, the Equinox offers lessons on its own Equinox Pond or the Battenkill River. You can also attend the Orvis Fly-Fishing School, the oldest of its kind in the country, and the Orvis Shooting School, located right in Manchester Village.

You can eat breakfast, lunch, and dinner at the Marsh Tavern, a darkish, cozy place that dates back to 1769. You can also enjoy cocktails on the tavern's terrace during July and August. For a more elegant dining experience, head to the grand Colonnade.

Some nights there is entertainment in the Marsh Tavern, and during the summer months a number of local performing art centers offer an assortment of concerts and theater productions. Come here if you love New England and all it offers. Your accommodations at the Equinox will be supremely comfortable; your choice of activities plentiful if you love exploring the countryside and participating in traditional sports.

Think of any name-brand clothing or sporting goods company and you'll find it in the outlet stores that line the roads leading into town. The stores are housed in attractive New England–style buildings of weathered wood and clapboard, in harmony with the surrounding countryside. If you have some wedding money you want to spend, you can easily fill the backseat of your car with bags full of bargains from Anne Klein, Liz Claiborne, Ralph Lauren, London Fog, Armani, Escada, and Donna Karan, to name a few.

The Equinox Resort & Spa

Location: In the center of Manchester Village, in southern Vermont's Green Mountains

Romantic Highlights: Sleigh rides; late evening nightcaps in the cozy Marsh Tavern; en suite Jacuzzis and fireplaces

Address/Phone: Historic Route 7A, Manchester Village, VT 05254; (802) 362–4700; fax (802) 362–1595

E-mail: reservations@equinoxresort.com

Web Site: www.rockresorts.com

U.S. Reservations: (800) 362–4747 or (866) 670–ROCK

Owner/Manager: A member of the Rockresorts collection; Gary S. Thulander, general manager

Arrival/Departure: Transfers via private car can be arranged at $85 per car, one-way, plus 15 percent gratuity.

Distance from Albany Airport: 64 miles (about 1½ hours)

Distance from Manchester Village: In the heart of town

Accommodations: 183 rooms and suites, including suites in the Charles Orvis Inn, next door.

Most Romantic Room/Suite: Try one of the new one-bedroom suites in the Charles Orvis Inn. Main building suites are also good.

Amenities: Toiletries, air-conditioning, telephone, clock radio, ironing facilities, cable TV, Wi-Fi, in-room movies, bathrobes, fireplaces (some), Jacuzzis (some); room service

Electricity: 110 volts

Sports and Facilities: Tennis (3 Har-Tru courts), swimming (indoor and outdoor pools), fishing, golf, Avanyu Spa, downhill skiing nearby, snowmobiling, cross-country skiing, biking, ice skating, snowshoeing, hiking, horseback riding, canoeing, off-road driving school, falconry school

Dress Code: Casual

Weddings: Can be arranged

Rates/Packages: $159–$929 per couple, per night; add $75 per person for breakfast and dinner or $95 for breakfast, lunch, and dinner. Honeymoon/Anniversary Package: $936–$1,060.50 per couple for 3 nights deluxe accommodations, flowers, champagne, massages, and use of fitness facility. Fireside Package: $945–$1,170 for 2 nights in fireplace suite, wine, breakfasts, and dinners.

Payment/Credit Cards: Most major

Deposit: 1-night deposit required to confirm reservation and will be applied to last night of visit. Refunds will be issued only if cancellation is received 30 days before your scheduled arrival date.

Government Taxes: Vermont rooms and meals tax

Service Charges: $19 per day

THE INN AT SAWMILL FARM
Vermont

At the Inn at Sawmill Farm, it's all about "rustic chic." Set on twenty rolling acres of pond-filled meadows in a valley that hunkers beneath Vermont's Green Mountains, the inn's twenty-one rooms and suites are located throughout the property—in a former barn (the main house), in the Farmhouse, the Ciderhouse, the Wood Shed, the Spring House, the Mill House, and the Carriage House (an eighteenth-century barn). On the grounds and inside the rooms, flowers reign exuberantly, a passion of owners Rodney Williams and his wife, Ione.

Several of the rooms have wood-burning fireplaces, Jacuzzis, and canopy beds. The Wood Shed, one of the most romantic cottages you'll find anywhere, is tucked under a spreading tree. It is a little gray-shingled house with a very private deck featuring a floor-to-ceiling window and French doors that look out to a bucolic pond. There is a wood-burning fireplace (a supply of wood is just outside), a king bed dressed in a blue duvet with rose medallions, and a beamed cathedral ceiling.

The spacious one-bedroom suite in the Carriage House is one of the few rooms where the decor strays from the floral theme. Decorated in the Federal style in more subdued neutral tones, this suite is utterly private with tall arched windows and a wrap-around deck overlooking the two-acre trout pond and gardens.

The Inn at Sawmill Farm is definitely a family affair. Williams, a well-known architect from New Jersey, and his wife, Ione, an interior decorator with a penchant for upbeat florals, purchased the property in 1967 to use as their ski and country home. It didn't take long before they realized that this was just too good a place to ever leave, so they converted it into an inn with lounges, a library, a game room, a bar, three dining rooms, and guest rooms spread throughout the property.

Today son Brill, an expert in wines, oversees the food and beverage side of the business and maintains a fabulous 28,000-bottle wine cellar. Early on, he developed a love for fine wines and was one of the first in New England to celebrate the wines of boutique winemakers like Phelps and Ridge in California. His wines represent the best wineries from all over the world.

Brill also serves as the inn's chef, so if you're at a loss as to what to choose, he is more than happy to help you find the perfect fit. Sister Bobbie Dee Melitor helps out in the administration of the property.

Flowers are everywhere. Even the pretty china has roses running around the edge. There are numerous gardens, fresh flowers on the table, flowers on the fabric and drapes and wallpaper—a virtual garden of delight. A huge fireplace in the main lounge serves as a gathering place for guests, especially on a brisk afternoon.

The dining room by day is cheerful with white beams and red-and-white toile wallpaper. By night it waxes romantic with linens, sparkling crystal chandeliers hanging from the rustic beams, original period paintings, and candles.

Breakfast is worth getting up for. It may consist of a yummy concoction of shirred eggs and English muffins, with tomato coulis, scallions, and cheese, a specialty of Chef Brill, and of course there is always a delicious selection of pastries.

A four-course prix-fixe dinner at $42 includes a choice of three appetizers, soup, a selection of entrees, and dessert. Local fare is used whenever available. For example, you might have sautéed breast of squab with leeks and a reduced port wine sauce; roast loin of venison with braised cabbage and fresh black truffle sauce; or native partridge with Armagnac-soaked prunes and lentils with porcini mushroom–scented sauce.

There are two ponds, a pool set on a gentle hill overlooking one of the ponds, and a tennis court. Just a half-mile away the Mount Snow Golf Course treats golfers to good golf on a pretty, rolling layout. For those who want to improve their game, the Original Golf School at Mount Snow uses the Accelerated Golf Method, with one golf pro assigned to every four students.

Nearby there are 20 miles of hiking trails, snowboarding, downhill and cross-country skiing, mountain biking, and an Orvis-endorsed fly-fishing school.

If you are a couple who like to hike or mountain bike, there are several trails in the area. Pack a picnic and find a pretty spot in the woods or by a stream to take a break.

The Inn at Sawmill Farm

Location: In the foothills of the Green Mountains in southern Vermont in the village of West Dover

Romantic Highlights: Fireplaces, private cottages with decks overlooking a pond, candles, Jacuzzis, canopy beds, music, sleigh rides

Address/Phone: P.O. Box 367, Crosstown Road, West Dover, VT 05356; (802) 464–8131, (800) 493–1133; fax (802) 464–1130

E-mail: sawmill@sover.net

Web Site: www.theinnatsawmillfarm.com

U.S. Reservations: (800) 493–1133

Owner/Manager: The Williams family; Bobbie Dee Melitor

Arrival/Departure: Most rent a car and drive. The inn is 4½ hours, 213 miles, from New York City; 2 hours, 117 miles, from Hartford, CT; and 1½ hours, 68 miles, from Albany, NY

Distance from Albany International Airport: 1½ hours

Distance from Manchester Airport: 1 hour

Accommodations: 21 hotel rooms, 10 in the main house, 11 fireplace rooms in nearby buildings: 3 in Ciderhouse, 4 in Farmhouse, 1 each in the Spring House, Wood Shed, Mill House, and Carriage House

Most Romantic Room/Suite: Private cottages, like the Wood Shed

Amenities: Air-conditioning, hair dryer, radio, CD player, alarm clock, ironing facilities, robes and slippers, designer toiletries, woodburning fireplaces, whirlpool tubs. There are no phones or televisions in rooms but they are available in public areas.

Electricity: 110 volts

Sports and Facilities: Outdoor pool, pond, tennis plus golf, hiking, fishing, boating, mountain biking, fitness club, skeet shooting, horseback riding; the Mount Snow Ski area and golf course are 2 miles away; massages can be arranged

Dress Code: Casual

Weddings: Can be arranged

Rates/Packages: Rooms start at $395 per night including breakfast and dinner. A Honeymoon Package priced from $2,100 per couple includes 4 nights, breakfasts and dinners, champagne, fruit, a picnic lunch (or sleigh ride), and 2 massages. "Dinner by Design" (rates from $840) includes accommodations for 2 nights, breakfast, and a special dinner created just for you with Brill.

Payment/Credit Cards: Most major

Deposit: 1-night deposit within 10 days of booking, full payment within 30 days of arrival during peak seasons (winter and summer). Prepay in full within 7 days before arrival during shoulder seasons.

Government Taxes: 9 percent sales tax

Service Charges: 15 percent

WOODSTOCK INN & RESORT
Vermont

If you are dreaming of a honeymoon in New England—with warm fires crackling and snow falling on the mountains, or brilliant fall foliage shading a village green lined by pristine clapboard houses, or perhaps lazy summer days strolling on woodland trails—your fantasies will turn into reality when you arrive in Woodstock, Vermont. At the heart of this beautiful little town of only about 2,500 people lies the stately Woodstock Inn & Resort, a lovely inn built by Laurance S. Rockefeller in 1969 on the site of the original inn and tavern, which dated back to 1793.

It's a resort you can enjoy all by itself. The impressive facilities include a putting green located in the courtyard of the inn; the Woodstock Country Club, with its superb golf course, Woodstock Health & Fitness Center, and Ski Touring Center; the nearby Suicide Six ski area; and many planned activities. But just outside your door is the delightful village of Woodstock, with all its eighteenth- and nineteenth-century homes, interesting shops, covered bridges, and historic places like the Billings Farm & Museum, an active historical museum and working dairy farm depicting what farm life was like in the nineteenth century, and the Marsh-Billings-Rockefeller National Historical Park.

Furnished in Colonial style, with soft reds, greens, and blues, the rooms—fifty recently renovated—are bright and cheery, many opening onto a central courtyard, where the putting green is located. Many have fireplaces—just ask and the staff will lay the logs for you. Beds are covered with handmade quilts and hand-loomed coverlets; bookshelves are filled with hardbacks and paperbacks; and built-in cupboards and bureaus give you plenty of storage space. You also have white louvered blinds that you can close when you wish privacy, as well as modern tile and marble baths.

The lobby area is most inviting, especially on a cold day when the massive, 10-foot fireplace is blazing away. Exceptional original artwork in various styles ranging from primitive to contemporary is located throughout the inn along with antique fixtures, lamps, and furniture.

You can dine in the main dining room at tables elegantly appointed with fine linen and gas lamps or enjoy a more casual meal in the Eagle Cafe. Particularly appealing is Richardson's Tavern, where you can settle into a comfortable sofa in front of the fireplace and sip a cognac before heading to your room. The cozy bar area is a popular gathering place.

Just a five-minute walk down South Street from the inn is the Woodstock Country Club. Here you'll find the 6,001-yard, eighteen-hole, Robert Trent Jones–designed golf course. It's narrow and lined with more

than eighty bunkers and has some nasty water hazards guaranteed to give wild hitters more than a few nightmares—the Kedron Brook comes into play on all but six of the eighteen holes. (You might want to leave your driver in the car.) It's also one of the most interesting little courses you'll find in New England.

The 40,000-square-foot recently refurbished Woodstock Health & Fitness Center, located about 1 mile farther south from the Woodstock Country Club, has two indoor tennis courts, two squash courts, two racquetball courts, a 30-by-60-foot lap pool, a whirlpool, a gym, and a croquet court. Tennis buffs can enjoy ten outside tennis courts. Spa treatments include massages, facials, manicures, and pedicures.

In the winter the golf operations turn into the Woodstock Ski Touring Center. Ski trails lace the golf course and beyond, and equipment for sale or rent occupies the space where in the summer you find golf bags, balls, and accessories.

The personal, user-friendly Suicide Six ski area, which opened in 1937, has twenty-two trails in addition to the Face, which is served by two chairlifts and a beginner area with a J-bar. Although the more advanced skiers may prefer to head to nearby Killington, Suicide Six is still a good choice for skiers of all levels who want a pleasant, challenging ski experience. Here you'll find a ski school, ski shop, cafeteria, and lounge-restaurant in the Base Lodge.

Other activities at your fingertips include hiking, biking, horseback riding, fishing, and cultural performances (Dartmouth College's Hopkins Center for the Performing Arts is just a half-hour's drive away). The inn serves morning coffee and afternoon tea and cookies in the Wicker Lounge, a greenhouselike lounge.

Your best bet, if you want to play golf or ski, is to look into a package that includes these activities. Otherwise you will be charged for the use of many of the sports facilities. For example, greens fees are $40.00–$85.00 per person; tennis is $10.00–$20.00 per person, per hour, and inn guests pay $8.00 per person for the use of the racquetball or squash courts. The use of the pool, sauna, steam room, whirlpool, exercise room, and croquet court is complimentary for Woodstock Inn guests.

The Woodstock Inn & Resort is a comfortable, friendly hotel boasting a staff that is eager to see to it you have everything you need. It has just enough spit and polish to make it a top-rated property, yet is not pretentious or stuffy. It's a place you'll want to come back to on your first anniversary.

Woodstock Inn & Resort

Location: Centrally located in Vermont near the New Hampshire border

Romantic Highlights: En-suite fireplaces; village setting

Address/Phone: Fourteen the Green, Woodstock, VT 05091-1298; (802) 457–1100; fax (802) 457–6699

E-mail: email@woodstockinn.com

Web Site: www.woodstockinn.com (reservation requests accepted on-line)

U.S. Reservations: (800) 448–7900

Owner/Manager: Chet Williamson, president and general manager; Paul Ramsey, inn manager

Arrival/Departure: Daily air service available from New York, Hartford, and Boston to Lebanon, New Hampshire; taxi and car rentals available at Lebanon Airport

Distance from Lebanon Airport: 15 miles; 138 miles from Albany; 148 miles from Boston

Distance from Woodstock: In the heart of town

Accommodations: 144 rooms and suites, 23 with fireplaces

Most Romantic Room/Suite: The fireplace rooms or Suites 304 and 349

Amenities: Toiletries, air-conditioning, telephone, clock radio, ironing facilities, cable TV, VCR, bathrobes, fireplace (some), concierge services, room service, valet parking

Electricity: 110 volts

Sports and Facilities: Putting green, outdoor pool, 12 tennis courts (2 indoor, 6 clay, 4 all-weather), 18-hole golf course, 2 squash courts, 2 racquetball courts, lap pool, whirlpool, ten-station Nautilus room, aerobics room, steam baths, saunas, croquet court, ski trails, Alpine ski center, horseback riding, biking, hiking, fishing

Dress Code: Casual; jackets customary and encouraged in dining room; blue jeans, T-shirts, and swim shorts not permitted on golf course or tennis courts

Weddings: Can be arranged

Rates/Packages: $209–$615 per couple; $139–$460 during value season; add $69 per person per day for MAP; Classic Romance: $749 per couple, includes 2 nights' accommodations, breakfast daily, 1 dinner for two, champagne, and special gift. Tennis, golf, and ski packages available.

Payment/Credit Cards: Most major

Deposit: 2-night deposit to confirm reservation. Refunds will be issued only if cancellation is received 1 week before your scheduled arrival date. Cancellations are subject to a $30 processing fee.

Government Taxes: 7 percent Vermont rooms and meals tax

Service Charges: Not included

THE GREENBRIER
West Virginia

The Greenbrier, a venerable bastion of Southern gentility and great golf, is a destination in itself—a place to come for golf, tennis, hiking in the great outdoors, and other gracious pleasures, such as afternoon tea, carriage rides, late-night hot chocolate, croquet, and horseback riding. Mineral baths, an array of spa treatments, good food, and dancing in the cocktail lounge are all part of the scene here.

Grooms will have to pack their ties and jackets and brides will get to wear their favorite fancies. At The Greenbrier tradition reigns, and dressy attire is required for dinner at two of the resort's six restaurants. Black tie is also acceptable.

When the rich and famous traveled here in the mid-1800s to revive themselves in the famous mineral waters and socialize with their peers, they told their friends they were going to the "Old White." The guest book of this stately grande dame includes such historical greats as Dolley Madison, Andrew Jackson, Thomas Edison, and John F. Kennedy. At least twenty-six presidents have come here to take in the fresh mountain air and Southern hospitality.

The original 400-foot-long building is gone, but in its place a majestic Georgian-style structure with pillars and rows of windows sits like a great European castle in the midst of a sea of green pine. Most impressive.

This is not exactly a place you'd describe as intimate or cozy. Any resort that claims to sit on 6,500 acres is major stuff. However, accommodations such as the cottages and suites give you all the privacy you want along with a generous dash of luxury.

The public and private rooms are truly grand. The designer Carleton Varney orches-trates all the interior decoration, including the creation of new fabric and wallpaper designs every year. Each of the hotel's 803 rooms and suites has its own unique decor. Yards and yards of brightly flowered fabric, richly swagged and draped around the high windows; bed canopies and pillows; upholstered chairs and chaises; and bedspreads create surprising riots of fresh color against walls and carpets of reds, emerald greens, and yellows. No fainthearted application of color here! Furnishings are a combination of traditional period antiques and antique reproductions, along with gilt-framed mirrors, paintings, and Oriental carpets.

In the lofty lounge, in spite of the dramatic black-and-white marble floor and high columns, chairs and tables have been arranged in intimate, inviting groupings conducive to a quiet chat, a game of backgammon, or afternoon tea, to the accompaniment of chamber music.

If you want to hide away in your own cottage, ask for accommodations in one of the guest houses. The cottages are airy and roomy, and each has its own porch, fireplace, oversize tub, wet bar or kitchen, separate parlor, and dressing room.

With the staff of 1,800 outnumbering the guests, you can be totally decadent and do nothing but allow yourself to be pampered. If your journey here has been a long one, perhaps the first place you should visit is the Spa. In addition to a Greek-inspired, Olympic-size pool ringed with pillars and patterned tile work, you'll find whirlpool baths, saunas, herbal wraps, and massages—over twenty different treatments.

For the more energetic there are aerobics classes, exercise equipment, and other instruments designed for hard labor. There are guided hiking excursions along the miles of mapped and unmapped trails on The Greenbrier grounds and on nearby Kate's Mountain and plenty of tennis courts, indoors and outdoors, along with three great golf courses. Winding through the rolling countryside at the base of the starkly beautiful Allegheny Mountains, these courses give golfers a visual gift as well as a challenge. Newer golfers may prefer the picturesque, gentle-on-your-score Meadows course. The more competent links mavens can tee off on the championship Nicklaus layout or The Greenbrier, a traditional favorite.

Golf packages are one of the better deals here, giving you unlimited golf, use of a practice range, a clinic, and daily club cleaning and storage as well as breakfast and dinner. It is quite a bargain, as the cost to a nonguest for just playing the course is more than $300 with cart.

For a special romantic day, The Greenbrier's Romantic Rendezvous takes you on a Victorian carriage ride on the grounds and ends at their gazebo, where a waiter serves you lunch. The cost for this treat is $287 per couple.

When it comes time to eat, you have a lot of choices. The Main Dining Room, the largest of the eateries, is an elegant affair with chandeliers, pillars, and ornate plasterwork. Meals, featuring continental and American cuisine, are served with a flourish. The presentation is a work of art. Be sure to save room for the chocolate truffles.

The Drapers Cafe is fun, colorful, and informal. Here you can get breakfast in season, lunch, and dessert and good things from the soda fountain. For a cozy, intimate meal, try the Tavern Room, which specializes in American food, seafood, and rotisserie selections. (Although rates include breakfast and dinner, you'll pay a surcharge to eat here.)

If you are coming from the golf course, you can stop at Sam Snead's for fine dining in a casual setting. You can also catch the latest sports events on TV along with afternoon food and beverages at Slammin' Sammy's, adjacent to Sam Snead's.

There is also the Lounge for cocktails and dancing and the Rhododendron Spa Cafe. In other words, there are plenty of places to eat, suitable for whatever mood you're in.

Many of the vegetables and fruits come from the local markets, and there are local specialties such as fresh trout. The Tavern serves its own ice cream, made daily. Especially popular at breakfast are the warm, homemade muffins and buckwheat cakes. And if you're into watching what you eat, The Greenbrier has introduced its Greenbrier Spa Cuisine, with one-third the calories and low-fat.

You won't have to go very far if you want to shop. There is a major shopping arcade right in the main building, with stores like Orvis, the Carleton Varney Gift Gallery, and the Greenbrier Gourmet Shop. There is also another group of craft shops on the grounds, selling some really good handicraft items.

The Greenbrier

Location: On a 6,500-acre estate in the Allegheny Mountains, in White Sulphur Springs, West Virginia

Romantic Highlights: Victorian carriage ride followed by private lunch in gazebo; sleigh rides in the Allegheny foothills; fireplaces

Address/Phone: White Sulphur Springs, WV 24986; (304) 536–1110; fax (304) 536–7834

Web Site: www.greenbrier.com

U.S. Reservations: (800) 624–6070

Owner/Manager: Ted J. Kleisner, president and managing director

Arrival/Departure: Amtrak offers train service to The Greenbrier from New York and Chicago, with intermediate stops in Philadelphia, Wilmington, Baltimore, Washington, D.C., Indianapolis, and Cincinnati.

Distance from Greenbrier Valley Airport, in Lewisburg: 12 miles (15 minutes)

Distance from Washington D.C.: 250 miles southwest

Accommodations: 803 rooms, 33 suites, 97 guest houses

Most Romantic Room/Suite: Guest houses (Paradise Row or Spring Row) or Garden suites

Amenities: Air-conditioning, hair dryer, clock radio, minibar, toiletries, bathrobes, wet bar or kitchen in some suites, TV, fireplace in guest houses

Electricity: 110 volts

Sports and Facilities: 3 golf courses; 10 indoor and outdoor tennis courts; indoor and outdoor swimming pools; mountain biking; falconry academy; horseback riding; trap and skeet shooting and sporting clays; croquet; whitewater rafting trips; hiking, jogging, and fitness trails; fishing; bowling; sleigh rides; Golf Digest Academy and Off-Road Driving School; 43,000-square-foot spa

Dress Code: Casual by day; jacket and tie for dinner, except in golf club restaurant

Weddings: Can be arranged

Rates/Packages: From $237 per person (double occupancy), including breakfast and dinner. Honeymoon packages are from $540 per couple per night, including breakfast, dinner, champagne, and a photo. However, if you're into golf or tennis, you'd do better to take the golf or tennis packages.

Payment/Credit Cards: Most major

Deposit: $300–$600, depending on time of reservations

Government Taxes: 6 percent sales tax; 3 percent occupancy tax

Service Charges: $28 per person per day

AMANGANI
Wyoming

The minute you enter the expansive lobby area at Amangani, a feeling of peace takes over. This is fitting, since the name Amangani means "peaceful home." The resort faces west, with sweeping views of the Snake River and Teton mountain ranges from virtually every vantage point.

Everywhere you go a zenlike atmosphere permeates, managing to convey both rusticity and elegance at the same time. Large openings lead from one high-ceilinged room to the next, with few doors blocking the flow of movement and energy.

Rawhide chairs cushioned in faux fur, original Western art, and pine stumps that serve as cocktail tables fill the common areas.

Suites are spacious with stone, remote-controlled fireplaces; cowhide chairs with simulated wolf fabric; and modern, sleek furnishings. The expansive bathrooms feature twin vanities, separate toilet and shower rooms connected by a deep soaking tub big enough for two, all with stunning views of the mountains and the valley. Floors are a rich redwood.

A separate, open dressing area includes twin benches and robes and slippers. The shower is trimmed in slate and faces the mountains. In fact, there's very little you can do at Amangani where you are not in sight of the mountains.

Sliding glass doors lead to a large deck complete with iron outdoor furniture and a sculpture designed by a Western artist (each deck features a different design). A large window seat flanked by pillows and a chenille blanket presents a cozy spot to read your favorite novel. Pull up the silk gauze shades and gaze up at the stars. Better yet, during the spring and summer (and even in the winter if you don't mind the chill) take the telescope that's provided in every room and head out to the deck for stargazing. With few lights and the town of Jackson on the other side of a bend in the road, you'll have no trouble spotting the constellations.

At night take advantage of the "peaceful pillow" placed by your bed. Made of flaxseeds and relaxing lavender, the soothing eye pillow is sure to help you nod off.

Because of its location, Amangani showcases some stunning sunsets. Take it all in while relaxing in the lounge with its two-story window wall and wood-burning fireplaces, or go to the adjacent library where you'll find a huge collection of books on Native American culture and Western art as well as CDs, videos, and games.

The main deck leads to a heated outdoor pool and whirlpool with—you guessed it— views of both the Snake River range and the Tetons. Radiant-heat floors in the deck areas ensure snow melts instantly, allowing you to walk barefoot comfortably from pool to whirlpool.

Amangani's only restaurant, the Grill, serves breakfast, lunch, and dinner. The mood is comfortable elegance as you dine amidst specially commissioned artwork and slate and black terrazzo furnishings. The menu changes seasonally and offers regional cuisine that features venison, elk, and buffalo. Everything is made from scratch at the Grill, with the country's freshest vegetables brought in from California. Vegetarian options are always available.

In the health center there are four treatment rooms where you can enjoy everything from a hydrating salt glow to an herbal wrap. There's also a small fitness center and studio (one-on-one classes and trainer sessions are available), and ladies' and men's locker rooms, each with a steam room and showers.

The stone steam room is one of the best we've seen. The harsh sound of the steam as it permeates the room is drowned out by soft, New Age music, and a squirt bottle filled with eucalyptus is available should you want your steam bath to have a hint of mint. Some treatments can be performed in the privacy of your suite.

When it's time to venture out, there's a vast array of activity at your beck and call. During the winter, both Jackson Hole and Grand Targhee Ski areas offer some of the best Alpine skiing in North America. In Teton Village at the Jackson Hole ski resort, you'll find a private ski lounge exclusively for Amangani guests. Enjoy a cocktail or a cup of hot cocoa after a long day of skiing. Half- and full-day snowmobile tours to Granite Hot Springs give you the chance to explore the abundant wildlife and natural surroundings; then relax in a 105-degree natural pool.

A trip to the National Wildlife Art Museum includes a tour of thirteen galleries and the chance to ride a horse-drawn sleigh through the National Elk Refuge just across the street. The refuge is home to thousands of elk during the winter, so be sure to bring your camera.

During the summer, the nearby Snake River is perfect for rafting, kayaking, and fly-fishing. A wildlife safari through Jackson Hole with a naturalist guide provides the chance to see hundreds of bird species including bald eagles.

Like the other properties in the Amanresorts collection—Amangani is the only U.S. property—the staff is impeccably trained, the service superb. The staff ratio at Amangani is three per room, which means you'll enjoy a nice combination of individualized attention and a respect for privacy. With a cocoonlike ambience of peace and tranquility and an ecosystem waiting to be explored outside the door, it's easy to see why so many Amanresorts guests keep coming back for more.

Amangani

Location: Atop East Gros Ventre butte in Jackson Hole, Wyoming, with meadows and grazing land below, the Snake River Range to the southwest, and the Grand Teton Range to the north

Romantic Highlights: En-suite fireplaces, expansive outdoor decks in every suite, heated outdoor pool and whirlpool, awe-inspiring views of the mountain ranges

Address/Phone: 1535 North East Butte Road, Jackson Hole, WY 83001; (307) 734–7333; fax (307) 734–7332

E-mail: amanganires@amanresorts.com

Web Site: www.amangani.com

U.S. Reservations: (877) 734–7333

Owner/Manager: Gay Heywood, general manager

Arrival/Departure: Daily service available to Jackson Hole Airport, Jackson, Wyoming, from several major U.S. hubs. Amangani provides complimentary shuttle service to and from the airport to all guests.

Distance from Jackson Hole Airport: 10 miles (20 minutes)

Distance from Jackson: 5 miles (10 minutes)

Accommodations: 29 superior rooms, 8 deluxe suites, and 4 Aman suites including the Grand Teton Suite

Most Romantic Room/Suite: The Grand Teton Suite, with a wraparound deck and views of both the Snake River Range and the Grand Tetons

Amenities: Air-conditioning, hair dryer, telephone, cable TV, VCR, CD player, ironing facilities, robes, toiletries, 24-hour room service, minibar, fireplace, sports equipment storage, complimentary shuttle service to and from the airport and to and from Jackson Hole

Sports and Facilities: Outdoor heated pool and whirlpool, health center, downhill and cross-country skiing, ski skating, snowshoeing, snowboarding, dogsledding, sleigh rides, snowmobiling, ice skating, hiking, mountain biking, horseback riding, whitewater rafting, canoeing, kayaking, hot air balloon rides, golf, tennis, fly-fishing, gift shop

Dress Code: Comfortably elegant

Weddings: Depending on the season, weddings can be arranged for guests anywhere on the property.

Rates/Packages: From $525–$1,300 per room, per night

Payment/Credit Cards: Most major

Deposit: Secure with credit card; first and last nights' deposit paid at least 15 days before arrival

Government Taxes: 6 percent sales tax

Service Charges: 10 percent

SNAKE RIVER LODGE & SPA
Wyoming

The Snake River Lodge & Spa offers a quiet respite from the hustle and bustles just outside your door where a wealth of mountain activities await, from skiing and snowshoeing in winter to hiking and kayaking in two of the country's best national parks in summer.

Within the resort, the elegant Avanyu Spa is an oasis of relaxation. Enter the spa's grand double doors and the first thing you'll find is a heated pool surrounded by rock formations. During the winter, jump in, swim underneath the divider, and you'll find yourself outdoors surrounded by gorgeous snowy mountain scenery without feeling a pinch of cold. Follow the outdoor heated pathway past the cascading waterfalls and enjoy a soak in the outdoor hot tub.

The 17,000-square-foot spa features men's and ladies' levels each with saunas, steam rooms, and awe-inspiring views of the Grand Tetons. After indulging in an Avanyu Stone Massage, which uses hot and cold stones to relax you and relieve stress, head back to your lounge for a soak in the oversized whirlpool and watch the skiers (or paragliders, depending on the season) as they glide down the mountain. For die-hard sports fans, the men's lounge boasts its own oversize whirlpool with a giant-screen TV set right in front of it.

Winter visitors will appreciate the ski-in service complete with an overnight ski valet. Head down to the valet each morning to pick up your gear and you'll find boots that are not only dry but warm and toasty, too. The Saddlehorn Nordic Center is right across the street from the lodge and serves as the village's one-stop shop for everything from cross-country ski lessons to snowshoe rentals and dogsledding excursions. Summer brings trips to Grand Teton and Yellowstone national parks where you can bike, hike, or go on a safari and get up-close views of the animals as they emerge from their winter hibernation.

The lodge's only restaurant, Gamefish, happens to be one of the best in town, open for breakfast, lunch, and dinner. The menu features local fish and wild game along with Wyoming-raised Angus steaks. If you'd rather venture out, Teton Village has numerous restaurants all within walking distance. Spend one evening in the town of Jackson where you'll find a slew of restaurants and nightspots.

Stop in at the Cowboy Bar and learn to two-step, or head to the Jackson Hole Hat Company and get a custom hat-fitting from owners Marilyn and Paul Hartman. The pair crafted those used in Broadway hits including *Annie Get Your Gun* and *Oklahoma*.

Back at the lodge you'll find the entire property reflects its earthy mountain setting. Oversize brown and deep-red leather sofas and chairs, wood tables, and whimsical hand-carved bears dot the lobby and bar area.

Rooms are simple but elegant with large windows; soft, overstuffed down comforters, and locally made wood furniture. Bathrooms have granite countertops, marble-tile floors, and jet tubs. By far the best feature of the rooms is the bed with a perfectly chosen mattress, not too hard, not too soft. It was so comfortable, we even peeked to see if we could find out who made it. No luck. Along with soft, delicious linens, Snake River's bedding provides a haven for sweet dreams.

Snake River Lodge & Spa is for those whose idea of a perfect resort is one where a location offering an endless array of year-round activity is coupled with a world-class, in-house spa and a five-star-worthy restaurant.

Snake River Lodge & Spa

Location: Nestled in the heart of Teton Village, Jackson Hole's premiere ski resort, with the famous Teton Mountain Range as a backdrop; both Grand Teton and Yellowstone National Parks nearby

Romantic Highlights: Couples' massages with views of the Grand Tetons; indoor/outdoor hot tubs; heated indoor/outdoor pool with cascading waterfalls; en-suite fireplaces

Address/Phone: 7710 Granite Loop Road, Teton Village, WY 83025; (307) 732–6000

E-mail: Through the Web site (use the link on the site)

Web Site: www.rockresorts.com

U.S. Reservations: (800) 445–4655

Owner/Manager: Bruce Grosbety, general manager

Arrival/Departure: Daily service available to Jackson Hole Airport from several major U.S. hubs; taxi and car rentals available at airport

Distance from Jackson Hole Airport: 25 minutes

Distance from Jackson: 12 miles (15 minutes)

Accommodations: 88 hotel rooms, 40 luxury suites/condominiums

Most Romantic Room/Suite: Any third- or fourth-floor luxury king-size room or executive king for best views.

Amenities: Air-conditioning, hair dryer, telephone, cable TV, ironing facilities, robes, toiletries, 24-hour room service, minibar, kitchen, fireplace in suites

Electricity: 110 volts

Sports and Facilities: Lobby bar, indoor and outdoor heated pool, hot tubs, sauna, spa and fitness center, ski-in and ski valet service, downhill and cross-country skiing, ski skating, snowshoeing, snowboarding, dogsledding, sleigh rides, snowmobiling, heli-skiing, ice skating, hiking, biking, horseback riding, white-water rafting, canoeing, kayaking, hot air balloon rides, golf, tennis, fly-fishing

Dress Code: Casual

Weddings: Can be arranged

Rates/Packages: $120–$409 for rooms, $449–$1,700 for suites/condominiums

Payment/Credit Cards: Most major

Deposit: Varies with season

Government Taxes: 7 percent sales tax

Service Charges: 4 percent resort fee

CANADA

THE FAIRMONT BANFF SPRINGS
Alberta

Modeled after a Scottish baronial castle, the Fairmont Banff Springs reigns over the majestic mountains and hills that surround it. This massive stone hotel—with its steeply pitched green roofs and gables topped by finials of gold and its gray granite walls, turretlike wings, and arched passageways—would be right at home perched in the Alps. Built in 1888 by the Canadian Pacific Railroad to provide its passengers with an oasis of opulence, it has enough rooms to accommodate a king, a queen, and their entire court.

Called "Castle in the Rockies," grand features include king-size fireplaces, massive wrought-iron chandeliers, and print fabrics in deep rich tones. The Fairmont Banff Springs invites you to have it both ways: the wilderness experience—trail rides, hiking, and biking—along with luxuries like a full-service spa, fireplaces, minibars, and tons of shops. Certainly its appeal has attracted its share of notables over the years, including Clint Eastwood, John Travolta, Alec Baldwin, Woody Harrelson, and Meg Ryan.

A truly four-seasons resort, in the summer flowers overflow in hanging baskets and thrive happily in the gardens, golfers head to the tees, hikers and bikers hit the trails, and white-water rafters swoosh down the swollen rivers.

In the winter the fireplaces get cranked up, the ski tows start running, and cross-country skiers head out on the miles of trails. And any time of year it's an easy walk to the center of Banff, where a number of shops and cafes beckon to browsers and buyers.

Rooms and suites located in the main building and in the adjacent Manor House are furnished in mostly Victorian style in deep reds, greens, and browns. Unique heritage accessories such as glass bottles, leather-bound books, and brass candlesticks are placed here and there. Views are of the mountains, the pine forests, and the golf course.

A $75 million restoration and renovation program has resulted in a stunning grand lobby, expanded kitchen facilities, restaurants, public areas, and shops. Guest rooms have been refurbished and an arrivals entrance welcomes visitors in grand style. On the picturesque eighteen-hole championship Stanley Thompson–designed Golf Course, which winds along the valley at the base of the mountains and along the Bow River, wildlife often calls the shots. Elk are at times as plentiful as geese. This is especially true in the fall, rutting season, when the big guys get all charged up and herd together all the females they can bully. Rangers are called almost on a daily basis to shoo the elk to the sidelines. (A word of caution: Heed posted warnings and don't try to approach an elk with a camera or a club. The bulls can get testy.)

If you want to kick back and head into the hills, Holiday on Horseback offers hourly and two- to six-day overnight pack trips from its base near the hotel. After a four- to five-hour ride through some pretty spectacular countryside, you'll reach Sundance Lodge, a two-story log house with a wide veranda. The lodge has several bedrooms. Beds are very comfortable and food is plentiful—perhaps a ham or roast beef with all the trimmings and homemade pie. In the evening guests gather around the campfire to swap tales and roast marshmallows. The lodge is solar heated and remarkably warm and cozy. Farther up the trail is

Halfway Lodge, for folks who want something even more rustic and a longer trip.

The Fairmont Banff Springs participates in the Heritage Mountaineering and Interpretive Hiking Program, offering hikes led by certified mountain guides and naturalists.

At the end of a day's hiking or riding, or just anytime for that matter, the full-service recently renovated Willow Stream Spa and Fitness Centre, a $12 million dollar 35,000-square-foot facility, pampers you with aromatic wraps, refreshing facials, scrubs, baths, and hour-long massages. There is a sauna, Jacuzzi, inhalation room, and steam room as well as a 105-foot saltwater pool divided into lanes for doing laps. In another area mineral water cascades in silvery sheets into three massage pools heated at different temperatures; from there you can step into a larger therapeutic mineral pool and then relax on the cushioned lounges.

Outside there is another heated pool open year-round and a large Jacuzzi. Willow Stream also boasts a fully equipped cardio- and strength-conditioning fitness center and an aerobics theater where daily classes are scheduled. Views of mountains and dense stands of pine all around complete the blissful picture.

Relax in the lobby where 20-foot windows overlook the Sulphur Mountain Range and extensive skylights frame mountains and sky. Or try the Rundle Room (formerly the hotel lobby), which has been transformed into an elegant guest parlor with vaulted ceilings, huge windows, and antique furnishings. With seventeen restaurants and lounges—including the Banff Shire Club featuring gourmet cuisine in a private club-style setting; Grapes, a European bistro and wine bar; and Samurai, where you can make a meal out of their California rolls— the only decision you have to make when it comes time to eat is do you turn right or left out of the elevator.

You can spend a week, a month, or more at The Fairmont Banff Springs and never tire of things to do or see.

The Fairmont Banff Springs

Location: Nestled in the mountains at the confluence of the Bow and Spray Rivers in the Canadian Rockies

Romantic Highlights: Castlelike features; awesome views; fresh mountain air; fireplaces; spa treatments and massages for two

Address/Phone: P.O. Box 960, Banff, Alberta T1L 1J4, Canada; (403) 762–2211; fax (403) 762–5755

Web Site: www.fairmont.com/banffsprings/

U.S. Reservations: (800) 441–1414

Owner/Manager: David Roberts, regional vice president and general manager

Arrival/Departure: Shuttle service available from Calgary Airport

Distance from Calgary Airport: 80 miles (1½ hours)

Distance from Calgary: 80 miles

Accommodations: 770 rooms and suites

Most Romantic Room/Suite: Tower rooms featuring a spiral staircase leading to a loft, which may have a round bed, a Jacuzzi, and great views of the valley

Amenities: Tea/ coffeemaker, minibar, TV, radio, hair dryer, bathrobes, iron/ironing board, toiletries; some with fireplaces, parlors, oversize whirlpools, saunas

Electricity: 110 volts

Sports and Facilities: Willow Stream Spa and Fitness Centre features cascading waterfalls, mineral whirlpools, indoor and outdoor saltwater pools, solaria, steam rooms, saunas, and various treatments;

18 holes of championship golf, 5 tennis courts, hiking, biking, horseback riding, bowling, rollerblading, white-water rafting, canoeing, fishing, interpretive walks, rock climbing, mountaineering, skiing, heli-skiing, snowboarding, ice skating, dogsledding, tobogganing, horse-drawn sleigh rides, curling, hockey. A retail shopping area contains 15 speciality and boutique stores.

Dress Code: Resort casual; jacket and tie requested in the Rob Roy Room during summer months

Weddings: Can be arranged

Rates/Packages: Canadian Rockies Experi-

ence package includes accommodations, meals, unlimited sports, gratuities, and sight-seeing. Summer package is priced from $671 per room, per day; winter from $693. Outdoor activities include golf, canoeing, cycling, fishing, hiking, Heritage Mountaineering and Interpretive Hiking Program, sleigh rides, ski lift tickets.

Payment/Credit Cards: Most major

Deposit: By credit card

Government Taxes: 12 percent

Service Charges: Sometimes included

Entry Requirements for U.S. Citizens: Passport and photo ID

THE FAIRMONT CHATEAU LAKE LOUISE
Alberta

Built in 1913 this white stucco resort is huge, with sweeping vistas of the snow-topped mountains that cradle a stunning glacier-fed turquoise lake. Even at night the lake glows, a shimmery, glassy surface framed by the jagged steep cliffs, pine-clad hills, and striated rock formations that have shifted over thousands of years to slant toward the water. Dark blue velvet skies ringed by patches of misty clouds sparkle with stars. The resort twinkles with tiny white lights, creating an outdoor wonderland. Then daylight. The lake, not large, is a watercolor of reflections fanning out from the narrower end, where the glacier lies receding in the distance.

From the beginning the Fairmont Chateau Lake Louise was built to appeal to guests with outdoor interests. Its orientation to one of the most beautiful lakes in North

America and its setting of manicured lawns and gardens surrounded by densely forested mountains laced with hiking, biking, skiing, and horseback riding trails, rock faces to climb, and rivers to conquer hold enough interests and challenges to appeal to people of all skill levels.

Some come simply to soak up the scenery and enjoy a variety of dining experiences. Famous guests have included Queen Elizabeth II, Mary Astor, John Barrymore, Cary Grant, Prince Rainier of Monaco, and many of today's Hollywood celebrities.

With close to 500 rooms and suites, the Fairmont Chateau Lake Louise could hardly be called your cozy inn in the Rockies. Yet within its walls there are intimate spaces, comfortable sofas, warm-paneled wood lounges, and fireside groupings. Built to celebrate the outdoors, the hotel has immense arched windows that frame the mountain peaks and paths that lead to the water's edge and along it.

Rooms and suites are spacious and oriented toward the lake or the mountains. Some have balconies and oversize whirlpool tubs. High ceilings, rich, thick carpets in greens and reds, hand-painted folk art on each guest room door, chandeliers, brass fixtures and wood paneling are featured in public rooms and guest accommodations. Special touches include such items as books, glass bottles, and candlesticks. A shopping arcade sells everything from Canadian sweaters and fleeces to jewelry and Irish goods, including wool capes, sweaters, and crystal.

Restaurants include Walliser Stube, specializing in Swiss Alpine cuisine—the fondue and raclette are excellent. For casual dining there is the Poppy Brasserie, serving breakfast, lunch, and dinner, and the Glacier Saloon, where the Old West comes alive. The Fairview Dining Room features world-class cuisine, and in the Victoria Dining Room you can experience grand dining in a European atmosphere punctuated by beautiful chandeliers, linens, and china. Backpackers can stock up at the Chateau Deli on water, sandwiches, soups, and desserts; cocktails are available in the Lobby Bar.

Recalling the time one hundred years ago when Swiss guides arrived in the area, greatly boosting the hiking and mountain climbing activities, the Fairmont Chateau Lake Louise has launched its Heritage Mountaineering and Interpretive Hiking Program. There are hikes for all levels, from those just moderately fit to the highly experienced. Certified mountain guides and naturalists take you on a wonderful journey of from four to ten hours.

"Prepare to leave civilization," cautions naturalist guide Bruce Bembridge in a hushed tone. The snow continues to fall

through the trees, the ice on the path melts into dark wet patches. Snow clings to spiderweb threads hanging from pine branches like Christmas tree icicles. You continue walking down the hill, finally reaching the wide open grounds that lead to the entrance of the hotel. You have left the tiny blue flowers poking through the snow, the views high up and through the spruce and firs of Lake Louise, the teahouse perched on a mountain peak, the chipmunks gathering and cracking nuts. It's all so breathtakingly beautiful.

The Fairmont Chateau Lake Louise

Location: In Banff National Park in the Canadian Rockies

Romantic Highlights: Awesome views of crystal-clear lake and mountains; horse-drawn sleigh rides; fireplaces; moonlight skating

Address/Phone: Lake Louise, Alberta T0L 1E0, Canada; (403) 522–3511; fax (403) 522–3111

Web Site: www.fairmont.com

U.S. Reservations: (800) 441–1414

Owner/Manager: David M. Bayne, general manager

Arrival/Departure: Shuttle service available from Calgary Airport

Distance from Calgary Airport: 120 miles (2½ hours)

Distance from Banff: 36 miles

Accommodations: 550 rooms, including 83 suites; 26 rooms with whirlpools; 4 split-level suites with balconies

Most Romantic Room/Suite: Junior Suites on upper floors with sitting areas and lake views; the Belvedere Suites, two-level accommodations with balconies overlooking lakes and mountains; Room 303 with its coffered ceiling, wide balcony, and wood paneling is especially grand; Room 536, decorated in the Victorian style, with an elegant living room, fireplace (non-working) flanked by bookcases, and a bathroom, powder room, and Jacuzzi.

Amenities: Minibar, hair dryer, TV, dressing table, toiletries, coffee/tea facilities, iron/ironing board, robes, fan

Electricity: 110 volts

Sports and Facilities: Recreation center with indoor pool, whirlpool, steam rooms, weights and exercise equipment; walking, hiking, canoeing, fishing, mountaineering, rock climbing, dogsledding, Alpine and cross-country skiing, ice skating, river rafting, golf, guided snowshoeing expeditions, snowboarding, heli-skiing, horse-drawn sleigh rides, hockey, broom ball, guided trail rides and overnight horseback adventures, arcade and video room, art classes

Dress Code: Resort casual; jacket and tie required for Fairview Dining Room

Weddings: Can be arranged

Rates/Packages: Canadian Rockies Experience package priced from $471 (summer); from $364 (winter) per person, per day includes accommodations, meals, unlimited sports, gratuities, and sight-seeing. Romance packages available, like the "Love & Hugs" package: Unwind at 5,680 feet above sea level with the "Silk and Bubbly" room delivery, featuring sparkling wine, chocolates, a bath treat, and a teddy bear. Rates start from $139 in winter and $289 in summer per person, per day, based on double occupancy in a Fairmont room and include breakfast in bed, or the alpine buffet, and complimentary valet parking. Outdoor activities include canoeing, cycling, fishing, hiking, Heritage Mountaineering and Interpretive Hiking Program, sleigh rides, ski lift tickets.

Payment/Credit Cards: Most major

Deposit: By credit card

Government Taxes: 11 percent

Service Charges: Sometimes included

Entry Requirement for U.S. Citizens: Passport and photo ID

THE FAIRMONT JASPER PARK LODGE
Alberta

It began as a tent city in 1915 in the 4,200-acre Jasper National Park, becoming a lodge in 1922, a place where people could escape and reconnect with nature. And they came: the Kennedys, John Travolta, Marilyn Monroe, Bob Newhart, and many others who could afford the best.

Today The Fairmont Jasper Park Lodge has grown: more cottages, more facilities, a wonderful main lodge with enormous lounges, shopping arcade, dining rooms, golf clubhouse, and outdoor swimming pool and Jacuzzi. Still, although it now has close to 450 rooms and 9 places to eat and drink, it has emerged with its integrity intact. It continues to appeal to anyone who appreciates cool mountain air, walking along lakeshore paths, going to bed hearing the plaintive calls of elk, skipping stones across a white-blue translucent lake, sitting in front of a crackling fire drinking hot chocolate, and heading out to the golf course, ski trails, or other outdoor pursuits for fresh air and exercise.

The Fairmont Jasper Park Lodge, a comfortable enclave of log cabins and cedar chalets, features spacious, well-appointed rooms with all the amenities you could wish for, including padded hangers, mini-fridge, TVs, down duvets, king-size beds, large picture windows, pine armoires, and colorful burgundy, green, and brown print fabrics. Some rooms open onto decks or patios; some have fireplaces and oversize whirlpool baths. One thing is certain, you may be stomping around the grounds and surrounding mountains in your wool socks and hiking boots, but when it comes time to eat or hit the sack, you'll find nothing rough about your accommodations.

Cabins range in size from three bedrooms, each with private bath, to Milligan Manor, with eight bedrooms, nine baths, and a 900-square-foot living and dining room. Point and Overlook, older cabins loaded with charm, feature several well-appointed bedrooms, lofty living room, kitchen, and dining room (Bill Gates and his family rented one of these on a recent vacation). Since all rooms in these suite cabins are complete in themselves, with en-suite baths and outside entrances, they can be rented singly but are also ideal for a group of couples who desire private bedrooms but the use of a central living, dining, and kitchen area.

Those seeking privacy can book their own suite that sits on a bluff overlooking the water and comes with a living room, fireplace, and a whirlpool tub-for-two. Other options include the Whistler Cabins, featuring enormous vaulted ceiling living rooms with fireplaces and kitchenettes with refrigerators and microwaves; French doors open onto decks overlooking the lake.

Golfers will find the Stanley Thompson–designed golf course challenging but very playable. Tees on the course, which meanders along the shores of Lac Beauvert, are oriented to mountain peaks and some holes require driving over water. All but three of the holes are fenced to keep elk off the fairways and greens.

Restaurants range from the elegant Edith Cavell Dining Room, serving gourmet cuisine, to the Tent City, a pub offering billiards and shuffleboard and pub-style food. When dining at the Edith Cavell, be sure to try the mushroom chowder; it's the best. Also good is the filet of Alberta beef tenderloin on a Yukon Gold potato cake, the fresh lemon curd flan, and the birch and apple cider–basted British Columbia salmon filet. Fresh herbs and vegetables grown in Jasper's greenhouse are used in food preparation; breads and pastries are freshly baked.

All the mountain-oriented sports and activities are available at Jasper, including the Heritage Mountaineering and Interpretive Hiking Program and horseback riding. For a memorable adventure arrange a rafting trip with Mount Robson Whitewater Rafting, about forty-five minutes from the hotel in Valemount, B.C. Operated by the Cinnamon family, this company has more than twenty years' experience in taking venturesome travelers down the spectacular Fraser River, the longest river in British Columbia. At the end of the trip, chow down on some of the best veggieburgers or hamburgers you'll ever taste—the recipe is a secret.

The Fairmont Jasper Park Lodge is a peaceful place. Listen carefully as you walk along the paths and through the pines. Shhh. You may be able to hear the soft tread of the eclectic group of early adventurers who explored the land and climbed the mountains.

The Fairmont Jasper Park Lodge

Location: On 903 acres in Jasper National Park, a UNESCO World Heritage Site and Canada's largest Rocky Mountain National Park

Romantic Highlights: Awesome views; fresh mountain air; fireplaces; wildlife all around

Address/Phone: P.O. Box 40, Jasper, Alberta T0E 1E0, Canada; (780) 852–3301; fax (780) 852–5107

Web Site: www.fairmont.com

U.S. Reservations: (800) 441–1414

Owner/Manager: Amanda Robinson, general manager

Arrival/Departure: Shuttle service available from Calgary Airport

Distance from Calgary Airport: 256 miles (4½ hours)

Distance from Edmonton: 225 miles

Accommodations: 446 rooms, suites, cabins, and chalets

Most Romantic Room/Suite: Number 467 (Athabasca) known as the "Honeymoon Cottage"; Whistler Cabins also good

Amenities: Bathrobes, coffeemaker, minibar, TV, radio, hair dryer, iron/ironing board, umbrellas, scale, toiletries, turndown service; some with fireplaces, oversize whirlpool baths

Electricity: 110 volts

Sports and Facilities: Walking, hiking, fishing, mountaineering, rock climbing, dogsledding, Alpine and cross-country skiing, ice skating, river rafting, biking, heli-hiking, canoeing, sleigh rides, canyon ice crawling, snowmobile tours; 18-hole golf course, 4 tennis courts (hard surface); game room and fitness center with exercise equipment, steam room and whirlpool, year-round heated outdoor pool, Miette hot springs; billiards; guided snowshoeing expeditions, trail rides, and overnight horseback adventures

Dress Code: Resort casual

Weddings: Can be arranged

Rates/Packages: Canadian Rockies Experience package includes accommodations, meals, unlimited sports, gratuities, and sight-seeing. Summer package is priced from $697; winter packages from $475 per room, per day. Outdoor activities include golf, canoeing, cycling, fishing, hiking, Heritage Mountaineering and Interpretive Hiking Program, sleigh rides, ski lift tickets.

Payment/Credit Cards: Most major

Deposit: By credit card

Government Taxes: 11 percent

Service Charges: Sometimes included

Entry Requirements for U.S. Citizens: Passport and photo ID

LA PINSONNIÈRE

Quebec

This small inn, which lies between the Laurentian Mountains and the tidal flats of the St. Lawrence River, is a real find for those honeymooning in Canada. La Pinsonnière, which means "house of the finches," sits about 200 feet up a bluff overlooking the river, which at this point is 15 miles wide. This sprawling white manor house, with its pointed towers and garden setting ringed by tall trees, would seem equally at home on the Loire River in France's château country.

Jean Authier, along with his daughter, Valérie, La Pinsonnière's manager, are committed to providing their guests with an exceptional place to stay and dine. Their restaurant, with its French-trained chef, has already received a number of awards and has gained a reputation for serving some of the finest cuisine in Canada.

In addition to the hotel business, the Authiers have an avid interest in the arts. Contemporary paintings by Quebec artists, many for sale, hang in the dining room and in other places throughout the inn.

Each of the rooms has a personality all its own; several have been recently redecorated. For example, one has a king-size brass bed, fireplace, private sauna, and large whirlpool tub. Another is a vision of romantic Victoriana, with white wicker and rattan furniture, a white marble bath, lace duvet cover, and puffy white cushions.

Five rooms have been recently enlarged and transformed into sumptuous deluxe rooms with king beds, living rooms, breathtaking views, and lavish bathrooms with fireplaces and saunas.

Some rooms are decorated in muted traditional colors and feature Queen Anne–style furniture, brass lamps, and wing chairs; others are light and airy, decorated in soft sea colors with rattan and pine furniture and French doors leading to terraces overlooking the river.

Large marble baths with designer soaps, fluffy down duvets, classical music, and chairs you can really sink into and fall asleep in, add up to accommodations that are comfortable but not obtrusive.

La Pinsonnière is located in the Charlevoix region, an area known for its rugged cliffs, rolling hills, coves, and exceptional river views. A late afternoon pleasure

for the inn's guests is to sit on the terrace of the hotel's lovely large patio and watch the sun set over the tops of the tall cedar, spruce, and birch trees. You can also follow the path that leads down through a cedar forest to the inn's private, rugged beach, a great place for a picnic. Going down the 226 steps is easy. Going up you'll find rustic benches where you can stop and rest or just sit for a while.

The inn may be small, but it still offers a lot of choices for active couples. There is a tennis court, indoor pool, and massage therapists who can pamper you with a variety of soothing treatments.

In the warmer months, you can hike on the trails in the surrounding hills, take a whale-watching cruise, and play golf at nearby Murray Bay. Cruise up the Saguenay Fjord, the world's southernmost fjord, and marvel at the spectacular scenery of sheer rocky cliffs plunging dramatically down to the river. Or visit the artists' town of Baie Saint Paul, a pleasant drive from the inn, where you can browse through about twenty galleries featuring Charlevoix and Quebec painters. There are also many summer theater productions and concerts held nearby.

If you come in the winter, you can cross-country and downhill ski at Mont Grand Fonds, go snowmobiling, ice skating, and dogsledding and at the end of the day curl up in front of a crackling fire in your room or in the lounge.

Want an adventure? In the warmer months you can climb into a red isothermic suit and head off by boat for the world of the belugas and blue whales that inhabit the Saguenay Marine Arctic Park.

Vistas from La Pinsonnière's restaurant, as well as from most of the rooms, are expansive. Large windows afford marvelous views of the rivers, hills, and trees. Dining by candlelight at a beautifully appointed table is a special pleasure. Cuisine centered on continental fare with an emphasis on French cooking includes dishes such as ravioli croustillants de crabe en velouté de cidre, foie gras de canard poelé aux poires confites, and wild mushrooms served in a delicate sauce. In 2001 the restaurant was awarded the Table d'Or du Quebec as the best restaurant in the province. A prix-fixe dinner is about $55 (U.S.) for three courses, $70 for five courses, $100 for seven courses, plus tax and service charges. The Authiers' 13,000-bottle wine cellar is impressive, and you are invited to participate in frequent wine tastings. A new a la carte menu has been added.

An exquisite romantic hideaway, the inn is a member of the prestigious Relais & Châteaux group.

La Pinsonnière

Location: On the banks of the St. Lawrence River, in the picturesque Charlevoix region north of Quebec City

Romantic Highlights: Private fireplaces; terraces above the river; whirlpool baths for two

Address/Phone: 124 Saint-Raphael, La Malbaie (Cap-à-l'Aigle), Charlevoix, Quebec G5A 1X9, Canada; (418) 665–4431; fax (418) 665–7156

E-mail: pinsonniere@relaischateaux.com

Web Site: www.lapinsonniere.com

U.S. Reservations: (800) 387–4431; Relais & Châteaux, (800) RELAIS–8

Owner/Manager: The Authier family

Arrival/Departure: There is a very small airport, St.-Irenée, about 3 miles from the inn; free pickup can be arranged.

Distance from Quebec International Airport: 95 miles

Distance from Quebec City: 90 miles

Accommodations: 25 rooms, including 1 suite

Most Romantic Room/Suite: Room 312, which has a rosewood king-size bed, whirlpool bath for two, and sauna with a spectacular view of the St. Lawrence River; Room 211, a creamy white confection with king-size bed, fluffy down comforter, double whirlpool, fireplace, marble bath, and deck

Amenities: Hair dryer, toiletries, fireplace (some rooms), TV, telephone, robes, ceiling fans, air-conditioning, safe, and classical music; some have minibars

Electricity: 110 volts

Sports and Facilities: Indoor pool, hiking, beach, tennis, kayaking, skiing, skating, sauna, whale-watching, massage therapy

Dress Code: Casually smart; jackets are not required for dinner but are appreciated.

Weddings: Can be arranged

Rates/Packages: Can$144–$360 (US$180–$450) per couple per night (low season); Can$210–$450 (US$170–$360) (high season—warmer months and holidays); Can$80 (US$65) breakfast and dinner

Payment/Credit Cards: Most major

Deposit: 50 percent of total cost of stay required; balance due on arrival; refundable if canceled 15 days or more prior to date of arrival

Government Taxes: $2.00 per night; 7 percent federal; 7.5 percent provincial

Service Charges: Included

Entry Requirements for U.S. Citizens: Passport and photo ID

THE CARIBBEAN, BAHAMAS, AND BERMUDA

CAP JULUCA
Anguilla

Cap Juluca's dazzling white towers, turrets, and arches, set against the dense greens of the foliage and clear turquoise of the Caribbean waters, create a fairy-tale village straight out of Arabian Nights. Nothing but brightly hued blossoms of bougainvillea and waving palm fronds comes between you and your view of the sea from your oversize terrace or turret patio. Set on 179 acres, all rooms and villas are just steps away from the white, sugary sand crescent beach; no building is higher than the palm trees.

The exteriors of the buildings, with their parapets and domes, are dramatic enough, but wait until you get inside. Rooms are really large—at least 16 feet by 16 feet—and one-bedroom suites go up to 2,500 square feet with private pool. Villas, with up to five bedrooms, have private pools set in an enclosed red-tiled garden courtyard. You can rent bedrooms and suites in the pool villas, or you can rent the entire villa yourself for complete privacy.

Bathrooms are outrageously opulent, with tons of marble, double sinks, showers, and bidets. Some have double-size bathtubs with headrests; some open onto a private walled solarium furnished with chaises and a table. Louvered windows let the sea breezes slip through, yet preserve your privacy. You can lie back and catch the sun wearing as little as you want or nothing at all.

Rattan furniture with thick cushions, king-size beds, fine linens, potted palms in clay pots, dark Brazilian walnut doors and trim, white walls, and ceramic tile floors in various muted colors provide a sumptuous setting for romance. Unique accessories, such as wooden bowls and sculpture, leather, and clay, as well as beautiful area rugs, inlaid mirrors, and artwork, many imported from northern Africa, are found in some rooms; others lean toward a more European feeling, with traditional period furnishings and accessories.

There are three tennis courts, and the pro schedules round-robin tournaments every week. There is also a fitness center and a croquet court set up British style. A new spa is located adjacent to the main house. Complimentary water sports include waterskiing, sailing, and sailboarding. You can also go scuba diving (this is extra), or if you want to set off on your own "True Love" cruise, you can charter a yacht.

No one will intrude on your privacy, even while you're on the beach—unless, of course, you lower a flag from your beach umbrella. This means you would like someone to come over and see what you want, whether it be a clean towel or another Sea Breeze. Intimate "garden rooms," partitioned with hedges, are located around the pool. If you want service, just ring a bell.

Cap Juluca's beaches are long and very walkable. The main beach stretches along Maundays Bay for about a mile. Go around the eastern end of the headland and there is another 2-mile beach running along Cove Bay. In the center of Maundays Bay beach is an Olympic-size pool set back from the beach, which is surrounded by white market-style umbrellas and tables along with many lounge chairs—a popular gathering place.

Many guests, especially those who have terraces with great sea views, prefer to have breakfast brought to their room. Fresh fruits and juices, muffins and banana bread, and steaming coffee or tea are beautifully set up on your patio table complete with linen and china. You also get a summary of the latest news from the *New York*

Times faxed that morning from the States (just in case you've missed it).

One night you may wish to order a West Indian dinner served on your patio. Linger over a bottle of wine from the resort's extensive wine cellar, and see if you can spot the lights of St. Martin or tiny Saba twinkling across the water.

Cap Juluca has three open-air restaurants: the casually elegant Pimms, Kemia featuring international fare, and the more informal George's. Pimms is tucked into the corner of the protected eastern end of the cove and sits just 6 feet from the water's edge. George's is located midway along Maundays Bay beach and is open all day for casual dining. Kemia is located next to Pimms.

After dinner kick off your shoes and walk hand in hand back to your room along the moonlit beach and be lulled to sleep by the sound of waves rolling up on the shores. Or linger at your table at George's for some dancing under the stars.

When you come to Anguilla, don't expect a roaring nightlife. After all, an island where the 30-mile-an-hour speed limit is reinforced by a series of speed bumps and the airport allows only prop planes to land is not a swinging place. Come here if you like to picnic on an uninhabited island or drift away in a hammock in a garden perfumed with the scents of frangipani, jasmine, and orchids.

Cap Juluca

Location: Along Maundays Bay, on the southern coast of Anguilla

Romantic Highlights: Sugar-white crescent beach; palatial bathrooms, some with private solarium, some with private turrets; massages for two en suite

Address/Phone: P.O. Box 240, Maundays Bay, Anguilla, Leeward Islands, British West Indies; (264) 497–6666; fax (264) 497–6617

E-mail: capjuluca@anguillanet.com

Web Site: www.capjuluca.com

U.S. Reservations: (888) 8–Juluca; fax (305) 466–0926

Owner/Manager: Cap Juluca Holdings, Inc., owner; Dion Friedland, chairman of the board; Eustace Guishard, general manager

Arrival/Departure: Anguilla is reached via scheduled air service from San Juan (50 minutes) or St. Martin (5 minutes) or via ferry from Marigot in French St. Martin (25 minutes). Guests are met on arrival. You can also take the Cap Juluca "Sea Shuttle" from Juliana Airport, St. Martin (scheduled service), or by private charter boat from the same area.

Distance from Wallblake Airport: 8 miles (15 minutes)

Distance from Marigot, St. Martin: 8 miles (25 minutes by ferry); 5 miles from the Valley (capital)

Accommodations: 58 luxury rooms and junior suites; 7 suites; 6 pool villas

Most Romantic Room/Suite: For privacy try the end units: Pool Villa 19 and a room or suite in Villa Building 12

Amenities: Air-conditioning, ceiling fans, private walled terrace, toiletries, refrigerator, stocked starter selection minibar, kitchen in villas, butlers available

Electricity: 110/220 volts

Sports and Facilities: Spa, 3 Omni-surface tennis courts (2 lighted), croquet, sailboarding, waterskiing, snorkeling, scuba diving, Hobie-Cats, kayaks, Sunfishes; Olympic-size pool, 6 villa pools, 3 miles of beach; extra charge for use of motor cruiser, and mono-hull sailing dinghies

Dress Code: Casually elegant and sophisticated; no jacket or tie required

Weddings: Can be arranged

Rates/Packages: Spring/fall: $490–$1,685; Summer: $380–$1,240; Winter: $750–$2,615, including full European breakfast, tennis, water sports, entertainment, use of fitness center, tea, sorbet on beach, 30-minute massage for two, group Tai Chi class for two, and daily butler service in all pool suites

Payment/Credit Cards: Most major

Deposit: Deposit within 2 days

Government Taxes: 10 percent (except for package where tax is included)

Service Charges: 10 percent (except for package where service charge is included)

Entry Requirements for U.S. Citizens: Return ticket and proof of citizenship required; passport best

Closed: September–late October

CURTAIN BLUFF
Antigua

If there is a pot of gold at the end of one of Antigua's most winding, bumpy roads, it has to be Curtain Bluff. It's worth every torturous mile it takes to get you to this superb little resort, which seduces you from the moment you arrive. Consistently rated as one of the best resorts in the Caribbean for almost forty years, Curtain Bluff rises from a narrow peninsula between two beaches, marking the place where the Caribbean and Atlantic meet, and giving you nonstop ocean views from every room. Bougainvillea, hibiscus, oleander, royal palms, and every other tropical flower you can think of line walkways, hug buildings, and fall in great clouds of blossoms from trellises and walls. And wherever you go, you never lose sight of the sea.

Some of the two-story buildings are spread out along the beach whereas the villa suites climb gently up the slope of the peninsula. At the top of the bluff sits the home of the owner, Howard Hulford. It's the crown to Curtain Bluff's string of pink and white buildings and the site of weddings as well as cocktail receptions honoring Curtain Bluff's guests.

There was nothing much on the land when Hulford bought the property, but he brought seeds and cuttings from plants he liked from everywhere, started his own nursery, and soon had the grounds flourishing with palms, flowering shrubs, and other tropical plants. Today Hulford says he enjoys spending at least an hour a day tending to his fledgling seedlings and newly grafted shrubs. This attention to detail by a man who once flew planes for a living is just part of the story and helps explain the beauty and seductive influence Hulford and his beautiful wife, Chelle, have created at Curtain Bluff.

All the rooms and suites are decorated with impeccably good taste by Chelle in soft pastels and natural textures—clay pots, baskets filled with flowers, red tile, and an abundance of plants and real art. Rooms are airy and large with spacious patios, rattan furniture, puffy pillows, and natural fiber rugs on the Italian-tile floors. Large sliding doors, which glide like butter, open onto a spacious, well-furnished seaside patio. Ceiling fans (even in some bathrooms) along with louvered side windows let the sea breezes slip in and keep the rooms fresh and pleasantly cool. There is no air-conditioning, nor is it needed.

White walls and high, vaulted cedar ceilings distinguish the executive multilevel suites. In addition to the seaside patio, there is another, flower-filled open-air patio with walls just high enough to give you total privacy. A roomy hammock big enough for two is slung across a corner. A dining area, bedroom, bath, and another patio are located on the top level.

All the suite bathrooms are large and luxurious, with lots of tile and marble. They boast twin vanities, endless shelf space, a bidet, a walk-in, no-curtain shower, and a large tub.

Dining is on an open terrace, where a band plays every evening. Dance under a spreading tamarind tree and a canopy of stars. Chef Christophe Blatz is adept at preparing delicious American and European cuisine. Ingredients are the freshest you can find in the Caribbean: Fish is delivered every day and is filleted right on the property.

Curtain Bluff has an impressive 25,000-bottle cellar. Dust off a bottle of 1983 Louis Roederer Cristal and toast your bride, or try a bottle of '83 Dom Perignon or an '81 Taittinger Brut Reserve.

On Wednesdays you can warm up to reggae at the beach party, which is held at the bay beach. Lunch is served at the beachfront restaurant, where a lavish buffet tempts you with salads, fish, pasta, and meat dishes. Or, if you want to eat in the privacy of your room or on your patio, just order room service. It's all included in the price.

Straddling the peninsula, the two beaches offer something for everyone. The waters off the ¾-mile beach on the Caribbean side are calm, gentle, and great for swimming. You can sailboard, snorkel, sail, or just laze away the hours on the beach. On the other side the Atlantic stirs up more surf and the winds beckon to sailors and those looking for a little more excitement. A swimming pool, overlooking the bay beach, has a seating area in the water.

Tennis is big here, with four superbly maintained Laykold courts. Lessons, clinics, round-robins, tournaments, and just friendly play keep the action rolling. There's a good-size stadium for spectators to watch their favorite players as well as a squash court and a croquet field.

The fitness center is well equipped with Trotter treadmills, steppers, and the latest in health and fitness equipment. Aerobics classes are held on an adjacent deck.

There are no TVs in the rooms, but there is Television House, perched high on stilts near the tennis courts and fitness center. Guests gather here to watch events like the Super Bowl and the Kentucky Derby.

The ages and interests of guests range from older, well-heeled traditionalists to active, younger couples. You'll see a lot of Brits here, especially during January and February.

At first glance Curtain Bluff may seem a bit pricey at $4,500 to $6,000 for a week (in the deluxe rooms). But everything is included (except wine by the bottle), even the scuba diving and the deep-sea fishing. Curtain Bluff is for those who love a beautiful, warm place by the sea where they can get away and totally unwind while a superb, dedicated group of people see to it that nothing interferes with this vision of what paradise should be.

Each year Curtain Bluff closes down for three months in order to refurbish and refresh. Perhaps this is one reason nothing here ever looks tired or worn. A recent addition on the beach contains glamorous suites.

Curtain Bluff

Location: Situated on Antigua's south shore, on a private peninsula jutting out into the water

Romantic Highlights: Dancing under the stars; hammocks for two on your own private patio (executive suites)

Address/Phone: P.O. Box 288, Antigua, West Indies; (268) 462–8400; fax (268) 462–8409

Web Site: www.curtainbluff.com

U.S. Reservations: (888) 289–9898

Owner/Manager: Howard W. Hulford, owner and chairman, board of directors; Robert S. Sherman, managing director; Calvert A. Roberts, general manager

Arrival/Departure: Taxi to and from airport. Local regulations prevent hotel from sending drivers.

Distance from V. C. Bird International Airport: 15 miles (35 minutes)

Distance from St. John's: 9 miles

Accommodations: 72 rooms and suites with king-size beds, all with terraces and all overlooking the sea: 18 deluxe rooms and 54 suites (including 40 junior suites)

Most Romantic Room/Suite: The Terrace Room, with its huge terrace, one-bedroom suites, and Presidential Suites

Amenities: Hair dryer, wall safe, ceiling fans, bathrobes, telephone, fresh flowers daily, minibars in suites and rooms

Electricity: 110 volts

Sports and Facilities: 4 tennis courts, squash court, putting green, swimming pool, fitness center; waterskiing, sailboarding, scuba diving, snorkeling, sailing, croquet, deep-sea fishing, swimming, aerobics (land and water), yoga, and Pilates

Dress Code: Elegantly casual; long pants and collared shirts for men (no jeans)

Weddings: Can be arranged

Rates/Packages: All-inclusive rates include accommodations, 3 meals daily, all bar drinks, afternoon tea, hors d'oeuvres, tennis, weekly beach party, entertainment, mail service, and water sports including scuba diving. $850– $2,300 per couple, per night (mid-December to mid-April); $625–$1,700 (mid-season); $595–$1,500 (May 10–July 22)

Payment/Credit Cards: American Express, Visa, MasterCard, personal check, traveler's check

Deposit: 3-night deposit

Government Taxes: 8.5 percent

Service Charges: 10 percent

Entry Requirements for U.S. Citizens: Passport

Closed: August–October

JUMBY BAY RESORT
Antigua

"Jumbie" in colloquial Antiguan means "mischievous spirit" and, indeed, this tropical haven lives up to its name. There are surprises around every corner, from the tile-walled garden showers to glimpses of the rare Spanish sheep and Hawksbill Sea Turtles who live here. Playful, casual, seductive, Jumby Bay, managed by Rosewood Resort, entices with soft warm starry nights, riotously brilliant tropical foliage, wild orchids, and stunning white sand beaches that ring the 300-acre island.

After arriving at Antigua's V.C. Bird International Airport, you are met and whisked by private catamaran across the narrow stretch of water that separates Jumby Bay from the mainland. As you pull up to the dock, you'll see red roofs hiding amidst lush tropical greenery. Except for some private homes and a handful of multi-million dollar estates, most of the Mediterranean-style buildings are part of the resort.

First open in the 1980s, Jumby Bay is now owned by a committed group of home-owners dedicated to maintaining the low-key elegant style and panache the resort is known for. To get a great overview of the island, climb to the top of the lookout tower and you'll see villas, beaches, tennis courts, an original sugar mill, the old Estate House, a beach pavilion, a dock, and the sports area—the heart of this tranquil resort. Linking them all are brick paved "roads" reserved for bikes, pedestrians, and golf carts. From the time you arrive, your mode of transportation is a sturdy Caloi bicycle or a four-seater golf cart.

Two-story white buildings with red roofs are arranged in clusters along the beach and around pools. The two-suite villas are set alongside Pond Bay House, an old Spanish-style house overlooking a long beach; junior suites are located in Pond Bay House; other villas are located along paths leading from the main beach to the Estate House, where you'll find the restaurant and library. There are a handful of luxurious private houses nearby that are available for rent.

Brilliant flowers looking like ads for Miracle-Gro are everywhere. Huge ceramic and clay pots sitting in romantic courtyards are filled with flowering plants, orchids, and palms. Inside, the ceilings are high, with fans slowly moving the air gently around the room. Walls are decorated with original art-work and tile murals; fresh cut flower arrangements sit on counters and in the bathrooms. Baskets in all shapes and sizes are artfully arranged and French doors frame

the gardens just outside while louvered doors made of Brazilian walnut let in the breezes.

White plaster walls and ginger-colored tile floors complement the king-size, mahogany four-poster beds, some draped with British Colonial–style, filmy white canopy of netting. Polished amboa wood, cane chairs, and loveseats dressed in quiet beiges and creams create an elegant under-stated look. Skylights help make the rooms bright and sunny. Private verandas are set with teakwood chairs, tables, and chaises.

The bathrooms are incredible. There are two showers, indoor and out, both big enough for two. The indoor shower has dual showerheads and glass mosaic tiles. The outdoor showers are set in lushly planted gardens. In many, one entire wall is devoted to "The Shower." It has no sides—just a beautifully decorated wall of colored ceramic tile. You stand somewhere under the showerhead, which comes out of the tiled wall, and the splashing water is absorbed by the gardens located on either side. Look up and you can see the stars through the skylight. Baths also feature twin golden limestone vanities, bamboo acces-sories, oversized closets, and personal safes.

No one locks doors at Jumby Bay. There's no need to. Bowing to the need many have to stay connected, rooms come with satellite TV and personal computers with Internet access. Still, no one will intrude on your pri-vacy while you're in your room. Telephones are located elsewhere in cozy booths and mini telephone lounges placed at strategic areas throughout the property. If you have a call coming in, they'll find you and direct you to the nearest phone.

Dinner is served in the Estate House where tables are set with white linens, fine porcelain, crystal, and bowls of floating petals. Dating back to the 1700s, the Estate House was once an English sugar plantation. Its courtyard, with tiles, flowers, arches, and columns, resembles an Italian palazzo. Upstairs the very clubby Estate Bar is unabashedly romantic, with intimate seating areas, deep-green velvet settees, and chaise lounges lit seductively by carved and painted pineapple lamps, a perfect place for an after-dinner single-malt Scotch or cognac.

A balanced choice of American, European, and Asian-influenced dishes are offered by Australian-born Executive Chef Joel Wilkinson. Many of the fresh herbs, fruits, and vegetables are grown in Jumby Bay's own nursery. As night falls on the island, candles are lit at the tables on the Estate House terrace that overlooks the gardens and the sea beyond. A band provides soft music for listening and dancing.

Breakfast can be delivered to your room or you may eat in the open-air Verandah Restaurant just steps from the main beach and the boat dock. Lunch and afternoon tea are also served on the Verandah's open-air terrace. Cocktails are available at the Verandah Bar, located at the Beach Pavilion, and the Beach Bar located midway down Jumby Bay Beach.

During the day, there are plenty of things to do. Pack a picnic and head to Pasture Beach, a smaller and more private beach than the main one. Explore the island on your bike or on foot; plant yourself under a thatched umbrella with a cool drink; hang out in the hammock with a good book; play tennis or croquet; perfect your putting; go waterskiing or windsurfing; work out in the fitness room; or paddle out in one of the sea kayaks. Morning snorkel trips are offered weekly and snorkeling lessons can be arranged. Spa services are available including in-room massages and other treatments.

Jumby Bay Resort

Location: A 300-acre private island just 2 miles north of Antigua in the Caribbean Sea

Romantic Highlights: Idyllic private island; some villas have private plunge pools; secluded beaches; hammocks for two; picnics on the beach; garden showers

Address/Phone: P.O. Box 243, St. John's, Antigua, West Indies; (268) 462–6000; fax (268) 462–6020

Web Site: www.jumbybayresort.com; www.rosewoodhotels.com

U.S. Reservations: (888) ROSEWOOD

Owner/Manager: Peter Bowling, managing director

Arrival/Departure: Met by Jumby Bay representative at airport and taken to private pier for 10-minute catamaran cruise to island

Distance from V.C. Bird International Airport: 15 minutes

Distance from St. John's: 5 miles

Accommodations: 40 suites and 11 villas with private plunge pools

Most Romantic Room/Suite: New Jumby Bay Suites; luxury villas by beach (#s 32–36) with king beds and garden shower; also house rentals—Blue Pelican has its own pool and is near Pasture Beach

Amenities: Air-conditioning, ceiling fans, hair dryer, safe, satellite TV, personal computers with Internet access, CD player, minibar, butler trays, Italian linens, bathrobes, designer toiletries, flashlights, umbrellas, coffeemaker, fresh flowers daily, kitchens, 24-hour security, 24-hour room service, 4-seater golf cart

Electricity: 110 volts

Sports and Facilities: 4½ miles of hiking trails, biking trails, 3 tennis courts, putting green (2 floodlit), several pools (private and shared), sunfish, water skiing, sea-cycling, windsurfers, floats, snorkeling, beaches, croquet

Dress Code: Casual during the day; casual cocktail attire evenings; jacket and tie suggested for dinner in high season, but not required

Weddings: You can now rent out the entire resort for your own private island wedding (price available upon request). Good locations are the old sugar mill, which is on a crest in the center of the island; the Great House, which overlooks the water and Pasture Bay Beach. There is also a tower that overlooks the entire island, which is worth considering.

Rates/Packages: Rates are "all-inclusive" and include accommodations, 3 meals daily, all bar drinks, welcome champagne, departure bottle of rum, airport taxi service and boat transportation to and from island, hors d'oeuvres, tennis, croquet, weekly beach party, weekly sunset cruise, use of bicycles, entertainment, mail service, and non-motorized water sports. Daily rates for ocean-view rooms, $700–$1,200; suites, $950–$2,950; villas, $1,800–$3,500; and private residence rates are available on request. Two If by Sea, a 7-night package, includes a special romance turn-down service with rates from $5,095 to $10,450.

Payment/Credit Cards: Visa, MasterCard, American Express

Deposit: 3-night deposit; 30–45 days cancellation depending on period of year

Service Charges: 10 percent (no tipping)

Government Taxes: 7 percent; $20 departure tax

Entry Requirements for U.S. Citizens: Return ticket and proof of identity. Passport best.

ONE&ONLY OCEAN CLUB
Paradise Island, The Bahamas

From the moment you are greeted with a bubbling glass of fine champagne by warm, hospitable people, you know your honeymoon at this small, intimate resort on Paradise Island is off to a good start.

Once part of billionaire Huntington Hartford's holdings, the One&Only Ocean Club just continues to get better without losing its sense of intimacy and elegance.

Since Kerzner International acquired the property in 1995, this little jewel has seen some changes, including a seaside restaurant, Dune, as well as a spa, championship golf course, and ongoing room renovations, all costing a cool $100 million. Always fresh and quietly exclusive, the One&Only Ocean Club continually burnishes its reputation for providing guests with superb service and luxurious accommodations appealing to those seeking European ambience in a tropical setting.

Whether you are staying in one of the oceanfront rooms or suites in the new Crescent Wing, in a room in the Hartford Wing, or in one of the spacious villas, you are sure to be pampered by services and amenities fit for a king. Regal, king-size beds, softly colored pastel linens and fabrics, sink-in-your-toes carpeting, noiseless central air-conditioning, designer ceiling fans, stocked minibars, and 27-inch TVs are just the beginning. Bathrooms have state-of-the-art appointments with imported marble, tile vanities, bidets, scales, and many other features you'd expect to find in fine European hotels, right down to the customized toiletries and bottled water. And something you probably wouldn't find across the "pond"—irons and ironing boards!

But that's not the total picture. Add twenty-four–hour room service, a maid who cleans your rooms three times a day, complimentary shoeshines, free shuttle transportation on Paradise Island, use of the bicycles, and a wonderful fruit basket in your room and you have a pretty good idea of what's yet to come.

One of the unique features of the One&Only Ocean Club is the terraced Versailles Gardens flanked by beautiful old trees, tropical flowers, and shrubs that are tiered like a wedding cake up a gentle hillside. At the top is a fourteenth-century French cloister that was imported from Europe and rebuilt stone by stone by Hartford. With its marble columns, arches, and statues, it is a lovely place to relax and enjoy the beauty of the gardens and the sea. (It's also a great place to have a wedding ceremony.)

For tennis players there are nine Har-Tru courts, lighted for night play and free to guests, a teaching pro, and a well-equipped pro shop. For pool loungers there is a pool adjacent to both the tennis courts and a delightful open-air restaurant serving lunch and cocktails. The soft, white, sandy beach, one of the prettiest in the Bahamas, is set in a protected cove lined with palms and tropical plants. A full-service spa offers a variety of rejuvenating treatments.

With the opening of the totally rebuilt Ocean Club golf course, golf in the Bahamas was brought to an entirely new level. When Tom Weiskopf designed his brilliant links-style course, he made sure the crystalline sea was hardly ever out of sight. Here water, sand, and wind play key roles. Cart paths snake through the fairways, tall palms poke up into the sky, and bunkers with deep, soft, white sand lie in wait everywhere.

Breakfast, lunch, and dinner are served in the chic Dune beachfront restaurant created by internationally renowned chef and restauranteur Jean-Georges Vongerichten. Serving as a focal point, the kitchen is encased in transparent blue glass, reflecting and mirroring the blue of the sky and the water and geometrical designs around the room. The cuisine makes good use of the fresh local produce and seafood as well as herbs grown on the property. Menu choices reveal a Pacific Rim influence but are international in scope. For a casual drink by the sea, there is a bar set into the hill overlooking the beach.

Because Kerzner International owns about 75 percent of Paradise Island, you are close to the action, glitter, and glitz of the mega-size Atlantis, located less than a mile down the road. At the Atlantis there are twelve different restaurants and a 30,000-square-foot casino complete with Las Vegas–style shows. The casino is open twenty-four hours a day for the slot machines and from 10:00 A.M. to 4:00 P.M. for the gaming tables. If you crave some action, this is the place to come, courtesy of the One&Only Ocean Club, which runs a free shuttle every half-hour until midnight.

One&Only Ocean Club

Location: On Paradise Island off the northern edge of Nassau, New Providence Island

Romantic Highlights: Terraced Cloister Gardens; seaside dining in Dune; massages in the open-air oceanfront pavilion; hammocks for two; fountains and gardens

Address/Phone: P.O. Box N4-777, Nassau, Bahamas; (242) 363–2501; fax (242) 363–2424

E-mail: info@oceanclub.com

Web Site: www.oneandonlyoceanclub.com

U.S. Reservations: (800) 321–3000

Owner/Manager: Kerzner International, owner; Russell Miller, general manager

Arrival/Departure: Paradise Island Airlines leaves from Miami, Ft. Lauderdale, and West Palm Beach twice a day and lands 5 minutes from the One&Only Ocean Club. Delta, Kiwi, American, and United also fly into Nassau. Transfers can be arranged.

Distance from Paradise Island Airport: 1 mile (5 minutes); Nassau International Airport, 15 minutes

Distance from Nassau: 3 miles (10–15 minutes)

Accommodations: The Crescent Wing features 40 beachfront rooms and 10 beachfront suites; the Hartford Wing features 50 rooms, 4 suites, and 4 2-bedroom cottages. There are also 3 new luxurious 3- and 4-bedroom villas.

Most Romantic Room/Suite: Suites overlooking ocean

Amenities: Hair dryer, toiletries, central air-conditioning, ceiling fans, iron and ironing board, 27-inch TV, DVD/CD player, bathrobes, scales, safe, bidet, minibar; 24-hour room service, laundry and valet service

Electricity: 110 volts

Sports and Facilities: 9 Har-Tru lighted tennis courts, 18-hole golf course, spa, sailing, swimming, snorkeling, Aquacat sailing, kayaking, cycling, croquet

Dress Code: Casual day; jackets required for dinner at Dune

Weddings: Can be arranged

Rates/Packages: $475–$6,500 per night

Payment/Credit Cards: Most major

Deposit: 2-night deposit; cancellation 15 days or more prior to arrival, no charge

Government Taxes: 12 percent room tax; $15 departure tax at airport

Service Charges: $3.00 housekeeping gratuity

Entry Requirements for U.S. Citizens: Proof of citizenship; passport best

SANDALS ROYAL BAHAMIAN SPA RESORT & OFFSHORE ISLAND
Nassau, The Bahamas

It's couples-only at this European-style Sandals Resort, where the elegance factor in this pink-and-white confection has been turned up several notches with huge Palladian windows, tons of marble, chandeliers, frescoed ceilings, fountains, and pillars everywhere.

If all those pillars that seem to float on the water and the huge, rather fearsome statue of Neptune that greets you at the entrance seem a bit excessive, the overall impression is nevertheless one of opulence and grandeur. Hard to argue with that.

Sandals Royal Bahamian has three large pools and two private minipools. Located in the middle of everything, the heated main pool comes with Jacuzzis, waterfalls, a swim-up bar, and even Neptune himself, spouting a stream of water out of his mouth. For cooling off you can sit under the misting pool. Work up a sweat in the Fitness Center on the penthouse level using snazzy exercise equipment like Lifecycle exercise bicycles, stairclimbers, treadmills, and Cybex weight machines, or show up for poolside aerobics classes.

Although the resort is located on the sea and has a moderate-size beach, the best beach is found on Sandals Cay, a private island reached by water shuttle just a half mile offshore. Besides the wonderful white sand, there is a pool with a swim-up bar, a Jacuzzi, and the Cafe Goombay. Sandals also offers a full range of water sports, including scuba diving.

Accommodations range from beachfront rooms in The Manor House to villas and suites. You can choose from twelve different styles of rooms and suites. The ultraluxurious Beachfront Royal Windsor Suite features a separate living room, oversize vanity, 27-inch color TV, Roman soaking tub, Italian-tile floors, and incredible views of the beach from the balcony. Some suites even come with 24-hour butler service and a VIP Rolls Royce limo ride to and from the airport.

Furnishings are traditional and elegant, with hand-carved mahogany four-poster king-size beds, flowing flowered fabrics, and comfortable upholstered chairs. Many rooms have balconies or patios.

There will be no need to go off the property when it comes to dining choices: Sandals Royal Bahamian has eight restaurants, ranging from the dazzling crystal room and French-inspired Baccarat restaurant to Spices, serving a medley of Caribbean and Mediterranean-inspired dishes. And there is the popular and casual Cricketers. If Cricketers looks like an authentic English pub, that's because it is; much of the interior was brought here piece by piece from Great Britain.

For late-nighters there is entertainment and a disco. The brash, neon-lit Carnival Resort and Casino, just down the road, is far enough away not to impinge on the romantic mood, yet close enough for those who want a night out to gamble.

For total pampering you can head to the 6,000-square-foot spa, where you'll find a wide choice of European-style services and treatments. Kur baths, Finnish saunas, reflexology, aromatherapy, deep-cleansing facials, and much more are offered here and are about the only items not included in Sandals's all-inclusive price.

Sandals Royal Bahamian Spa Resort & Offshore Island

Location: Cable Beach, Nassau, Bahamas

Romantic Highlights: Nonstop activities; one super spa; cooling off under the misting pool; sipping a deliciously wicked "Sex-on-the-Beach" at the resort's private island; free weddings

Address/Phone: P.O. Box CB-13005, Cable Beach, Nassau, Bahamas; (242) 327–6400; fax (242) 327–6961

U.S. Reservations: (800) SANDALS

Owner/Manager: Stephen Ziadie, general manager

Arrival/Departure: Sandals guests are met at the airport and escorted to the resort.

Distance from Airport: 15 minutes

Distance from Nassau: 5 minutes

Accommodations: 403 rooms, suites, and villas

Most Romantic Room/Suite: Grande Luxe Oceanfront rooms in The Manor House

Amenities: Air-conditioning, king-size beds, ceiling fans, hair dryer, generous kits of lotions and shampoo, telephone, clock radio, color TV, and safe; suites also with fully stocked wet bars, terry robes, and *New York Times* faxes; some have butler service

Electricity: 110 volts

Sports and Facilities: 3 freshwater pools, 2 mini-pools, 5 whirlpools, 2 tennis courts, fitness center, scuba diving, snorkeling, sailboarding, sailing, paddleboats, canoes, kayaks, golf (nearby), pool/billiard tables, volleyball, shuffleboard, croquet, waterskiing, full-service spa (services and treatments are extra)

Dress Code: Casual

Weddings: On-site wedding coordinators arrange all the details, including taking care of the paperwork, leading the couple through the process of getting the marriage license, flowers, music, and reception. "WeddingMoons"—Sandals's term—can be as intimate as a couple getting married in a horse-drawn carriage or under a gazebo with a best man and attendant "borrowed" from the Sandals staff, or it can be an even more elaborate affair, with a reception for a couple's family and friends. Stay 5 nights or more and weddings are free.

Rates/Packages: All-inclusive rates start at $380 per person, per night ($228 with 7-night stay)

Payment/Credit Cards: Most major

Deposit: Guarantee with credit card

Government Taxes: Included

Service Charges: Included

Entry Requirements for U.S. Citizens: Passport required

CAMBRIDGE BEACHES
Bermuda

It's about as far out on the island as you can get, but who cares? Cambridge Beaches, located on the western end of the island, has five Bermuda-pink pristine beaches and numerous little coves to discover that are tucked into the rocky ledges of the peninsula. With water on three sides, the resort's pink-and-white limestone cottages nestle into the nooks and crannies of the well-manicured tropical gardens above and along the shoreline. White roofs and louvers, mellow stone walls and steps turn golden in the late-afternoon sun, and lush, flowering oleanders and hibiscus have had many years to mature transform Cambridge Beaches into a magical world where dreams are made and fulfilled.

It's truly one of the world's premier hideaway resorts and one of Bermuda's most exclusive properties. There is a variety of rooms and suites, most with king-size beds and sitting areas, others with fireplaces, vaulted beamed ceilings, and French doors leading to large terraces and spectacular views of Long Bay, the Atlantic Ocean, or Mangrove Bay, dotted with sleek yachts riding at anchor, their stays slapping masts with low-pitched tings.

Rooms are individually decorated. Some have cheerful English chintz fabrics in warm pinks, sunny golds, and blues; traditional Queen Anne furniture; and marble baths. Some of the larger suites feature charming antique pieces and extended grassy terraces; others are contemporary in style. Most have whirlpool tubs. Attractive scenes of Bermuda decorate the walls. You have your own terrace, where you can enjoy a cozy, private breakfast or dinner, and from your door it's only a short walk to the beaches.

The 275-year-old Great House, overlooking Mangrove Bay, shelters a gracious lobby furnished with Bermuda and English antiques—it has that comfortable "been here a long while" feel, yet decor is light and pleasant. An adjacent library is filled with books and English tea is served in the living room each afternoon.

Downstairs you'll find the elegant Tamarisk Restaurant, where the food is a work of art. The chef, Jean-Claude Garzia, has won the prestigious MOF (Meilleurs Ouvriers de France), awarded to just eighteen French chefs worldwide every five years. Your plate may be decorated with fans of fresh fruit, delicate lacy butterflies of chocolate, or swirls of raspberry sauce in a pool of vanilla custard. The menu also includes island-style items such as baby shrimp curry pie with a light banana sauce, bouillabaisse, and pan-fried tenderloin with a Chambertin red wine and truffle sauce— all superb, as are the pastries, breads, and ice cream, which are made in Cambridge's own Pastry Shop.

The paneled Port O'Call Bar, with its cozy fireplace, is a perfect spot to hide out when the weather is cool. A cable TV provides news and sports fans with the latest broadcasts.

For lunch and more casual dining, the Mangrove Bay Terrace invites you to dine and dance under trees and night sky. Wrought-iron chairs and tables are set on the stone terrace, where you can see the harbor from just about anywhere you sit.

Enjoy casual fare alfresco at Breezes right on the water's edge at Long Bay Beach. Brilliant sunsets, endless stargazing, and soft surf make this a perfect place for special nights. A new dine-out option for those on the MAP plan gives you credit to dine anywhere you wish on the island.

Water sports activities at the resort's private marina are a short stroll from the Main House. Rent a boat and explore the private islands just off the coast or head to nearby Turtle Cove beach, pick up the phone at the bottom of the steps, and

order "room service." The resort has a number of boats you can use, including kayaks, sailboats, and motorboats. Cruise on a luxurious yacht, and watch the sunset while sipping a Sea Breeze.

Want to be pampered? Then treat yourself to a massage or facial at the two-level, 10,000-square-foot Wellness Center and Ocean Spa, where you can indulge in a choice of more than one hundred treatments and services. There's even a "His and Her" massage plus a special session designed for couples who wish to learn the art of massage. Relax by the lovely Ocean Spa pool, which is built under a retractable glass room—perfect for those cooler days—or work out in the fitness room, take a sauna, or decompress in the steam room. There is also yoga stretch and water aerobics.

If you can bear to leave the beach, check out the shops, art galleries, and other attractions in Hamilton. A free Cambridge Beaches ferry shuttles you to the city three times a week. You can explore Dockyard, located at this end of the island, or take a romantic horse-and-buggy ride in the nearby town of Somerset. Rent a moped or bicycle and ride off to discover the beauty of Bermuda. The speed limit on the island is 20 miles per hour, so you can really enjoy an easy, carefree spin on your wheels.

At Cambridge Beaches entertainment is not forgotten. There is music for listening and dancing every evening in season.

Cambridge Beaches

Location: On a 25-acre peninsula on Bermuda's western coast, near Somerset Village

Romantic Highlights: Dancing under the stars; boat ride to a private island for a picnic; 5 pink beaches to sink your toes into;

couples' candlelit massage; private breakfasts in your cottage; beach dinner for 2 on Turtle Cove or Morning Beach

Address/Phone: 30 Kings Point Road, Somerset, MA 02, Bermuda; (809) 234–0331; fax (809) 234–3352

E-mail: cambeach@ibl.bm

Web Site: www.cambridgebeaches.com

U.S. Reservations: (800) 468–7300

Owner/Manager: Michael J. Winfield, president; Richard Quinn, manager

Arrival/Departure: A 45-minute taxi ride from the airport costs approximately $65.

Distance from Bermuda International Airport: 17 miles

Distance from Somerset: 10-minute walk

Accommodations: 94 cottage-style rooms and suites, all refurbished in the past 5 years

Most Romantic Room/Suite: Cambridge Suites, which have a bedroom and separate living room with panoramic water views; suites with water views also good. Sunset Suite is superb. New Luxury Pool Suite with its own infinity plunge pool. North Rock Cottage with 6-foot tub with views of sunsets and ocean.

Amenities: Air-conditioning, ceiling fans, telephone, bathrobes, hair dryer, whirlpool, toaster, safe, mending kit, room service, free shuttle to Hamilton, cable TV, CD/radio, whirlpool tubs in bathrooms, many with glass showers, high-speed Internet access

Electricity: 110 volts

Sports and Facilities: Spa, fitness center, 3 tennis courts, croquet, heated indoor and outdoor pools, 5 beaches, snorkeling, scuba diving, sailing, sailboarding, kayaking, fishing, motorboating; putting green, golf nearby

Dress Code: Jacket and tie optional for Tamarisk Room—buttoned down, collared shirt required; smart casual for Terrace; casual for Breezes, on the beach. Resort wear recommended.

Weddings: Can be arranged; complimentary vow-renewal ceremonies. Proposal and Romance concierge (Nadja Talevi) in place to advise and create special occasions.

Rates/Packages: MAP rates per couple, per night include breakfast, dinner, afternoon tea, use of tennis courts, putting green, croquet, fitness center, beaches, pools, and ferry service to Hamilton, $495–$830 (high season); $345–$705 (low season/winter). "Heavenly Honeymoon Package" includes 5 nights in a deluxe suite with private terrace and water view; taxes; gratuities; daily gourmet breakfast, afternoon tea, and dinner; sunset sail; couples' candlelit massage; deluxe picnic basket; choice of mopeds, kayaks, or bicycles; and personalized photograph, $4,525 (high season). "Romantic Escape" and "Dream Wedding" packages also available.

Payment/Credit Cards: Cash, personal checks, Visa, Mastercard, American Express

Deposit: 2-night deposit at time of booking to cover first and last night's accommodations or 50 percent of packages; cancel 28 days or more prior to arrival for full refund of deposit minus $50 administration fee. Within 28 days, full deposit is retained by resort.

Government Taxes: 7.25 percent government tax; 4 percent energy surcharge

Service Charges: $18 per person, per night

Entry Requirements for U.S. Citizens: Passport required

THE REEFS
Bermuda

The Reefs, one of Bermuda's most romantic honeymoon resorts, has been consistently rated as one of the best on the island for a number of years. A $5 million renovation program added twelve suites, including three spectacular Pointe Suites, an arrivals area, and a porte cochere. Sitting high above the beautiful pink beach and coral reefs below, the salmon-hued low-rise lanai cottages ramble over the landscaped, terraced grounds. All have great views of the sea from the balconies.

Guest rooms are attractively furnished with rattan chairs, sofas, tables, and bed; bright tropical prints; area rugs on red-tiled floors; and cheery prints of Bermuda scenes. The Point, Junior, and Longtail suites have a king-size bed, a sitting area, and a private terrace where you can enjoy breakfast served on your table overlooking the sea. The Point Suites, at 690 square feet, are airy and spacious. Luxurious bathrooms have large Jacuzzis, rainwater showers, double sinks and step-down sitting areas facing private ocean-view balconies with outdoor Jacuzzis. Light sherbet colors in the decor echo the pink-tinged beaches.

The reception building houses an attractive lobby, comfortable lounge-bar, Grill 56, the main dining room, and a tropical conservatory, where you dine under a glass roof. In the warmer months, you can enjoy a candlelit dinner outside on the terrace under the stars, and there is often music for dining and dancing. The Reefs's delicious international cuisine is included in your room rate.

If you want to dine outside while the surf rolls in nearby, try eating at the Ocean Echo Terrace Grill or the casual, thatched-roof Coconuts, the beach-level restaurant (warmer months only) specializing in Cajun and Caribbean dishes.

The Reefs has the only infinity pool in Bermuda that overlooks the water and two all-weather tennis courts. There's a wonderful pink beach—one of Bermuda's best—and more to discover if you walk around the big black boulders that lie at the ends of the beach. Here you'll come upon more delightful small beaches tucked into coves, which continue along the shoreline. And, yes, the sand is really tinged pink from the bits of pulverized coral that have been mixed in over the years. In the summer, an activities director is on hand to help you plan your days. You can walk along the beach or rent a moped or go by bus or taxi to nearby Hamilton for some serious shopping.

The La Serena Spa offers a number of treatments, including the only authentic traditional Thai massage in Bermuda. The Reef's Thai massage therapist, Sudprani, was born in Thailand and learned her skills at the sacred Wat Pho Temple in Bangkok. Also on the spa menu are Thalgo facials, Reiki and Swedish massages, Balinese body scrubs, reflexology, Asian botanical treatments, pedicures, manicures, and other treatments.

The Reefs' traditions, such as serving tea each afternoon, are grounded in the British way of doing things, but the hotel is more informal than many other Bermuda hotels, more smart-casual in tone. Although the resort certainly appeals to a solid group of over-fifties who come back year after year, its lively mix of nightly entertainment, water sports, and fresh tropical decor attracts a large number of well-heeled young couples, as well.

The Reefs

Location: In Southampton, on the south shore of Bermuda

Romantic Highlights: Hillside rooms overlooking the sea; breakfast on your private balcony; private pink beach; dining on the beach

Address/Phone: 56 South Shore Road, Southampton SN 02, Bermuda; (441) 238–0222; fax (441) 238–8372

E-mail: generalinfo@thereefs.bm

Web Site: www.thereefs.com

U.S. Reservations: Islands Resorts Reservations Ltd., (800) 742–2008

Owner/Manager: David Dodwell, managing director; Neal Stephens, general manager

Arrival/Departure: A 25-minute taxi ride from the airport costs approximately $30.

Distance from Bermuda International Airport: 11 miles

Distance from Hamilton: 7 miles

Accommodations: 65 ocean-view guest rooms and suites, including 8 one- to four-bedroom cottages

Most Romantic Room/Suite: Pointe Suites; Sunrise Suite #340 with private ocean-view balconies and outdoor Jacuzzis

Amenities: Air-conditioning, ceiling fans, mini-fridge, hair dryer, coffeemaker, data-port, safe, iron and ironing board, bathrobes, umbrella, Taylor of London toiletries. Suites also come with king-size beds, flat-screen cable TVs, and VCR/DVD player. Cottage suites also have free long-distance access, toaster, microwave, and private patio with outdoor Jacuzzi. Dry-cleaning/laundry service, *New York Times* fax, and complimentary Internet access.

Electricity: 110 volts

Sports and Facilities: 2 tennis courts, infinity swimming pool, hot tub, beach, La Serena Spa, fitness center with Cybex equipment, bike and scooter rentals, snorkeling, kayaks, floats, shuffleboard, croquet, scuba diving, sport fishing, sailing, parasailing, jet skiing, glass-bottom boat cruises, horseback riding, golf at several nearby courses

Dress Code: Smart casual; no ties or jacket required at dinner

Weddings: Can be arranged

Rates/Packages: Rates are $284–$1,398 per couple, per night, including breakfast, afternoon tea, dinner, in-room beverages on arrival, and use of sports facilities. Romance Package, $3,634–$6,304, including 6 nights' accommodations, all of the above plus champagne, dinner for two on the beach, 4 hours on Boston Whaler departing from Somerset Bridge with picnic lunch, government tax, and service charges. Rates are about 40 percent less during winter.

Payment/Credit Cards: Most major

Deposit: 2-night deposit at time of booking

Government Taxes: 7.25 percent of nightly rate; included in Romance Package

Service Charges: 10 percent of daily rate (summer); $19 per person, per day (spring, fall, and winter) for a lanai and $21 for a suite; included in Romance Package

Entry Requirements for U.S. Citizens: Proof of citizenship; passport best or a certified U.S. birth certificate and photo ID

BITTER END YACHT CLUB
Virgin Gorda, British Virgin Islands

Don't let the name turn you off. This "Bitter End" could be your "Sweet Beginning." Artfully tucked into a cove on the northernmost tip of Virgin Gorda, one of the most picturesque of the British Virgin Islands, Bitter End Yacht Club (BEYC) is a perfect place for newlyweds who love to sail. You can combine your passion for a romantic setting with a few days' cruise aboard a bare boat or crewed yacht, exploring the neighboring islands. Or you can spend all your nights at the resort and venture out onto the gentle seas during the day.

World-class yachtsmen have known about this place for many years, and people like Jean-Michel Cousteau and Mel Fisher have rendezvoused often at this unique tropical haven, which has seventy deepwater moorings, two restaurants, and a host of water sports activities—all first-class from beginning to end.

Protected by coral reefs and beach-fringed cays, this secluded, idyllic spot can only be reached by boat. The white-sand beach, fringed by gnarled sea grape shrubs and palms, frames a lagoon that seems more like a large, clear, turquoise lake dashed with flashes of the bright-colored sails of sailboarders.

From the time of your arrival at Virgin Gorda's tiny airport—hardly large enough to hold your luggage—everything is handled by the Bitter End staff with great style. After you've gathered your luggage, you're whisked up and over the steep hills to a landing area about twenty minutes away. Then it's a five-minute boat ride across a brilliant Caribbean-blue lagoon, where you are met by a smiling staff member at the dock. (Those landing at Tortola come to BEYC via high-speed water taxi.)

Native stone lines the walkways and roads, and flowers and tropical plants, including fragrant frangipani, bougainvillea, hibiscus, oleander, and sea grape, wind along the paths and up the hillside. Colorful nautical flags fly from the rafters of the bar, from poles along the walkways, and just about everywhere. Buildings are decorated with whimsical gingerbread trim and iron grillwork and are connected by a series of garden courtyards. Blue-and-white-painted wrought-iron tables and chairs sit on brick-paved patios accented by tiered fountains and flowering plants. All very Mediterranean.

As the sun sets, you'll soon become aware that the lighting throughout the resort is seductively low. (Can this be due to the Caribbean-style electrical power or is it planned for romantics like you?) As you walk along the seaside paths to the dining room, you'll find the tiny flashlight you got at check-in extremely useful.

Because BEYC is actually the marriage of two different resorts, the styles of accommodations are quite different. There are rustic beachfront bungalows that blend into the hills, with their thatched roofs and weathered wood exteriors, and there are the more contemporary hillside North Sound Suites. The bungalows are much closer to the water than the suites—some are right on the beach—and are very Caribbean in feeling. You won't have a room key, because there are no locks. Nor are they needed. Open wraparound, palm-thatched verandas, ceiling fans, large walk-in showers, bamboo furniture, a tiled dressing area, and native art and quaint knickknacks lend a homey island feeling to the bungalows. Since most come with twin beds, request ahead to have them put together.

The deluxe 600-square-foot North Sound Suites, perched high over the water, are more spacious and luxurious, with vaulted ceilings, balconies, air-conditioning, two queen-size beds, and a very large marble inside/outside garden shower room. Connected by wooden walkways much like jungle catwalks, the suites have wood peaked ceilings and glass doors leading out to balconies, and they are attractively decorated in rich fabrics, native art, and grass-cloth walls.

The North Sound Suites and bungalows come equipped with a refrigerator and coffeemaker, and a comfortable sitting area. The choice is yours: Lie in luxury overlooking the harbor or pick a casual, native-style beachfront villa.

When it comes to water sports, you're in sailing heaven. There are enough Mistral sailboards, Sunfish, Lasers, Hobie Cats, Hunter 216s, Rhodes 19s, IC-24s, and outboard-powered skiffs to get the whole guest population of the resort out on the water at the same time.

There are daily escorted snorkeling trips, scuba lessons, dive trips, and lots of regattas. There is also the full-service Sailing School, a great way for new sailors to learn how to tell a *jib* from a *ready-about*. If you want to explore nearby shores, you can take one of the skiffs and chug over to other parts of the island for a picnic or a visit. For landlubbers a lovely pool and patio area is located on the eastern end of the resort, near the suites.

Well worth seeing is Anegada, known as Shipwreck Island. Also be sure to visit The Baths, giant granitelike boulders on the southwest coast. Take your bathing suit and swim in the pools located in, under, and around the huge rocks, some as high as 40 feet.

If you want the best of both worlds, you can live aboard one of the resort's Free-dom 30s, fully outfitted, sporty yachts that you can sail into the sunset for a few days or a few hours, returning to your home base for the evening. All meals are included, whether you eat on board or ashore.

BEYC has two restaurants. The Clubhouse, on the shore, serves breakfast, lunch, and dinner. You can eat inside, on the tree-shaded terrace, or on the veranda. The terrace bar, poised on the edge of the water, is a popular gathering place for guests to enjoy morning coffee or a late-afternoon cocktail.

Nearer the North Sand Suites is the dining room of the English Carvery, which is open for intimate candlelight dinners and dancing. You can also grab a quick snack or a light lunch at the English Pub at the Emporium, which serves pizza, hot dogs, and fish burgers.

Bitter End Clubhouse attracts top-notch Caribbean "jump-up" entertainers, and there is more romantic dinner music at the Carvery. Bitter End's steel band plays several nights a week, and there are beach barbecues and sunset and moonlight cruises.

With more than 200 staff for just eighty-five rooms, Bitter End gives you all the attention you want and need, but one of the best things of all is that it's done in a totally unobtrusive manner. You can wash your hair, take a walk on the beach, and when you return find a fresh towel in your room. Beds are turned down every night, and the beaches are raked every morning.

Although you will be surrounded by tempting things to do, you can find your own quiet spot on one of the secluded beaches and just sit back under a palm tree and watch a bananaquit, a perky yellow bird, eat sugar from your outstretched hand.

Bitter End Yacht Club

Location: Covers 25 acres along a mile of beach and waterfront on the North Sound of Virgin Gorda—the most protected and secluded deepwater harbor in the Caribbean

Romantic Highlights: Magnificent sailing; thatched-roof bungalows on the beach; opportunity to combine a yacht cruise with an island stay; sunset sail; private picnic via Boston Whaler on your own

Address/Phone: North Sound, Virgin Gorda, B.V.I.; (284) 494–2746; fax (284) 494–4756

E-mail: binfo@beyc.com

Web Site: www.beyc.com

U.S. Reservations: (800) USA–BEYC, (800) 872–2392, or (305) 468–0168; fax (305) 468–0156

Owner/Manager: Owned by the Hokin family for over 25 years; Grand Heritage Group, managers

Arrival/Departure: Transfers from Beef Island Airport, Tortola, or Virgin Gorda Airport, $50 per person, round trip

Distance from Virgin Gorda Airport: 30-minute drive or bus ride plus 10-minute boat ride

Distance from Spanish Town: 30 minutes

Accommodations: 87 rooms and suites, ranging from Beachfront Villas to North Sound Suites and live-aboard Freedom 30 yachts

Most Romantic Room/Suite: Beachfront bungalows for beach lovers; North Sound Suites for those who prefer luxury and a bird's-eye view of the water

Amenities: Air-conditioning (North Sound Suites only), ceiling fans, garden shower, hair dryer, coffeemaker, alarm clock, iron/ironing board, international adaptors, sewing kit, refrigerator, VCR (in suites), turndown service, shops and convenience store

Electricity: 110 volts

Sports and Facilities: Water sports galore: Mistral sailboards, Sunfish, Lasers, Hobie Cats, Hunter 216s, Rhodes 19s, IC-24s, and outboard-powered skiffs; snorkeling, kiteboarding, scuba diving, swimming pool, 3 beaches, fitness trail, marina, Blue Water Excursions

Dress Code: Very casual. Leave your cocktail dresses and sports jackets at home

Weddings: Can be arranged

Rates/Packages: From $490 per couple per night (spring–fall); $670 (winter); includes 3 meals and use of water sports equipment. A Honeymoon Package, 8 days/7 nights, is $3,430–$5,740 per couple. A package combining 5 nights on a yacht and 4 nights in the resort is priced from $3,920 per couple. Stay 7 nights or more on an Admiral's Package and meals, water sports, excursions, and activities are included (for example, introduction to sailing course, sunset sails, snorkeling trips, and Blue Water Excursions)

Payment/Credit Cards: Most major

Deposit: 3-night deposit; cancel 30 days prior to arrival date for refund (by September 1 for Christmas season)

Government Taxes/Service Charges: 18 percent

Entry Requirements for U.S. Citizens: Proof of citizenship; passport best

LITTLE DIX BAY

Virgin Gorda, British Virgin Islands

One of the most consistently appealing Caribbean resorts, Little Dix Bay was established over thirty years ago by Laurance S. Rockefeller, who visualized an ecological preserve and wilderness resort where privacy and solitude were paramount. Today Little Dix remains extremely romantic and seductive. It sits on 500 acres and has a lovely ½-mile crescent-shaped beach. The rooms and public areas are designed to blend into the surrounding gardens of flowering shrubs, sea grapes, and palms. Cottages containing two to eight rooms all face the sea. Some are on stilts and have cone-shaped roofs; others are more conventional. All have louvered-window walls designed to catch the cooling trade winds.

Coral reefs and a cove create a calm, safe "harbor" for swimming and water sports. In 1993 Rosewood Hotels & Resorts took over the operation of the resort, giving the property a major facelift, with new furniture and custom-designed fabrics, new lighting, telephones, redesigned bathrooms, and the addition of air-conditioning in all the rooms. To lend a Polynesian ambience, bamboo beds and other interesting furniture pieces were imported from Asia, and unique touches were added, such as wicker baskets and artwork. Throughout the renovation, great care and sensitivity were taken to preserve the harmonious pact Little Dix has had with nature. Colors reflect the natural island surroundings.

Cottages are constructed of native wood and stone with peaked wooden ceilings, circulating fans, and tile floors. Bamboo king-size beds; rattan furniture, including chaises roomy enough to hold two; and natural fiber area rugs are low-key yet elegant

enough to satisfy the most discerning of guests. Rooms are located in clusters of cottages, some on ground level. Shaded footpaths winding through the gardens link the cottages to the public areas.

With more than 300 on staff, the hotel provides excellent, yet not overpowering, service. They pay attention to the little things, like replenishing your ice bucket daily and providing an abundant supply of fresh towels.

Little Dix has three restaurants. The open-air Pavilion, which has four dramatic Polynesian-style pyramid roofs and a stone terrace, offers international and Caribbean specialties, lunch buffets, afternoon teas, and candlelight dinners. Rack of lamb, fresh salmon, red snapper, and grouper are served grilled or with wonderful light sauces. Guests often gather on the terrace early in the evening for cocktails as the sun sets. After dinner a band plays music for dancing under the open skies. The romantic Sugar Mill gives you the opportunity to get dressed up for a really lovely evening of good food, wine, and romance—the kind of night you always dreamed about.

The Sugar Mill restaurant, located in a rustic stone structure fashioned after a local sugar factory, is the resort's most intimate place to dine. Your table is just steps from the beach, and you can hear the waves softly lapping the shore as you enjoy fresh local seafood. Anegada lobster, tuna, mahimahi, snapper, and hand-cut steaks and chops are mainstays of the menu. The savory dinner selections are complemented with a la carte sides such as garlic-mashed potatoes and asparagus with hollandaise. The sinfully rich dessert menu changes daily.

Should you want to dine under the stars on the beach surrounded only by tiki torches, rustling palms, and the sound of gently lapping water, you can order from the Sugar Mill selections.

The open-air, ocean-view Beach Grill, where you can get light lunches and dinners, has been recently renovated in the low-key, elegant Little Dix style with floors made from locally quarried stone. Everything from fish to burgers to salads is served. Eat on the terrace or take your lunch to the beach.

At Little Dix the beach is right in your "front yard." Float the afternoon away on a rubber raft, or sit under an umbrella of palm fronds. Take a box lunch and umbrella and climb aboard the resort's water taxi, which will shuttle you to a secluded beach. Snorkel in Devil's Bay and explore Mosquito Island. Ask the boatman to drop you near the famous Baths, and spend a few hours climbing above, under, and around the huge boulders that create this unique natural phenomenon. Swim in the grotto pools and climb the path that leads from the beach to a hilltop restaurant/bar.

Guided snorkel tours are offered four times a week, and you can take Sunfish lessons, aerobic exercise, and even a tour of the gardens with the resident horticulturist. The tennis center offers complimentary clinics and round-robins twice a week, and movies are shown every evening in the large, open-air lounge.

Recently Little Dix Bay added a cliff-side spa, offering a variety of Caribbean-inspired treatments. The luxurious spa offers private treatment cottages, all with ocean views, and a special cottage for couples' treatments, including the sunset serenity treatment. You can enjoy massages followed by champagne and fresh fruit served at sundown while you relax in your private plunge pool located on your private veranda overlooking the water.

Your honeymoon package includes a sunset cocktail sail on the resort's trimaran Pond Bay and a ride on a Boston Whaler to Spring Bay for a picnic. Full-day sails to nearby areas as well as scuba diving, fishing charters, and beauty treatments are also available as optional choices.

Well-heeled guests have been coming here for years, appreciating the easy ambience and the excellent service—they treat it rather like their personal island club. During the winter months the guests tend to be on the more mature side. But in the spring—honeymoon season—the resort is popular with newly married young couples, many of whom have learned about the resort from their parents. (But beware: Christmas and Easter attract families.) Spring, summer, and fall are great times to come to Little Dix. Prices are lower, and the weather is great.

Little Dix Bay

Location: Northwest corner of Virgin Gorda, just off the Sir Francis Drake Channel

Romantic Highlights: Beachfront setting; dining and dancing under the stars; hammocks for two; secluded beaches

Address/Phone: P.O. Box 720, St. John, U.S.V.I. 00831-0720; (284) 495–5555; fax (284) 495–5661

Web Site: www.rosewoodhotels.com

U.S. Reservations: (800) 928–3000; fax (214) 758–6640

Owner/Manager: Managed by Rosewood Hotels & Resorts; Martein van Wagenberg, managing director

Arrival/Departure: Virgin Gorda can be reached via San Juan, Puerto Rico, Tortola, and St. Thomas. Shuttles are also available to and from St. Thomas and Caneel Bay.

Distance from Virgin Gorda Airport: 1 mile

Distance from Spanish Town: 2 miles

Accommodations: 98 rooms and 4 one-bedroom suites all facing the sea.

Most Romantic Room/Suite: Newly created beachfront suites with oversize soaking tubs and showers and separate bedroom and living room, or the elevated hexagonal rooms on the west side, near the beach

Amenities: Air-conditioning, ceiling fans, hair dryer, telephone, TV, minibar, refrigerator

Electricity: 110 volts

Sports and Facilities: Tennis day or night, scuba diving, snorkeling, sailboarding, sailing, Sunfish, kayaking, waterskiing, aerobics, fitness room, new spa

Dress Code: Informal during day; although jacket and tie are not required, most guests usually wear elegant attire when dining at Sugar Mill and long pants are required for men

Weddings: Can be arranged

Rates/Packages: From $325 per couple, per day; Romance Package, $4,200–$14,500, includes 7 nights accommodations, meals, trimaran day sail, sunset cocktail cruise, Spring Bay afternoon picnic, champagne and fruit, transfers, tennis, water sports, afternoon tea, water taxis to nearby beaches, guided snorkeling tour, Sunfish lessons, aerobic exercise, and massage for two

Payment/Credit Cards: Most major

Deposit: 50 percent of package, due 14 days from date of booking. If booking 30 days prior to arrival, credit card deposit required within 24 hours of booking.

Government Taxes/Service Charges: 7 percent room tax and 10 percent service charge. Meal plans, food, and beverages are subject to a 15 percent service charge.

Entry Requirements for U.S. Citizens: Proof of citizenship; passport best

PETER ISLAND RESORT AND YACHT HARBOUR

Peter Island, British Virgin Islands

Peter Island is an easy, twenty-minute boat ride from the Beef Island Airport on Tortola, just long enough for you to stretch travel-weary limbs and bask in the warm sun and fresh salt air. As you pull up to the resort's pier, you'll see deserted white sandy beaches, coconut groves, and low hills covered with cactus and bougainvillea.

There aren't a lot of buildings here, and what structures do exist are so unobtrusive, you have to look hard to find them. There

are only fifty-two rooms and two villas (Hawks' Nest and Crow's Nest), along with two restaurants, a lounge, library, reception area, fitness center, a new $6 million spa, and dive shop, on the entire 1,300-acre island. You'll find no Club Med sorts of "playmakers," no casino, no disco. What you will find is the opportunity to do pretty much what you want when you want to do it. If you like beaches, sun, and water sports, this island can be your nirvana. Like to sail? You can choose from a 42-foot yacht, Hobie Cats, 19-foot Squibs, and Zumas along with kayaks and sailboards. There are also power boats that can be chartered for deep-sea fishing.

If you feel a little green about sailing a Sunfish by yourself, don't worry. The instructor keeps an eye on everyone. "I've never lost anyone yet," he'll tell you with a smile as he helps you push your boat into the water.

Peter Island is an excellent place for snorkeling and scuba diving as well as sailing. Snorkeling gear is free to guests, and just offshore of the main swimming beach is a reef where you can see a wonderful assortment of colorful fish, shellfish, corals, and aquatic plants. All you have to do is to wade out, don your mask and fins, and paddle off.

Scuba lessons and dives are available for all levels. One of the most popular dive sites is the wreck of the *Rhone,* a nineteenth-century British mail ship, which was used as a location for the movie *The Deep.*

If you like to go exploring, you can climb the rocks at the end of the main beach, follow the fitness trail and see who is the most flexible and the strongest, and walk to the really isolated Reef Bay Beach around the corner, where you can find lots of shells, coral, and bits of sea glass. Take along a blanket and a picnic lunch and enjoy a few hours on your own.

Peter Island has four Tru-flex tennis courts along with a small tennis center. A pro is available (high season) to give you lessons or arrange partners if you're looking for a set of doubles. Also located at the tennis center is a paperback book exchange library.

One of my criteria for a great beach resort is a place where you can go from your room to the beach in twenty paces and walk on that beach (and others) for miles.

Peter Island passes the sand test. But there's more: king-size beds, attractive decor in the island mode, plenty of thirsty towels, lights bright enough for night reading, and a great view of the sea. You also have a minibar, a sitting area, a shower that looks into a small private garden, a double sink, a large walk-in closet, and lots of louvers that you can open to let in the breezes and the sounds of waves. Patios or balconies are furnished with beautiful teak lounge chairs. There are CD players in all rooms, but if you want to watch TV, you'll have to head to the library, tucked between the pool and the sea.

Great water views are revealed from the Tradewinds Restaurant and patio. For casual, beachfront dining, there is The Deadman's Beach Bar and Grill. Peter Island gets its fish daily from local fishermen, and the chef knows how to cook it! Especially good is the grilled tuna served with a homemade pineapple chutney. The resort also makes its own desserts and pastries. Fresh muffins in the mornings, great cookies with white chocolate chunks and macadamia nuts, and Key lime pie made the traditional way are all delicious.

For entertainment there is music by local bands for dancing or listening almost nightly on the open-air patio. Excursions to neighboring islands such as St. Thomas, Jost Van Dyke, and Tortola are also offered.

The resort's rates include breakfast, lunch, and dinner, a good thing since Peter Island's restaurants are the only game in town. For the best of both worlds, cruise around the British Virgin Islands aboard the resort's luxurious 41-foot sailing yacht *Silmaril* and spend the rest of the time on Peter Island.

Peter Island is for those who love beautiful beaches and water sports and don't need a lot of high-level activity. You're on your own here, with all the toys at your disposal.

Peter Island Resort and Yacht Harbour

Location: A private 1,300-acre island in the British Virgin Islands

Romantic Highlights: Private honeymoon beach; deserted beaches to explore on your own

Address/Phone: P.O. Box 211, Road Town, Tortola, B.V.I.; or P.O. Box 9409, St. Thomas, U.S.V.I: 00801; (800) 346–4451, (284) 495–2000; fax (284) 495–2500

Web Site: www.peterisland.com

U.S. Reservations: (800) 346–4451; fax (770) 476–4979

Owner/Manager: Wayne Kafcsak, managing director; Sandra Grisham-Clothier, general manager

Arrival/Departure: Those arriving at the Beef Island Airport are taken by private launch to Peter Island.

Distance from Beef Island Airport: About 4 miles by sea

Distance from Tortola: 4 miles

Accommodations: 52 rooms and suites: 32 with ocean or harbor view, 20 junior suites on beach; 2 villas

Most Romantic Room/Suite: Go for the beachfront suites

Amenities: Air-conditioning, ceiling fans, minibar, coffeemaker, double sinks, hair dryer, bathrobes, umbrellas

Electricity: 110 volts

Sports and Facilities: Sunfish, sailboard, kayaks, floaters, snorkeling gear, dive center, and fishing charters; 4 Tru-flex tennis courts (2 lighted); fitness trail; pool. The new spa has 10 treatment rooms and 2 outdoor seaside bohios.

Dress Code: Casual by day; casually elegant by night. No tie required at dinner, but collared shirts, pants, and shoes are required.

Weddings: Can be arranged

Rates/Packages: $550–$1,380 per couple per night, including meals, transfers, water sports, bicycles, tennis, and ferry transportation to Tortola; seven-night land-and-sea packages from $5,937 per couple, including meals. Romance package: per room, $2,668–$4,008 for 4 nights; $4,318–$5,658 for 7 nights including accommodations, meals, champagne, couples' massage, vintner dinner, day trip to neighboring island, unlimited use of island activities, sports facilities, transfers, and unlimited ferry service to and from Tortola.

Payment/Credit Cards: Visa, MasterCard, American Express

Deposit: Full payment required within 5 days of booking. No refunds on unused portions. Refunds available no later than 4 weeks prior to scheduled arrival.

Government Taxes: 7 percent

Service Charges: 10 percent

Entry Requirements for U.S. Citizens: Proof of citizenship necessary. Passport best.

LALUNA

Grenada

One of the newer resorts on Grenada, Laluna is rapidly becoming the trendy hideaway for young movers and shakers. Its sixteen adobe Balinese-style cottages are staggered up a hill with knock-out views of the sea. Decorated in chic minimalist Indonesia-meets-Italian style, the guest rooms feature king-size four poster Balinese beds, made up with fine Italian linens, and adobe-style walls hand-rubbed in rich golds, blues, and other earthy colors. All cottages come with private plunge pools and private verandas. Decks are framed in bamboo and windows are wood louvered.

There are four kinds of accommodations: cottage suite, cottage deluxe, beach cottage deluxe, and two-bedroom cottage. Certainly the beach cottages are the most romantic, close enough to the water to hear it lap up on the beach. Yet all the cottages are close enough to the sea to afford wonderful views with the wall of each cottage facing the sea, for the most part, open. Privacy is protected with filmy, natural cotton curtains. Cottages come with decks, private plunge pools, and funky open showers.

The thatched roof open-air restaurant that fronts the beach features Italian cuisine with a Caribbean flair and an emphasis on fresh fish, lobster, and seafood prepared by Laluna's European chef. Have a tropical drink at the Sunset bar or relax in the thatched-top, open-air lounge comfortably furnished with Indonesian sofas—very conducive to a doze or two. Just off the lounge is the pool, giving the whole place a sense of easy intimacy. You don't have to go far for anything—the beach, with hammocks or chaises, is just steps away.

Take time to explore Grenada, a pretty sprawling butterfly-shaped island, hilly and volcanic in origin and breathtaking in its jungly greenness. Not only is it one of the most picturesque of the Caribbean islands, perhaps equally important, mass tourism has not yet found its way here. Fluffy golden sand stretches for miles along Grand Anse, Pink Gin, Prickley Bay, and Bathway beaches, and the beach at Laluna is secluded and idyllic.

Don't come here if you're looking for non-stop nightlife. In Grenada there are no high-rise hotels or wide manicured concrete boulevards, and nightlife is limited to a couple of local clubs such as Fantasia 2001 and Le Sucrier in nearby St. George's, the capital city. There is, however, a weekly Rhum Runner Cruise, which is party time big time.

Grenada is small enough to be toured in one day. But I wouldn't advise it. Although the principal roads are in pretty good shape, if you veer off onto secondary routes, you may be in for a rough ride. Roads curve around hillsides, ramble around the irregular coastline, and find their way over some pretty steep hills. Everything in Grenada, it seems, is built on a hill. Your best bet is to explore Grenada in a number of mini-excursions, spread out over a few days.

There are rum factories to visit such as the River Antoine Rum Distillery, the Grand Etang National Park, and Annandale Falls. You can hike through the rain forest from Concord Falls to Au Coin and beyond that, Fontainbleu, where there is a lovely deep water pool cradled in a rock basin at the foot of a cascading 65-foot waterfall. The water is clear and cold, perfect for a refreshing swim. Although not a particularly rigorous climb, if you are timid about climbing over rocks and an occasional wet log, forget it.

Laluna

Location: Tucked at the base of a hill on a lovely white sand beach on the Caribbean island of Grenada

Romantic Highlights: Open-sided rooms facing the sea; dining by candlelight by the water

Address/Phone: Morne Rouge, P.O. Box 1500, St. George's, Grenada, W.I.; (473) 439–0001; fax (473) 439–0600

E-mail: info@laluna.com

Web Site: www.laluna.com

U.S. Reservations: (800) 4–LALUNA

Owner/Manager: Christine Nelles, general manager

Arrival/Departure: Taxis are available at the airport.

Distance from Point Salines International Airport: 15 minutes

Accommodations: 16 cottages

Most Romantic Room/Suite: Beach Cottage Deluxe

Amenities: Air-conditioning, TV, VCR, CD player, ceiling fan, minibar, tea/coffeemaker, computer modem outlet, in-wall safe, hair dryer, bathrobe, make-up mirror, private plunge pool

Electricity: 220 volts

Sports and Facilities: Swimming pool, beach, snorkeling, kayaking, mountain bikes. Golf, tennis, hiking, fishing, island tours can be arranged on request.

Dress Code: Comfortably casual

Weddings: Yes

Rates/Packages: From $310 per couple. Romance and wedding packages available

Payment/Credit Cards: Most major

Deposit: 3-night deposit by credit card due at time of reservation in order to confirm; balance due 30 days prior to arrival

Government Taxes: 8 percent

Service Charges: 10 percent

Entry Requirements for U.S. Citizens: Proof of citizenship; passport best

HALF MOON
Jamaica

Half Moon, in the exclusive Rose Hall area of Montego Bay, enjoys one of the most romantic settings in the Caribbean. Put this together with one of the best managers in the Caribbean, Richard Whitfield, and it's no wonder that this resort attracts a sophisticated, international clientele, including Sean Connery, David Bowie, Prince Charles, and George H. W. Bush. Set on 400 acres of manicured gardens bordering a mile-long, white crescent beach, most of Half Moon's stark-white, two-story, plantation villas and beach houses are quietly arranged along the edge of a lovely, palm-fringed beach. Gardens are interspersed among the buildings, which serve as a brilliant backdrop for the red and orange bougainvillea that climbs up the walls and hugs the arches. Some of the rooms open onto wrought-iron balconies; first-floor rooms have arched Palladian windows with French doors that open onto a seaside terrace. The villas are really superb, with private pools and gardens.

Golfing couples will enjoy the excellent par 72 championship golf course designed by Robert Trent Jones, and racquet players can challenge their partners on the squash or tennis courts and meet other couples at the tennis pavilion. There is a full-service health center with Nautilus and life fitness equipment as well as aerobics classes, and there are biking, horseback riding, and paths for walking. Swimmers and sun-bathers have a choice of several freshwater pools, located throughout the grounds, or they can head to the beach. You don't even have to get up when you want a drink pool-side or on the beach. Snorkeling, scuba diving, sailing, sailboarding, and deep-sea fishing are readily available, and if you want to totally relax you can try a sauna, a massage, or even an herbal wrap.

Your choice of accommodations includes deluxe rooms, suites, and villas, most strung along the beach and some set in the gardens. Rooms are airy and spacious, and most have sitting areas. They are furnished with white wicker and Queen Anne–inspired pieces made out of Jamaican mahogany. Black-and-white-tiled floors, sisal throw rugs and Oriental carpets, English flowered chintz, and authentic Jamaican art create an elegant yet exuberant mood, somewhat different from the usual Caribbean style. Worth considering are the newly renovated Hibiscus Suites, many with ocean views and a private beach area. The Royal Beachfront Suites are enclosed in their own garden courtyard with two pools and a central lounge reserved exclusively for Royal Suite guests, where continental breakfast and

evening cocktails are served each day.

Half Moon has four outstanding restaurants, the open-air Seagrape Terrace, the Sugarmill Restaurant, Il Giardino, and the Royal Stocks. Guests can select over one hundred different kinds of wines from several countries at any of the restaurants. The Seagrape specializes in Caribbean cuisine, and diners can sit on the tree-shaded seaside patio and enjoy dining by candlelight under the starry skies. If you're in the mood for chicken marinated in lime and fresh herbs, *duckanoo* (sweet potato dessert), or breadfruit vichyssoise, this is the place to come. During and after dinner there is a resident band for dancing well into the evening.

Under the direction of the German chef, Klaus, the Victorian-style Sugarmill Restaurant is located on the grounds of—surprise—a sugar plantation, where you'll find the remains of a 200-year-old water-powered mill. Here diners are treated to dishes such as freshly made pastas, prime rib, flambéed entrees, and shrimp stuffed with ripe bananas and cooked in coconut batter. You can dine on the open-air terrace or inside while enjoying live music for listening and dancing.

For a change of pace, you can order room service and indulge in a lazy morning with breakfast in bed. Try the coconut waffles, fresh fruits, and Blue Mountain coffee. A Night Owl menu is available from 10:00 P.M. to 1:00 A.M. Beach parties, floor shows with native entertainers, and steel drum bands are scheduled on various days. As if there weren't enough places to hang out, there is also the breezy, beachside bar.

Since the choices and quality of food at Half Moon are among the best in Jamaica, if not the Caribbean, take one of the plans that includes food as well as the various sports activities.

Half Moon

Location: On 400 beachfront acres in Rose Hall, Montego Bay

Romantic Highlights: Clusters of villas and suites, some with private pools; candlelight dining under the stars

Address/Phone: Rose Hall, Montego Bay, Jamaica, W.I.; (876) 953–2211; fax (876) 953–2731

Web Site: www.halfmoon.com

U.S. Reservations: (800) 626–0592

Owner/Manager: Richard Whitfield, managing director

Arrival/Departure: Complimentary transfer

Distance from Donald Sangster International Airport, Montego Bay: 6 miles

Distance from Montego Bay: 7 miles

Accommodations: 419, including rooms, suites, cottages, and villas; many with private pools

Most Romantic Room/Suite: Hibiscus Suites, Imperial Suites, Royal Suites, or beachfront cottages

Amenities: Air-conditioning, ceiling fans, hair dryer, minibar, cable TV, radio, double sinks (villas and Royal Suites)

Electricity: 110 volts

Sports and Facilities: 18-hole championship golf course, renovated by Roger Rolewich; David Leadbetter golf school; putting green; 13 tennis courts; 4 squash courts; scuba diving, snorkeling, sailboarding, sailing, paddleboats, glass-bottom boat, deep-sea fishing; horseback riding, bicycles; saunas; aerobics classes; 51 public/private pools total

Dress Code: Casually smart

Weddings: Wedding packages available

Rates/Packages: From $240 per room, per night

Payment/Credit Cards: Most major

Deposit: 3-night deposit required for confirmation

Government Taxes: Included

Service Charges: Included

Entry Requirements for U.S. Citizens: Valid passport

SANDALS RESORTS IN JAMAICA
Jamaica

Sandals Resorts packages romance with a capital "R." Starting in Montego Bay, Jamaica, with the first property, Sandals now has more than a dozen (and growing) spread out over several other islands, including St. Lucia, Antigua, and the Bahamas. The resort company's all-inclusive, couples-only concept continues to score a "ten" with honeymooners for a number of reasons.

For starters, their ultra-inclusive plan, whereby you pay one price up front for virtu-

ally everything, is a real winner. Accommodations, meals, snacks, bar beverages including name-brand liquors, water sports, tennis, golf, tips, and just about anything else you can think of are all rolled into the package. Since many young couples have a set amount to spend, knowing there will be no surprises when they check out provides a high level of emotional comfort. It also eliminates the "Do we have enough cash to eat here tonight?" kind of discussion. But no matter how good an idea, this wouldn't work unless the resorts themselves were really romantic and special. They are.

Guided all along the way by its dynamic founder and chairman, Gordon "Butch" Stewart, Sandals has attained a well-deserved reputation for consistently delivering what it promises: a "no problem" romantic holiday with all the bells and whistles. Standard with Sandals are king-size beds, beautiful decor, a whole range of sports and fitness facilities, every water sport you can think of, including scuba diving, and a staff that radiates as much good cheer as kids on their first day of summer vacation.

The fact that you can walk up to any of the bars and order a drink or food at will without having to sign a chit or pull out your wallet is a big plus. This also goes for the restaurants. You can eat at the same one every night or try different ones. You can order anything on the menu—wine, beer, mixed drinks—whatever you're in the mood for, and it's all part of the package.

There is a huge list of activities available to guests, all complimentary. On hand to keep the mood upbeat and arrange special activities and parties are the energetic Play-makers. If you like to be on the go from dawn to dusk waterskiing, hiking, or playing tennis or golf, you can participate in the vast array of activities on tap at any of the Sandals properties. And if you tire of the scenery where you're staying, you can hop on a shuttle and spend the day or evening at one of the other Sandals resorts as part of their Stay at One, Play at Six, Enjoy All concept.

You'll find many other young newlyweds to exchange wedding stories with on your honeymoon at Sandals, and since the resorts operate exclusively for couples, you won't have to share your pool space with any kids. Many couples marry here and go on to make friendships that may last a lifetime.

Each of the Sandals properties offers the same quality of services and amenities. Where you choose to stay, however, will depend on what is really important to you. Each place has its own unique allure:

Sandals Montego Bay, the oldest of the properties and one of the most intimate, enjoys a wonderful beach. Its 242 rooms and suites are located in two-story buildings and two-unit cottages that are literally a stone's throw from the sand. The lobby is not as elegant as those of the other properties, and the resort's location close to the airport can be a distraction. However, the staff and guests cheerfully make light of the occasional jets that zoom in and out by waving to them—a Montego Bay tradition. And being so close to the airport means you can land, clear customs, and be on the beach inside about a half-hour. The beachfront suite with separate sitting room, marble bath, four-poster bed, and patio with a private pool is wonderful. And especially good here are the restaurants.

The 187-room **Sandals Royal Caribbean** is also close to the airport and is set on seventeen acres fringed by a series of six white, sandy beaches. The rooms, which are located in two- and three-story pink-and-white buildings, are designed in the spirit of a traditional Georgian great house and are elegantly furnished with four-poster beds, English flowered chintz drapes and bedspreads, and classic mahogany furniture. The buildings, arranged around three nice little pools, are named after homes owned by British royalty and look to the sea.

If you love white sandy beaches and don't mind being a bit out of the way, try the 223-room **Sandals Negril Beach Resort & Spa.** Ask for the loft suites, which are set into the palms and gardens along a 7-mile, powdery, white-sand beach. It's about a ninety-minute ride from the airport and has a more laid-back ambience than the other Sandals resorts.

Set in a virtual Garden of Eden, **Sandals Grand Ocho Rios Resort & Golf Club** is a botanical wonderland of flowers, trees, and shrubs. Hammocks are hidden in little glades, small streams bubble through the ferns and grasses, and bridges span the waterways. Pools are action centers for high-energy sports like water volleyball and swimming races. There is also a smaller pool, hidden in the dense "jungle," where you can escape and simply loll around. If you're looking for a long stretch of white-sand beach, you may be disappointed; the beach here is small. The views from your oceanside room are great, though, and the satisfaction level of the property's guests is high.

Sandals Dunn's River Golf Resort & Spa resembles a posh establishment on the Italian Riviera. Rooms are located in two large, red-roofed, two- and six-story buildings facing the sea. Here the grounds have been sculpted, molded, and planted to the nines, creating a playground of pleasure. The largest pool in Jamaica, with its own waterfall—a replica of Dunn's River Falls—and swim-up bar, along with seaside gazebos, Jacuzzis, bridges, and a piano bar are spread out over a large area. The 250 rooms are elegantly furnished, and the beach is good.

You might assume, since the food is already included and paid for, that a place like Sandals could get away with providing rather average restaurants. Not so. At Sandals the restaurant side of the resort operation is first-rate. Dinners feature a la carte menus, and couples can dine alone or with other couples. Breakfast and lunch are buffets, but a nice Sandals touch is the "white glove" service—a waiter carries your tray to your table. Each resort averages four restaurants, and all offer a distinctly different dining experience, ranging from informal to elegantly casual. Most of the restaurants are oriented to the sea, and the Bali Hai restaurant at Sandals Royal Jamaican is actually on its own little island.

If you like Italian food, you can head to Cucina Romana, at Sandals Montego Bay, where you can dine on a freshly made pasta of your choice while enjoying the sunset view from your table on the open-air deck. Next door, at Sandals Royal Jamaican, the Courtyard treats its diners to fresh-grilled specialties. If the flair and flourish of a teppanyaki Japanese restaurant is tempting, you can try Kimonos at Sandals Negril. Here you'll dine on exotic Oriental entrees prepared right in front of you.

Sandals went all the way to Holland to find an authentic Indonesian chef for Bali Hai. Since the restaurant is located just offshore from Sandals Royal Jamaican, getting there via the resort's private launch is part of the fun. Once you arrive at the entrance of the ornate, carved-wood building, a hostess wraps a colorful silk scarf around you, your "costume" for the evening. Diners sit at long tables where hot and spicy as well as mild dishes (for more timid palates) are placed in the center for everyone to sample. Other chefs come from many countries including Israil (wait until you try his hummus) and the Czech Republic.

In the elegant category, Sandals Montego Bay's Oleander Room, brainchild of Horace Peterkin, the resort's enterprising general manager, has stenciling on the ceiling and a warm coral decor accented with brass lamps, chandeliers, and Palladian windows overlooking the sea. Most romantic. This is your chance to try some tasty Jamaican specialties.

Get hungry between meals? Each Sandals resort has an "anytime grill," open well into the night, offering snacks as well as made-to-order meals.

Dollar for dollar, the Sandals resorts offer a lot of value and a lot more unexpected pleasures.

Sandals Resorts

Location: Montego Bay, Negril, and Ocho Rios

Romantic Highlights: Couples only; nonstop activities and quiet hideaway places; romantic restaurants; Stay at One, Enjoy All program—use all the Sandals resorts at no extra charge

Address/Phone: In Jamaica, W.I.: **Sandals Montego Bay,** P.O. Box 100, Kent Avenue, Montego Bay, St. James; (876) 952–5510 or 952–5515; fax (876) 952–0816; **Sandals Royal Caribbean,** Mahoe Bay, Box 167, Montego Bay, St. James; (876) 953–2231 or 953–2232; fax (876) 953–2788; **Sandals Negril,** P.O. Box 12, Negril; (876) 957–5216 or 957–4217; fax (876) 957–5338; **Sandals Grand Ocho Rios,** P.O. Box 771, Ocho Rios, St. Ann; (876) 974–5691; fax (809) 974–5700; **Sandals Dunn's River,** P.O. Box 51, Ocho Rios, St. Ann; (876) 972–1610; fax (876) 972–1611

U.S. Reservations: (800) SANDALS

Owner/Manager: Gordon "Butch" Stewart, chairman of the board; Horace Peterkin, general manager, Sandals Montego Bay; Carl Hendricks, general manager, Sandals Royal Caribbean; Baldwin Powell, general manager, Sandals Negril; Michael Darby, general manager, Sandals Grand Ocho Rios; Louis Grant, general manager, Sandals Dunn's River

Arrival/Departure: Sandals guests are met at the airport and escorted to their resort. A new lounge has been built for guests at the airport offering Red Stripe beer and other refreshments.

Distance from Donald Sangster International Airport, Montego Bay: Driving time: Montego Bay 5 minutes; Ocho Rios 1¾ hours; Negril 1½ hours

Accommodations: Rooms, suites, bungalows: **Sandals Montego Bay,** 242 rooms and suites in nine categories; **Sandals Royal Caribbean,** 187 rooms in six categories; **Sandals Negril,** 223 rooms in six categories, including loft suites; **Sandals Grand Ocho Rios,** 522 rooms in five categories; **Sandals Dunn's River,** 250 rooms and suites in five categories

Most Romantic Room/Suite: At **Sandals Montego Bay,** the Presidential or Prime Minister Suites or the beachfront suite with the private pool (shared only with adjacent suite); **Sandals Royal Caribbean,** Grand Luxe Honeymoon Beachfront or Beachfront Royal Suites; **Sandals Negril,** Beachfront Honeymoon Suite or Beachfront Honeymoon One-Bedroom Loft Suites; **Sandals Grand Ocho Rios,** Penthouse Honeymoon Ocean-View Suite; **Sandals Dunn's River,** the Penthouse Honeymoon Suite or the one-bedroom Oceanfront Suite. These accommodations will run you approximately $500 more (for 7 nights) than the most inexpensive room but are worth it if you care to splurge a bit and like butler service.

Amenities: Air-conditioning, king-size bed, ceiling fans, hair dryer, generous kits of lotions and shampoo, telephone, clock radio, TV, minibar, and safe deposit box

Electricity: 110 volts

Sports and Facilities: Tennis day or night, scuba diving, snorkeling, sailboarding, sailing, Hobie-Cats, paddleboats, canoes, kayaks, racquetball, golf, pitch-and-putt golf, volleyball, basketball; pool tables, shuffleboard, horseshoes, croquet, Ping-Pong, aquatriking, squash, and waterskiing (only Negril); "Fit-Shape" program, exercise rooms, aerobics classes

Dress Code: Casual

Weddings: Over 500 weddings are performed annually at the various Sandals properties.

On-site wedding coordinators arrange all the details, including taking care of the paperwork, leading the couple through the process of getting the marriage license, flowers, music, and reception. "WeddingMoons"—Sandals's term—can be as intimate as a couple getting married at the beach or under a gazebo with a best man and attendant "borrowed" from the Sandals staff. Or it can be a more elaborate affair held at one of the Sandals villas with a reception for the couple's family and friends.

A Sandals wedding is free (excluding the $150 government fee) with a stay of 5 nights. The package includes preparation of documents, best man/maid of honor (if needed), wedding announcement cards, services of a justice of the peace or clergy, tropical flowers, wedding cake, champagne, personalized candlelight dinner, and wedding video. Options include special treats such as sunset cruise, reception, gift baskets, and upgraded villa accommodations.

There are many places a couple can choose to be married. Most popular are places like the gazebo at Sandals Montego Bay and the beach or the gardens in Sandals Grand Ocho Rios. Brides can bring their own dresses or use one provided by Sandals. One bride who got married in Sandals Dunn's River wore a white, two-piece swimsuit with her veil, gloves, and garter. The groom wore a pair of white shorts, a bow tie, a cummerbund, and a boutonniere attached to one of his shirt garters. Taking a quick dip in the Caribbean after the ceremony was "no problem."

Rates/Packages: $215 per person, per night; all-inclusive rates for 7 nights start at $1,806 per person

Payment/Credit Cards: Most major

Deposit: Guarantee with credit card

Government Taxes: Included

Service Charges: Included

Entry Requirements for U.S. Citizens: Valid passport

FOUR SEASONS RESORT NEVIS
Nevis

Once you hear the rustle of the swaying palms, feel the gentle breezes crossing the beach, and see the flourishing tropical rain forest from your private veranda, you will no doubt believe that you have landed in paradise.

Four Seasons Resort Nevis, which is part of the Four Seasons group of prestigious, upscale resorts in exotic locations around the world, lives up to its reputation for providing a bundle of services and luxurious appointments, such as the large marble baths and the Evian water sprayed gently on your face by attendants to cool you while you lounge on the beach or by the pool. But beware: This resort also delivers high prices and can make a serious dent in your budget.

One of the best things Four Seasons has going for it is its location—really spectacular, with a long, golden sand beach lined by what seem to be hundreds of tall, graceful palm trees that blend into the hillside beyond.

It also has an impressive, 6,725-yard, eighteen-hole Robert Trent Jones II golf course that climbs from sea level up the volcanic slopes of Mt. Nevis to the fifteenth hole, where, from your perch at about 1,000 feet above sea level, you will see some incredible views of the sea and craggy hills. The course takes you up and down the mountainside, over deep ravines, and along the ocean. What more could a golfer want! Perhaps a pro shop? Of course. Nothing is left to chance here.

Tennis players have a fancy complex of ten courts, a pro shop, and organized lessons and clinics. And if this isn't enough, there is a fully equipped health club, a new spa, a complete water sports center, two pools, Ping-Pong, croquet, hiking paths, and myriad other activities that may pull you away from your lounge on one of the most beautiful beaches in the Caribbean.

Occasionally even those with a passion for *plein air* find it necessary to come inside. Because the restaurants and lounges have been designed to ensure maximum exposure to the outdoor environment, even when you are technically indoors at the resort you can still enjoy a magnificent view, trade-wind breezes, and the sound of lapping waves.

Most of the public rooms are located in the sumptuous Great House, the heart of the resort. Many public rooms are open-air, with patios and terraces leading to gardens of tropical Nevisian flowers. The Library Bar is enclosed, cozy, and could have come straight from England—it even has a fireplace and paintings of tall ships. On the rare occasions when the sun is not shining, this is a wonderful place for cocktails before and after dinner.

The two-story bungalow buildings that stretch along the beach have rather uninspired architectural designs, but the interiors of the rooms and suites are spacious and decorated to the nines. Deep chestnut-brown armoires, carved headboards, brass lamps, and botanical prints contribute to the British ambience. The use of rattan chairs, tropical-colored fabrics and prints, and tile floors keep the rooms from looking too heavy. Fresh flowers and potted palms also help lighten it all up.

The bathrooms will really knock your socks off. They're simply superb, with lots of marble, double vanities, attractive lighting, and plenty of fluffy towels. The Four Seasons toiletries are especially fine.

There are two gourmet restaurants that serve Caribbean-inspired meat, fish, and seafood dishes and fresh fruits and vegetables: the more formal Dining Room, with its French doors, high ceiling and chandeliers; and the casual, open-air Nebe, a contemporary-style restaurant serving Mediterranean specialties and brick-oven pizzas. The Ocean Terrace overlooks the pool and the beach, and there is the Library Bar. A game area and entertainment lounge for children and teens, and a sports pavilion are also on the grounds.

Evenings you will be able to enjoy dancing and listening to local bands, including a steel drum group.

So if you don't mind blowing a lot of cash, be prepared to revel in one of the most ultraluxurious megaresorts in the islands.

Four Seasons Resort Nevis

Location: Set on 2,000 feet of beachfront on Nevis's leeward coast

Romantic Highlights: Catamaran cruise to private beach; candlelight dinners on your veranda

Address/Phone: P.O. Box 565, Pinney's Beach, Charlestown, Nevis, W.I.; (869) 469–1111; fax (869) 469–1112

Web Site: www.fourseasons.com

U.S. Reservations: (800) 332–3442

Owner/Manager: Martin Sinclair, general manager

Arrival/Departure: Most fly to San Juan for a quick flight to St. Kitts, where guests are met by a hotel representative and whisked to the private dock in Basseterre to board a boat for the 30-minute ride to the resort. Prior to boarding you complete check-in formalities and enjoy some refreshments. From Antigua and St. Martin you can fly direct to Nevis via regional carriers.

Distance from St. Kitts Airport: 20 minutes by boat; 6 miles by land

Distance from Charlestown: 1½ miles

Accommodations: 196 rooms and suites, each with a large veranda ranging from 120 to 160 square feet, overlooking the ocean, Nevis Peak, or the golf course. There are also more than 20 exquisite villas and homes for rent.

Most Romantic Room/Suite: The oceanfront Nelson and Hamilton Suites

Amenities: Air-conditioning, ceiling fan, toiletries, telephone, TV, VCR, DVD player, clock radio, ice maker, minibar, hair dryer, twin vanities, separate shower and tub, magnifying mirror, bathrobes, bath scale, 24-hour room service, Wi-Fi in lobby

Electricity: 110 volts

Sports and Facilities: 10 tennis courts (5 lighted), 18-hole championship golf course; health club, spa, massage therapies; beach, pool, snorkeling equipment, sailboards, kayaks, sailboats, sea cycles, catamarans, waterskiing, fishing, scuba diving; croquet, volleyball, shuffleboard, and hiking

Dress Code: Casually elegant

Weddings: Can be arranged

Rates/Packages: Romance in Paradise package, $774–$1,474 per room, per night, includes accommodations, flowers, champagne and truffles, candlelight dinner, breakfast, non-motorized water sports, unlimited golf and tennis, massage for two, transfers, and half-day catamaran cruise to private beach

Payment/Credit Cards: Most major

Deposit: Deposit with credit card

Government Taxes: 8 percent

Service Charges: 10 percent

Entry Requirements for U.S. Citizens: Proof of citizenship; passport best

HORNED DORSET PRIMAVERA HOTEL
Puerto Rico

The elegant Horned Dorset Primavera Hotel, which is hidden away on Puerto Rico's western shore, focuses more on relaxation than recreation and offers only a few facilities. The resort attracts solitude-seeking guests who want a small hotel with plush European standards. Located 2½ hours from San Juan, the Horned Dorset isn't the easiest of places to find. But once you do, you may never want to leave. And that is just part of its mystique.

Its name sounds like a weird kind of English pasta, but the hotel, directly on the pounding surf, is named after a breed of sheep raised on the grounds of the owner's upstate New York inn. No sheep are in sight; still, the setting is bucolic.

The grounds are lavishly landscaped with exotic plants. A recently built Spanish colonial hacienda with a curving split staircase brings you to the stunning, tiled-floor breezeway/lobby and an open porch cantilevered over to catch the sea spray. Below is a courtyard with a gigantic fountain, and beyond that is a large swimming pool with a wide lounging deck set up with Japanese umbrellas.

Off the lobby is a smaller, open dining terrace for breakfasts of warm banana bread, local fresh-ground coffee, finger bananas, papaya, and pineapple from local fields. Light lunches might feature fresh, grilled fish and a yummy salad. Drinks are served in the charming, wicker-furnished library, home to Pompideau, a pampered macaw in a huge cage.

The walk up the hacienda's stairway to dinner, with the tree frogs chirping a chorus, brings you to the second-floor dining room, where you are served a six-course, prix-fixe dinner by candlelight. A member of the elite Relais & Châteaux group, the resort serves fine, French-inspired cuisine. A typical dinner might include Carrot Soup, Lobster and Grilled Vegetable Salad, Passion Fruit Granité, Roasted Sierra with Red Wine Sauce, Radicchio and Celery Salad, Cheeses, and Papaya Soufflé with Lemon Sauce.

As you dine, romantic ballads are softly played in the background by a classical guitarist. You can sit by French doors that open onto a balcony overlooking the ocean and the tiny beach.

The tropical grounds are extremely quiet. No pets, no TVs, no radios, and no children are allowed on the property. What to do? How about lazing by the pool or reading a novel from the library? Fishing, whale-watching, and golf are only thirty minutes away and can be easily arranged. Or walk along an almost deserted beach for a couple of miles past a small fishing settlement.

Temptation in this languorous, lush bit of paradise lurks behind the mahogany-shuttered windows of well-appointed suites that match the plush public rooms in quality. There are handwoven rugs over tile floors, louvered and mullioned windows, roomy armoires, and large, lavish European baths with quirky features like big, old-fashioned tubs and brass antique shower fixtures.

Woodwork is from island artisans, and four-poster beds, claw-footed tubs, and some of the only bidets on the island are unexpected amenities. All units have individual air-conditioning, queen-size sofa beds in sitting areas, and furnished balconies looking out on the water and beach.

An ultraluxurious unit housing eight suites with plunge pools was finished in 1995, and in spring 2002, twenty-two 1,400-square-foot duplex suites were added. These stunning new suites all face the ocean and come with private plunge pools. Along with the new Mirador Villa, they are the most superb accommodations.

The Horned Dorset is located in a part of Puerto Rico you may not even have a clue exists: quiet, quiet, and, yes, quiet. No casinos, no discos, no glitz. Just the Straits of Mona separating you from another island far across the water.

Horned Dorset Primavera Hotel

Location: On 4 acres, tucked away on the west coast of Puerto Rico

Romantic Highlights: Small, intimate inn by the sea; cocktails on seaside veranda as the sun sets

Address/Phone: Rincon, Puerto Rico 00677; (787) 823–4030; fax (787) 823–5580

E-mail: PGH@coqui.net

Web Site: www.horneddorset.com

U.S. Reservations: (800) 633–1857

Owner/Manager: Harold Davies and Kingsley Wratten

Arrival/Departure: Transfers can be arranged from the San Juan or Mayaguez Airports.

Distance from San Juan International Airport: 120 miles (2½ hours); Mayaguez Airport, 6 miles (10 minutes)

Distance from Rincon: 5 miles

Accommodations: 52 suites and the Mirador Villa

Most Romantic Room/Suite: New suites with plunge pools

Amenities: Air-conditioning, hair dryer, marble bath, toiletries, ceiling fans, ice service, room service (breakfast)

Electricity: 110 volts

Sports and Facilities: Pool; water sports and golf nearby; scuba and deep-sea fishing can be arranged

Dress Code: Semiformal, evenings

Weddings: Can be arranged

Rates/Packages: $190–$290 per person per night (winter), $140–$230 per person (summer); Mirador Villa, $400 per person per night (winter), $325 per person (summer); $80 per person includes breakfast and dinner; Romance package, $3,350–$4,130 per couple (summer), includes 7 nights' accommodations, breakfast, dinner, transfers, and champagne

Payment/Credit Cards: All major

Deposit: Credit card deposit for 4 nights (winter); 1 night (summer); for refund cancel within 45 days of arrival date (winter); 15 days (summer)

Government Taxes: 9 percent

Service Charges: 15 percent on food and beverages; 3 percent for general service

HOTEL GUANAHANI & SPA
Saint-Barthélemy

You've got to hand it to the French, they took a rocky island just 11 miles long and turned it into one of the Caribbean's chicest destinations. St. Bart's (Saint-Barthélemy, French West Indies) is like an exquisite piece of jewelry wrapped in tissue inside a velvet box. In other words, it's a gem! From the time you land on the runway in your small plane, you quickly realize this is not your usual Caribbean destination (and not for those on a budget). St. Bart's is très French, très chic, très expensive. Here people speak French (and English), dress French, dine French, look French. There are no high-rises, no fast-food places, no casinos. The only things not French, it seems, are the weather, the houses— mostly white

with red roofs and gingerbread trim—and the incredible crystalline turquoise sea.

The Hotel Guanahani is the best place to stay if you've got your heart set on staying on the beach. It's the island's only hotel with two beaches and with sixty-nine bungalows, one of the largest. Painted in upbeat island colors and decorated with gingerbread trim, cottages have terraces, private gardens filled with bougainvillea, hibiscus, and palms, and many come with private pools. Most rooms face the sea. From your patio or terrace you can watch the brightly colored sails of perky windsurfers dart back and forth across the brilliant turquoise water.

The cottages may look very cute but there is nothing ho-hum about these digs.

Some interiors are elegantly vibrant with splashes of bright sunny colors; others feature rich mahogany floors, carved four-poster beds, and natural-colored fabrics. They come with all the modern extras today's luxury-minded traveler expects, like air-conditioning, ceiling fans, in-room safe, direct-dial phones, DVDs, satellite TVs, marble baths—you get the picture.

Suites are set on bluffs above two white sandy beaches dotted by palm-topped palapas. Each suite has a sitting room or area, a terrace, and garden; fourteen of the thirty-eight suites have private pools. We suggest you stay in an ocean-front one-bedroom pool suite or spring for La Villa, the three-bedroom villa containing a "love tub," Jacuzzi, and plenty of room to spread out.

The Hotel Guanahani & Spa has two white sand beaches, one on the calm reef-protected bay and the other, Marechal Beach, on the ocean side of Marigot Bay. You can also swim in two freshwater pools, relax in the large outdoor Jacuzzi, and play tennis on floodlit courts. There are plenty of water toys including windsurfers, snorkeling equipment, canoes, kayaks, pedalos, and fishing gear, all complimentary.

And just as the resort courts twosomes—two pools, two beaches, two tennis courts, twice-a-day maid service, tea for two—there are also two restaurants: the Indigo on the beach serving breakfast and lunch and Le Bartoloméo featuring fine French cuisine. There are also the bars: Beach Hut and Bartolomeo Piano Bar.

At Le Bartoloméo, the most elegant place to eat in the resort, Executive Chef Philippe Masseglia creates dishes that combine regional flavors with international flair. For example, there is Chilean sea bass with shiitake and bok-choy, coconut milk, and kefir lime; and lamb fillet with caraway, soft polenta, and sundried tomatoes; topped off by a soft chocolate cake or chocolate tart with caramelized bananas.

Besides chilling out in a hammock under the palms, windsurfing, getting massages in your room or in the new full-service Clarins Spa, one day you might rent a car and tour the island. It won't take long. It's so small, no matter what road you take, you'll probably wind up near where you started. Shops cozy up to the roadsides while homes with their exuberantly painted trim nestle into the lush green of the hillsides. Check out the stores and boutiques in the capital, Gustavia, and the small enclave of St. Jean, and linger at one of the small cafes.

Whereas on most Caribbean islands, if you want to marry they make it pretty easy—usually just a day or two of residency and you can say "I do"—not so on St. Barts. If you want to marry here, you are required to have been in residence on the island for six months. So what couples do to get around this is have a civil marriage at home before they come to the island for an ultra-romantic wedding ceremony and reception.

Exchange vows on the dazzling white beach in the coconut grove or in the gardens. Since the hotel has just a handful of weddings a year, they work hard to make it perfect.

Hotel Guanahani & Spa

Location: Nestled on 16 acres on the northeastern coast of the Caribbean island of Saint-Barthélemy, overlooking the Atlantic Ocean and the Grand Cul de Sac lagoon

Romantic Highlights: Views of the sea from your private patio or pool; dozing in a hammock under the palms

Address/Phone: Grand Cul de Sac 97133, Saint-Barthélemy, F.W.I.; 590–590–27–6660; fax 590–590–27–7070

E-mail: guanahani@wanadoo.fr

Web Site: www.leguanahani.com

U.S. Reservations: (800) 223–6800

Owner/Manager: Marc Thézé, manager

Arrival/Departure: Round-trip transfers between the airport and the hotel by the Guanahani's shuttle service are included in the room rates.

Distance from Saint-Barthélemy Airport: 10 minutes

Accommodations: 69 rooms in cottages including 31 suites, 14 with private swimming pools

Most Romantic Room/Suite: Bungalows with private garden pools

Amenities: Air-conditioning, ceiling fans, stocked minibar, in-room safe, hair dryer, direct-dial telephones, satellite TV, DVD, stereo system, terry robes, marble shower, 24-hour room service, *New York Times* fax, Hermès toiletries.

Electricity: 220 volts

Sports and Facilities: 2 pools, 1 with a Jacuzzi, 2 floodlit tennis courts, 2 beaches, spa, fitness center; scuba diving, deep-sea fishing, and private boat excursions can be arranged (extra charge)

Dress Code: Resort casual

Weddings: Can be arranged

Rates/Packages: From about $316 per room, per night including breakfast, non-motorized water sports, use of the fitness center, service charges, and airport transfers. A 7-night Romance Package including breakfast, grilled lobster lunch, gourmet dinner, 7-day car rental, 2 massages, cooking class, wine-tasting, half-day cruise or sunset cruise, and champagne is priced from about $3,871. Spree and spa packages also available. (Currency on the island is in Euros and U.S. currency is accepted island-wide).

Payment/Credit Cards: Most major (no personal checks)

Deposit: Credit card deposit

Government Taxes:

Service Charges: Included

Entry Requirements for U.S. Citizens: Proof of citizenship; passport best

ANSE CHASTANET
St. Lucia

There are no televisions, no room phones, nothing really to break the spell of tropical moonlight, refreshing sea breezes, and the scent of frangipani in this dense, green, jungly paradise that is the idyllic setting for Anse Chastanet. Your room may be wide open to lofty views of the blue-green pyramidlike peaks of the Pitons and the variegated blue sea. And this is exactly what Nick Troubetzkoy had in mind when he created Anse Chastanet.

Nick, an architect, and his wife, Karolin, have carved into the thick tropical forests on this remote hillside one of the world's most unique and romantic resorts. In the premium rooms there are no walls at all, so that you can easily hear the birds, the waves, and the rustling of palms. Waking up to see the cones of the two Pitons framed by the arches of your octagonal "tree house" can blow you away.

There are only forty-nine cottages, partially camouflaged by the foliage that rises like a thick green carpet from a lovely, coconut-palm-fringed beach. Thirty-seven of the cottages are staggered up the hillside, and twelve are located at the beach level. As you walk up the hillside to your cottage, you may wonder if the climb is worth it. It is. The higher you are, the better the view and the privacy.

Each room is fun and dramatically different not only in decor but in shape. Standard hillside rooms are rectangular and slightly smaller than the superior rooms, which are octagonal or rectangular in shape and feature two twins or one king-size bed. Beachside rooms are spacious, with either two double or one king-size bed, a bath with two sinks, a shower, and a large balcony or patio. Although these are just steps from the beach and probably the best choice for those who can't or don't want to climb the hill, they have garden, not ocean, views. It is the premium rooms located high up the hill that are so spectacular.

Even the showers are worth writing home about; many are as large as a garage. Ginger (number 14B) has a gommier tree growing right through it. Some open onto gardens, others to the sea. Most have no curtains or doors.

It's not just that the rooms are superspacious—7B is roughly 30 feet by 30 feet—it's the way they blend into the surroundings. Mahoe (number 14A), for example, is totally open on two sides. The only creatures that will share your private moments are the birds (which you'd expect would fly in and out, but they don't). You have mosquito netting, but you really don't need it.

Red-tile or wood floors, original art by Reina Nieland, a Dutch-Canadian artist who works in burlap and mixed media to create superb abstract collage, and woodcarvings by Lawrence Deligny, a St. Lucian artist, are located throughout the rooms and public areas. Simple but effective basket lamp shades with yellow insect repellent bulbs hang around the perimeters of the rooms, balconies, and restaurants.

If you can tear yourself away from your room, you'll find there's plenty to do here if you like water sports, hiking, or a massage. Located in a new beachfront building is the spa, Kai Belté ("house of beauty" in patois), where you can enjoy facials and body scrubs using natural fruits like mango and coconut. Professionally trained therapists offer a variety of massage treatments and reflexology at the spa or in your room. Also available at the spa are other beauty and body treatments, including body polishes, waxing, facials, pedicures, and manicures.

Among the resort's toys are fifty Cannondale bikes with all the accessories, which can be rented for a half or full day. Ten miles of trails lace the 500-acre property.

There is a palm tree or palm-roofed umbrella for every guest who wants some shade on the picturesque, volcanic sand beach, which seems to sparkle with diamond dust in the sun. At one end of the beach, you'll find the casual Trou-au-Diable restaurant and bar, two boutiques, and the scuba center.

Two other restaurants, a bar, and a reception area are located midway up the hill. Dining up in the Tree House Restaurant, you look through foliage and flamboyant trees down to the beach and the turquoise waters. Breakfast is served at the Piton Restaurant, on the same level as the Tree House.

Food is excellent, especially the fresh-grilled catch of the day, which might be red snapper or grouper. Fresh fruits and vegetables such as breadfruit and christophine as well as curries are very tasty. And be sure to try the banana pancakes, a house specialty.

One of the Troubetzkoys' major commitments is to the crafts of St. Lucia. A woodcarver has his own workshop area at the northern end of the beach; a pottery shop has been established on the grounds. The work of local and international artists is represented in many of the rooms.

For scuba enthusiasts the waters off the beach are brilliantly clean and clear, and a reef on the southern end of the beach was declared a marine preserve.

The resort's Dive Center maintains a staff of fully qualified dive instructors and offers a complete range of courses. Dive trips operate daily to sites around the island.

A must-do while you're here is an excursion with Menau, Anse's resident horticultural guide. He will take you to the ruins of an eighteenth-century French sugar plantation located off the resort's Anse Mamin Beach.

A complimentary water taxi, *Peace on Earth,* takes you to Anse Mamin and Soufrière. Or charter the resort's 37-foot yacht for a sail and snorkeling tour.

If you must have quick access to phones, TVs, and faxes, keep in mind the only public phones are found in the reception area midway up the hill and there's a fax machine in the office. That's it.

Anse Chastanet

Location: Situated on 600 hillside acres on the southwestern coast of St. Lucia

Romantic Highlights: Dramatic open rooms with spectacular views; huge open showers; candlelight dining and dancing

Address/Phone: P.O. Box 7000, Soufrière, St. Lucia, W.I.; (758) 459–7000 or (758) 459–7554; fax (758) 459–7700

U.S. Reservations: Ralph Locke Islands, (800) 223–1108 or (310) 440–4225; fax (310) 440–4220

Owner/Manager: Nick Troubetzkoy, owner and managing director; Karolin Guler Troubetzkoy, director of marketing and operations

Arrival/Departure: Pickup can be arranged at the airport

Distance from Hewanorra International Airport: 18 miles (1 hour); GFL Charles Airport (formerly known as Virgie Airport), 30 miles (1¾ hours)

Distance from Soufrière: 1½ miles

Accommodations: 49 rooms: 4 open-style, Premium rooms on hillside, with dramatic Piton views; 12 large, open Deluxe hillside rooms; 12 Deluxe beachside rooms with a garden view; 17 Superior hillside rooms with wraparound balconies; 4 Standard hillside rooms

Most Romantic Room/Suite: Room 7F, huge and open on two sides; 14B, wide-open room with a tree growing in the shower; 14A, four-poster bed and wide-open vistas

Amenities: Hair dryer, refrigerator, tea and coffee bar, ceiling fans, supersize baths (most), bidets (some)

Electricity: 220 volts

Sports and Facilities: Scuba diving; snorkeling, kayaking, sailboarding, Sunfish sailing, hiking, swimming; spa; tennis, table tennis; mountain biking; yacht charters

Dress Code: Men requested to wear long slacks or long-cut Bermuda shorts at Tree House Restaurant

Weddings: Can be arranged. Wedding package priced at $695, with a number of options.

Rates/Packages: Double room, including breakfast and dinner, $465–$795 (winter); the breakfast and dinner plan is optional in the shoulder and summerseasons; double room $260–$555, meals not included (spring and fall); $210–$485 (summer)

Payment/Credit Cards: Most major

Deposit: 3 nights in winter; 2 nights in summer and shoulder seasons; all weekly packages must be prebooked and prepaid in full.

Government Taxes: 8 percent

Service Charges: 10 percent

Entry Requirements for U.S. Citizens: Proof of citizenship; passport best

LADERA

St. Lucia

Looking for a place that is small, secluded, dramatic? Try Ladera, which runs along a mountain ridge 1,100 feet above the sea. The views just don't get much better. If the poolside scene seems familiar, you may be recalling it from *Superman II,* which was filmed here. On one side you have the rain forest, mango trees, and the mountains, on the other, your three-sided villa opens full up to stunning views of the sea, the gardens, and the green-clad Pitons. Being that high up in your luxurious "tree house" has another advantage: cool breezes that ruffle the netting draped over your four-poster bed and lull you to sleep.

Designed by architect John Di Pol, who used polished tropical hardwoods, massive beams, stone, and terra-cotta tiles, the bungalows seem to disappear beneath the lush foliage, as though part of the natural things all around. With the open wall, gardens and flowers are inside and outside at the same time. Coconut shells define the perimeter of the gardens and a leaf motif is imprinted in a masonry floor outdoors. Wooden doors feature ornate carvings.

Furnished with an eclectic mix of French furniture, hand-carved wooden pieces, wicker, local-designed fabrics, and accessories and art by local artisans, each of the rooms is different. All have open-air bedrooms, plunge pools, some with waterfalls,

and refrigerators with complimentary "welcome stock" and coffeemaking facilities. Although there are large villas that sleep up to five people and come with two or three bedrooms, the deluxe one-bedroom suites offer the same wonderful views.

Water tumbles out of a shell into the vanity basin, molded in the shape of a clam shell; piles of colorful pillows of green, gold, and red plaid fabric are distributed around the rooms on chairs, sofas, and beds; polished floors of greenheart wood are enhanced by woven rugs; and tiled see-through baths—though private—still reveal fabulous views. There are no CD players, TVs, or radios in the rooms, nothing to interrupt the songs of the birds and rustling of the palms. However, there is a television room for guests to use.

If you have to be smack on the beach, Ladera is probably not for you—although there is a nice beach just ten minutes away, and the resort offers a complimentary beach-shuttle and use of snorkeling equipment.

Ladera has one of the best places to eat and drink in St. Lucia, the multi-tiered indoor/outdoor Dasheene Restaurant and Tcholit Bar. The cuisine, which can loosely be described as "Caribbean Original Fusion," is creatively prepared under the direction of executive chef Orlando Satchell.

The new Ti Kai Pose Spa features a full-line of spa treatments available in the spa or in the privacy of your open-air suite. Treatments include massages, body polish and wraps, aromatherapy, manicures, pedicures, and beauty treatments.

There are plenty of outdoor activities to keep you busy in the area. You can hike in the rain forest, snorkel or scuba dive, sail, horseback ride, deep-sea fish, play golf, or swim. Take time to visit the sleepy port town of Soufrière. There isn't much there in the way of shopping, just a few small stores selling souvenir items like T-shirts and jewelry, but you'll be rewarded with wonderful photo opportunities: fishing boats tied up along the beach, sun-faded houses with gingerbread trim, and boats arriving to unload their produce and fish.

If you can tear yourself away from your hilltop haven, take a trip to see the sulfurous moonscape-like terrain of the Soufrière volcano with its boiling mud and steaming trails.

Ladera

Location: Atop a steep hill in the southern part of St. Lucia just two miles from the old banana port of Soufrière

Romantic Highlights: "Open-wall" rooms offering breathtaking views of the Pitons mountains, rain forest, and sea; private plunge pools; dining under the stars

Address/Phone: P.O. Box 225, Soufrière, St. Lucia, W.I.; (758) 459–7323; fax (758) 459–5156

E-mail: Ladera@candlw.lc

Web Site: www.Ladera.com

U.S. Reservations: Karen Bull Associates (800) 738–4752; fax (404) 237–1841

General Manager: Robert Stewart

Arrival/Departure: GFL Charles Airport (formerly known as Virgie), to or from $80 per couple, one way; Hewanorra Airport (UVF), to or from $65 per couple, one way

Distance from Soufrière: 10 minutes

Accommodations: 6 villas, 19 suites

Most Romantic Room/Suite: 1-bedroom suites

Amenities: Hair dryer, refrigerators with basic stock, coffeemakers, toiletries, adaptors

Electricity: 220 volts (Ladera has adapters/converters available)

Sports and Facilities: Pool and private plunge pools, Ti Kai Pose Spa, hiking, guided day trips, nature walks, water sports (10 minutes away), golf nearby

Dress Code: Casual

Weddings: Can be arranged. Wedding packages are available from $900–$1,150.

Rates/Packages: From $280 per couple, per night, including breakfast. All-Inclusive packages available from $1,522 per person, 5 nights, including suite, meals, most beverages, spa treatment, and transfers.

Payment/Credit Cards: Most major credit cards

Deposit: 2-night deposit to guarantee booking. Cancellation must be at least 21 days prior to arrival to avoid forfeiting deposit.

Government Taxes: 10 percent

Service Charges: 8 percent

Entry requirement for U.S. Citizens: Passport

Note: Ladera is closed from mid-September to early October.

SANDALS RESORTS IN ST. LUCIA
St. Lucia

Sandals has brought its couples-only, ultra-all-inclusive concept to St. Lucia, with three Sandals resorts: Sandals Regency St. Lucia Golf Resort & Spa at LaToc; Sandals Grande St. Lucien Spa & Beach Resort; and Sandals Halcyon Beach.

The first thing one couple I spoke to said you should do when you get to **Sandals Regency St. Lucia**—"even before the obvious honeymooner thing"—is to make dinner reservations. Said this newly married couple, who spent their June honeymoon at Sandals Regency, "While we certainly never experienced a shortage of food at the resort, we found that there was limited seating at the specialty restaurants, especially the French place, La Toc, and Mario's, the Italian restaurant at the Halcyon resort." (At Sandals Regency St. Lucia you're allowed full access to the other Sandals resorts on the island including the restaurants and facilities; a free hourly shuttle runs between the resorts.)

They said they loved Sandals Regency St. Lucia for a number of reasons: "Here you don't have to deal with kids and singles. If you do feel like socializing with others, you have something instantly in common with the other guests—you share the same wedding date. So not only is everyone in the best mood of their lives, but you can feel free to trade wedding stories from what went perfectly right to where Uncle Ralph's hairpiece flew during the Electric Slide." They added, "If you feel like making a party out of it, you can join others with the Sandals' 'Playmakers,' who organize everything from aqua aerobics to beer-chugging contests."

The couple added, "One extra that we did indulge in was a sunset cruise. It's one of the few things you have to pay extra for,

arranged through Sandals. It was a three-hour cruise on a large catamaran fully equipped with a stocked bar, a guitarist you can sing along with if you choose to, and a breathtaking view of the island at sundown. It turned out to be one of the most memorable parts of our honeymoon."

The larger of the company's three properties on the island, Sandals Regency St. Lucia sits on 155 acres and boasts a huge, sprawling pool with waterfalls, a swim-up bar, whirlpool baths, bridges, and a pavilion. The property has 327 rooms, offering twelve categories in various locations and configurations including 56 villas on Sunset Bluff. Two-story town houses, with a living room and patio upstairs and a bedroom downstairs, are set high along a bluff at one end of the property and come with marble baths, minibars, four-poster beds, and sitting areas; some also come with private plunge pools. Other rooms and suites are located closer to the ½-mile beach and near the golf course. Some of the villas are two-story; some also have plunge pools. Although the villas are more private, if you want to be near the action, go for the Grande Luxe Beachfront rooms and suites.

Sandals Regency St. Lucia has several restaurants and bars, two pools, a fitness center, and a whole boatload of sports options, including golf on the premises, as well as a disco and nonstop other activities.

You can choose from the elegant La Toc restaurant, where the emphasis is on French cuisine, or try Japanese food at Kimonos, steak and ribs at Arizona, or Caribbean and Creole items at the Pitons Restaurant. You can eat inside by candlelight; outside, under the stars by the sea or by the pool. At night entertainment kicks in with theme parties, disco dancing, billiards, and a piano bar.

The newest Sandals on St. Lucia opened in 2002 on its own seventeen-acre peninsula at the north end of the island, 15 miles from Castrie's GFL Charles Airport (formerly known as Virgie Airport) on Gros-Islet. **Sandals Grande St. Lucien Spa & Beach Resort** has two wonderful white sand beaches, spa services, and four pools, including a lagoon-style pool where couples can swim right up to their rooms. Rooms come with king beds, designer baths, and private verandas.

Sandals Halcyon Beach is a smaller, more intimate Sandals and has abundant, lush tropical gardens. Like many of the Sandals, among its most popular features is a vast, spectacular swimming pool in classic Sandals style. This Sandals has three restaurants and a total of seven bars. The Pier Restaurant is set out over the water and offers fine dining in a special setting.

Although you may find little impetus to leave the properties, if you do decide to explore, there's much to see. St. Lucia, with its starkly beautiful Pitons, reminiscent of upside-down ice cream cones, is blessed with more than 19,000 acres of verdant rain forest. Reminiscent of Fiji or Kauai, with its steep hills and valleys carpeted with rich tapestries woven of palms, banana trees, bamboo, flowering plants, and other tropical foliage, St. Lucia is cut by streams and waterfalls plunging into deep pools curtained with giant ferns and fringed by golden sand. Dark volcanic-grained beaches sparkle like diamonds in the sun.

Most visitors make a trip to the famous La Soufrière volcano and Sulphur Spring. The last eruption here took place 200 years ago, leaving a smoking crater with more than twenty-one bubbling black pools of water that resemble liquid tar. Hydrogen sulfide, a stinky but nonpoisonous gas smelling like rotten eggs, continually rises from somewhere deep in the earth, creating these boiling pools that are thought by some to have health benefits (when cooled down sufficiently, of course).

The whole scene is like a set from *Star Wars.* As you peer over the top of the rim and look down over this most inhospitable landscape, you can occasionally see someone bravely trekking over the grayish ground and rocks. (Don't try it—that stuff is hot.)

At Morne Coubaril Estate, a fifty-acre working plantation and museum, you can stroll through the attractive gardens and see reconstructed houses similar to those the original plantation workers lived in, small cramped affairs with mud floors and walls papered with newspaper. Here you can see how cocoa is harvested, dried, pulverized, and molded into chocolate sticks; you can also watch workers at the coconut "factory," where coconuts are processed and every part is put to some practical use, including the fiber of the shell, which is used in mattresses.

Sandals Regency St. Lucia Golf Resort & Spa; Sandals Grande St. Lucien Spa & Beach Resort; Sandals Halcyon Beach

Location: All on white sandy beaches in St. Lucia

Romantic Highlights: Couples only, all-inclusive plan, nonstop activities and quiet hideaway places, romantic restaurants, secluded villas with private plunge pools; Stay at One, Play at Three program gives you use of other Sandals resorts' restaurants and facilities at no extra charge

Address/Phone: Sandals Regency: P.O. Box 399, Castries, St. Lucia, W.I.; (758) 452–3081; fax (758) 452–1012 ; **Sandals Grande:** P.O. Box GI 2247, Pigeon Island Causeway, Gros-Islet, St. Lucia, W.I.; (758) 455–2000; fax (758) 455–2001; **Sandals Halcyon:** P.O. Box GM910, Castries, St.

Lucia, W.I.; (758) 453–0222; fax (758) 451–8435

Web Site: www.sandals.com

U.S. Reservations: (800) SANDALS

Owner/Manager: Baldwin Powell (Sandals Regency); Konrad Wagner, general manager (Sandals Grand); Lennox Dupal (Sandals Halcyon)

Arrival/Departure: Sandals guests are met at the airport and escorted to their resort.

Distance from GFL Charles Airport (formerly known as Virgie Airport): 10 minutes; Hewanorra International Airport, 75 minutes

Accommodations: 780 rooms, suites, villas (327 at Regency, 283 at Grande, 170 at Halcyon)

Most Romantic Room/Suite: 1-Bedroom Sunset Oceanview Suites and Grande Luxe Beachfront Suites (Regency)

Amenities: Air-conditioning, king-size bed, ceiling fans, hair dryer, generous kits of lotions and shampoo, telephone, clock radio, color TV, safe; suite concierge service also includes terry robes, upgraded amenity kit, fully stocked wet bar, sitting area, mahogany four-poster bed, daily *New York Times* fax, and services of dedicated suite concierge

Electricity: 110 volts

Sports and Facilities: Several freshwater pools and whirlpools, fitness centers, tennis, scuba diving, snorkeling, sailboarding, sailing, Hobie-Cats, aquatriking, waterskiing, paddleboats, kayaks, golf, pool, volleyball, darts, shuffleboard, table tennis, lawn chess, nearby 9-hole golf

Dress Code: Casual

Weddings: On-site wedding coordinators arrange all the details, including taking care of the paperwork, leading the couple through the process of getting the marriage license, flowers, music, and reception. "Wedding-Moons"—Sandals's term—can be as intimate as a couple getting married at the beach or under a gazebo with a best man and attendant "borrowed" from the Sandals staff.

Rates/Packages: All-inclusive rates for 7 nights start at $3,920 **Sandals Grande;** $3,867 **Sandals Regency;** $2,772 **Sandals Halcyon**

Payment/Credit Cards: Most major

Deposit: Guarantee with credit card

Government Taxes: Included

Service Charges: Included

Entry Requirements for U.S. Citizens: Proof of citizenship; passport best

WINDJAMMER LANDING VILLA BEACH RESORT & SPA
St. Lucia

You can reach Windjammer by land or by sea. Either way, you'll be impressed with this little seaside "village" of white villas with red roofs and white adobe turrets and arches reminiscent of Mykonos in the Greek islands. Narrow, winding brick paths, which meander up the hillside to the villas, are lined with a profusion of flowering bougainvillea, hibiscus, and oleander. Since the villas are clustered together comfortably, there is room on this 66-acre resort to explore: to poke around the nooks and crannies defined by the villas, gardens, pools, restaurants, and beaches.

Shuttles take you up and down the hill to and from your villa to the beach, pools, and restaurants. But you'll find it tempting to laze away the day at your own private plunge pool, which is set in a tiled courtyard surrounded by flowers. From here the views of the sea and the hills in the distance are magnificent.

The one-bedroom villas, with 1,200 to 1,300 square feet of space, are a perfect choice for a romantic hideaway. The living rooms are large and airy, furnished with wicker furniture with pastel fabric cushions that contrast nicely with the red-tile floors and thick, round arches and windows. Cocoa straw mats, hand-painted tiles, and original art along with fresh flower arrangements add splashes of color to the white plaster walls, and lofty ceilings are light, pickled pine. There is a lovely tiled terrace with a dining area as well as a good-size kitchen. Baths are spacious and some have tubs and showers open to the sky. Taking a shower together while gazing out to a sailboat far out at sea can be a real turn-on. It does rain occasionally, allowing some water to seep into the tub/shower area, but that only enhances the sense of being outdoors that (in my estimation) far outweighs being totally dry-docked.

If you hate air-conditioning—I'm in that camp—you can open the door to your patio as well as the louvered windows to allow the ever-present breezes to waft through. Still, for those who must be mechanically refreshed, Windjammer's AC works very well and is amazingly quiet.

Water sports on the grounds are complimentary, including an introductory scuba lesson. You can join in the aerobics, participate in the waterskiing contest, go on a snorkeling trip, or take part in a sailing regatta. There are fashion shows, games in the main pool, beach volleyball, water polo, and calypso lessons. Tennis courts are lighted for night play.

Windjammer has six places to eat and drink. Dragonfly serves buffet breakfast daily and Asian-meets-West Indies cuisine for dinner when the candlelit restaurant is very romantic. Jammers, a split-level casual restaurant on the beach, is popular for cocktails and lunch; Café Labrelotte is the place to go for ice cream, sandwiches, and coffee; The Upper Deck features seafood specialities and a "Captain's Table Menu."

A wood-fired oven set into the wall is a feature of Papa Don's Taverna, where you can enjoy a variety of healthy items in keeping with the resort's new spa. (And you can still order a pizza and have it delivered to your room.)

Want a very private dinner for just the two of you? Just ask the kitchen staff to prepare and serve a special meal on your terrace. Start with Chilled Breadfruit Vichyssoise and follow it up with a Mille-Feuille of Fresh Mahimahi with a Saffron Cream Sauce and a Panache of Vegetables.

Windjammer Landing Villa Beach Resort & Spa

Location: Set on a hillside on Labrelotte Bay, on the northwestern coast of St. Lucia

Romantic Highlights: Private dinner on your garden terrace overlooking the sea; your own plunge pool

Address/Phone: P.O. Box 1504, Labrelotte, Castries, St. Lucia, W.I.; (758) 456–9000; fax (758) 452–9454

E-mail: reservations@windjammer-landing.com

Web Site: www.windjammer-landing.com

U.S. Reservations: (800) 743–9609; L.R.I. (Loews Representation International), (800) 223–0888

Owner/Manager: Anthony Bowen, general manager

Arrival/Departure: Round-trip transfers included in Honeymoon package

Distance from Hewanorra International Airport: 32 miles (1¾ hours); 5 miles (20 minutes) from George Charles Airport

Distance from Castries: 5 miles

Accommodations: 232 rooms and suites in 126 villas: 31 one-bedroom villas; 28 two-bedroom villas; 27 three-bedroom villas; 3 four-bedroom villas; 21 standard rooms; 21 deluxe rooms; 16 estate villas

Most Romantic Room/Suite: One-bedroom villas (2 have private Jacuzzis overlooking the bay)

Amenities: Hair dryer, air-conditioning, cable TV, ceiling fans, bathrobes, in-room safe; villas have fully equipped kitchen, microwave, blender, and coffeemaker

Electricity: 110 volts

Sports and Facilities: 4 pools, Serenity Health Spa, beach, PADI scuba program, snorkeling, waterskiing, sailboarding, fitness center, aerobics; golf nearby

Dress Code: Casually elegant

Weddings: Windjammer's wedding package, $699 per couple

Rates/Packages: $175–$355 per room/villa, per night

Payment/Credit Cards: Most major

Deposit: Three-night deposit at time of booking.

Government Taxes: 8 percent

Service Charges: 10 percent

Entry Requirements for U.S. Citizens: Proof of citizenship; passport best

Note: With an extensive children's program, Windjammer is understandably popular with families. So if having kids around on your quiet romantic interlude is not on your wish list, I would suggest you check with the hotel as to what weeks are for the most part kid-free.

PARROT CAY
Turks and Caicos

From the time you are met at the airport and whisked by private boat across the incredibly turquoise sea, feeling the breezes shake out the rigors of your travel, the sun warming your skin, you will sense you are in for a very special experience. Parrot Cay, a 1,000-acre private island paradise in the Turks and Caicos, British West Indies, is ringed by more than 3 miles of dazzling white beaches and planted with cactus, feathery casuarina pines, and tropical plants and flowers, all native to the island. It is a place that soothes, restores.

Since its opening in 1998, Parrot Cay has quickly become an island playground for celebs like Julia Roberts, Sandra Bullock, Paul McCartney, Barbra Streisand, Demi Moore, Donna Karan, Bruce Willis, and Britney Spears, people who covet their privacy and appreciate low-key luxury. Shell paths and raised wooden walkways brushed by the grasses and fibers of wetlands lead to the villas, a beachfront infinity pool, the Lotus Restaurant and the Mediterranean-style main hotel, which presides over a hillside, just a five-minute walk from the beach.

You don't come here for nightlife or blackjack or shopping, nor do you come for pool volleyball, dance contests, or limbo shows. There are no tent cards, activity boards, gilded columns. What you do have are private plunge pools, dreamy beds encased in gauzy fabric, Evian water delivered by butlers, a $200 Shirodhara Ayurvedic warm oil treatment, iced hibiscus tea, warm sand, privacy. Peace. And you don't have to pack much. Here on Parrot Cay, life is purposely simple, a study in refined, minimalist chic.

Rooms, villas, and beach houses are spread out along the beach and in the main building. Beach villas feature spacious, lofty living rooms decorated in soft whites and neutrals with pickled-pine vaulted ceilings, custom-designed natural timber and woven wicker furniture with slip-covered off-white cushions and pillows. Lights are created with curved sheets of handmade glass, and fiber carpets dress the dark wood floors. The natural, timeless look is arranged according to *feng shui* principles.

In the bedroom king-size four-poster beds are enveloped by a filmy white voile that billows softly when the wind from the sea wafts through the screened doors. Screened sitting rooms, living rooms that open to large decks with plunge pools and views of the water, kitchens, and every electronic gadget a tech-nut could want—flat screen TV, CD and DVD/VHS players, and fax machine—create an oasis of luxury.

In the bathrooms there are thick polished pine vanity tops and two showers. A limestone wall encloses an outdoor shower "room": when the faucet is turned on, water tumbles over a slab of rock in a shower-like stream. An indoor shower big enough for two features large rainheads.

The wood decks have plunge pools, wood chaises with thick cushions, an outdoor shower, and an umbrella table. A hammock big enough for two lures you to lie back and watch the clouds drift across the moon and the stars—just about as close to heaven as you can get.

Every detail from the stone flower container on the large slab of thick wood that sits on the coffee table to the flowing white organdy curtains reflect the superb taste of Christina Ong, the Singapore-based owner. Everything man-imposed is designed to serve as a backdrop to nature, to the endless blue sea, the rich greens, reds, yellows and blues of the flowering shrubs just outside, and the fleeting colors of the tropical birds (ironically the island has no parrots).

Parrot Cay has sixty rooms, suites, beach houses, and villas. Although the beach villas are the most luxurious accommodations, for half the price you can have a room in the main hotel that has views of the water, a balcony, and the same good taste in decor.

Executive Chef Tippy Heng showcases his talents with Mediterranean-inspired dishes tinged with hints of Asia like seared tuna, pink on the inside, lightly grilled on the outside. The Terrace Restaurant in the main hotel is open for breakfast and dinner, whereas the more casual poolside Balinese-style Lotus Restaurant, featuring weathered wood louvers and views of the pool and the sea, serves breakfast, lunch, and dinner. On some evenings you can listen or dance to live music.

The treatments and rituals offered by COMO Shambhala, a deluxe, 6,600-square-foot holistic retreat housed in simple wooden cottages set on a crest overlooking the water and wetlands, center on a philosophy to impart peace and harmony. Many of the massage therapists come from Bali. Gentle, soft-spoken, they are very good at what they do. Yoga is offered each day and there are a variety of massage therapies available, including an Indonesian-style treatment using traditional Javanese essential oils and combining rolling and long kneading strokes to bring renewal.

You can try the Thai massage, Shiatsu,

Indian Head Massage, Reiki, and reflexology; there are also special rituals and baths, facial and beauty treatments, Pilates, and meditation. Ayurvedic therapies include the Maharaja Odyssey with two therapists working together, Ahbyanga, a four-hand massage, Ubtan, an herbal power scrub, and Shirondhara where a stream of warm herbal oil is poured over your forehead. Couples can book Shambhala's two private pavilions, which have a double outdoor tub, deck, and treatment rooms for two. A special menu, low in fat and energizing, is offered in both restaurants.

Parrot Cay has a well-equipped gym, an infinity-edged pool, a number of water toys such as kayaks, windsurfers, and canoes, two tennis courts, and bikes. You can use a golf-style cart to take you anywhere you want to go on the grounds, including the boat dock from which the shuttle to Provo and the snorkeling and diving excursions depart. Parrot Cay's private launch can take you island hopping, perhaps to Iguana Island inhabited by prehistoric-like creatures.

Parrot Cay

Location: On an idyllic private island in the Turks and Caicos

Romantic Highlights: Walks on the long white sand beach; four-poster bed swathed in white voile; private pools; decks on the beach; booking Shambhala's private cottage for massages and relaxing

Address/Phone: P.O. Box 164, Providenciales, Turks and Caicos, B.W.I.; (649) 946–7788; fax (649) 946–7789

E-mail: res@parrot.tc

Web Site: www.parrot-cay.como.bz

U.S. Reservations: (877) 754–0726

Owner/Manager: Crawford Sherman

Arrival/Departure: Guests are met by the resort and taken by private launch to Parrot Cay.

Distance from Providenciales Airport: 35 minutes by boat

Accommodations: 60 rooms, suites, beach houses, and villas

Most Romantic Room/Suite: Bungalows with private garden pools

Amenities: Air-conditioning, ceiling fans, stocked minibar, hair dryer, direct-dial telephones, modem port, TV, DVD and CD players, radio, tea and coffee facilities, terry robes, marble shower, 24-hour room service, *New York Times* fax, and COMO Shambhala toiletries.

Electricity: 220 volts

Sports and Facilities: COMO Shambhala Spa, pool, water craft, fitness facility, snorkeling, beach

Dress Code: Resort casual

Weddings: Can be arranged

Rates/Packages: From $390 for rooms; from $1,320 for beach houses per night including airport transfers, breakfast, and use of non-motorized sports

Payment/Credit Cards: Most major (no personal checks)

Deposit: 3-night deposit covering the first and last two nights of stay by credit card or bank wire transfer

Government Taxes: 10 percent

Service Charges: 10 percent

Entry Requirements for U.S. Citizens: Passport or birth certificate and photo ID such as a driver's license

POINT GRACE

Turks and Caicos

The elegant stone work of the intimate Point Grace casts a faint pink glow against the wide-open azure blue sky. In front, within view of the terraces of the oceanfront suites, 12 miles of sandy beach fan out in either direction along an impossibly clear turquoise sea.

Inspired by British colonial and planters' estate homes, Point Grace, with its balustrades and wide, sweeping stairways reflected in the garden pool, is simply stunning. Apparently no expense has been spared in the creation of these side-by-side twin palaces with their blush-hued domes, green shutters, columns, and lofty spacious suites. Details tell all.

The resort has thirty-two spacious suites housed in two four-story beachfront buildings along with a few cottages that face the pool area. Accommodations range from a 1,080-square-foot one-bedroom cottage to two- and three-bedroom suites and the penthouse. Much of the hardwood and hand-carved teak furniture, as well as the silk, cotton, and linen fabrics, has been imported from Bali, Java, and other exotic places. Special features include Turkish marble floors and hand-carved mahogany doors along with much original artwork and antiques such as 200-year-old wall hangings from India, Indonesian wedding chests, and leather-bound books.

In addition to air-conditioning, ceiling fans, direct dial telephone—things you'd expect—these villas come with cable TV with DVD and CD player, safe, kitchen with granite counters and Sub-Zero refrigerator, washer and dryer, two bathrobes per person (a thick Frette terry cloth and a light Indonesian cotton), and king-size beds that are lavishly dressed in Frette linens.

Then there are the little niceties. Like when you arrive back in your room after dinner and find your bed turned down and an oil lamp glowing softly on the bureau, or opening your fridge to find it stocked with juices, water, and soft drinks. Or the excellent selection of CDs and books in the bookcase. And, oh yes. There are secretarial services, in-room fax machines, babysitting, additional maid and butler services, private in-room chefs, and personal fitness trainers.

The entire property is lushly landscaped with palms, tropical shrubs, and flowers, some quite unusual. There is a Monkey Nut Tree that produces small pink trumpetlike flowers, several traveler's palms, a cacti garden, yuccas, Alexander Palms, and Chinese Fan Palms as well as brightly colored bougainvillea and hibiscus.

Breakfast and lunch are served on the terrace or patio gardens just off the main reception area and there is an espresso machine where you can help yourself to a variety of coffees at any time of day. Dinner is in Grace's Cottage where the chef has created quite a stir on the island with his creative and tasty cuisine. I'm not sure which I liked best: the carpaccio of tuna with poached scallops, dry vermouth, and a leek fondu or the hot chocolate soufflé with homemade chocolate ice cream.

The $2.5 million penthouse—the 7,200-square-foot, four-bedroom "Nonsuch"—simply knocks your socks off. An Indonesian *bale* bed on one of the suite's two roof terraces, custom-made Mandalay lamps (brass floor lamps with fans) in the

Grand Salon, a grand piano, computer-operated sunshades, a cabinet crafted from a canoe, a tented bed bathed in muslin, silk pillows—the opulence goes on and on. There is even a massage room and a dressing room with mahogany cabinets and custom-made Indonesian brass work.

Point Grace is about in the middle of the beach. Club Med is a forty-minute speed walk away at one end; the frenetically busy all-inclusive Sandals Beaches resort, where I saw enough kids to fill a day care center, is a thirty-minute walk in the other direction. In between, except for a few low-key resorts, private homes, and empty spaces, there really isn't much going on. So aside from walking the beach, water sports including incredible diving opportunities and snorkeling off Smith Reef and Coral Garden, and soaking up the sun, there's not a whole lot of action on the island. There is just one small casino and a handful of small clubs where local bands entertain. Of course you can visit the Conch Farm, play golf at the Provo Golf Club for about $120 a round (a five-round pass is $450); or grab your binoculars and go bird-watching. But if you're looking for a happening nightlife, this is probably not your cup of tea.

For others, it may be just perfect. One couple fulfilled a dream by getting married on the beach at Point Grace. They walked down an aisle created by flower-filled conch shells and exchanged marriage vows and red roses just as the sun raked its streaks of orange and red across the skies. Thanks to help from the resort's staff in the months prior to the event, everything went like a Swiss watch (Point Grace was the result of the vision of a Swiss developer, after all).

To choose the menu for the small reception, sample menus had been exchanged via e-mail, a picture of what the bride wanted for her bridal bouquet was scanned and e-mailed to a Turks and Caicos florist, a cake was chosen, and legalities were reviewed. After the couple agreed on the guest list—only a handful of close friends and family would be invited—invitations were sent out.

In order to comply with island laws, the couple arrived three days before the wedding date (the law requires forty-eight hours residency). In that time, Pamela Ewing, Point Grace's wedding coordinator, helped the couple get their wedding license, went over the ceremony with the minister, and met the couple's guests who arrived on Thursday. The couple was married on Saturday and after the guests returned home on Monday, the newlyweds stayed on at Point Grace for a two-week honeymoon in their oceanfront suite (a complimentary upgrade by Point Grace).

The honeymoon was everything they dreamed it would be. "We weren't looking for nonstop activities. We simply wanted to relax and unwind in a beautiful place. We really enjoy each other's company," said the bride.

Point Grace

Location: Set in the center of a spectacular, wide white-sandy crescent along Grace Bay, in Providenciales

Romantic Highlights: Stunning views of beach from stone balcony; returning after a candlelight dinner to find your bed turned down, an oil lamp glowing softly on the bureau

Address/Phone: P.O. Box 700, Providenciales, Turks and Caicos Islands, B.W.I; (649) 946–5096; fax (649) 946–5097

E-mail: Tracy@pointgrace.com

Web Site: www.pointgrace.com

U.S. Reservations: (866) 924–7223

Owner/Manager: Valerie Hudson, general manager; Lucas Chanter, resident manager

Arrival/Departure: Transfers can be arranged

Distance from Providenciales International Airport: 15 minutes

Distance from Providenciales Center: 10 minutes

Accommodations: 32 oceanfront suites and cottages

Most Romantic Room/Suite: Oceanfront villas

Amenities: Air-conditioning, ceiling fans, cable TV with DVD and CD player, hair dryer, safe, kitchen with refrigerator, washer and dryer, bathrobes, king-size bed

Electricity: 120 volts

Sports and Facilities: Pool, beach, Hobie-Cats, kayaking, windsurfing, snorkeling, 26-foot Chris-Craft for island tours; complimentary membership (and shuttle) to nearby Provo Country Club where golf and tennis are available

Dress Code: Resort elegant

Weddings: The basic ceremony including legal fees and minister, cake, champagne, dinner for two, flowers, CD music, photograph, and services of the wedding coordinator averages about $850.

Rates/Packages: Rates start at $395–$1,795 per night including daily cocktail hour, use of the business center, transfers, shuttle to golf and tennis club, and nonmotorized water sports. Penthouse rates from $4,200.

Payment/Credit Cards: Most major

Deposit: 50 percent required within 10 days of booking; balance due 30 days prior to arrival

Government Taxes: 9 percent plus $15 departure tax

Service Charges: 10 percent

Entry Requirements for U.S. Citizens: Passport or birth certificate and photo ID such as a driver's license

Closed: Three weeks in September

CANEEL BAY
St. John, U.S. Virgin Islands

With 5,000 acres of tropical jungle around you, there is plenty of room to spread out on Caneel Bay, one of Laurance Rockefeller's most beautiful creations. He discovered this pristine, jungle-covered island in 1952 when he was on a sailing trip. After purchasing a good portion of the island, he set about to personally oversee the building of Caneel Bay, insisting that it be a low-key, ideal vacation resort for those who wanted to escape to a peaceful, natural retreat.

Over the years many couples have started their married lives here, and their children have come after them on their honeymoons. It's traditionally been ranked as one of the best honeymoon resorts in the world, the kind of place "old money" likes—elegance without the glitz or bells and whistles.

In 1993, the upscale Rosewood Hotels & Resorts took on its management and undertook a multimillion-dollar renovation project, redecorating just about everything except the scenery.

The cottages, which are constructed of natural stone and weathered wood, are spread out along the fringes of the beaches and in the gardens and manicured lawns. Designed to blend into the lush tropical plants and trees that surround them, the cottages have louvered windows that let in the cooling sea breezes and wonderful views of the beaches or gardens. For those who prefer a more controlled environment, air-conditioning has recently been installed in all cottages. The new decor emphasizes a palette brought in from the outdoors, including corals, blues, and greens. Accessories and furniture also echo nature's design in clay, cane, bamboo, and local hardwood. There are six categories of rooms: courtside, tennis garden, ocean-view, beachfront, and premium as well as Cottage 7, a luxury villa popular with visiting bigwigs.

On the whole, the rooms are not super-luxurious, nor are the baths mega-marble marvels. But with Caneel's setting and amazing natural assets, who can complain?

If you come here for a week's honeymoon, you will be able to plunk yourself on a different beach every day, but the alluring Honeymoon Beach may seem most appropriate. At Caneel your day spreads out before you like a sybaritic feast of wonderful things to do and see. If you love nature, you'll have miles of trails to follow that wind through the 5,000-acre Virgin Islands National Park. At night you can take walks along the pathways, which are softly lit with low mushroom lights to aid hikers, joggers, and strollers. Need to relax? The Self Centre, a spa for physical and mental well-being sits high atop Honeymoon Beach and offers yoga, Pilates, t'ai chi, m'ai chi (water aerobics eastern-style) and for couples, "The Rhythms of Relationships" course featuring yoga, touch, and meditation exercises designed to heighten each other's connection as well as their physical and mental needs. This one is perfect for newlyweds.

Feel adventurous? Then take a jeep or boat to other islands or to Caneel's sister property, Little Dix Bay on Virgin Gorda. Ask Caneel to pack a picnic lunch for you, and spend a relaxing day on your own. You can also head to Cruz Bay for shopping and browsing. There are several excellent shops in this little town along with some good restaurants.

Tennis players will be in racquet heaven, with eleven courts surrounded by tropical gardens in the terraced Tennis Park. The resort offers complimentary clinics and private lessons, and there is an on-staff pro and a fully stocked shop.

Water sports abound. Stop at the Beach Hut and get a Sunfish or sailboarder and sail off into the calm waters in the bay. You can go snorkeling either by yourself or with a guide or charter a boat for deep-sea fishing. The best snorkeling is off the north end of Caneel Beach, where you can see bright green parrot fish, funny-looking needlefish, and sinister moray eels tucked into crevices of coral. The brilliant world underwater also comes to life through the eyes of Lucy Portlock, the staff marine biologist, who personally escorts guests on weekly snorkel tours through the island's undersea treasures.

More than 1,400 different kinds of plants and trees flourish on Caneel's property. The resort's horticulturist, Oriel Smith, will take you on a tour of the grounds.

Caneel's three restaurants and terrace lounge look out over the sea. Turtle Bay Estate House, a gourmet restaurant reminiscent of a grand plantation house, invites you to enjoy open-air all-day dining while looking out over gardens to the deep turquoise sea beyond. At the Caneel Bay Beach Terrace, a casual, open dining room along the beach, you can indulge in a sumptuous lunch buffet every day. From your table in Equator, which is set in the ruins of an ancient sugar plantation, you can see the twinkling lights of St. Thomas across the water; the Caneel Bay Bar provides a casual, comfortable place to meet friends and relax with a cool rum punch.

Meals are included in some packages. Those on daily rates should budget for the meal plan: $90 per person per day for breakfast and dinner; $110 for all meals.

At night there is live music for dancing under the stars while the torches set in the lush foliage turn the resort into a tropical wonderland.

Caneel Bay

Location: Situated on a private, 170-acre peninsula on St. John

Romantic Highlights: A different beach for each day; natural splendor of a national park surrounding the resort; candlelight dining amid flower-bedecked ruins

Address/Phone: P.O. Box 720, Cruz Bay, St. John, U.S.V.I. 00831-0720; (340) 776–6111; fax (340) 693–8280

Web Site: www.rosewoodhotels.com

U.S. Reservations: Rosewood Hotels & Resorts, (800) 928–8889; fax (212) 758–6640

Owner/Manager: Rosewood Hotels & Resorts, management company; Rik Blyth, managing director

Arrival/Departure: Caneel Bay can be reached via San Juan, Puerto Rico, and St. Thomas. Caneel Bay's regular ferry service operates between downtown St. Thomas and Caneel Bay several times each day.

Distance from Cyril E. King Airport: 12 nautical miles (40 minutes)

Distance from Cruz Bay: 3 miles

Accommodations: 166 rooms and cottages. All have terraces; many have king-size beds.

Most Romantic Room/Suite: Secluded Cottage Point area

Amenities: Ceiling fans, air-conditioning, minibar, hair dryer, bathrobes, TV, in-room safe

Electricity: 110 volts

Sports and Facilities: 11 tennis courts (5 lighted), pool, boating, sailing, snorkeling, and swimming

Dress Code: Casual during the day; men required to wear slacks, collared shirts, and closed-in footwear in evening; jackets required during height of winter season for dinner in Turtle Bay Estate House restaurant

Weddings: Can be arranged

Rates/Packages: $325–$1,150 per couple, per night includes use of nonmotorized boats, snorkeling gear, shopping trip to St. Thomas, tennis and weekly clinics, scuba clinic, and garden walk; the Allure Package, $4,600–$11,625 per couple, includes 7 nights' accommodations, champagne, massage for two, a private starlit dinner, a private sunset champagne picnic, self center treatment, and more. Meal plans are $80 for breakfast and dinner or $100 for three meals.

Payment/Credit Cards: Most major

Deposit: Three-night deposit; balance due 30 days prior to arrival

Government Taxes: 8 percent

Service Charges: 10 percent

Entry Requirements for U.S. Citizens: Proof of citizenship required when traveling between the United States and the British Virgin Islands

MEXICO

MAROMA RESORT & SPA

Cancun

From the time you arrive at the small, elegant Maroma, you are completely pampered and left alone. Yet the Maroma "family" makes you feel as though anything is possible; all you have to do is ask. And for the most part, it's true!

Marked by a plain wooden gate off the Yucatán Peninsula's main corridor, a rutted, single-lane path winds through jungle, past flowering trees and around iguanas sunning themselves. In a small clearing is a cobblestone driveway, at the end of which is an elegant whitewashed hacienda. A small reflecting pool and an assortment of honking geese and ducks greet you.

Upon entering the open-air, tiled foyer, you are welcomed by a charming hostess and a frosty Maroma Margarita (with a delicious secret ingredient). The hostess asks if you have any special requests and tastes: When would you like your fresh coffee or tea to arrive in the morning? What are your favorite foods and drinks? What special activities would you like arranged?

A quiet, secluded estate of loosely linked suites and elegantly lighted walkways set around a pretty blue-tiled swimming pool fed by a gurgling fountain, Maroma is a collection of one- and two-story buildings, some topped by thatched palapa roofs made of native palm fronds.

Past the pool is the large, breezy main building, El Sol, with high ceilings, winding staircases, and terra-cotta tile floors. Inside are a small bar and a casually elegant dining room, flanked by a slate terrace with a large Jacuzzi and steps leading to a beach of fine, soft white sand.

The new 6,365-square-foot Kinau Spa offers a full range of spa treatments in unique environments. Enjoy a massage in the outdoor palapa or in a private garden. Get 360-degree views of the sea and jungle from a rooftop yoga and meditation pavilion. Each element in the building has been aligned to the stars to ensure positive energy flow for a peaceful mind, body, and spirit. Yucatan-inspired spa cuisine is served poolside or in your treatment room.

Your room, designed to appeal to the senses, is furnished with handsome Mexican colonial furniture, rich fabrics, and original artwork. A silky, translucent netting cascades from the ceiling and flows over the bed to a floor of large, honey-colored tiles. Thick cloth curtains frame the entrance to a room-size sunken tub and a shower made of golden ceramic tiles.

The beach is quiet and mostly deserted. At one end of the mile-wide cove is a secret sulphur spring that feeds into the shallows. Find it by digging your toes in the talc-soft sediment. You'll know you're there when you smell the pungent sulphur. The jungle that surrounds Maroma is home to monkeys, anteaters, possum, foxes, and a variety of exotic birds.

Maroma, Spanish for "somersault," is named for the swirling currents beyond the offshore reef, a mixing of tidal currents and upwellings that first bedeviled Mayan seafarers trading along the coast and at the nearby island of Cozumel. It's odd that such a quiet, serene place like this should be named after a turbulent waterway.

La Maroma, the namesake ocean current, however, poses no problem for the snorkeler or swimmer. The water sports concession is run by a Mexican-French family. They are expert guides to the local waters and are full of charm and a love of this area.

The relaxed restaurant host chats easily with all the guests, recommending things to do and telling stories about Maroma. Under his laid-back but attentive eye operate a cast of smiling, expert servers.

The menu at Maroma clearly caters to an international crowd. The elegant but pricey fare includes appetizers like lobster in filo on balsamic-perfumed tomato compote and duck mousse with green peppercorns and entrees such as mosaic of fish and shellfish with caviar, beef tenderloin medallions with Roquefort, and an array of chicken, pork, lamb, and duck dishes. If you have a taste for heat, ask for the *chnee-pek,* Mayan for "dog's nose." This salsa—a combination of onions, habañero chiles, and tomatoes—will spice up any meal.

The servers will encourage you to use your imagination and ask for whatever dish you're in the mood for. If the ingredients are in the kitchen, they'll be happy to make you a custom meal. Another tip: When it's not busy, ask to have a flambéed coffee drink prepared for you and taken up to the Mirador, a private rooftop alcove with sweeping views of the moonlit beach. For lunch the strip steak with Oaxaca cheese and roasted poblano chilies is hearty and delicious. Breakfast is leisurely and lovely and offers all kinds of choices, ranging from the compote of pineapple marmalade, dripping with honey and spiked with cinnamon, to custom egg dishes and pancakes with bananas and pecans. As the sun is fading on the beach, order margaritas, chips, and the incredible guacamole.

If you're looking for a real traditional Mexican meal, you're best off heading to a restaurant in nearby Playa del Carmen. About twenty minutes south on the main strip, this is the shopping and nightlife hub of the area. Playa's shopping district is filled with roaming European backpackers and tourist couples from the occasional cruise ships that dock there. Along the main drag, wall-to-wall shops sell jewelry, clothes, hammocks, and all manner of gifts and souvenirs. Music trickles out from bars and eateries. Several of the restaurants have mariachi bands that wander through the outdoor tables—a Mexican-vacation must.

But some guests never feel the urge to leave Maroma. And it's not hard to understand why. Like the peacocks that roam the walkways prowling for bugs, like the ducks and geese that have made their home at Maroma, honeymooners at Maroma may find that it's really quite pleasant to stay just where they are.

Maroma Resort & Spa

Location: On the east coast of the Yucatán Peninsula, 20 miles south of Cancun

Romantic Highlights: Small, intimate property with 520 acres (much of it jungle); a secluded beach; king-size beds draped with silky netting, private terrace with hammock

Address/Phone: Carretera Cancun Tulum Km51 Riviera Maya, Solidaridad Quintana Roo, CP 77710, Mexico; 52–998–872–28200; fax 52–998–872–28220

E-mail: reservations@maromahotel.com

Web Site: www.maromahotel.com

U.S. Reservations: (866) 454–9351

Owner/Manager: Orient Express Hotels

Arrival/Departure: Complimentary transfers are provided in a comfortable, air-conditioned Maroma car.

Distance from Cancun Airport: 20 minutes

Accommodations: 45 rooms; 6 suites; 1 3-bedroom villa

Most Romantic Room/Suite: The 1-bedroom suite on the 3rd floor overlooking the ocean and jungle

Amenities: Hair dryer, toiletries, telephone, 24-hour room service, bottled water

Electricity: 110 volts

Sports and Facilities: Snorkeling, Hobie-Cat sailing, sailboarding, scuba diving, deep-sea fishing, horseback riding; library with TV and VCR; boutique; spa, pool, fitness/wellness center; beach bar; golf courses nearby. Visits to Tulum, Cozumel Island, and day and overnight excursions to Chichen Itza, Sian Ka'an Biosphere Reserve, Merida, and Tikal.

Dress Code: Casually elegant

Weddings: Can be arranged

Rates/Packages: Rates including breakfast, transfers, and 1 snorkeling trip, $410–$1,500 per couple, per night; 5-night Romance Package, $2,530–$4,455 including champagne, breakfast, dinner with wine, snorkeling trip, Temazcal spa treatment per person, Kaftan per person, a hand-crafted pewter picture frame, sunset cruise, and transfers

Payment/Credit Cards: Most major

Deposit: Guarantee with credit card; cancel within 15 days of arrival to avoid a 1-night penalty charge in low season. In high season 15 days are required and the penalty is 2 nights. At Christmas, New Year's, and Easter, a 21-day cancellation is required and the penalty is 2 nights.

Government Taxes: 10 percent IVA, 2 percent hospitality tax, $17 departure tax

Service Charges: 10 percent, rooms; 15 percent, restaurant

Entry Requirements for U.S. Citizens: Passport

THE RITZ-CARLTON, CANCUN
Cancun

Cancun, with its very large hotels and booming commercial areas, may not be everyone's margarita, but anyone who appreciates luxury, pampering, and just the finest in accommodations and service can totally "get into" this superb resort. Once you step onto the marble floors of the elegant lobby, check in, and see where you'll be spending the next few nights, you may find you'll have little desire to do much more than lounge on the beach or by the two sparkling pools. You could take a day to visit the Mayan ruins at Chichen-Itza or Tulum. And you could go shopping. That is if you can drag yourself away from all the good things at the Ritz.

The Ritz-Carlton, Cancun has received a lot of awards for everything from service to overall excellence since its opening more than six years ago. You really can't go any-where on the property without feeling special. In addition to soft corals and golds, sparkling chandeliers, sweeping drapes, Oriental carpets, and highly polished traditional furniture, there are flowers everywhere.

Rooms are beautifully furnished in traditional French furniture upholstered in light brocades and prints. They come with marble baths and full-length French doors lead to spacious balconies overlooking the sea.

On the patios and dining terrace, the cobalt blue market umbrellas are offset by red-tile floors and white chairs and lounges. The cobalt theme is subtly repeated in the crystal water goblets in the dining room, where plushly upholstered chairs in coral fabrics and beautiful appointments such as Chinese vases and original art help create a quietly elegant place for that special dinner.

The coral and cream hotel may have 365 guest rooms and suites; still its design, roughly in the shape of a "U" facing the sea, with the public areas in the center, makes it feel like an intimate boutique hotel. You can get from your room to the beach in no time at all. The elevators are zippy; everything works.

There are four restaurants: The Caribe Bar & Grill, offering light meals and tropical drinks; The Club Grill, featuring regional specialties; El Cafe Mexicano, for casual dining including meals on the oceanfront terrace; and the elegant Fantino, the most formal of the four places to eat. Fantino's white-and-gold brocade chairs and beautiful china and crystal set the mood. The Lobby Lounge with its white wicker chairs, puffy cushions, potted palms and ornate marble floors, almost Moroccan in style, provides a pleasant place for cocktails and entertainment.

At the Ritz, you'll find yourself looking forward to your next meal. Everything is so good, so beautifully presented—starting with breakfast, where you may choose, for starters, fresh papaya, oranges, berries, mango, and pineapple served in a half shell of coconut or the Papaya Smoothie, a meal in itself.

For dinner you might have risotto of lobster, apple and foie gras Napoleon with black pepper and honey vinegar, savory bread soufflé with tequilla sauce, and porcini with white truffle butter. Certainly a dessert like warm black and white chocolate almond cake will satisfy the most demanding sweet tooth.

For those who want to get in on the latest craze, check out the new Cigar Lounge, which, by the way, is as popular with women as with men. Here you can select your smoke from a fine selection of Cuban cigars as well as sip a variety of tequilas, ports, and cognacs. The decor—burgundy leather chairs, wood paneling and original oil paintings—simply adds a bit of humph, humph to the whole scene.

If tequila is one of your passions, you'll have plenty of opportunity to indulge. Thirty of Mexico's finest tequilas can be found at the Lobby Lounge, many quite rare. Want to learn more about this national beverage? The Ritz's "tequiller" holds daily tasting sessions where you can get the scoop on its history and production.

The Ritz-Carlton, Cancun is a perfect setting for romance. You can arrange a private candlelight dinner for two on the beach or on your terrace; wake up late and have breakfast in bed; or sit under a beach cabana and enjoy some quiet time. But be warned: you may never want to leave.

The Ritz-Carlton, Cancun

Location: On the Caribbean Sea at the tip of the Yucatán Peninsula in Cancun

Romantic Highlights: Private candlelight dinner on the beach or poolside; massage on the beach; private patios overlooking the sea

Address/Phone: Retorno del Rey 36, Zona Hotelera, Cancun, Quintana Roo, Mexico; 52–9881–0808; fax 52–9885–1015

E-mail: ritz-carlton-cancun@rc-cancun

Web-Site: www.ritzcarlton.com

U.S. Reservations: (800) 241–3333

Owner/Manager: Tony Franzetti, general manager

Arrival/Departure: Arrangements can be made for pickup at the Cancun Airport.

Distance from Cancun International Airport: 15 minutes

Distance from Cancun: In the hotel zone

Accommodations: 365 rooms including 50 suites and 57 Ritz-Carlton Club rooms.

Most Romantic Room/Suite: A suite on the Ritz-Carlton Club floor; Executive Oceanfront Suite also great

Amenities: Air-conditioning, hair dryer, telephone, toiletries, 24-hour room service, two-line telephone with fax connection, TV, minibar

Electricity: 110 volts

Sports and Facilities: 2 outdoor pools, whirlpool; 3 tennis courts, health center, saunas, water sports, massage therapy, gym, golf nearby

Dress Code: Casually elegant

Weddings: Can be arranged

Rates/Packages: $249–$550 per room per night; three-night honeymoon package from $1,224

Payment/Credit Cards: Most major

Deposit: Guarantee with credit card

Government Taxes: 10 percent federal tax; 2 percent lodging tax

Service Charges: Not included

Entry Requirements for U.S. Citizens: Passport

HOTEL VILLA DEL SOL
Zihuatanejo

It's only 4 miles from Ixtapa, but this small gem is quite different, indeed, from Ixtapa's hotel strip. It has a beauty of a beach sheltered by a dense canopy of palms and framed by a carpet of tropical foliage that begins at the edge of the beach, rising up into the hills behind. Nestled in this greenery are seventy suites in adobelike two-story casitas, including fourteen luxury Lagoon Suites and a two-bedroom Presidential Suite. Winding stone walkways lead from the cottages to the two palapa-roofed bar/restaurants and the beach. Water runs in a meandering channel from the main fountain, along the paths, and into the pool.

Once you've had time to let the magic of Villa del Sol sink in, you'll be hooked. From the time you step up into the lofty, palapa-topped reception area and pass through to the gardens just beyond, you've entered the Mexican version of the Garden of Eden, and in this garden everything works: from the high-tech faucets that glide open like butter to the attractive lights that line the walkways. Created by Helmut W. Leins, who came to Mexico twenty-five years ago from

Germany, Villa del Sol combines the casual and colorful ambience of Mexico with the superb service-oriented traditions of Europe.

Passionate about details, Helmut says he sleeps in every room at least once a year. This way he knows if everything is as it should be. It's only when you stay here that you notice how well thought out it all is—subtle things like soap dishes, towel bars, and shelves are all perfectly placed.

Each of the suites is unique and appointed with authentic Mexican artifacts, such as wooden masks, terra-cotta pots, and ceramic birds. Suites come with separate sitting areas, terraces or balconies, and luxurious baths with large walk-in showers. The newest Lagoon Suites are vast with vaulted ceilings and private infinity plunge pools. With views of the pool, lagoon, and ocean, it's water, water everywhere. Adobe walls and great wooden beams and sliding doors carry out a definite Mexican mood. Some have thatched roof bathrooms open on one side to the gardens—yet private. The decor is in soft natural colors, a perfect setting for the colors of the artwork, flowers, sky, and sea just outside.

Rooms are decorated in rich, Mexican-loomed fabrics and enhanced by colorful handmade Mexican tiles. Terra-cotta and white ceramic tile floors are accented by area rugs; beds are draped in filmy white gauze; and a hammock is strung in a corner of each patio, providing a pleasant retreat for an afternoon siesta.

Villa del Sol's beachfront suites are about as romantic as it gets. The problem is, once you've seen them, you'll not want to leave. These suites are pure Mexican magic at its best. Each has a large patio smack on the beach with a hammock for two as well as a table and chairs; you can wake up slowly there to fresh coffee and croissants each morning. Sitting areas open onto a wide deck with a blue-tiled plunge pool. A lounge for two, padded and comfortable, is the perfect place to catch a snooze. King-size canopied beds and extra-large baths and views of orange-flamed sunsets take the romance level up another notch. Red-tile floors, fresh flowers, shelves, and roomy closets all add to the wonderful ambience.

If one wants to nitpick (and that's all it is): A few of the bungalows in this cool jungle setting are a bit on the dark side, especially those that front the gardens. The heavy tropical vegetation overhanging the roofs tends to keep sunlight at bay—and enhance the privacy. But this is a minor thing and will soon be forgotten once you settle in. The majority of suites including the beachfront suites are quite open and spacious.

A large round palapa-thatched roof, which looks much like a giant sombrero, houses the boat-shaped Orlando's Bar.

The white-sand beach, shaded by palms and palm-frond umbrellas, is set up with comfortable lounges with thick cushions, where you can chill out and snooze. Want a frosty margarita? Just signal the beach attendant, and it will be brought to you in speedy fashion. Generally the waters off La Ropa,

unlike the rougher beach areas in neighboring Ixtapa, are very swimmable. You can also cool off in one of the resort's four pools including a stunning cobalt-hued infinity pool overlooking the beach. The beach is pure sand. No rocks, coral, or rough places to hurt your feet so you can walk and swim with ease even when it's dark.

There are two lighted tennis courts, which, like everything else on the property, are well maintained. A fitness center is equipped with basic exercise equipment and spa services are available.

Dining at the Villa del Sol under the palapa roof is just about everything you could want: excellent, well-prepared food, candlelit tables by the sea, and warm smiles from those who serve you. Mediterranean fare is served at casual La Cantina Bar & Grill at the north end of the beach. Eat at the bar, on the large wooden deck, or inside near the open kitchen. Each Friday, enjoy a Mexican Fiesta featuring a sumptuous buffet and symphonic mariachi music. The waiters will set up a private table on the beach set with linens and china for lunch or dinner when you can stargaze by candlelight.

Nearby lies picturesque Zihuatanejo. Still very much a sleepy fishing village in spite of the tourism influx at nearby Ixtapa, here you can still watch the fishermen bring in their daily catch, and you can stroll down decorative brick-paved streets past small shops and cozy little restaurants. If you crave a bit of lively nightlife, you can head to Ixtapa. But then, who really wants to leave the Villa del Sol for very long?

Hotel Villa del Sol

Location: On palm-lined La Ropa Beach in the sheltered bay of Zihuatanejo, 150 miles northwest of Acapulco on the Pacific Coast

Romantic Highlights: Lovely 600-foot white

crescent-shaped private beach; private terrace with hammock; garden mini-pools; candlelight dinner on the beach—wonderful when the moon is full

Address/Phone: P.O. Box 84, Playa La Ropa, 40880 Zihuatanejo, Gro., Mexico; 52–755–554–2239 or 52–755–554–3239; fax 52–755–554–2758 or 52–755–554–4066

E-mail: hotel@villasol.com.mx

Web Site: www.hotelvilladelsol.com

U.S. Reservations: (888) 389–2645

Owner/Manager: Helmut Leins, owner/director

Arrival/Departure: Taxis are available at the airport; transfer can be arranged when booking

Distance from Ixtapa-Zihuatanejo International Airport: 15 minutes

Distance from Zihuatanejo: 5 minutes; from Ixtapa, 10 minutes

Accommodations: 70 individually designed rooms and suites, including 35 luxury suites

Most Romantic Room/Suite: Beach suites, each with a private terrace with ocean view, double chaise lounge, extra-large hammock, and mini-pool

Amenities: Air-conditioning, ceiling fans, king-size bed, in-room safe, TV, minibar, terrace, hammock, telephone, laundry and valet service. Suites have a living room area, minibar, bathrobes, private fax, phones, satellite TV, stereo, and CD player. Some have whirlpool or mini-pool. Services include room service, *New York Times* fax, massages, and beauty salon.

Electricity: 110 volts

Sports and Facilities: Beach, waterskiing, snorkeling, sailboarding, sailing, 4 freshwater pools; 2 lighted tennis courts with full-time tennis pro; two 18-hole golf courses in Ixtapa; scuba diving, spa services, deep-sea fishing, and horseback riding can be arranged

Dress Code: Casual; casually elegant for dinner at Villa del Sol restaurant; informal at La Cantina

Weddings: Can be arranged

Rates/Packages: From $270 (summer); from $365 (winter). During winter the meal plan for breakfast and dinner is mandatory ($60 per person per day in summer).

Payment/Credit Cards: Most major

Deposit: Two-night deposit

Government Taxes: 17 percent

Service Charges: 10–15 percent suggested

Entry Requirements for U.S. Citizens: Passport

LA CASA QUE CANTA
Zihuatanejo

La Casa Que Canta, "the house that sings," is one of those rare finds in Mexico, a small, intimate, five-star inn perched atop a cliff overlooking the Pacific. The clusters of pink-hued adobe-like casitas with terraces and thatched roofs that look like giant mops atop little blockhouses are staggered down the hillside so that you get a great view of the sea from each room.

Eclectically and creatively furnished with authentic Mexican artifacts and furniture, the suites have chairs with arms that are brightly painted to resemble birds and legs carved like feathers. A colorful striped animal (could it be a pig or a tapir?) sits on the floor balancing a carved bird on its back. A large terra-cotta bird with real, brightly colored feathers sits on a table, one of the many cleverly designed lamps scattered here and there in the public areas and suites. Furniture painted by well-known Mexican artists such as Frida Kahlo and Diego Rivera, mermaids, and ceramic angels along with tons of plants and Mexican tapestries and paintings add beauty and a sense of fun to La Casa Que Canta.

Your suite, with its bedroom, sitting room, and separate patio, is home to a number of valuable and whimsical art pieces: hand-painted desks, folk art from Erongaricuaro and equipale chairs. All these wonderful things are set against a background of creamy white walls and bed linens and red-tile floors edged with shiny, polished pebbles. Wood louvered doors open out to the terraces, which are partially thatched and have two extra-long lounge chairs, colorfully painted wrought-iron tables and chairs, a cushioned sitting area, lamps, and hammocks. In the harbor below you'll see a scattering of beautiful yachts—picture-postcard stuff. Don't look for a TV: There isn't one—but who needs it, with such views? (If you really need a quick catch-up on the world outside, there's a TV in the "theater room.") Your bath has a granite counter with double vanity, a pink-marble walk-in shower, a walk-in closet, separate toilet with bidet, and oversize bath towels.

Other resorts might be able to duplicate the decor (although I doubt it, unless the designers are prepared to spend years searching for interesting Mexican art and furniture pieces), but a more stunning setting would be hard to find. Your terrace, the pool, the dining room, the various terraced rooms tucked into the descending hill-side—everything—sits over the sea, which continually crashes into the wet, dark, jagged rocks at the base of the cliff. There is a saltwater pool as well as a Jacuzzi cut into the rocks near the bottom of the cliff. The freshwater pool, near the top of the cliff, is constructed so that the water seems to simply slip over the side of the pool down to the sea. You can quite happily while away the entire day sitting on the patio here, enjoying the scenery and sun.

In the evening when you come into your room, you'll find a floral surprise waiting for you: an elaborate pattern of flower petals on your bed, perhaps shaped into a heart. You also might find flowers tucked into washcloths, in soap trays, and on your bedside table.

La Casa Que Canta is but a two-minute walk to Playa La Ropa, a lovely white sandy beach with good swimming.

Meals are served outdoors overlooking the bay or in a palapa-palm-frond–thatched structure, where you'll also find a reception area, lounge, and bar. Dining hours are relaxed. You can eat anytime after 8:00 A.M., and Mexican specialties, salads, and grilled items are offered at both pool terraces. Like tequila? The resort features twelve different brands. Try a frosty and yummy quanabana margarita, or go for a cold Corona, the local beer, which goes great with the bar's new selection of Mexican tapas at the Terrace Bar.

Enjoying cocktails and dinner on the terrace at night is about as romantic as it gets: The soft, yellow lights play on the lofty, palm-thatched ceilings, and endless views of the sea are punctuated by the winking lights of Zihuatanejo in the distance. Light peeks through the holes of large round terra-cotta pots and gently glows from hanging wicker shades; there are enough private cozy sitting areas tucked here and there for couples who want their own space.

Just five minutes away is Zihuatanejo, a charming fishing village nestled into the curve of a bay cut sharply into the hills. Small white houses with red-tile roofs, a variety of fishing vessels anchored in the bay or pulled up on the shore, and a small population of happy, easygoing people makes this a fun place to visit. If you crave some modern-day action, the beach resort area, Ixtapa, is just a ten-minute drive around the corner.

This all may seem familiar if you saw the movie *When a Man Loves a Woman,* starring Meg Ryan and Andy Garcia, which was filmed here. A glance at the guest book says it all: A honeymoon couple writes, "La Casa Que Canta was the best place to start the first day of the rest of our lives." Another says simply, "Wow! Pure magic."

La Casa Que Canta

Location: On a cliff above Zihuatanejo Bay adjacent to Playa La Ropa, near the center of Zihuatanejo

Romantic Highlights: Views, view, views; intimate suites with private plunge pools; wonderful small terraced places where you can drink or dine

Address/Phone: Camino Escenico a la Playa la Ropa, 40880 Zihuatanejo, Gro., Mexico; 52–755–555–7030; in Mexico: 01–800–7109–345, (888) 523–5050; fax 52–755–554–7040

E-mail: lacasaquecanta@prodigy.net.mx

Web Site: www.lacasaquecanta.com

U.S. Reservations: (888) 523–5050 or 52–755–555–7000; fax 52–755–554–7900

Owner/Manager: Jacques Baldassari, owner; Teresa Arellano, and Ana Maria Frias, management committee

Arrival/Departure: Transfers from Ixtapa/Zihuatanejo Airport can be arranged

Distance from Ixtapa-Zihuatanejo International Airport: 12 miles (20 minutes); 35-minute flight from Mexico City

Distance from Zihuatanejo center: 5 minutes

Accommodations: 24 suites, each with its own living room and terrace; suites range in size from 800 to 1,733 square feet; 10 suites have private pools; there are 11 master private pool suites and 3 terrace rooms

Most Romantic Room/Suite: Private pool suites

Amenities: Air-conditioning, fans, bidet, large walk-in shower, magnifying mirror, toiletries, hair dryer, telephone, in-room safe, minibar, bathrobes; room service, massages available

Electricity: 110 volts

Sports and Facilities: 2 pools (1 freshwater "infinity" pool, 1 saltwater), saltwater Jacuzzi, Center of Well Being with 4 treatment rooms for massage therapy, most water sports, horseback riding; golf and tennis nearby

Dress Code: Casually elegant

Weddings: Can be arranged

Rates/Packages: $375–$915 (Penthouse pool suite) per couple per night; Master Pool Suite, from $615

Payment/Credit Cards: Most major

Deposit: Two-night deposit; refund if canceled 30 days prior to arrival date (60 days for Christmas and Easter)

Government Taxes: 17 percent

Service Charges: 10 to 15 percent suggested

Entry Requirements for U.S. Citizens: Passport

EUROPE

HOTEL GOLDENER HIRSCH

Austria

The Hotel Goldener Hirsch is pure Austrian, from the puffy duvets to the quaint, wrought-iron folk art lamps that decorate the rooms. If you are coming to Austria for your honeymoon and want a historic inn in the heart of Salzburg, try this one. You'll know you're there when you spot among the many beautifully wrought hanging signs along the narrow street the one with a gold deer atop an ornate golden circle—Goldener Hirsch stands for "gold deer." From the time you check in at the elaborately carved front reception desk and follow the bellman to your room on a rather circuitous route, you'll begin to realize that this is indeed a unique place.

The Goldener Hirsch is not just one building but a combination of interconnected buildings that stand smack on one of the most elegant streets in the baroque, historic heart of Salzburg. The Getreidegasse is lined with trendy boutiques and antiques shops, and just down the street is Mozart's birthplace; close by is the Festspielhaus (Theater).

Each of the sixty-nine rooms and suites is individually furnished with cozy sitting areas, a conglomeration of antiques, and masterpieces of rural art. On the beds are those wonderful creations of European refinement—goose-down duvets and fine, soft linens. Headboards, desks, tables, and bureaus are likely to be mellowed orange pine. The baths are modern, and rooms come with comfortable amenities such as telephone, TV, radio, and minibar.

There is no way you can spend a night here and not be touched in some way by the rich heritage of this fine old inn. Its character and place in the world are due in part to the work of a very special lady, Countess Walderdorff. She is the one who rescued the centuries-old structure from its sad state of disrepair and began its reconstruction during the difficult years following World War II. During the renovations the countess supervised every detail of the hotel's rebirth, from the hand-wrought iron light fixtures to the specially made china.

Almost from the first day it opened its doors, the Goldener Hirsch became known as the "in" place for notables to stay and be seen when they came to Salzburg. Heads of state and the elite of the world have come to overnight and sup at this famous hostelry, among them the Duke and Duchess of Windsor, Herbert von Karajan, and Leonard Bernstein.

Enjoy a quiet cocktail at the bar before sitting down to dinner. You can try local specialties and delicious draught beer in the rustic Herzl-Taverne. Indulge in all kinds of good things at the hotel's Goldener Hirsch restaurant, one of the best in Austria. Ask the hotel manager, Herbert Poecklhofer, to recommend his favorite dishes and he may suggest that you try the goose liver and *tafelspitz* (a boiled beef dish). Top it all off with a delectable caramel soufflé and caramel and walnut pancakes.

The Goldener Hirsch is not a particularly elegant place, nor is it one that offers much in the way of entertainment or activities. It doesn't need to. It's friendly and charming, and imagine: The whole wonderful city of Salzburg is right outside your door, with just about everything within easy walking distance. There are museums to explore, concert performances to attend, romantic little restaurants to try out, shops to browse, and endless, interesting streets to discover.

Hotel Goldener Hirsch

Location: In the heart of Salzburg, on elegant Getreidegasse

Romantic Highlights: Antique beds; Old World charm in fifteenth-century inn; the magic of Salzburg

Address/Phone: Getreidegasse 37, A–5020, Salzburg, Austria; 43–662–80840; fax 43–662–843–349

E-mail: welcome@goldenerhirsch.com

Web Site: www.goldenerhirsch.com; www.luxurycollection.som/goldenerhirsch

U.S. Reservations: Starwood Hotels & Resorts, 888–625–5144

Owner/Manager: Herbert Poecklhofer, manager

Arrival/Departure: Taxi from airport or train station

Distance from Munich International Airport: Approximately 84 miles (2 hours); 3 miles (10 minutes) from Salzburg Airport

Distance from Salzburg: Located in heart of town

Accommodations: 65 rooms, 4 suites

Most Romantic Room/Suite: Room 23 with its antique painted bed is charming; suites are roomier

Amenities: Hair dryer, minibar, TV, telephone, radio, toiletries, air-conditioning, room service, valet service

Electricity: 220 volts

Sports and Facilities: Guest privileges at Gut Altentann Golf & Country Club with payment of greens fees; other sports nearby include tennis, swimming, skiing, squash, and horseback riding

Dress Code: Informal by day; jacket and tie for men appreciated for dinner

Weddings: Can be arranged

Rates/Packages: From €232 (US$290) per couple, per night, including taxes

Payment/Credit Cards: Most major

Deposit: Guarantee with credit card, except festival period

Government Taxes: Included

Service Charges: Included

Entry Requirements for U.S. Citizens: Passport

HOTEL SCHLOSS FUSCHL
Salzburg

What about a fairy tale castle for a romantic getaway? The red roof atop the white square tower of the Hotel Schloss Fuschl rises above the greenery and gardens set on the edge of the hotel's private lake. Built in the fifteenth century as a hunting lodge and used as a summer residence by Salzburg archbishops, there can be no more romantic place to stay. You sleep within thick medieval castle walls; you look out over the deep blue Lake Fuschl ringed by tree-covered mountains. Perfect.

There are eighty-four rooms and suites with views of the lake or castle park. Oriental carpets, marble fireplaces, original oil paintings, vaulted ceilings, and richly upholstered sofas establish a sense of well-heeled elegance. In one of the suites, a large marble bathroom is lit by a crystal chandelier and a branched candelabra is placed near a huge tub roomy enough for two.

In fact there are several silver candelabras and chandeliers throughout, as well as gilded mirrors, silk and tapestry draperies, unique period pieces like a grandfather clock, antique desks, silk bed coverings, and high thread count linens.

Public rooms are in the main castle, and the lounge, characterized by a massive fireplace, antiques, ornate vaulted ceilings, brown tooled-leather chairs, bar, and exquisite tapestries, is a place you will want to linger.

Serving haute cuisine, the Castle Restaurant reveals views of the lake and the mountains through gold-draped windows. Chairs are upholstered in silk damask, candles are everywhere and floors are covered with Oriental carpets. A specialty of the chef is fresh fish caught from the crystal clear Lake Fuschl like char, rainbow trout, and bream. In fact the hotel's fishery smokes its own fish, a special treat for guests. On the menu you might find roast salmon trout with white onion–tomato ragout, and a liquid chocolate soufflé with elderberries.

For more casual dining try the Jagdhof Restaurant serving regional cuisine in a bistro-style environment. Another dining venue that is popular for events such as wedding receptions is the Waldhaus room. There is also the Wintergarden for breakfast, the Blue, Pink, and Yellow Salmon, the Castle Bar, and the barbecue bar at the lakeside beach.

On a balmy summer day unwind on one of the cushioned chaises on the lakeside terrace, take a swim, or sail. The hotel also has a hilly nine-hole golf course with drop-dead views of the lake and mountains; and there is a tennis court, boat rentals, indoor pool, Finnish sauna, solarium, whirlpool, and fitness center. In the winter cross-country skiing is available at Gaissau-Hintersee.

On Golf Course Schloss Fuschl, when you tee off from the first hole, a par-three, where you are hitting way down to a green framed by a lake and snow-topped mountains, you know you're in for an exceptional experience. The scenery doesn't get much better.

Submit to a day of pampering at the spa where white walls, tropical greenery, arches, and flowers enhance the experience. There are six treatment rooms and a pretty marble swimming pool and spa services include thalassotherapy and hydrotherapy, facials, massages, and other body treatments.

The castle is a perfect backdrop for a wedding. You can marry in a pretty, private chapel on the grounds, then have the reception in one of the grand rooms in the castle or on the terrace.

Although you can easily spend your entire vacation at the castle, we suggest you take time to explore Salzburg, a city of great beauty and Italian-inspired architecture, often referred to as the "Rome of the North." Wherever you walk in the city, you will be surrounded by a kaleidoscope of cultures revealed through costume, dancing, and music. Stroll through the gardens of the seventeenth-century Mirabell Palace and along the narrow Getreidegasse, where fanciful metal and gilded signs created a maze of color and ironwork. See where the children were filmed in the *Sound of Music* and the theater where the Von Trapp family sang their last concert.

This is Mozart country, birthplace of Wolfgang Amadeus Mozart (1756–1791). Mozart's birthplace, a yellow building at Getreidegasse 9, contains a museum displaying family portraits, Mozart's violins, two of his pianos, and numerous letters, personal belongings, and music—more than

800 original compositions of Mozart's original 8,000 works still exist. A larger house at Makartplatz 8 is where Mozart composed more than 150 works.

Coming to Salzburg without attending at least one Mozart concert would be like going to Vienna and skipping the opera. Concerts are held somewhere almost every night. At the Stiftskeller St. Peter Restaurant, you can enjoy a candlelit table and between courses prepared from seventeenth- and eighteenth-century recipes, listen to Mozart music performed by Salzburg artists in traditional costumes.

Editor's note: At press time we learned that the hotel was in the process of being totally renovated. It will reopen July 1, 2006, and promises to be better than ever.

Hotel Schloss Fuschl

Location: Set in an 85-acre park on the shores of Lake Fuschl just outside Salzburg on the northern edge of the Alps

Romantic Highlights: Dinner on the lakeside terrace; bath by candlelight; dinner in the Castle Restaurant; private chapel

Address/Phone: A-5322 Hof bei Salzburg, Austria; 43–6229–22–53–0; fax 43–6229–22–53–531

E-mail: schloss.fuschl@arabellasheraton.com

Web Site: www.luxurycollection.com; www.arabellasheraton.com

U.S. Reservations: Luxury Collection (800) 325–3589

Owner/Manager: Herbert Laubichler-Pichler

Arrival/Departure: Fly into Salzburg via Austrian Airlines and connect with Tyrolean Airways for the short flight to Salzburg. (800) 843–0002; www.austrianair.com

Distance from Salzburg Airport: 30 minutes

Distance from Salzburg: 12 miles

Accommodations: 84 rooms and suites

Most Romantic Room/Suite: Romy Schneider's suite, with elegant gold-hued decor

Amenities: Air-conditioning, hair dryer, telephones, cable TV/VCR, radio, CD player, alarm clock, ironing facilities, robes and slippers, designer toiletries, oversize tubs, room service

Sports and Facilities: 9-hole golf course, tennis court, boat rentals, paddle boats, indoor pool, sauna, solarium, steamroom, whirlpool, fitness center, and spa. Cross-country and alpine skiing, sailing, mountain biking, horse riding, and hiking are available in area.

Dress Code: Casual to dressy

Weddings: Can be arranged

Rates/Packages: From $340 per couple, per night including breakfast; Romance Package from $285 includes breakfast in bed, flowers, and champagne (minimum 2 nights' stay)

Payment/Credit Cards: Most major

Deposit: Full prepayment is required 35 days prior to arrival. Cancellations within the 14-day period will result in a forfeiture equal to the rate of the first night

Government Taxes: Included

Service Charges: Included

Entry Requirements for U.S. Citizens: Passport

Note: Closed November–March

THE GROVE
England

If an eighteenth-century grand country house that was once home to the Earls of Clarendon can be called fun and funky, the designers of The Grove have managed to do this. Opened in 2003 as a resort, you couldn't ask for a better setting. Meadowlands, wetlands, lakes, and rolling hills and glades spread out below and around this impressive brick estate. There is an enormous walled garden, greenhouses, golf course, outdoor pool, and spa with a stunning black mosaic indoor pool.

But for the moment, it is the interior decor that can send you over the top. If you expect grand traditional furnishings—crystal chandeliers, gilt mirrors, oil paintings of stiff old ancestors—you're in for a surprise. Perhaps shock is the better word.

For starters, the lobby is modern in feeling and it's only when you actually take time to look around that the unusual artwork everywhere starts to catch your eye. Globe purple allium are casually arranged in black cone-like glass vases and sit in a row on a long glass table; a period chair upholstered in blue silk sits against the wall; and a blue crystal chandelier twinkles overhead. Floors are darkly varnished wood; walls are painted a deep eggplant/black.

Everywhere there are contrasts: traditional pieces with a twist juxtaposed with contemporary pieces. Look outside and you'll see metal hoops set on end on the grounds with tiny metal men balancing inside, a motif that is repeated in shadowbox art on a much smaller scale. Giant acorns sit randomly under a tree and bursts of spidery glass lights on top of stakes stick up in the gardens like pointy flowers.

The decor continues to be playful yet at the same time sophisticated in a series of connecting rooms. Giant cobalt blue urns sit on a table behind a blue upholstered, elaborately carved Victorian sofa against a backdrop of black columns, black walls, and white moldings. Comfy red velvet sofas form a seating group against walls of curved mirrors, while a row of tall white vases parade along a ledge, softly lit by a pinky glow; the neutral-hued reception area is enhanced by a curved glass table topped by several clear glass globes of varying size holding live hibiscus blossoms. Stools or "tables" of wood stumps sit next to a stark metal sculpture resembling a plant stake, and glass vases of lilies sit on a beautiful polished period wood chest of drawers.

Getting off the elevator in the older part of the mansion, you are greeted by narrow halls that wind and twist around corners and are hung with heavy black velvet drapes with gold borders. Wall lights that look like long witches' brooms hung upsidedown emanate just enough light to cast shadows. Call it spooky, call it creepy, call it fun, call it sexy. It's all in how you see it. (Some say there are ghosts here, but friendly ones.)

Pushing aside the drapes, you open the door to your room, entering another world, almost like a secret hideaway. Room #40 is all creamy with a chrome and lucite four-poster king bed draped with white gauzy fabric. There is a mirror-fronted armoire, white sofas, and chairs arranged around a fireplace. Black pillows and a brown throw accent the whiteness of the room. The huge bathroom has both a large shower and a footed tub sitting in the center.

Another room features a chrome, lucite, and black four-poster bed with posts topped by ostrich feathers. Black filmy drapes can be drawn around the bed, enveloping you in a dark cocoon; a large flashy poppy painting dominates the wall. Rooms in the newer West Wing are quieter, more conservative with a minimalist flair. (The West Wing contains a conservatory and an orangery, as well as conference facilities.)

All rooms come with 32-inch or 42-inch wall-mounted plasma TV screens, DVD and CD players, designer linens, air-conditioning, high-speed Internet and e-mail access; many have balconies or terraces, fireplaces, and tubs for two.

Meals are served in the Glasshouse where the buffet offers a wonderful assortment of international cuisine from sushi to pasta. You can also try Colette's, an elegant a la carte restaurant; the Stables, located adjacent to the pro shop; and the Potting Shed, open in-season near the pool. Drinks are served in the Glasshouse Bar, the Drawing Rooms, and the Stables Bar.

On the grounds is a beautiful golf course designed by Kyle Phillips whose last project, the Kingsbarns at St. Andrew's, Scotland, was voted one of the Top Fifty courses in the world. It is managed by Troon Golf, a company that really knows how to make a golf course and facilities work (it manages more than 150 golf courses around the world). The track has interesting water features and dog legs, as well as carries over wetlands. The clubhouse incorporates the former stables and there is a large terrace dining area, changing areas, restaurant, and pro shop. I found the pro and his staff to be extremely helpful and friendly. As Troon has on staff a full-time agronomy expert, you can expect the course grounds to be in superb shape. They are.

The Sequoia, a day spa with thirteen treatment rooms, includes a VIP suite for couples, therapeutic saline water vitality pool, large indoor pool, fitness studio, aerobic studio, Jacuzzi, and relaxation rooms. In-room massages are available.

Since The Grove is so new, it is still evolving. For example, because of its sheer size both inside and outside, better signing for getting around would be welcome. The outdoor pool is quite a walk from the hotel; you have to cross the parking lot and go into the walled garden so you'll need to bring everything you need on the first run. The children's center is also at the far corner of the property.

There is some talk about putting a restaurant in the greenhouse near the pool, which seems like an excellent idea. Still, for all its idiosyncrasies, The Grove is a refreshing addition to the English hotel scene, one that people of any age should enjoy, especially those who love the unexpected.

As Martin Hulbert of the design firm Fox Linton Associates put it, "We wanted to create something fantastic but also familiar, almost as though the family had never left the house. This is informal living—a new take on country house living."

Sure is. This is Groovy Grand at its best.

The Grove

Location: Set on 300 acres of private Hertfordshire parkland just 40 minutes from Central London

Romantic Highlights: Late night cocktail in the Library; four-poster beds topped with ostrich feathers; fireplaces; strolls in the Walled Garden

Address/Phone: Chandler's Cross, Hertfordshire, England WD3 4TG; 01923–807807; fax 01923–221008

E-mail: info@thegrove.co.uk

Web Site: www.thegrove.co.uk

U.S. Reservations: Leading Hotels of the World (800) 223–6800

Owner/Manager: Matthew Dixon, general manager

Arrival/Departure: Most arrive by private car or taxi; pickup can be arranged

Distance from Heathrow Airport: 30–40 minutes

Accommodations: 211 guest rooms, 16 suites

Most Romantic Room/Suite: Numbers 40 and 26 in the older part of the building

Amenities: Hair dryer, in-room safe, designer toiletries, bathrobes, plasma screen TV, air-conditioning, DVD/CD, high-speed Internet and e-mail access, data-ports, ironing facilities, daily newspaper,
24-hour room service, valet parking

Electricity: 220 volts

Sports and Facilities: Championship golf course, Sequoia Spa, two pools, fitness studio, Jacuzzi, tennis courts, walled garden, croquet lawn

Dress Code: Smart casual

Weddings: Yes

Rates/Packages: From £240 (about $450)

Payment/Credit Cards: Most major

Deposit: By credit card

Government Taxes: 17.5 percent

Service Charges: Not included

Entry Requirements for U.S. Citizens: Passport

HARTWELL HOUSE
England

Just because it looks like it would cost a king's ransom doesn't mean it actually does. In fact, Hartwell House, though certainly appealing to the well-heeled, is one of the more reasonably priced Grand Estate–style hotels I've come across. Apparently King Louis XVIII thought so, too. Exiled from France when Napoleon was flexing his muscles, King Louis leased the estate in 1809 at a grand sum of £500 per year.

Large enough to accommodate more than 130 people who came with him to keep him company, Louis made Hartwell House his residence for the next five years. Since that time Hartwell House has been altered by three architects, damaged by fire, and used as a school. Today, after a meticulous restoration by Historic House Hotels, Hartwell House stands as one of Europe's most gracious country house hotels.

Located about an hour's drive from London's Heathrow Airport, Hartwell House lolls in contented splendor amid rolling manicured lawns accented by topiary. Beyond these grounds cows graze peacefully, held back from nibbling the lush lawns by a ha-ha, an "invisible," ditchlike barrier.

Rooms and suites are in the main building as well as in Hartwell Court, a group of charming eighteenth-century coach houses that also contain the Hartwell Spa and a series of meeting rooms.

Although every room is different, each has a sitting area. Some rooms have four-poster canopy beds. Some have fireplaces. All have marvelous bathrooms with all the expected amenities.

Louis's former bedroom, now called the King's Room, looks out over the south lawns and pastures and is almost too opulent to leave. You can perch on the sofa, pour two glasses of sherry from the decanter on the coffee table, sit back, and gaze out over the bucolic scene just outside your high bay windows. Cows find shelter from the sun under groves of trees; two children dash across the lawns to hide behind one of the tall, chipped yew hedges—probably not unlike the scene Louis himself viewed when he had time to muse.

History permeates this room, for peering down on you from their lofty perches on the walls are the life-size oil paintings of some very important-looking aristocrats from King Louis's days.

Although Hartwell's Georgian interiors date from the 1740s, with much use of the ornate rococo style, I did not find the house to be dark or imposing. Decorators have lightened the look with soft pastel colors.

Large mullioned windows let in plenty of light, and ceilings and walls are high. Superb plasterwork details include leaves and flowers in ivory against pale pastel backgrounds on walls and ceilings, and balusters on the unique Jacobean staircase create interest with their wood-carved, not-so-flattering figures of influential people.

The Great Hall, a masterpiece of English baroque design, features an elaborate carved fireplace. Just a few steps away is the oak-paneled bar, where you can sip your Pimms while gazing at original paintings of the eighteenth-century gardens of Hartwell by Spanish painter Balthazar Nebot.

There are three dining rooms, decorated in soft golds and greens, with artfully designed ceilings, chandeliers, and draperies. The library at Hartwell is appointed with many antiques and period pieces, including some objects that were in the original house.

Cuisine, created by Chef Daniel Richardson, includes imaginative dishes such as layered terrine of home-smoked duck and chicken with globe artichokes and truffle dressing; filet of Scottish beef with creamed spinach and celeriac, confit shallots and garlic, a parsley puree, and a Cabernet Sauvignon jus; and three apple puddings: tarte tatin, apple and cider mousse, and crispy apple dishes with sorbet served on lemon custard.

For something more casual there is the Spa Buttery, open for breakfast, lunch, and afternoon tea, and the Spa Bar, open daily until 7:00 P.M.

At Hartwell there is plenty to keep you busy without leaving the grounds. Take time to stroll through their lovely park. It features a number of pavilions and monuments, including a statue of Hercules and an obelisk.

The Hartwell Spa, modeled after an orangery, is just 100 yards from the main building. It has a swimming pool, a steam room, a whirlpool bath, saunas, and a gym, along with the bar and small restaurant—a great place to relax with coffee, breads, and the London Times after an early morning workout. The pool is surrounded by an arcade furnished with comfortable lounges. Treatments include facials, massages, reflexology, aromatherapy, and detoxifying algae wraps.

The rococo-style Morning Room, the Drawing Room, and the Library overlook the gardens. The sunny roof terrace, once used by King Louis's buddies for growing vegetables and keeping rabbits and chickens, gives you a great view of the countryside. Or on a cool day, after a brisk walk, you can retreat to the warmth of the Great Hall and the comfort of the highly plumped couches in front of a crackling fire while you sip a glass of brandy or sherry or a cup of tea. Highly civilized.

Hartwell House makes an excellent base for exploring the English countryside. Within easy driving distance are places like Blenheim Palace, Waddesdon Manor, Claydon House, Windsor Castle, and Stowe Landscape Gardens. The Vale of Aylesbury is picnic country. Ask the hotel staff to pack a picnic lunch for you. They can fill your hamper with good things like smoked salmon and lemon, avocado and prawns, fruits, lobster salad, strawberries and cream, scones, and wines and champagne.

Lord Byron, thinking Louis a bit foolish to leave Hartwell, even if it was to assume his throne, wrote, "Why wouldst thou leave calm Hartwell's green abode . . . Apician table and Horatian Ode?" And the spa wasn't yet built in Louis's day!

Hartwell House

Location: Set on 90 acres in the Vale of Aylesbury, Buckinghamshire, 50 miles northwest of London

Romantic Highlights: Gracious country estate; fireplaces; elegant dining; gardens; serpentine walkways; lake; wonderful spa

Address/Phone: Oxford Road near Aylesbury, Buckinghamshire HP17 8NL, England; 44–1296–747–444; fax 44–1296–747–450

E-mail: info@hartwell-house.com

U.S. Reservations: (800) 98–PRIDE (Pride of Britain)

Owner/Manager: C. A. Jonathan Thompson, director and general manager

Arrival/Departure: Guests can be met by prior arrangement at London Heathrow Airport; nearest rail stations are Aylesbury and Thame & Haddenham Parkway

Distance from London Heathrow International Airport: 35 miles

Distance from London: 50 miles

Accommodations: 30 rooms and suites in the main house; 16 rooms and suites in Hartwell Court

Most Romantic Room/Suite: King's Room (15); Queen's Room (12); in Hartwell Court (46 or 47), a ground-floor suite opens onto a private garden

Amenities: Hair dryer, telephone, TV, bathrobe, toiletries, magnifying mirror, pants presser

Electricity: 240 volts

Sports and Facilities: The Hartwell Spa with pool, whirlpool spa bath, steam room, sauna, treatment rooms, and gym; 2 tennis courts, jogging track

Dress Code: Jackets required (but not ties) evenings in the dining room

Weddings: Small wedding receptions can be arranged

Rates/Packages: Room rates from about £270 (US$486) per couple with early morning tea, service, and VAT. Winter and Spring Champagne Breaks, £340–£540 (US$612–$972) per couple per night (minimum 2 nights), including room, early morning tea, breakfast, dinner, champagne, service, and VAT; Historic House Summer Breaks from £340–£540 (US$612–$972) per couple, including all of the above plus admission to one of the historic properties in the area, such as Blenheim Palace. Spa packages also available. (The hotel welcomes children 8 years of age and older.)

Payment/Credit Cards: Visa, MasterCard

Deposit: Guarantee with credit card

Government Taxes: Included

Entry Requirement for U.S. Citizens: Passport

LE MANOIR AUX QUAT' SAISONS

England

Those who dream of honeymooning in a centuries-old stone manor house and have the wherewithal to pay the bill should head to Le Manoir aux Quat' Saisons. England has a lot of wonderful castles and estate hotels, but you'd have to look far and wide to find a place with as much going for it as this one: romantic rooms, idyllic setting, superb service, convenient location near the Cotswolds and London, plus one of the best restaurants in all the kingdom.

Once a favorite country retreat of Lord Coventry, trusted servant of James I, and a refuge for public officials in high standing, this magnificent estate became a hotel in 1984 when Raymond Blanc opened Le Manoir. During the past few years, the property has been totally refurbished, and a garden wing and two glass conservatory dining rooms have been added.

One of the most unique accommodations, designed by Michael Priest, is located in the fifteenth-century dovecote, a round, stone tower with a conical pointed roof. The bathroom has a huge antique tub on feet that has been painted with fanciful pink and white doves and flowers. A great shower gives you the option of steam superjets coming at you from all sides. A wide, soft pink–carpeted staircase winds up to the second level, where a queen-size bed is topped by "garlands" of white-and-pink fabric swags held aloft by white doves suspended from the ceiling by invisible wires. The thick walls of the tower are painted in a warm yellow and decorated with pretty pictures hanging from wide pink ribbons. There are also a skirted dressing table, a cabanalike pink-and-white-striped tented "closet," and a small leaded window opening onto the gardens. The only downside of this blissful romantic bower is its size—it's a bit tight; other suites are roomier. But for sheer romance this is a honeymoon favorite.

Hollyhock is in the main building and was the bedroom of one of the former owners of the estate. It is extremely spacious, furnished with a couch, chairs, dressing table, desk, coffee table, and large, canopied bed. A number of leaded windows open onto the courtyard. Also popular are the two-story garden suites, Lacy and Peony, which have a sitting room on the lower level along with a furnished patio; the bedroom is upstairs. All are exquisitely decorated with a combination of traditional English furniture, antiques, artwork, chintz, and French accents.

New rooms arranged around a garden courtyard combine clean contemporary lines with antique accents. Broad bands of off-white textures wrap around walls, mirrored tables and twentieth-century artwork complement hand-hewn beams and geometrical tapestry carpets.

Flowers are lavishly spread through the public areas and guest rooms. An in-house florist has her own cutting garden and flower house tucked into the corner of the property. A recent addition to the hotel, a Japanese garden, may seem a bit out of sync with the English gardens, but somehow it fits. A delicate mist of water falls from hidden places between the trees that overhang the pond, and a Japanese teahouse welcomes those who want to stop and be soothed.

Throughout the grounds you'll find a number of original sculptures. A bronze work of birds rising through the reeds is particularly appealing. Many are for sale, as the gardens serve as an excellent showcase for artists such as Judith Holmes Drewry and Lloyd Le Blanc. Prices range from about $300 to more than $50,000.

Walk through the three acres of vegetable gardens and you'll begin to understand why the food here is so good. The thirty or so chefs who prepare the meals each day use only the freshest of ingredients. Baby zucchini picked just minutes before serving, with blossoms still attached (to stuff with crabmeat and truffles); beetroot, runner beans, artichokes, leek, spinach, tomatoes—more than one hundred varieties of vegetables, herbs, and fruits planted here supply the hotel with most of its produce. Meat comes from a local butcher just down the road. The hotel has expanded its kitchen and restaurant facilities, adding a patisserie and bakery, a new cookery school, and a cocktail bar. Take a peek in the kitchen, and on the shelves you'll see huge glass jars filled with plums, cherries, raspberries, and other fruits.

But having the right ingredients is just the beginning of the road leading to a Michelin two-star rating. It takes a great chef like Raymond Blanc to complete the picture: Blanc's list of credits fill a page and more. His kitchen, the heartbeat of the hotel, turns out creations that not only look like works of art but titillate taste sensations you never knew you had. Your meal may also seem to be priced like an art object (hors d'oeuvres such as pressed duck confit and foie gras in a truffle gelée costs about $36; entrees such as pan-fried wild salmon fillet on a sorrel sabayon will set you back about $47; homemade sorbets on a waffle "painter's palette" cost around $23), but look at it this way: Sure it costs a lot, but here you're not just paying for dinner, you're investing in a delectable memory guaranteed to last a lifetime. If you come to the hotel and can't afford to try the restaurant, you might as well go somewhere else.

Meals are served in three different dining rooms: the original one and two new conservatory rooms, which are pleasant and pretty year-round.

Lest you be tempted to simply loll on the grounds and take in the never-ending vistas of pure English countryside, there is a croquet court and a garden courtyard, enclosed by hedges. You can go biking, walking, or fishing or arrange with the concierge to play golf or go horseback riding. And Le Manoir is in a great location for exploring the Cotswolds, Oxford, and other historic and interesting places, such as Blenheim Palace, the Royal Shakespeare Theatre, and Windsor Castle.

Le Manoir aux Quat' Saisons combines the country charm of merry old England, the cuisine of France, and the technical expertise of today's engineering: a real winner! Now if the price of a room here in 1474—about 95 cents for a week—could be matched today, you'd really be in heaven.

Le Manoir aux Quat' Saisons

Location: In a small country village between the Chilterns and the Cotswolds

Romantic Highlights: Cocktails on the terrace overlooking the meadows and gardens; a stroll through the tranquil Japanese gardens; sleeping in a round, stone, medieval dovecote

Address/Phone: Church Road, Great Milton, Oxford OX44 7PD England; 44–1844–27–8881; fax 44–1844–27–8847

E-mail: info@blanc.co.uk

Web Site: www.manoir.co.uk

U.S. Reservations: Relais & Châteaux, (800) RELAIS–8

Owner/Manager: Raymond Blanc, chef-patron; Tom Lewis, general manager

Arrival/Departure: Pickup at London's airports can be arranged; from Heathrow via private limousine (about $135 per car); from Gatwick Airport (about $235); helipad on grounds

Distance from London Heathrow International Airport: 40 miles (under 1 hour); Gatwick, 55 miles (1½ hours)

Distance from Oxford: 8 miles south

Accommodations: 32 rooms and suites

Most Romantic Room/Suite: The 2-story Dovecote Suite, built in a fifteenth-century dovecote; Hollyhock, a spacious room with a four-poster bed in the main building; and the 2-story suites in the new garden wing, Lacy and Peony

Amenities: Hair dryer, TV, telephone, radio, terry robes, sewing kit, heated towel bar, bidet, double sinks, toiletries, magnifying mirror, full-length mirror, padded hangers, trouser press; daily newspaper, fresh fruit,

Madeira, mineral water, 24-hour room service, fresh flowers, VCR on request

Electricity: 220/240 volts

Sports and Facilities: Latex tennis court, croquet, pool, bicycles, walking trails, fishing; riding and golf nearby

Dress Code: Country elegant

Weddings: Can be arranged; gardens and terraces make lovely setting

Rates/Packages: £465–£895 (US$888–$1,700) per couple per night for a suite; £275–£395 (US$525–$754) per couple per night for a room; rates include a French breakfast.

Payment/Credit Cards: Most major

Deposit: $150 per couple per night; cancel 2 weeks prior to arrival date for full refund

Government Taxes: Included

Service Charges: Included

Entry Requirements for U.S. Citizens: Passport

CHÂTEAU DE LA CHÈVRE D'OR

France

For pure romance you can't beat it. Perched on the rocks of the ancient hilltop village of Eze, this Relais & Châteaux property is a jewel. Château de la Chèvre d'Or appears to be carved into the rocky side of a cliff, suspended between sea and sky and awash in romance and mystery. From your balcony poised 1,200 feet above the sea, you can see far out to the Mediterranean. To your right are the lights of Nice, and the beaches and misty piece of land, long a playground of the smart and stylish, called Cap Ferrat; somewhere out to the left is Monte Carlo. It all spreads out below you, this feast of

international chic, which is, in fact, but a few minutes down the hill.

But caught up here in your own hideaway away from it all, you may never want to leave this little piece of heaven.

The hotel is not far from the entrance to Eze Village, which is a good thing since no cars are allowed in the small town. You'll park (or take a taxi) to the entrance and walk up to the hotel with help from the staff with your bags.

From its lofty rock pedestal, Eze, a twisty, rocky, little place that 1,000 years ago was designed for horse and donkey traffic and quite certainly not for cars, consists of narrow cobblestone alleys banked by artsy little shops, multilevel terraces, clouds of bougainvillea tumbling over the rocks, and brilliant seascapes framed by ancient stone arches.

The furnishings and appointments of the Chèvre d'Or are far from medieval. Canopy beds, fireplaces, Oriental carpets, heavy beamed ceilings, crystal chandeliers, wrought-iron trim, and French doors opening onto private terraces or balconies cast their spell.

Each of the thirty-three rooms and suites is different. Some are located in the mansion itself, others are tucked away in separate buildings that, with their rugged stone walls, arches, winding steps, tile, and billowing flowering vines, appear to have been here for hundreds of years. Which they have.

Fill your en-suite marble Jacuzzi with bubbles, light the candles, open the Cristal, and slip into the water to soak and soothe in sensuous pleasure; gaze out to the sea and the stars and the lights of the Riviera. Later light the fire and cuddle up.

The swimming pool is set in a flower-filled courtyard overlooking the sea—pure joie de vivre.

French cuisine reigns at La Chèvre d'Or gourmet restaurant where the food is as special as the mind-blowing setting. Dishes are so artfully presented you won't know whether to eat them or paint them. Rich, sensual chocolate desserts are guaranteed to add to your love handles. For more casual fare try Le Grill du Château for a quick lunch. The bar-lounge features stone walls, large fireplace, and a lovely medieval-style beamed ceiling.

The whole world of the French Riviera is minutes away. Try your luck at the Monte Carlo casino, swim and sun on the beach at Nice, shop in the stylish boutiques and speciality shops, play golf, tour the palace of Monaco's royal family, and visit towns along the Riviera and in Provence like Antibes, Mougins, Cagnes sur-Mer, and Vence. It's magic.

Château de la Chèvre d'Or

Location: In the medieval hilltop village of Eze above the Mediterranean between Nice and MonteCarlo

Romantic Highlights: Views, views, views; private balconies overlooking the French Riviera; soaking in a Jacuzzi tub looking out to sea

Address/Phone: Côte d'Azur (Moyenne Corniche), Rue du Bani, 06360 Eze-Village, France; 33–492–106–666; fax 33–493–410–672

E-mail: reservation@chevredor.com

Web Site: www.chevredor.com

U.S. Reservations: (800) RELAIS–8 (735–2478)

Owner/Manager: Thérèse Blay, general manager

Arrival/Departure: By taxi available at airport

Distance from Nice Côte d'Azur Airport: About 12 miles (30 minutes)

Distance from Nice: 10 miles (15 minutes)

Accommodations: 33 rooms and suites

Most Romantic Room/Suite: La Suite, an elegant gold-and-white confection with glass window walls and marble whirlpool for two overlooking the sea, marble floors, Oriental carpets, and hand-painted ceilings; suites overlooking sea

Amenities: Air-conditioning, toiletries, hair dryer, TV, telephone, minibar, safe, bathrobes

Electricity: 220 volts

Sports and Facilities: Pool, fitness center, free access to the Borfiga Tennis Club (five-minute walk), golf and beaches nearby

Dress Code: Casually elegant; jackets preferred for men at dinner in La Chèvre d'Or restaurant

Weddings: Can be arranged

Rates/Packages: €260–€1,650 (US$337–$2,062) low season—March, April, November; €370–€2,550 (US$462–$3,187) high season—Easter and from May to end of October; per couple, including taxes and service

Payment/Credit Cards: Most major

Deposit: 1 night

Government Taxes: 1 euro (US 94 cents) per person, per day city tax

Service Charges: Included

Entry Requirements for U.S. Citizens: Passport

Closed: Late November–early March

CHÂTEAU EZA

France

Like the legendary Camelot, Château Eza stands in a medieval hilltop village awash in romance and mystery. But while King Arthur's domain was an invention of British folklore, this exquisite, intimate hotel tucked away in a 1,000-year-old fortress village is very real. Modern-day Lancelots and Guineveres will love this castle of stone, the former residence of the Swedish royal family.

Try your luck at the Monte Carlo casino, spend the day at the Nice beach, shop where the beautiful people shop, play golf, and visit small towns and markets such as Antibes, Mougins, Cagnes-sur-Mer, and Vence.

Narrow stone passages and walkways lead to ten guest accommodations. All have modern conveniences such as air-conditioning and fine baths, and the rooms are enhanced by charming fireplaces, stone walls, beamed ceilings, balconies, and the pièce de résistance: the views.

Each room is thematically different: There is a quaint room perched on the cliff's edge overlooking the mountains, and there is an intimate, romantic room with a canopy bed, fireplace, and balcony as well as a very grand Louis XVI chamber with a separate dressing area fit for a queen. La Suite du Château, a three-room suite with a floral and ivy theme, has a bedroom with loft, sitting room, separate dressing room, private terrace with outdoor Jacuzzi, and spectacular sea view.

Another suite is especially dramatic, with high ceilings, arches, columns, and an enormous iron bed. Take your pick! All the rooms were recently renovated.

Although there are no sports facilities on the property, within the walled city of Eze there is the Jardin Exotique, filled with cacti as well as gift shops, art galleries, and restaurants.

Dinner at Château Eza is served in either the indoor glass dining room or outdoor terrace atop the cliffs. It is considered one of the most romantic dining spots in the world.

The wine list is extensive. Although dinner for two with wine is on the high side of $220, a special lunch menu with wine costs about $80.

The staff at the hotel is efficient, friendly, and helpful; restaurant service, excellent.

You would need a time machine to travel back more than a thousand years to the medieval era—unless, of course, you chose to visit Château Eza. Here, on a spellbinding cliff overlooking the Mediterranean, all the romance and chivalry of King Arthur is yours, albeit for the modern-day equivalent of a king's ransom.

Situated midway between Nice and Monte Carlo, Château Eza is conveniently located on the Moyenne Corniche (the middle road running between the two cities), allowing guests easy access to the many attractions of the famous Côte d'Azur—provided they can tear themselves away from the breathtaking views.

Château Eza

Location: Situated inside the medieval village of Eze on the Moyenne Corniche between Nice and Monaco, on the Côte d'Azur

Romantic Highlights: Seductive views of the Mediterranean, the stars and lights of the Riviera and Cap Ferrat; regally appointed themed rooms; champagne breakfasts on your balcony; narrow cobblestone pathways winding between ancient stone buildings draped in masses of bouganvillea

Address/Phone: 06360 Eze Village, Côte d'Azur; France; 33–493–411–224; fax 33–493–411–664

E-mail: info@chateaueza.com

Web Site: www.chateaueza.com

U.S. Reservations: (800) 507–8250

Owner/Manager: Terry Giles, owner; Stephen Chaline, general manager

Arrival/Departure: By taxi, available at airport or private transfers on request

Distance from Nice-Côte d'Azur Airport: 12 miles

Distance from Nice: 8 miles (15 minutes)

Accommodations: 4 suites; 6 guest rooms

Most Romantic Room/Suite: Le Suite du Château

Amenities: Air-conditioning, safe, TV, DVD player, Wi-Fi, telephone, hair dryer, toiletries, bathrobes, minibar

Electricity: 220 volts

Sports and Facilities: Beach 10 minutes away

Dress Code: Men should wear a jacket at dinner.

Weddings: One of their specialties

Rates/Packages: Rates per couple: about $507–$870; suites $870–$1,015 including breakfast, service charge, and taxes.

Payment/Credit Cards: Most major

Deposit: 1-night deposit; for stays 3 nights or more, 50 percent deposit; 15-day cancellation notice for full refund less cancellation fees

Government Taxes: Included

Service Charges: Included

Entry Requirements for U.S. Citizens: Passport

Closed: Mid-November–mid-December

DOMAINE DES HAUTS DE LOIRE

France

A long drive winding through tall trees to the Domaine des Hauts de Loire sets the tone of this nature-oriented Relais & Château hotel. Before you have even reached the entrance, you see swans and ducks gliding on a small lake and trails that invite you to walk deep into the woods. Gardens and terraces surround the main lodge and the carriage house. A pointed tower rises above the three-storied stone building; gables and French doors let in plenty of light; and an orangery and greenhouses are located near the lake. A bench, perfect for two, sits on the bank close to the water.

Close to historic chateaux and castles, such as Chambord and Chenonceaux, and in the heart of the Loire wine country, Domaine des Hauts de Loire makes an ideal base for exploring the region, its gardens, country markets, and villages. All around the property are neat farms and small villages.

As grand estates go, the Domaine des Hauts de Loire is fairly modest in its appointments. The flower arrangements are casual, perhaps a bouquet of cosmos or peonies, and the entrance is relatively small. Yet the polished floors in the sitting room, the silk tapestry-upholstered chairs, gold-leaf mirrors, long draperies, Oriental carpets, and crystal chandeliers leave no doubt that this is a place where people come who expect the best.

Rooms and suites are located in the main lodge and an adjacent carriage house, my choice for those looking for privacy and luxury. Unique room features include skylights, beams, terraces, sitting areas, and antique armoires. A circular staircase curls up through the tower to the upper floors in the lodge.

Once the hunting lodge for the Count of Rostaing, the hotel, which was constructed in several stages between 1845 and 1865, is built on the site of a feudal castle. The castle once covered 1,400 acres. Much of that land is now occupied by small working farms.

The restaurant is characterized by massive beamed ceilings, a series of French doors leading out to the stone terrace where meals are served in the warmer months, and a fireplace. Many come here from Paris and the countryside to enjoy the cuisine, which is certainly up to Relais & Châteaux standards in not only its food but its service as well. I particularly enjoyed the chestnut soup with mushrooms, scallops, and peas; and the Viennoise de Saint Jacques aux Poires. Portions for the five-course meal are not overwhelming, making it possible to savor each thing you eat.

The wineries, vast green fields, rivers, chateaux, and castles of the Loire Valley are all around. I suggest you drive along Route N152, which runs atop a levy-like embankment along the Loire River, and follow the wine route, which winds through the vineyards in the high land above the river. You'll pass huge fields of corn, kale, wheat, and cabbage, and skirt neat little villages such as Cangey and Le Clos Lucé where narrow streets twist around old stone buildings and lace curtains hang in the windows.

You'll see trees filled with mistletoe hanging like giant pom-poms (as if you needed an excuse to kiss), and you'll pass many lovely chateaux and wineries, many with cellars cut deep into the rock.

From the early Middle Ages through the eighteenth century, drawn by the beauty of the countryside, the mild climate, and rich river valley, French royalty came to the Loire valley to build magnificent castles, many as vacation retreats. You'll find more than fifty castles strung out along the 150-mile stretch of the Loire from Angers to Orléans. For example, there is the grand Angers with its seventeen stone towers and moats, the sixteenth-century Azay-le-Rideau, Blois, Chambord, Villandry, lovely Chenonceaux, which spans the Cher River, and Usse, a fairy-tale castle of white towers, which is said to have inspired the legend of Sleeping Beauty.

While in the Loire Valley, browse through one or more of the outdoor markets. Each town seems to have its own market day, so stop by a visitor's center for more information.

Domaine des Hauts de Loire

Location: In a grove of trees in the Loire Valley

Romantic Highlights: Private patio overlooking the countryside; dinner on the stone terrace by the swan-studded pond; long walks on paths in the woods

Address/Phone: 41150 Onzain, France; 33–0254–20–7257; fax 33–0254–20–7732

E-mail: hauts.de.loire@wanadoo.fr

Web Site: www.domainehautsloire.com

U.S. Reservations: (800) 735–2478

Owner/Manager: Pierre-Alain Bonnigal, general manager

Arrival/Departure: Most arrive by private car. For those who wish to come by air, there is a helicopter landing pad on the property.

Distance from Charles de Gaulle Airport: 120 miles; 2½ to 3 hours

Distance from Tours train station: 24 miles

Accommodations: 35 rooms and suites

Most Romantic Room/Suite: The rooms and suites in the Carriage House are more private and better appointed. Number 27 on the 2nd floor comes with a large bath with a skylight; 38, a somewhat smaller coral-hued room, has great beam features and a skylight; 39 decorated in red-and-white toile, has beams, skylights, a small balcony, and tub for two; 35 is very large and comes with a balcony overlooking the gardens, a separate sitting area, and tub for two; and 40, a gold-and-white room on the ground floor has a private entrance, sitting room, terrace, and very comfortable sitting area.

Amenities: Direct-dial phones, television, minibar, air-conditioning (some), terry robes, turndown service, full-length mirror, hair dryer, fine toiletries, in-room safe

Electricity: 220 volts

Sports and Facilities: Tennis court, outdoor pool, fishing pond, walking trails, bicycle paths. Golf and ballooning can be arranged.

Dress Code: Smart casual for lunch; coat and tie appreciated for dinner

Weddings: Yes

Rates/Packages: From about $110

Payment/Credit Cards: Most major

Deposit: By credit card; Rooms are guaranteed until 6:00 P.M. unless a deposit has been paid to hold the reservation.

Government Taxes: Included

Service Charges: Included

Entry Requirements for U.S. Citizens: Passport

Note: Closed December 1–mid-February

HOTEL DE MOUGINS

France

Just down the road from the Provençal town of Mougins, it looks like it has been here forever: an old farmhouse surrounded by four country villas in the midst of fragrant flower gardens. In reality, Hotel de Mougins is new, making it the best of both worlds. Warm terra-cotta stucco walls and arches, red-tile roofs, bougainvillea spilling over trellises, and courtyard gardens lend a sense of timeliness, yet modern amenities like state-of-the-art bath and light fixtures, direct-dial telephones, in-room safes, and coral marble vanities are incorporated throughout this charming boutique hotel.

If quality is in the details, this property is top of the line. Tile floors, white antiqued furniture; Provençal fabrics in yellows, blues, and corals; wicker and wrought iron; French doors leading to balconies; built-in armoires; and white-tiled showers make the rooms extremely pretty and comfortable. From your balcony you see peaks of cypress poking up into the sky, groves of mimosa trees, fig trees, bursts of lavender and rosemary, and stone walls.

There is a lovely pool, a number of gardens, and an outdoor patio under the trees furnished with wrought-iron furniture.

Coté Jardins offers both superb food and romantic, intimate ambience. You can dine under century-old ash trees, at poolside, or in the blush-colored dining room. Start the day with one of their flaky croissants, fresh fruit, and a cup of café au lait. From here it only gets better. Dinner might be tendresse de filet de boeuf aux mangues en parfum de poivre de Séchuan (beef filet), croquettes de céleri, with crème brûlée aux gousses de vanille for dessert. In the summer there are two bars and Le Pool-house, an outdoor grill by the pool.

Gravel paths lead from the main building, through the gardens, and to the pool and rooms, a bit hard on heels and difficult going for wheelies; still, the pebbles are so in keeping with the area, I'm not sure I would want to see anything different. After all, you can always wear flat shoes and call a valet for your luggage.

There is a tennis court on site and a choice of several excellent golf courses close by. Next door is the celebrated Golf Country Club de Cannes-Mougins, an easily walkable, scenic, rolling course with a sixteenth- century clubhouse occupying what was once an olive oil production facility.

The Royal Mougins Golf Club, a dramatic course with all the bells and whistles, five tee boxes, lots of bunkers, water, and elevations, undulates and rolls with great abandon. Holes with names like Angel's Dive, Le Lac, and Roller Coaster give you a fair idea of what to expect.

One day, make sure you visit Mougins, a lovely, hilly little town filled with delightful restaurants, art studios, craft shops, galleries, and gift stores.

Hotel de Mougins

Location: Set into the hills surrounding Cannes in the residential district of Saint-Basile

Romantic Highlights: The scent of mimosa and lavender drifting over the gardens; views of the countryside over tall cypresses from your terrace; breakfast on your patio

Address/Phone: 205 Avenue du Golf, 06250 Mougins, France; 33–92–92–1707; fax 33–92–92–1708

U.S. Reservations: (800) 888–4747

E-mail: info@hotel-de-mougins.com

Web Site: www.hotel-de-mougins.com

Owner/Manager: Alain Delporte, general manager

Arrival/Departure: Arrangements can be made for pickup at the Nice-Côte d'Azur Airport.

Distance from Nice-Côte d'Azur Airport: 10 miles

Distance from Cannes: 3 miles

Accommodations: 48 rooms, 2 junior suites, 1 suite

Most Romantic Room/Suite: Suites

Amenities: Air-conditioning, hair dryer, safe, pants press, toiletries, minibar, reading lamps, full-length mirror, telephones, satellite TV

Electricity: 220 volts

Sports and Facilities: Tennis, pool, *boules;* golf next door

Dress Code: Informal

Weddings: Can be arranged

Rates/Packages: €160–€240 (US$208–$312) including buffet breakfast per room; €110–€150 (US$143–195) per person for room, breakfast, and lunch or dinner, double occupancy

Payment/Credit Cards: Most major

Deposit: Credit card

Government Taxes: Included

Service Charges: Included

Entry Requirements for U.S. Citizens: Passport

HOTEL PLAZA ATHÉNÉE
France

From the champagne raspberry specialty drink, red toy bear, red umbrellas in La Cour Jardin, and red geraniums in the window boxes, red reigns at the Hotel Plaza Athénée on Twenty-fifth Avenue, Montaigne, where beautiful people stride into the lobby carrying shopping bags from Dior, Chanel, Pucci, and other haute-couture houses, which are all within walking distance. Here people check in with luggage from Louis Vuitton and Goyard, where tiny soft leather draw-string purses hover around $100. What an address!

For more than ninety years, the hotel has welcomed the Vanderbilts, the Rockefellers, Jackie Kennedy, and CoCo Chanel. But not to rest on its past, the Hotel Plaza Athénée is one of Paris's most hot hotels. A refurbishment in 1999 and 2000 married the traditional classical style of the hotel to modern technology and current fashion trends.

Essentially the Plaza is designed in two distinct styles: The first six floors are decorated in Louis XV, Louis XVI, and Regency styles. Fabrics re-created from eighteenth-century designs, flowing silk curtains, stylish furniture reproductions in natural wood, marquetry, or stained to coordinate with the room colors, set the mood. Accessories like gilded mirrors, period lamps, chandeliers, and oil paintings in keeping with the period enhance the elegant look.

Designed to attract a hip, younger clientele, Plaza Athénée swung from Louis XV splendor to the chic, sleek Art Deco style when it redecorated the top two floors in keeping with the rebirth of this 1920s movement. Fun, sometimes bright, sometimes muted but usually accented by black, the fashionable rooms are light and clean. Furniture is streamlined wood and glass; fabrics recall prints of the period, including some leopard-motifs. All rooms come with modern technology, including Internet and e-mail access via television, cable channels, VCR and CD players, two-line telephones, and fax modems. You can choose feather, foam, or ergonomic pillows from a pillow menu and decide whether you prefer a duvet or blanket. The Royal Suite even has a private fitness facility with a view of the Eiffel Tower.

There are five dining venues: Restaurant Plaza Athénée, decorated in the distinctive Louis XV–style where renowned chef Alain Ducasse spins his culinary magic; La Cour Jardin, a popular courtyard restaurant open for lunch and dinner in season; Le Relais Plaza an informal Art Deco–style bistro; and La Galerie des Gobelins, a tea and chocolate lover's promised land; and Le Bar du Plaza Athénée.

At night Le Bar du Plaza Athénée and adjoining La Galerie des Gobelins heats up with movers and shakers and wanna-be-trendsetters who come to see and be seen. Le Bar du Plaza Athénée is a happening place for hip Parisians who gather around the iceberg-like, sandblasted glass bar illuminated with cool blue light or settle into cushy leather club chairs. The director of Le Bar, Thierry Hernandez, has created a superb selection of fantasy drinks like "flower power"—a blue non-alcoholic cocktail with a basis of flower extract topped up with oxygen-enriched water; champagne served in buckets overflowing with blue ice cubes that light up, and stylish "gel" cocktails—a square of delicious spirits presented in much the same way as sushi. The hotel's signature Rose Royale is made with champagne and fresh raspberry purée and the "Bubblegum" is studded with strawberry pieces and pink Malabar chewing gum (very sweet but no, you cannot blow bubbles with it).

The fitness and health center provides massage and beauty treatments and equipment is state of the art with Cybex equipment, a sauna, and a steam room.

Just outside, the beautiful City of Lights is yours to discover. Take shopping. In Paris, shopping is a movable medley of discovery. From an astonishing array of chic boutiques and trendy designer shops to big name haute-couture houses and art galleries, as well as department stores, bookstores, shopping arcades, and food marts. For those who love to shop and browse, Paris is about as good as it gets.

Even with a map, it's easy to lose your way, but who really cares? Wandering through the fashion boutiques of Saint Germain des Prés, the designer workshops of Le Marais, and the "Golden Triangle's" high temple of fashion along Rue du Faubourg Saint-Honoré and Place de la Madeleine, there is hardly any place in Paris where you won't find something irresistible, perhaps a sexy bustier, a whimsical creation from John Galliano, a sophisticated Chanel suit, a Dior dress, Louis Vuitton bag, or a scarf from Hermès.

A whisper of silk in drifts of celadon, ivory, and rose from one of Paris's fine lingerie shops promises close encounters of the right kind. Looking for that little model of the Eiffel Tower, some small crystal baubles, or postcards for the folks at home? You'll find them at the arcade shops along the Rue de Rivoli, a souvenir junkie's paradise. When you crave a croissant, a cafe au lait, a bit of pastry, or something more filling, there's always a cafe or clever little restaurant just around the next corner.

Charge up your batteries for a long leisurely stroll along the Champs Elysées, a broad, tree-shaded boulevard lined by sidewalk cafes, trendy stores, and restaurants. From the Arc de Triomphe at the north end to the Place de la Concorde at the Seine, the festive frenzy spins fast. Check out stores like Naf Naf, Swatch, the Virgin Megastore, and the colorful cosmetic emporium Sephora, with its merry amalgam of every conceivable kind and color of cosmetics. Back at the Plaza Athénée, rub elbows with the rich, the beautiful while sipping a Rose Royale.

Hotel Plaza Athénée

Location: In the heart of Paris just steps from the Champs Elysées and the Eiffel Tower on the chestnut tree–lined Avenue Montaigne, home to haute-couture fashion houses

Romantic Highlights: Sipping a Rose Royale (champagne and fresh raspberry purée) in Le Bar du Plaza Athénée; candlelight dinner in Restaurant Plaza Athénée; views of the Eiffel Tower from your balcony

Address/Phone: 25 Avenue Montaigne, 75008 Paris, France; 33–153–67–6665; fax 33–153–67–6666

E-mail: reservation@plaza-athenee-paris.com

Web Site: www.plaza-athenee-paris.com

U.S. Reservations: (866) 732–1106 or (800) 223–6800

Owner/Manager: Francois Delahaye, general manager

Arrival/Departure: The hotel can arrange a limo transfer or guests can take a taxi.

Distance from Charles de Gaulle Airport: 20 miles (40 minutes)

Accommodations: 187 rooms and suites

Most Romantic Room/Suite: Duplex suite with its own private fitness room, sauna, and a terrace with an amazing view of the Eiffel Tower; the Art Deco Suite with red décor—a favorite among celebs; and the newly refurbished Royal Suite

Amenities: Air-conditioning, hair dryer, telephones, cable TV/VCR, radio, CD player, alarm clock, robes and slippers, designer toiletries, room service, plasma TVs in some suites

Electricity: 220 volts

Sports and Facilities: Fitness center, sauna, massages, Shiatsu, steam room, yoga, tae-bo

Dress Code: Casual to dressy

Weddings: Can be arranged

Rates/Packages: From about $677 per room, per night

Payment/Credit Cards: Most major

Deposit: Guaranteed with credit card

Government Taxes: Most included

Service Charges: Not included

Entry Requirements for U.S. Citizens: Passport

LE MEURICE

France

From the moment you step into the gilded eighteenth-century reception hall enhanced by live orchids and massive flower arrangements, you feel like royalty. After all, this is the hotel where Queen Victoria, the Sultan of Zanzibar, King George VI, and the Grand Duchess of Russia stayed, along with American "royalty" such as Elizabeth Taylor and Richard Burton. Very upper crust.

In the early 1900s the King of Spain, Alphonse XIII, came to stay, bringing his own furniture. Le Meurice was considered the place to stay, especially among prominent artists and intellectuals, a tradition that continues today. Recent guests have included David Schwimmer, Robin Williams, and Liza Minnelli.

In 1998 two of France's most distinguished architects began a two-year renovation project, heading up a group of master artisans numbering more than 500 people. Friezes, plaster ceilings, wall paintings, columns, colorful mosaic floors, glass doors, and other features were restored and rooms were reconfigured to bring Le Meurice back up to the heights it enjoyed for a good part of two centuries.

From the public rooms to the private guest rooms, eighteenth-century elegance is celebrated with lovely crystal chandeliers, rare marbles, high ceilings, tall windows, gilded mirrors, and luxuriously upholstered furniture. Colors throughout are upbeat, sunny yellows, off-whites, rose, salmon, and green, and motifs are primarily floral, a reminder of the Tuileries Gardens just across the street.

There are more than thirty different room and suite designs. For over-the-top accommodations, the kind where heads of state and the impossibly rich stash their Louis Vuittons, there is La Belle Etoile suite built on the seventh floor of the hotel with the largest terrace (2,969 square feet) I've ever seen and 360-degree views of Paris—the Arc de Triomphe, Place de la Concorde, Nôtre Dame, the Opéra Garnier, the Eiffel Tower, the whole city. Simply stunning, especially at night. There are lots of windows, but since they are reflective, your privacy is maintained. The price. Well, on the rate sheet, it states "on request," which you know has to be très cher. It is. About $14,725 per night. But that includes breakfast.

The rooms and suites for less lofty subjects feature five decorative styles: Louis XVI, Empire, Academy (streamlined and business-like), Trianon Gardens, and Parisian Apartments, intimate, dormer-style rooms.

Furnished with authentic antiques and art from Sotheby's and Christie's, rooms feature a lavish use of French and Italian fabrics—at least one hundred yards are used per room. Some rooms have painted ceilings of clouds and sky, marble fireplaces, and canopied beds; all have marble baths. Modern necessities are not forgotten. There are two phone lines with fax and Internet access, and minibars.

Enjoy a light meal or afternoon tea in the light and airy Le Jardin d'Hiver, which glows softly under the Art Nouveau–style glass roof. The blue and yellow decor, leaded glass and mirror doors, potted palms, blue-and-white mosaic floor, nineteenth-century-style tables and chairs and garden ambience evoke the Empress Eugenie–era teas given by Princess Mathilde. Be sure to try the fresh-baked Viennese bread or go for the chocolate breakfast, a study in decadence with chocolate muffins, chocolate cookies, hot chocolate, and more.

More formal meals are served in Le Meurice, which sparkles with two Michelin stars along with Louis XVI–period crystal chandeliers, antique beveled mirrors, tall windows, piles of draperies, wall and ceiling paintings. The china by Limoges is inspired by the mosaic patterns on the floor.

Breakfast features the hotel's famous chariot de confitures made in a traditional manner by Chutelin in Grasse. I especially liked the rose leaf and the pear, which went perfectly with a freshly baked flaky croissant.

Sit in a leather chesterfield armchair and sip champagne in the Fontainebleau Bar or head to the Caudalie Spa for a massage, sauna, soak in the marble Jacuzzi, or a workout on the fancy exercise equipment. Vinotherapy massages are all inspired by grape seed extracts.

I could soak up the art for days, ponder the light filtering through the high windows and flittering off the crystal chandeliers, the sumptuous brocades, the pure luxury of it all, but then just outside the entrance, Paris awaits. Within walking distance you'll find the Louvre, Tuileries Gardens, the Rive Gauche (Left Bank), the Palais Royale, trendy shops including Cartier, Colette, Baccarat, and Lalique as well as those haute-couture greats such as Yves Saint Laurent, Christian Dior, and Chanel.

Le Meurice

Location: Paris overlooking the Tuileries

Romantic Highlights: Candlelight dinner under a painted ceiling of floating angels in a blue sky; chocolate breakfast; Dom Perignon at the bar Fontainebleau

Address/Phone: 228 Rue de Rivoli, 75001 Paris, France; 33–14458–1006; fax 33–14458–1019

E-mail: reservations@meuricehotel.com

Web Site: www.meuricehotel.com

U.S. Reservations: Leading Hotels of the World (800) 223–6800

Owner/Manager: Dominique Borri, general manager

Arrival/Departure: Most arrive by private car or taxi; pickup can be arranged

Distance from Charles de Gaulle Airport: 40 minutes

Distance from Orly Airport: 30 minutes

Distance from Gare du Nord (Eurostar station): 10 minutes

Accommodations: 160 rooms and suites including 25 full suites and 11 junior suites

Most Romantic Room/Suite: Ask for a room overlooking the Tuileries, the Marco Polo Suite, tucked under the eves on the 6th floor is also a kick. Decorated in the style of a tent from the Napoleonic period, fabrics in soft shades of blue are draped from the ceiling and cover the walls. The large open bath features an antique tub.

Amenities: Walk-in closets, separate vanities, air-conditioning, two-line telephone, Internet access, terry robes, turndown service, wet bar and mini-fridge, full-length mirror, hair dryer, 24-hour room service, fine toiletries, in-room safe. Stereo equipment and fax machines on request.

Electricity: 220 volts

Sports and Facilities: Caudalie Spa

Dress Code: Smart casual for Le Jardin d'Hiver; coat and tie preferred for Le Meurice.

Weddings: Yes

Rates/Packages: From about $650 per

room, per night; "Romance in Paris" (about $1,719), includes garden suite accommodations, American breakfast, rosé champagne, pink flowers, pink petits fours, two bathrobes, use of the health club, late check-out

Payment/Credit Cards: Most major

Deposit: By credit card

Government Taxes: Included

Service Charges: Not included

Entry Requirements for U.S. Citizens: Passport

LES HAUTES ROCHES
France

This has to be one of the most unique hotels in the world. The fifteen troglodyte rooms of Les Hautes Roches are actually former cave dwellings carved into a craggy tuffeau cliff facing the Loire. Once thought to house monks from the Marmoutier Monastery, this "castle in the rocks" is now far from primitive thanks to the hard work and dedication of the owner, Philippe Mollard, who turned a tumble-down property into a four-star hotel in 1989.

From 1855 to 1975 le Domaine des Pentes (the original name) served as a winery, producing the Vouvray appellation wines; the rooms were also used to grow mushrooms and store the famous "Lanternois" wine the French writer, Rabelais, favored. Later the property was used as a storage area. It was finally abandoned and wildly overgrown when Mr. Mollard found it and set in motion an extensive renovation.

Today this property is stunning. Rock ceilings, arches, tuff walls, stone fireplaces, and deep-set windows are juxtaposed against drapes of flowing chintz and brocade in cheerful colors of golds, reds, and yellows. King-size beds crowned with silk, paintings in gold frames, fine linens, and antiques are all very trendy, enough so to be featured in a Fox network special.

Each guest room is different, twelve are in caves reached by carved stone steps with ornate iron banisters. Some rooms feature large sitting areas, fireplaces, stone ceilings, and canopy beds. The most private room and the one with the best view is at the end, number 16. You have to walk up some steps to get there, but once the views grab you, it will hardly matter.

A restored Renaissance manor house and its modest-sized eighteenth-century castle contains the reception area, dining room, and bar that extends into the cliff. A pool furnished with chaises, chairs and umbrella tables, gardens, and a garden terrace all overlook the river.

Tables in the pretty dining room are set with fine linens, china, crystal, and candles. The cuisine features regional specialties like fresh fish accompanied by a good selection of Loire Valley's finest wines.

You can spend the day relaxing by the pool and gardens, dining on the terrace. But at some point you will want to go exploring. After all, you're in the heart of the Loire wine country. The wineries, vast green fields, rivers, chateaux, and castles of the Loire Valley are all an easy drive from Les Hautes Roche. In fact right next door within walking distance is the Marc

Brédif winery with its mile-long caves where thousands of bottles of wine dating from 1874 are stored.

Roads are good, well marked. I suggest you drive along Route N152, which follows the Loire River—the "Route Historique de la Vallée des Rois (kings)"—with more than forty castles, chateaus, and historic homes. Have a picnic lunch beside the river. You'll find a perfect spot just 4 miles from Onzain. Another good route, the "Route des Vignobles," winds through the vineyards that blanket the higher grounds on both sides of the river.

The 150-mile stretch along the Loire from Angers to Orléans is home to many magnificent castles built by French royalty from the early Middle Ages through the eighteenth century. For a special rush, take a tour of the valley in a hot air balloon.

Les Hautes Roches

Location: In a grove of trees in the heart of the Vouvray vineyards in the Loire Valley, less than a 3-hour drive from Paris

Romantic Highlights: Retreating to your private cave overlooking the Loire; summer dining on the terrace

Address/Phone: 86, quai de la Loire 37210 Rochecorbon, Vouvray, France; 33–0–247–52–8888; fax 33–0–247–52–8130

E-mail: hautesroches@relaischateaux.com

Web Site: www.leshautesroches.com

U.S. Reservations: (800) 735–2478

Owner/Manager: Philippe Mollard, owner; Didier Edon, general manager

Arrival/Departure: Most arrive by car from Paris or Tours. You can also take the speedy TGV train directly to Tours and on arrival rent a car to continue your journey. For those who wish to come by air, there is a helicopter landing pad on the property.

Distance from Charles de Gaulle Airport: 130 miles (about 3 hours)

Distance from Tours train station: 5 miles

Accommodations: 15 rooms

Most Romantic Room/Suite: Room 16 at the end is very private with a good view of the Loire River; also good views from 8–12, 14, and 15.

Amenities: Direct-dial phones, TV, Internet access, hair dryer, fine toiletries

Electricity: 220 volts

Sports and Facilities: Swimming pool, hiking; golf, mountain biking, fishing, hunting, waterskiing, horseback riding, canoeing, kayaking, rafting, and ballooning can be arranged.

Dress Code: Smart casual for lunch; coat and tie appreciated for dinner

Weddings: Yes (during low season only)

Rates/Packages: €130–€260 (from about $190)

Payment/Credit Cards: Most major

Deposit: 1-night deposit guaranteed by credit card

Government Taxes: Included

Service Charges: Included

Entry Requirements for U.S. Citizens: Passport

Note: Closed end of January to end of March

LONGUEVILLE HOUSE

Ireland

Irish eyes smile on those who stay at Longueville House, a lovely manor house hotel located in the southwestern part of the county. This grand creamy pink-hued mansion sits on 500 wooded acres with streams and ponds that create a countryside haven for those who love walking, fishing, and, in the fall, hunting. A listed Heritage Georgian Manor house dating from 1720, Longueville has a magnificent sweeping wooden staircase that goes from the entrance hall to the top rooms on the third floor, and a fabulous dining venue, the Presidents' Restaurant.

Longueville, which is owned and managed by the O'Callaghan family, is definitely a family affair. Aisling, the effervescent and efficient hostess, will greet you warmly along with her husband, William, chef and owner.

Each of the twenty rooms has its own personality. Some have king-size beds with canopies and tufted sofas. Long windows are framed by flowing drapes, and fabrics, wall coverings, and upholstery are fresh and elegant.

Presiding over the kitchen for the well-known Presidents' Restaurant, William O'Callaghan draws on as much locally produced ingredients as possible; most of the dishes Chef O'Callaghan creates in his kitchen come from area farms, rivers, and gardens. Meals are complemented by a selection of wines from Longueville's 150-vintage wine cellar. The warmly romantic restaurant features salmon-colored walls lined with oil paintings. Crystal, candles, and white linens set the mood.

An ornate restored glass conservatory provides another, less formal place to eat. Its tables overlook the river.

In addition to using Longueville as a base to explore scenic southwestern Ireland, the Blackwater River Valley, a fisherman's paradise, is known for its wild salmon and brown trout. Walking trails wind through the property. There are several golf courses nearby including the famous links at Ballybunion.

Longueville House

Location: In the rolling countryside 3 miles west of Mallow overlooking the Blackwater River Valley

Romantic Highlights: Dining by candlelight in a Victorian conservatory; long walks through the gardens and the scenic wooded estate grounds; drinks by a log fire in the elegant dining room

Address/Phone: Mallow, County Cork, Ireland; 353–22–47156; fax 353–22–47459

E-mail: info@Longuevillehouse.ie

Web Site: www.longuevillehouse.ie

U.S. Reservations: (800) 323–5463

Owner/Manager: The O'Callaghan family, owners and innkeepers

Arrival/Departure: Most arrive by car via the N20 highway; transfers can be arranged

Distance from Cork Airport: 28 miles (45 minutes)

Distance from Cork: 22 miles (35 minutes)

Accommodations: 20 rooms and suites including 2 suites, 5 mini-suites, and 13 rooms

Most Romantic Room/Suite: Vineyard Suite, Blackwater Suite

Amenities: Thermostat-controlled heating, hair dryer, iron/ironing board, tea trays, direct-dial phone, satellite TV, toiletries

Electricity: 220 volts

Sports and Facilities: Walking, fishing, shooting (from November–February)

Dress Code: Smart casual

Weddings: Can be arranged and can accommodate 38 guests overnight and cater for events up to 100 guests. All other guests stay in local B&Bs in Mallow town, which is 3 miles away. Current laws do not allow Irish hotels to host wedding services on site, but these can be arranged at a local church or registry office.

Rates/Packages: From €180 (about $242) per room per night, including breakfast

Payment/Credit Cards: Most major

Deposit: By credit card

Government Taxes: Included

Service Charges: Discretionary

Entry Requirement for U.S. Citizens: Passport

Note: Closed February to mid-March

EXCELSIOR PALACE HOTEL
Italy

The Excelsior Palace Hotel is a great find, offering excellent value and service in Rapallo, one of Italy's most popular resort areas. The grand turn-of-the-century Excelsior Palace, set on a piece of prime waterfront land on the Italian Riviera, has been restored and is now an excellent choice for those looking for romantic yet reasonably priced accommodations overlooking the Mediterranean. Once a popular gathering place for the international beau monde, it has welcomed Ernest Hemingway, Rita Hayworth, and Eleanora Duse.

Marble halls are punctuated with huge vases of flowers; a grand health club features spacious granite baths; most of the bedrooms and suites boast balconies and a view of the sea through large sliding glass doors; rooms are more spacious than many of the pricier digs in the area. Furnishings are tasteful, understated, and upbeat, with light-colored print fabrics and white-painted French Provincial–style furniture.

The Yachting Bar and dining rooms flow out on the lovely terrace with its white balustrades, candlelight, and wrought-iron tables and chairs—a perfect place to sip your Pellegrino or Campari while gazing out at the deep blue water and the yachts riding at anchor in Rapallo Bay. Enjoy traditional Italian cuisine in the Lord Byron restaurant and regional and Mediterranean dishes in the Eden Roc. Or venture into historic Rapallo and try one of the many delightfully intimate restaurants; dance the night away at Happening (a disco on the hills above the town) or Villa Porticciolo (a seafront disco); or savor delicious fresh fish at Ristorante Eden.

Hike the trails that wind along the coast and in the national park; take a boat from Rapallo around the peninsula to Camogli, passing Portofino and S. Fruttuoso, and instead of taking the boat back, hike through the park back to the hotel. Explore the caves at Isolona, visit the many shops and galleries in Rapallo and Portofino, and explore ancient castles. The beautiful Ligurian coastline, the Cinque Terre, and Genoa are not far away.

One of the oldest golf courses in Italy is less than a mile from the hotel, and a variety of water sports including waterskiing and scuba diving can be arranged through the concierge. For those who want it both ways, you can stay a few days in the hotel and extend your vacation cruising on a chartered yacht stopping at such ports as Naples, Portofino, Capri, Ischia, and Venice.

Excelsior Palace Hotel

Location: On the Portofino Coast overlooking the Mediterranean

Romantic Highlights: Seaside balconies; boat trips along the coast; Old World elegance

Address/Phone: Via San Michele di Pagana, 8-16035 Rapallo, Portofino Coast (GE) Italy; 39–0185–230–666; fax 39–0185–230–214

E-mail: excelsior@thi.it

Web Site: www.excelsiorpalace.thi.it

U.S. Reservations: Preferred Hotels and Resorts Worldwide (800) 323–7500 and JDB Associates (800) 346–5358

Owner/Manager: Aldo Werdin, general manager

Arrival/Departure: Shuttle service available from Genoa Airport on request

Distance from Genoa Airport: 18 miles; Milan, 90 miles

Distance from Portofino: 3½ miles

Accommodations: 114 rooms; 17 suites; most with sea views

Most Romantic Rooms/Suites: Junior suites

Amenities: Air-conditioning, hair dryer, toiletries, in-room safe, minibar, turndown service, cable TV

Electricity: 220 volts

Sports and Facilities: Beach Club; health and fitness club with indoor heated pool, sauna, steam bath, Jacuzzi, gym with sea views, massages, thalassotherapy, beauty treatments, sunbed; beach, water sports; tennis, golf course, horseback riding, boat excursions, and hiking trails within 1 mile of hotel

Dress Code: Resort casual

Weddings: Can be arranged

Rates/Packages: Room rates from €380 (US$475) per couple per night, including breakfast, taxes, and service charges. Sea, Beauty, and Relax packages available

Payment/Credit Cards: Most major

Deposit: By credit card

Government Taxes: Included

Service Charges: Included

Entry Requirements for U.S. Citizens: Passport

HOTEL DANIELI
Italy

To stay at the superdeluxe Hotel Danieli is to embrace the romantic heart and soul of this unique city of gondolas and canals, flower boxes, and footbridges, cathedrals, and ancient architecture. As with every corner of Venice, every nook and cranny of the Danieli begs to be photographed. The fourteenth-century palace of the Doge Dandolo is the central building of three attached wings that house 233 restored rooms and suites of varying vintage, decor, and views, but all definitely in the deluxe category.

Arriving by private water taxi right to the doorstep of the hotel, you walk into what is now a covered courtyard foyer with a gorgeous, golden stairway leading up to the rooms (elevators, of course, are always there for the travel weary). The lobby is sublime, darkly opulent, and unforgettable, with its marble arches, ornate ceilings, breathtaking Venetian glass chandelier, and huge fireplace. The ghosts of such eminent and historic guests as George Sand, Charles Dickens, and Richard Wagner can easily be conjured up as you sip a drink in the Bar Dandolo.

Right outside the front door is Venice itself. If you haven't already prearranged a package of sight-seeing and excursions, the concierge will be happy to help you arrange a gondola ride, a guided city sight-seeing tour, an excursion to the islands of the lagoon—Murano, Burano, and Torcello—to see the famed Venetian glass being made (with plenty of opportunity to shop), to visit the school of lace-making, and to tour the ancient cathedral of Torcello.

When you want to take a break from sight-seeing, you can spend the afternoon at the world-renowned Venice Lido (beach). A free water taxi takes you over to the Excelsior Lido Hotel to swim and sunbathe at the swimming pool or right on the beach, with its rows of cabanas. You can try your hand at the nearby casino or take in a round of golf.

On more than one morning, you may very well forgo a breakfast served in your room to eat at the hotel's open-air (in good weather) rooftop Terrace Restaurant to take in the early morning Venetian light and the breathtaking views of the lagoon.

Hotel Danieli

Location: Prime location on Venice's famed lagoon next to the Doge's Palace and near the entrance to the Grand Canal. Situated right in the heart of the city, it is a 2-minute walk to St. Mark's Square.

Romantic Highlights: Venice's opulence and history are combined in this authentically elegant Grand Hotel of the world, which once hosted visiting royalty and ambassadors (and continues to do so).

Address/Phone: Riva degli Schiavoni, 4196, 30122 Venice, Italy; 39–041–522–6480; fax 39–041–520–0208

E-mail: danieli@luxurycollection.com

Web Site: www.luxurycollection.com/danieli

U.S. Reservations: (800) 325–3535

Owner/Manager: Starwood Hotels & Resorts

Arrival/Departure: By air to the Marco Polo Airport, just outside of Venice, and then by private water taxi from the airport to the hotel; by train (Santa Lucia Station), then 20 minutes by boat

Distance from Marco Polo Airport: 45 minutes by boat

Distance from Venice Center: In the heart of the city

Accommodations: 233 deluxe rooms of varying vintage, decor, and views, including 11 suites and 197 double rooms

Most Romantic Room/Suite: 6 suites, 5 junior suites, and 52 double rooms are available with wonderful lagoon views

Amenities: Air-conditioning, hair dryer, minibar, shaver outlets, TV with international programs via satellite, direct-dial telephone, toiletries; robes and slippers in all rooms; room service

Electricity: 110/220 volts

Sports and Facilities: In season there are many sporting options on Venice Lido. The concierge can arrange tennis, horseback riding, golf, waterskiing, sailboarding, and yachting. Free boat service to the Lido is available.

Dress Code: Casually smart for daytime; dressier in the evening

Weddings: Can be arranged

Rates/Packages: From €440 (US$550) per couple per night for a luxury romance package including accommodations, breakfast, flowers, and Italian spumante; minimum stay, 2 nights.

Payment/Credit Cards: Most major

Deposit: Guarantee with credit card; cancel up to 24 hours in advance without penalty

Government Taxes: 10 percent

Service Charges: Included (at client's discretion)

Entry Requirements for U.S. Citizens: Passport

VILLA D'ESTE
Italy

The ultimate vacation resort on Lake Como, one of the loveliest lakes in the world, is Villa D'Este. Built as the summer residence of Cardinal Tolomeo Gallio in the sixteenth century, this impressive, neoclassical pleasure palace sits amid twenty-five acres of gardens, manicured lawns, magnolias, and towering trees. Once you pass through the elegant entrance, you will have everything you need to enjoy a relaxed, yet fun-filled honeymoon. In addition to the heart-stopping lakeside setting framed by the high ridges of the mountains, the resort boasts a full range of sports and fitness facilities, several restaurants, and a cozy piano bar.

As you come into the palatial lobby, with its high, vaulted ceiling, graceful white columns, wide double marble staircase, and fine period furniture, you enter another world, where you will be pampered like royalty, but not so much so that it becomes overbearing. The staff here strikes just the right note between service and respect for your privacy.

Each of the 88 spacious rooms and 70 suites and junior suites is different, and many, including those rooms located in the Queen's Pavilion, have balconies overlooking the lake. Rooms are elaborately decorated with rich, jewel-like fabrics and colors. Chandeliers, comfortable uphol-

stered chairs and sofas, luxurious full drapes pulled back with golden cords and brocade ties, Renaissance-style artwork, and plush carpets give you accommodations fit for a king and queen.

Clark Gable, Paul McCartney, Ali McGraw, Woody Allen, Arnold Schwarzenegger, John Cleese, and Carly Simon have all stayed here, along with other notables. It's a good place to unwind and fall in love all over again with the person you care most about.

In 1875 Franz Liszt remarked, "When you write of two happy lovers, let the story be set on the banks of Lake Como." No doubt he had in mind strolls along the shore in the moonlight and serene afternoons lying on the banks when he wrote this. But today this is only part of what you can do here. For active couples there are plenty of options. One of the resort's useful novelties is its large, freshwater pool, which actually floats in the water on its own island, just off the water's edge. There are also an indoor pool and a children's pool as well.

There are eight tennis courts as well as a squash court, waterskiing, sailing, and even hang gliding, along with various sports lessons and clinics scheduled throughout the week. Take a canoe and spend a peaceful afternoon paddling along the waters. If staying fit is on your agenda, you'll find the gym well equipped with the latest exercise and weight-lifting equipment. Or relax in the Turkish baths or saunas and get a soothing massage. Golf enthusiasts can practice their putting on the special green located on the villa grounds and later get in a game at a course just down the road.

All the dining facilities, and there are several options, are oriented toward the lake. In good weather meals can be served outdoors, for example, at the large, open Grill Room, set under a canopy of leafy, ancient plane trees. The walls are dense, green hedges, and the views are of the shimmering lake. At breakfast you can order a specially prepared omelet from the trolley and watch it being cooked or you can ponder your choices from the lavish breakfast buffet. Head to the terrace or sit poolside for lunch and enjoy a selection of fresh fruits, salads, fish, and pastas.

At night the Veranda restaurant raises its windows, which are electronically controlled, to shelter diners from the night breezes and turns up the romance factor with candles, lots of fresh flowers, and soft lights. The presentation of food is a work of art: Grilled salmon is served with red, green, and yellow peppers in the shape of leaves, and a lemon tartlet arrives in a pool of vanilla custard laced by a delicate pinwheel pattern of chocolate and strawberry sauce. You almost hate to stick your spoon into it and disturb the fragile beauty of that confection. But when you do, you'll scrape every last drop from your plate. It's just too good. After dinner, mellow out at the piano bar or dance the night away on the lake terrace.

If you should wish to venture out, you can visit the nearby quaint medieval villages with red-roofed buildings and narrow, winding streets and explore ruins of centuries-old castles and fortresses. One of the best ways to see the area is to take a boat ride around the lake, where you will see spectacular villas.

Villa D'Este

Location: Set on 25 acres on the western shore of Lake Como

Romantic Highlights: Spectacular lakeside setting; floating pool; dancing under age-old trees in the foothills of the Alps; watching the sun set over the lake and the mist waft down from the mountains

Address/Phone: Via Regina 40, 22012 Cernobbio, Lake Como, Italy; 39–031–3481; fax 39–031–348844

E-mail: info@villadeste.it

Web Site: www.villadeste.it

U.S. Reservations: Leading Hotels of the World, (800) 223–6800 or (212) 838–3110; fax (212) 758–7367

Owner/Manager: Jean-Marc Droulers, chairman and CEO; Ezio Indiani, general manager

Arrival/Departure: You can arrange for pickup by the hotel at the airport, but check rates. The resort is easily accessible by car (car rental at airport); helipad at hotel.

Distance from Malpensa Airport: 27 miles (45 minutes); Linate 28 miles (50 minutes)

Distance from Como: 3 miles; Cernobbio is less than 1 mile; Milan, 35 miles

Accommodations: 88 rooms and 70 junior suites. Many have balconies overlooking the water; others face gardens.

Most Romantic Room/Suite: Most of the rooms in the nineteenth-century Queen's Pavilion and suites in the main building overlooking lake

Amenities: Hair dryer, telephone, in-room safe, toiletries, air-conditioning, whirlpool tub, minibar, satellite TV, Internet connection, room service

Electricity: 220 volts

Sports and Facilities: 8 tennis courts (6 clay, 2 manteco), squash court, gym, putting green, jogging route with 15 checkpoints, sauna, Turkish bath, 3 pools (2 outdoor, 1 indoor); waterskiing, sailing, canoeing, sailboarding; golf 20 minutes away; spa with health and beauty treatments

Dress Code: Casual sports clothes during day; evening: jacket and ties required for men in the Veranda Restaurant

Weddings: Can be arranged; outside terrace popular

Rates/Packages: €465–€770

(US$580–$960) per couple per night, including buffet breakfast. "Romantic Stay" from €1,605–€2,244 (US$2,006–$2,805) per couple per night, includes 3 nights' accommodations, breakfasts, 3 dinners or lunches per person, flowers, plus use of most of the sports facilities

Payment/Credit Cards: Most major

Deposit: Guarantee with credit card

Government Taxes: Included

Service Charges: Included

Entry Requirements for U.S. Citizens: Passport

Closed: Mid-November–February

POUSADAS
Portugal

If you ever wondered what it would be like to live like a duke or countess or even a king or queen; to dine in a baronial stone hall, walls hung with priceless tapestries; to gaze from your hilltop terrace over the red-tiled roofs and fields of the world below; or to sleep in a bed topped by a crown of gold and crimson–velvet drapes, then catch the next jet to Portugal and check into a pousada. Dotting the countryside are forty-four pousadas, a network of unique places to stay, created in some of the country's most historic castles, palaces, monasteries, and regional structures. Most occupy the highest sites in their area and boast exceptional views of hills, mountains, lakes, and rivers.

From the Pousada de Sao Teotoio in the north, which is built inside the thirteenth-century fortress town of Valenca, to the cliff-top Pousada do Infanta on the southern coast, the pousadas range from the very opulent, including former castles and convents, to much simpler places chosen for

their exceptional location—perhaps on a lake or overlooking a river valley. Government owned and operated by Enatur, most pousadas average fifteen rooms. Many have swimming pools, some are located in the middle of medieval walled villages; others peer out over the sea.

Pousadas (derived from the Portuguese verb "pousar," to lodge or repose) were created not only to save some of these wonderful buildings but to provide places to stay where travelers are treated as honored guests. For example, there is the small riverside regional Pousada de Vale do Gaio, a modest, peaceful place where you wake to the sound of a cock's crowing and have breakfast on an outdoor terrace overlooking a shimmering river. Then there is the grand Pousada de D. Joao IV, with its age-burnished walls, once a royal convent. Original frescos and wall paintings have been beautifully preserved; rooms are arranged around the interior courtyard gardens.

There is nothing shabby or slipshod about any of the places in the furnishings, linens, toiletries, or service. Everywhere I went I was impressed by the consistency of the amenities and the cuisine, all the more remarkable when you consider that converting a thick-walled monastery to a first-rate hotel could not have been easy. It is obvious that a great deal of money has been spent to do the job right.

Cuisine served in the pousada restaurants includes a combination of regional specialties and continental dishes presented with flair and creativity. Fresh fish, cataplana de mariscos (seafood cooked in a special pan), steamed lobster, fish stew, frango na pucara (chicken cooked in a clay pot), and cozido a portuguesa (meat stew) are particularly tasty.

Here are details about a few of Portugal's pousadas:

Castelo Obidos, Obidos (north of Lisbon). Hugging the edge of the thirteenth-century walled town, this is the smallest of the pousadas and perhaps the most romantic. Three rooms are in tower suites with dramatic views of the countryside. Tapestries, dark-wood antique furniture, candles (electrified), and thick stone walls provide the proper medieval ambience. 9 rooms.

Castelo de Alvito (southeast of Lisbon). This fifteenth-century mellow stone castle with towers, turrets, and ramparts has hosted kings and queens. Now mere mortals can enjoy royal quarters with modern conveniences. The castle has a lofty reception room, stunning swimming pool, amphitheater, and resident brace of peacocks that strut their stuff around the grounds. The dining room serves regional dishes and wines from Alentejo, including oven-roasted fish, and pork with coriander. 20 rooms.

Pousada D. Maria I, Queluz (5 miles from Lisbon). This posh pink-and-white confection was once a residence for the king's court. For a peek at what life was like in the eighteenth century among the rich and titled, just across the street is the Queluz National Palace, with its splendid gardens and museum. The pousada is perfect for those who want to enjoy Lisbon during the day but prefer to escape the hustle-bustle of the city in the evening. The excellent restaurant, Cozinha Velha, is housed in the former royal kitchens. Rooms are spacious and furnished with handsome wood furniture and rich brocades. 24 rooms; 2 suites.

Pousada de Santa Luzia, Elvas (on the border of Spain and Portugal). With its airy and comfortable rooms decorated in light pastel colors and cheery painted furniture, this pousada is a good stopover location for those crossing the Caia border. See the 843-arch Amoreiras aquaduct nearby. Good restaurant and large pool and deck. 25 rooms.

Pousada de Sao Francisco, Beja (southeast of Lisbon). A converted thirteenth-century monastery with a lovely swimming pool, gardens, and tennis court. Restaurant has a deserved reputation for superb fish dishes. 37 rooms.

Pousada de D. Joao IV, Vila Vicosa (east of Lisbon). In the sixteenth-century this richly endowed complex was the Royal Convent of Chagas de Cristo. Many of the original altars, tiling, and artwork have been preserved and incorporated into the public and private rooms. Theme rooms include the Astronomy Room and the Painter's Room. Exceptional fresco of the Last Supper in dining room; after dinner fun in the billiard room. 33 rooms; 3 suites.

Pousada de Rainha Santa Isabel, Estremoz (east of Lisbon close to Spanish border). D. Dinis once lived in this thirteenth-century palace with his wife, Queen Isabel. Today a fine pool with a generous-size terrace and gardens tempt guests to laze the day away, yet there is a lot to see in this walled town. The dining room with its vaulted ceiling has been the setting for many royal meals. 23 rooms; 3 suites.

Pousada de Palmela, Palmela (south of Lisbon). This converted hilltop fortress with stunning views of Lisbon served as the headquarters of the Portuguese Knights of St. James in the thirteenth century. In modern times it has hosted such dignitaries as the President of France and the Queen of Denmark. Glassed-in cloisters overlook a wisteria-clad courtyard. Thick walls and smallish windows create interesting window seats in many of the guest rooms. Some furnishings date back to fifteenth century. Imaginative cuisine. 27 rooms; 1 suite.

Pousada D. Afonso II, Alcacer do Sal (south of Lisbon). Storks nest on poles just outside the entrance to this restored castle, which sits high above the Sado River. Guests enjoy fine views from their balconies of the countryside and red-roofed houses. Interesting mix of antiques and modern furnishings and artifacts. Beautiful gardens, pool, and archaeological museum on grounds. Very good restaurant. 31 rooms; 4 suites.

Pousadas

Locations: If you want to explore Portugal by car, to travel at your own pace, and experience a special place to stay and dine each evening, try plotting your itinerary through the countryside from pousada to pousada. Some are in or on the edge of town; others are in the middle of nowhere (or so it seems).

Romantic Highlights: Red-tile roofs and clusters of white houses in the green-clad moors glimpsed through rectangular spaces between the crenelated walls; huge silk-draped beds; fireplaces; gardens; history, history, history

Address/Phone: Avenida Santa Joana Princesa, 10A PT 1749–090 Lisbon, Portugal; 351–218442000; fax 351–218442085

E-mail: info@pousadas.pt or guest@pousadas.pt

Web Site: www.pousadas.pt

U.S. Reservations: Marketing Ahead (800) 223–1356

Owner/Manager: Enatur

Arrival/Departure: Most guests fly into Lisbon and rent a car.

Distance from Airports: Varies

Accommodations: 9 to 51 rooms and suites

Most Romantic Room/Suite: Some favorites: The Terrace Suite at Pousada de Evora, where jasmine winds over the wrought-iron balcony; a Tower Suite at Castelo Obidos; Room 108 at Pousada de Rainha Santa Isabel, a kingly room with a blue-and-gold canopy bed; Painter's Suite at the Pousada de D. Joao IV

Amenities: Hair dryer, telephone, radio, laundry service, toiletries; most have satellite TV; minibar, restaurants; some have air-conditioning, fireplaces, whirlpool tubs

Electricity: 220 volts

Sports and Facilities: Most have swimming pools and gardens

Dress Code: Casually smart

Weddings: Can be arranged

Rates/Packages: From $142 per room, including breakfast. Special interest packages available.

Payment/Credit Cards: Most major

Deposit: Guarantee with credit card

Government Taxes: Included

Service Charges: Included

Entry Requirements for U.S. Citizens: Passport

GLENEAGLES
Scotland

When it first opened, aristocrats and/or the hopelessly rich flocked to this venerable estate in the Scottish countryside. The golf courses quickly gained worldwide reputations as the finest in the realm. Today Gleneagles is a first-rate resort appealing particularly to those who love to be active, for there is a lot to do here on this sprawling property. With three championship golf courses plus the "Wee" nine-hole course, a full-blown equestrian center, tennis, falconry school, health club and spa, even an off-road driving school, plus a number of other sports and activities, those with an itch to see and do are sure to be blissfully happy.

The setting in the wild and wonderful heather-clad Perthshire hills is magnificent, a perfect venue for those who love to hike and ride and enjoy the outdoors. Shimmering lochs and rivers invite anglers to fish in the fresh, cool waters. Equestrians will find some of the most spectacular riding country in Europe at their doorstep, and a complete riding school with horses and instruction for every level and discipline.

Ever wanted to learn the fine art of falconry, one of the world's most aristocratic sports? At Gleneagles you'll find the British School of Falconry right on the grounds, where you can try handling and flying Harris hawks. Or what about popping a clay pigeon out of the sky? At Gleneagles' Shooting and Fishing School set smack on a grouse moor, you can learn how to master this unique sport.

Golfers can't help but love Gleneagles. Besides the original King's and Queen's Courses, there is the 2014 Ryder Cup venue PGA Centenary Course, an eighteen-hole layout designed by Jack Nicklaus opened in 1993. And for those who want to brush up on their game or even learn how to play, there is a superb golf academy. Tuition is included in some of the package plans.

Other activities are located at The Club. Here you'll find a pool, Jacuzzi, hot tubs, sauna, Turkish baths, gym, squash courts, snooker tables, croquet, bowls, pitch-and-putt course, tennis, and bicycles. All these things are free to Gleneagles guests. There is also The Spa, where you can enjoy a wide number of therapies and treatments such as aromatherapy and massages. Except for those on a special package, these treatments cost extra.

Lest you think Gleneagles is all about fun and games, there is more. Guests have a choice of five places to eat and drink including the Andrew Fairlie Gleneagles, The Strathearn, The Dormy Clubhouse Restaurant & Bar, The Bar, and The Club. You can choose from a wide assortment of cuisine ranging from Scottish specialties to Continental. Try grouse, salmon, kippers, scones and cream, and venison.

Rooms and suites are uniquely decorated with sensual fabrics and spacious bathrooms; comfortable upholstered chairs and sofas are covered in soft muted tones. You'll find highly polished wood tables and desks, brass lamps, leather stools, silk-lined walls, hand-woven carpets, and a few rooms have four-poster canopy beds. In the summer full-length French doors can be opened to let the fresh breezes in. For the colder months some suites have working fireplaces guaranteed to banish winter chills.

The new Whisky Suites blend the original furniture with classically contemporary features, such as lighting and bed heads with a subtle mix of silks, chenilles, and weaves to reflect the changing seasons of Scotland. Bathroom suites come with underfloor heating and feature a black-and-white tile design; some baths have free-standing tubs and walk-in showers.

Gleneagles' grounds are beautifully landscaped with gardens, trees, and lawns. Take your camera and walk or cycle along the paths or venture farther over the moors and hills. Ask the kitchen to pack a picnic for you and discover a special glade by a lake where you can have lunch.

In the summer, daylight hours are long and can last until 10:00 or 11:00 P.M., giving you plenty of time to explore the countryside where you can see hundreds of castles. For some local flavor, attend the local Highland Games or sheepdog trials. And remember, if you can tear yourself away for a day or two, Glasgow and Edinburgh are only an hour by car and well worth a visit.

Gleneagles

Location: On 850 acres north of Edinburgh in Perthshire, gateway to the Highlands, only an hour drive from Glasgow and Edinburgh

Romantic Highlights: Walks into the heather-covered hills; fireside cocktails after a brisk horseback ride; fireplace suites; serenade by bagpipers for newly married couples

Address/Phone: Auchterarder, Perthshire PH3 1NF, Scotland; 44–1764–662–231; fax 44–1764–662–134

E-mail: resort.sales@gleneagles.com

Web Site: www.gleneagles.com

U.S. Reservations: (866) 463–8734

Owner/Manager: Diageo plc, owner; Peter J. Lederer, CBE, managing director

Arrival/Departure: Arrangements can be made for private transfer to the hotel. Resort sales at Gleneagles will provide guests with a selection of private transfer options, starting from £100 (about $160). Gleneagles train station is 1 mile from the resort and all trains are met by the hotel's minibus (no charge).

Distance from Edinburgh Airport: 40 miles (under 1 hour); taxi or limousine can be arranged

Distance from Glasgow Airport: 55 miles (1 hour); taxi or limousine can be arranged

Distance from Perth or Stirling: approximately 20 miles

Accommodations: 269 rooms, including 16 suites

Most Romantic Room/Suite: Suites are ideal. The Royal Lochnagar is the best suite and costs a king's ransom (prices are available from resort sales upon request)

Amenities: Hair dryer, interactive TV with wireless keyboards and Internet access, minibar, toiletries, telephones, terry bathrobes, trouser press

Electricity: 220 volts; 110-volt adaptors available upon request in all rooms

Sports and Facilities: 4 tennis courts, 3 championship 18-hole golf courses, 1 9-hole course, riding, shooting, 2 squash courts, gym, falconry, fishing, mountain biking, spa, pool, snooker, jogging, off-road driving, hiking (it's a good idea to book sports activities such as golf when making reservation)

Dress Code: Smart casual

Weddings: Can be arranged; garden weddings are particularly lovely; bagpipers can be arranged to serenade newlyweds

Rates/Packages: General rates per room, per night including accommodations, full Scottish breakfast and VAT from £265 (about $503) for rooms; from £629 (about $1,195) for suites. Special Break packages available.

Payment/Credit Cards: Most major

Deposit: Guarantee with credit card

Government Taxes: Included

Service Charges: None

Entry Requirements for U.S. Citizens: Passport

THE WESTIN TURNBERRY RESORT & SPA
Scotland

For couples craving tees for two in a romantic setting, The Westin Turnberry Resort & Spa is perfect. From the craggy rock-strewn coast you can see the grand Edwardian country house, its distinctive red roof and gables standing along the crest of a hill, its white exterior glowing gold as the sun sets. Many come here to the Westin Turnberry Resort for the unrivaled golf experience on two of the world's most beautiful links courses. Indeed the views are breathtaking from the greens and fairways—the distant shore of Ireland, Ailsa Craig, the Isle of Arran, the sea, the lighthouse, the dunes. Magic.

Others come to enjoy the many outdoor activities available on the property, such as clay pigeon shooting, archery, horseback riding, off-road driving, tennis, and falconry, all available at the Outdoor Activity Center. For example, you can team up with your mate for the blind driver's obstacle course. One sits in the driver's seat and is blindfolded while the other gives verbal instructions to guide the blindfolded driver through a tricky course defined by orange cones. "Everyone does it differently," says the instructor, who also sits in the front seat ready to jump in if needed. "Turn right 20 degrees, turn left 5 degrees, now straight ahead," you say to help your mate drive the course. It's fun.

And if you are up for some more excitement, test your driving skills in a four-by-four off-road Jeep Cherokee, where you will be told to navigate over logs, through ruts at a 45-degree angle, and up to the hubcaps in a brook.

The heart of the property is the sprawling main hotel, which dates from 1906 when it opened as a social and sporting retreat for the British elite. Turnberry flourished during the golden age of the railroad, and was acquired by the Glasgow and South Western Railway. It was easily reached by train with guests arriving at a handsome station just minutes from the hotel.

During World Wars I and II, Turnberry was converted to an airfield. You can still see remnants of the runways peeking through the gorse on some of the fairways. In 1951, after a major redesign by MacKenzie Ross, the new Ailsa course emerged from the ravages of war, which had imposed concrete bunkers, runways, hangars, and utility buildings on the site, and the layout came to be recognized as one of the top 5 in Europe.

If exceptional links golf turns you on, you are in the right place. From the time you tee off, you may very likely have to deal with strong winds sweeping from the direction of Ailsa Craig. But as soon as you turn towards the sea after the third hole, the views will take your breath away. From the fourth hole to the eleventh, you follow the shoreline defined by dunes, grasses, and craggy rocks—with the lighthouse standing sentry on the edge. With carries over cavernous drops, shots through narrow gorse-protected openings, and impossible recoveries should you stray off course, the Ailsa is a beauty.

If there is a serious rival to the Ailsa, it is its sibling, Kintyre, opened in 2001 by Colin Montgomerie. With seven holes running along Bains Hills, a stretch of land extending along the Ayrshire coastline, from the elevated eighth to the eighteenth, you'll play one magnificent ocean-view hole after another. The par four, eighth hole facing head on to the sea is simply spectacular. Your caddie will tell you where to hit it, which is a good thing as you can't see the green nestled somewhere over a ridge below. Your second shot, typically a delicate wedge, flies down to the green. Go too far and you'll run off the back, where deep bunkers and nasty stuff awaits. This is definitely a pull-out-your-camera hole.

The Kintyre, with its tough pot bunkers, sweeping wetlands, and the narrow gorse-bordered fairways is unique in links layouts in that there are serious elevations, especially from the thirteenth tee. For golfing couples Turnberry, which is managed by Troon Golf, is a winner.

Near the clubhouse there is the Colin Montgomerie Links Golf Academy, an impressive facility with two indoor/outdoor teaching areas featuring GASP computerized digital videos, simulators, and swing analyzers; an open-air driving range; a short game pitching area; putting course; and the nine-hole par three and four Arran Academy course.

For those who love to be pampered, there is the Turnberry spa. It, too, commands stunning views of the sea. There are eleven treatment rooms, a fitness studio, and a large indoor pool with a waterfall and panoramic windows where you can relax in the chaises or soak in the Jacuzzi all the while enjoying the nonstop scenery. Several treatments and services are offered including hot stone therapy, Reiki, aromatherapy, hydrotherapy, holistic body care, and facials.

In addition to the rooms in the main hotel, there are more very comfortable rooms located in several lodges set in a village-like cluster at the base of the hill, just across from the golf courses. All guest rooms are fully equipped with all modern conveniences such as hair dryer, in-room safe, direct-dial phones, TVs, and Internet connections.

Enjoy classic Scottish specialties like filet of buccleuch beef Wellington or wild salmon in the Turnberry Restaurant overlooking the sea and golf course, or try the Tappie Torrie in the clubhouse, where the cuisine is remarkably gourmet. The Terrace Brasserie features spa cuisine.

Nearby explore Scotland's countryside. Visit the birthplace of Robert Burns, Culzean Castle, and the Isle of Arran, and stop at a local pub for a pint of Caledonia.

The Westin Turnberry Resort & Spa

Location: Nestled on 800 acres of Scotland's rugged southwest Ayrshire coast overlooking the Irish Sea

Romantic Highlights: Walks along the dunes; the plaintive sounds of bagpipers; views of the sea

Address/Phone: Ayrshire KA269LT, Scotland; 44–0–1655–331–000; fax 44–0–1655–331–706

E-mail: turnberry@westin.com

Web Site: www.westin.com/turnberry

U.S. Reservations: Westin Hotels (800) WESTIN–1

Owner/Manager: Starwood Hotels, owner; J. Stewart Selble, general manager

Arrival/Departure: Most arrive by private car or taxi; pickup can be arranged.

Distance from Glasgow Airport: 50 miles (one hour)

Accommodations: 221 rooms and suites

Most Romantic Room/Suite: Robbie Burns suite is Turnberry's most elegant and romantic room with a separate bedroom with heavenly king-size bed and large living room offering a full bar, dining table, and spacious balcony from which you can sip champagne while watching the glorious sunset over the Isle of Arran.

Amenities: Hair dryer, in-room safe, designer toiletries, bathrobes

Electricity: 220 volts

Sports and Facilities: Two championship golf courses, the Ailsa and Kintyre; the 9-hole (par 3/4) Arran Academy course; Cairngorms putting green; Culzean Pitch and Putt; the Colin Montgomerie Links Golf Academy; 2 tennis courts; spa with 78-foot pool, whirlpool, bio sauna; Outdoor Activity Center with archery, game fishing, shooting, horseback riding, off-road driving, quad biking, mountain biking, and falconry

Dress Code: Smart casual

Weddings: Yes

Rates/Packages: Romantic Getaway from about $240 per room, per night, including champagne, chocolates, and breakfast; golf and spa packages also available

Payment/Credit Cards: Most major

Deposit: By credit card

Government Taxes: Included

Service Charges: Not included

Entry Requirements for U.S. Citizens: Passport

BEAU-RIVAGE PALACE
Switzerland

You could not find a more romantic setting: a sparkling lake rimmed by dramatic snow-capped mountains, gardens, and Lausanne, both a beautiful town and sophisticated city with cobbled streets, a historic cathedral, and the headquarters of the International Olympic Committee. Since the mid-nineteenth century Lausanne has been a popular retreat for the discreetly wealthy and famous. Many came to stay at one of the finest hotels in Europe, the Beau-Rivage Palace.

Opening in 1857, this Belle Epoque hotel sits just high enough up the hill running from the shores of Lake Léman (Lake Geneva) to afford stunning views of the lake and the mountains, while providing an oasis of privacy from the busy lakefront just below. The exterior of the hotel is grand, its ornate balconies and terraces graced by bright yellow awnings, the domed conservatory tucked at the end of the formal gardens. Inspired by the neo-Baroque movement, the

Palace wing was added with its magnificent Art Nouveau elements in 1908.

The Beau-Rivage comes with an impressive pedigree—even the dogs have a history here. Walking along the garden path, I passed a little hill with small tablet-size plaques inscribed with names like "Toots 1940–57" and "Bouh Chan." This is the resort's dog cemetery, dating from the World War I–era when well-heeled people lived here for long periods and brought their pets with them.

Built when details like ornate Corinthian marble columns, coffered ceilings, inlaid marble floors, finely wrought lacey iron railing, and tall arched windows represented the height in elegance, no expense was spared. When the new Palace wing was added in 1908, Zurich artist Otto Heberer was commissioned to paint the exquisite Rotunda fresco and an artist from Paris was brought in to create the beautiful stained-glass windows that surround the hotel's main staircase.

The Beau-Rivage has none of the heaviness often found in properties of similar vintage. Rather the mood swings from whimsical to casual to burnished elegance. Colors are upbeat—gold, tangerine, lime, lemony yellow, sage. You may not be up for the approximately $5,000 per night for the Imperial Suite with its huge stone terrace, super-size Jacuzzi tub with gold fixtures, chandeliers, gilt mirrors, and silk tapestry upholstery (this was the suite booked by Phil Collins when he got married), but other rooms and suites—though on a much smaller scale—are just as well furnished and have the same views.

Sure, you'll have to forgo the gold fixtures on the tub, but you'll hardly notice; each room is a unique gem with incredibly comfortable beds, high-thread count linens, and all the amenities you could ask for, including push-button shades.

Start your day with freshly baked croissants, pastries, fresh fruit, and hot dishes, perhaps an omelet. From your table in Le Cafe Beau-Rivage, you'll have views of the lake, so you may wish to linger over your coffee. Just outside is the beach grill where teak slat tables and chairs are brightened with yellow and dark green print linens and white market umbrellas. Tables are set amidst the gardens and under flower-covered trellises.

The hotel's gourmet restaurant, La Rotonde, also with views of the water, was just awarded a Michelin star, so you can expect superb cuisine prepared by executive chef Didier Schneiter, who oversees a staff of more than fifty chefs. The wood-paneled English Bar is very clubby and rich in feeling with Oriental carpets, polished dark wood floors, and cozy tables and banquettes inviting you to enjoy an after-dinner cognac. The BaR offers another venue for sipping whiskies, beer, and wine and is more Art Nouveau in feeling with Tiffany lamps and sunny upbeat colors.

The cupola-topped Rotonde Room, which is often used for wedding receptions and other elegant functions, can take your breath away. With its superb frescoes, huge domed glass ceiling, soaring columns, ivory sculptures, chandeliers, and the bas-relief sculptures of classical figures and flowers, being here is like being inside an enormous Fabergé egg.

For quiet reading and relaxing, slip off to the Library, but take time to look up at the gold and ochre ceiling. It's wonderful. From here you are within walking distance of the Olympic Museum next door, and steps away from the small harbor and the flower-lined waterfront promenade, as well as the hotel's pier constructed on the lake shore in front of the property when the Beau-Rivage was built.

Nearby is plenty to see and discover. Stroll through the narrow cobbled streets of the old city; visit the Saturday morning market, the Olympic Museum, and the hilltop cathedral; drive to Montreaux stopping at the waterfront Chateau de Chillon castle. Or take a cruise on a sleek steam-powered hundred-year-old boat.

Beau-Rivage Palace

Location: Set in 10 acres of gardens on the shores of Lake Léman (Lake Geneva) in the resort town of Lausanne

Romantic Highlights: Balconies overlooking Lake Léman and the Swiss and French Alps; Jacuzzi tubs for two with views of the lake; dinner on the terrace

Address/Phone: Place du Port 17-19, CH-1000 Lausanne-Ouchy 6, Switzerland; 41–21–613–3333; fax 41–21–613–3334

E-mail: reservation@brp.ch

Web Site: www.brp.ch

U.S. Reservations: (800) 735–2478

Owner/Manager: Francois Dussart, general manager

Arrival/Departure: Limousine service from the airport can be arranged; the train station is 5 minutes away. The hotel has a fleet of Rolls Royces and a London-style taxi.

Distance from Geneva International Airport: 35 minutes

Distance from Zurich International Airport: 2 hours

Distance from Lausanne train station: 5 minutes

Accommodations: 169 rooms and suites, including 29 suites

Most Romantic Room/Suite: The junior suites with views of the lake and Jacuzzi tubs for two, especially the 7 top floor suites; the luxurious Imperial Suite with its enormous balcony is over-the-top luxury.

Amenities: Direct-dial phones, television, high-speed Internet access/modems, Wi-Fi, minibar, air-conditioning, bathrobes and slippers, turndown service, full-length mirror, hair dryer, fine toiletries, in-room safe, remote controlled lights and shades, special sockets for U.S. voltage, twice-daily maid service, whirlpool tubs in most rooms

Electricity: 220 volts

Sports and Facilities: New spa, gym, 2 tennis courts, indoor/outdoor pool, 15-mile walking path along lake, swimming. Golf and lake excursions can be arranged.

Dress Code: Casually elegant

Weddings: Yes

Rates/Packages: From about $400 per room, per night; suites from about $800

Payment/Credit Cards: Most major

Deposit: By credit card .

Government Taxes: Included

Service Charges: Included

Entry Requirement for U.S. Citizens: Passport

ASIA AND
THE PACIFIC

BEDARRA ISLAND
Australia

When you hear an Australian say, "Going troppo, mate," he or she could be heading to Bedarra Island, a sunny tropical bit of paradise located just off the northern coast of Queensland—Great Barrier Reef territory. For this cheery saying means you're going to a place guaranteed to provide lots of hot sun, sand, and sea. Bedarra offers all this and more—or less, depending on how you look at it. It's secluded; it's quiet. Very quiet. Here there are no schedules to follow and very little in the way of nightlife.

A white, sandy oasis in the middle of a brilliant turquoise sea, Bedarra Island is a small, intimate resort. Staying here is much like staying at the home of a wealthy relative who just happens to be out of town: Members of the staff are in attendance and have been told to do everything in their power to keep you happy. And they do!

At this sybaritic destination, besides being waited on, you're quite welcome to help yourself to anything you desire, at any time. If you want something special, all you have to do is ask. Caviar? They'll bring it. An omelet at three in the afternoon? They'll cook it. Want to go over to nearby Dunk Island for some action? They'll get the boat fired up. You just name it.

Your multilevel villa is yours alone. Crafted from native timbers, it sits on stilts amid lush gardens. Ceilings are high, with exposed beams; floors are made of highly polished wood. The bright, airy decor reflects the colors from outside. Linens are smooth and lovely; pillows are puffy, soft down. (If you want something different, just ask.) Towels are thick and thirsty and are changed often.

Each of the fifteen villas has a balcony, a good place to enjoy your welcome bottle of champagne while gazing out at the sea. Only a few steps from the beach, each villa comes with a king-size bed and a separate lounge area with CD stereo system, TV, video, and fully stocked complimentary minibar.

Since Bedarra is a very private island, you'll have no trouble finding innumerable places to be alone. Discover hidden coves; walk in the lush rain forest that flourishes alongside the beaches; or float side by side on rubber rafts. Swing gently in one of the hammocks slung between palms on the beach, or ask for a picnic hamper filled with delicious food and champagne to take with you to a secluded spot.

Although Bedarra's chefs find new ways to tempt you daily, they also make a point of asking if you have any personal requests. The open bar, which is available to you twenty-four hours a day, is stocked with domestic and imported beers, champagnes, fine vintage red and white wines, spirits, and liqueurs.

The restaurant, which is round and constructed of local woods, overlooks the gardens and turquoise lagoons, a perfect setting for that special romantic dinner. Enjoy the excellent cuisine and be sure to top it all off by indulging in a delectable Pavlova (a meringue dessert). There are only fourteen other couples at most, so if you're looking for a lively nightlife with lots of socializing, this might not be the place for you to come. If, however, a serene, beautiful natural setting and lots of pampering by an extremely competent and caring staff appeal, then Bedarra is worth the trip.

Bedarra Island

Location: On Bedarra Island, 3 miles off the tropical northern Queensland coast

Romantic Highlights: Very, very quiet private island; lovely beaches

Address/Phone: P.O. Box 1033, Bedarra Island via Townsville, Queensland, Australia 4810; 61–2–8296–8010; fax 61–2–9299–2103

E-mail: travel@voyages.com.au

Web Site: www.poresorts.com

U.S. Reservations: Voyages (800) 225–9849

Owner/Manager: Voyages, owner; Jackie McKeown, resort general manager

Arrival/Departure: Private resort launch transfer to and from Dunk Island airstrip

Distance from Dunk Island Airstrip: 15-minute launch ride

Distance from Cairns: About 108 miles from Cairns to Mission Beach, from there by launch or plane to Dunk Island, then by launch transfer to Bedarra Island

Accommodations: 16 private, two-level and split-level villas crafted from native timbers

Most Romantic Room/Suite: Villa Number 1 is the most secluded. The Point, with a large deck, private plunge pool, and spacious outdoor living area.

Amenities: Hair dryer, toiletries, air-conditioning, ceiling fans, ISD telephone, radio, ironing facilities, TV, VCR, bathrobes, CD stereo system

Electricity: 240 volts

Sports and Facilities: Tennis, use of motorized dinghies, island hiking, paddleskis, sailing, swimming, snorkeling, fishing, sailboarding. Guests may use sporting facilities at nearby Dunk Island, just 15 minutes away, at no extra charge.

Dress Code: Casual

Weddings: Can be arranged

Rates/Packages: All-inclusive rates, from AU$1,050 (US$784) per person per night, includes accommodations, 3 meals daily, open bar, snacks, tennis, water sports, and laundry. "Romantic Moments" package from AU$4,555 (US$3,404) includes 5 nights' villa accommodations, meals, open bar, massage, and transfers. Stay 7 nights and receive an 8th night free.

Payment/Credit Cards: Most major

Deposit: Credit card guarantee; no charge for cancellation made 30 days prior to arrival date; less than 30 days, a 1-night charge

Government Taxes: Included

Service Charges: None

Entry Requirements for U.S. Citizens: Passport

HAYMAN
Australia

Hayman, a long, low, sprawling property with reflecting pools filled with swans, tropical gardens, waterfalls, and palm-lined beaches, is designed for romance. The Great Barrier Reef is close by, but you may find it hard to tear yourself away from your Hayman Island paradise. Situated at the tip of the Whitsunday Islands, this luxurious 244-room resort is the only place on the 960 acres. And what a place!

It takes a bit of doing to get here, but it's worth it. First you have to get to Australia; then you can fly from Sydney, Brisbane, Cairns, or Townsville to Hamilton Island, where you board a sleek yacht for the hour-long cruise to Hayman. While onboard, you enjoy complimentary flutes of bubbly and get all the registration formalities out of the way so that you can head right to your room on arrival.

The resort, which stretches along a cove on the southern part of Hayman Island, fronts a beach. Some say the waters around this island offer some of the finest sailing in the world. Hayman, 3 miles in length and 2 miles wide, is shaped like a crescent with mountains running along its spine, punctuated by a tall peak standing 820 feet above sea level. The island is covered with a dense blanket of native eucalyptus trees, and the Australian bushland goes right to the edge of the white beaches. In 2002 Hayman completed an AU $30 million development program that included refurbishing the rooms and introducing new Palm, Pool, Beach, and East wings with new room categories.

All rooms, suites, and penthouses have either private balconies or terraces with views of the pools, lagoons, and beaches or gardens. Rooms are low-key but elegant, decorated in soft pastels, natural textures and rich woods that complement the tropical setting. All rooms come with large glass patio doors, white sliding louvers, handwoven rugs and dhurries, original paintings and sculpture, comfortable upholstered chairs and sofas, and lavish marble baths. The one-, two-, and three-bedroom penthouses on the top floor of the East Wing are each decorated in a different style, accented with a stunning selection of furnishings and objets d'art. You can choose from a variety of themes including Italian, Moroccan, Queensland, English, and French.

You don't have to be water-oriented to be enraptured by the dazzling freshwater pool floating in the midst of a huge saltwater lagoon—it's seven times larger than an Olympic pool. There is also an intimate pool surrounded by palms, tropical gardens, and fish ponds. Here you'll have as much privacy as you want. Wander through exotic gardens and along the beaches and never see another soul.

In addition to a full range of water sports facilities and five tennis courts, Hayman has an excellent health spa with full massage and beauty facilities, as well as computerized workout equipment, such as rowing machines, aerobicycles, and treadmills, along with spas, saunas, and steam rooms. Want to be pampered? Indulge in a Swedish or aromatherapy body massage.

Many things make Hayman an exceptional resort, but its proximity to the Great Barrier Reef really sets it apart. This incredible natural wonder is more than 1,200 miles long and is made up of 2,000 individual reefs and 71 coral-based islands. Snorkelers and scuba divers universally classify the reef as the ultimate underwater experience. The waters around Hayman churn with fish of all shapes and colors, and even for a rank novice it is a thrill to glide above and through their world. If you prefer to stay dry, you can opt for a glass-bottom boat ride or a helicopter or seaplane excursion, which will take you directly over the reef.

Hayman has its own marina and offers chartered fishing excursions aboard the *Sun Aura,* a 40-foot game-fishing boat. Since these waters offer some of the finest fishing in the world, you might get lucky and catch some dinner, which the Hayman chefs will be happy to prepare for you.

In all there are four restaurants, each one featuring its own unique fare. There is also an extensive wine cellar of more than 35,000 bottles. There is the Oriental, where you can try Moreton Bay "bugs," a cross between lobster and crab, served in an outstanding black bean sauce. The menu includes food selections from China, Malaysia, Thailand, and Japan. Fresh herbs from the resort's gardens are used in preparation of the meals. Hayman bakes its own breads and makes chocolates and ice creams. La Trattoria is a lively, informal, indoor/outdoor Italian bistro featuring pastas, salads, and antipastos at moderate prices. Azure, a dining venue fronting the beach, offers contemporary Australian-style dining specializing in fresh regional seafood prepared in an open kitchen and served inside or outdoors on an enlarged deck extending over the beach. The Beach Pavilion offers daily blackboard specials, barbecues, snacks, and drinks. And there is always room service, available at any hour. After dinner you can enjoy nightly performances by resident and guest artists.

Hayman's guests give the staff high marks for professionalism, friendliness, courtesy, and dedication. These, combined with an idyllic setting and superb facilities, add up to a top-notch honeymoon resort.

Hayman

Location: 20 miles from the Australian mainland, on 726 acres of one of the Whitsunday Islands

Romantic Highlights: Private dinners for two on beach or in tropical gardens; themed penthouses filled with antiques; island picnics and snorkeling on Bali Hai and Langford Reef

Address/Phone: Great Barrier Reef, QLD 4801, Australia; 61–7–4940–1234; fax 61–7–4940–1567

E-mail: reserve@hayman.com.au

Web Site: www.hayman.com.au

U.S. Reservations: Leading Hotels of the World, (800) 223–6800, (800) 4–HAYMAN

Owner/Manager: Mulpha Australia Limited, owners; Roger Wright, general manager

Arrival/Departure: Fly Jetstar, Qantas, Virgin Blue to Hamilton Island, where guests board one of Hayman's 3 luxury yachts for the hour-long trip to the island. A minibus will pick you up at the wharf for the 5-minute ride to the resort complex.

Distance from Hamilton Island Airport: 1 hour by boat plus 5 minutes by minibus

Distance from Hamilton Island: 25 miles (approximately 1 hour)

Accommodations: 244 rooms, including 11 penthouse and 1 beach villa

Most Romantic Room/Suite: Beach villa

Amenities: Air-conditioning, TV, Movielink, telephone, ceiling fan, minibar, in-room safe, refrigerator, tea/coffeemaker, hair dryer, toiletries, robe and slippers

Electricity: 240 volts

Sports and Facilities: Snorkeling, catamarans, sailboarding, paddle skiing; use of 5 tennis courts, golf target range, putting green; billiards, table tennis, badminton, and hiking. Scuba, fishing, and yacht trips can be arranged.

Dress Code: Casual during the day; casually elegant for dinner at the restaurants

Weddings: Exquisite setting for garden weddings

Rates/Packages: From AU $620 (US$476)

Payment/Credit Cards: Most major

Deposit: 1 night; cancellation 1 week prior to arrival for full refund

Government Taxes: 10 percent

Service Charges: Not included

Entry Requirements for U.S. Citizens: Passport

BORA BORA LAGOON
RESORT & SPA

French Polynesia

A full moon rises over Mt. Otemanu, the crenellated peak that inspired the legends of Bali Hai. The moon's rays shimmer on the glassy lagoon like a king's ransom of silver. This is the vision that awaits when you step onto your *lanai* (terrace) at the Bora Bora Lagoon Resort & Spa, an exclusive enclave set on a private isle off Bora Bora. Many consider Bora Bora to be the loveliest island in French Polynesia, with its mountaintops soaring heavenward like the skyline of an emerald city. Here a necklace of barrier reef is clasped around a perfectly blue, perfectly clear lagoon.

The resort is located on Motu Toopua, an islet in the lagoon that's just five minutes by boat from Bora Bora's main town, Vaitape. There are no roads, no electricity (the hotel uses generators), just twelve acres of tropical gardens and views of the mountains, reefs, and fields. After arriving by private launch at the hotel's long pier, you're taken to the main building, constructed of lava stone and bamboo, with local *aito* logs supporting the roof. Here you're welcomed with a lei and refreshing drink of coconut water.

You'll stay in Tahitian-style *farés* (bungalows, pronounced fa-RAY, Tahitian for "home"), with peaked roofs thatched with pandanus palm leaves. One wall is made up of louvered panels that you can slide open to the views and prevailing breezes. Each room offers a king-size bed and separate bath with a deep soaking tub and shower as well as a TV and DVD. The most romantic quarters are the over-water bungalows, built on stilts above the opalescent lagoon. A small stairway leads down to the water, so you can swim right from the deck.

Inside, the rooms reflect Polynesian chic, with tapa cloth hangings, coconut-shell inlays, and lovely floors of lustrous yucca wood streaked with a yellow and brown grain. Decorator fabrics come from French Polynesia. The most unusual piece of furniture is the glass coffee table: The top slides back so you can feed morsels of bread to the multicolored fish that gather below . . . an unusual twist on a "floor" show. The underwater spectacle is even illuminated at night!

The so-called beach bungalows are actually located in the gardens. Although they have the exact same decor as the over-water accommodations, they lack the magic of the sea-moored *farés*.

The rooms and facilities at the resort continue to be updated. The latest renovation took place in 2004.

The resort has two different restaurants, including the Otemanu Room for formal dining. Once a week the resort schedules a Tahitian feast, a Polynesian buffet, and a folkloric dance show.

Bora Bora Lagoon offers plenty of activities—and delicious ways of doing nothing at all. A quarter of a mile of white-sand beach stretches alongside the transparent waters, and there's a marvelous pool that flows right to the edge of the tiles—the largest swimming pool in French Polynesia. Practice your strokes on the two lighted tennis courts (racquets and balls are available if you didn't bring your own). At the fitness center you'll find exercise machines and free weights. Learn to paddle an outrigger canoe, or opt for a massage in your own room or at the spa facility. The new Marù Spa offers a variety of treatments and services.

Feel adventurous? You can also choose from a roster of intriguing excursions (which cost extra) each day. Tops on your list should be a four-wheel-drive expedition around Bora Bora. Dauntless Land Rovers crash through jungle, revving up steep, rocky, muddy, pothole-wracked tracks to some dynamite scenic overlooks. For thrill seekers there are the shark feeds. Wearing snorkel gear, you watch safely from the shallows as dive masters serve up chunks of raw fish to black-tip sharks, which circle just a jaw's breadth away. Other activities include helicopter tours and snorkel excursions.

Exciting as these excursions are, your most vivid memories will be of the spectacular scenery in Bora Bora.

Bora Bora Lagoon Resort & Spa

Location: Motu Toopua, a small, roadless coral island within the Bora Bora Lagoon

Romantic Highlights: Tahitian-style *farés* (bungalows) built on stilts right over the lagoon; private island setting; magnificent views of the Bora Bora mountainscape; unusual adventures like shark-feeding expeditions

Address/Phone: Motu Toopua; B.P. 175, Vaitape, Bora Bora, French Polynesia; 689–60–40–83; fax 689–60–40–01

E-mail: bblr@mail.pf

Web Site: www.boraboralagoon.com

U.S. Reservations: Orient Express Hotels, (800) 860–4095; Leading Hotels of the World, (800) 223–6800

Owner/Manager: Bernard Sarme, general manager

Arrival/Departure: At Bora Bora Airport, you are whisked to the resort across the lagoon on a private motor launch.

Distance from Bora Bora Airport: 15 minutes

Distance from Vaitape: 5 minutes by boat

Accommodations: 50 over-water bungalows (6 over water at end of pontoon); 18 beach bungalows; 5 garden lagoon bungalows; 3 suites and 1 presidential villa

Most Romantic Room/Suite: Over-water bungalows

Amenities: In-room safe, minibar, air-conditioning; electric ceiling fan, hair dryer, telephone, in-house video system, TV, double sinks

Electricity: 220 volts

Sports and Facilities: 2 tennis courts, Marù Spa, swimming pool, outrigger canoes, pedalboat, snorkeling, sailing, windsurfing, fitness center; deep-sea fishing, waterskiing, parasailing, jeep safaris, sunset sails, massages, sharkfeeding, and scuba diving can be arranged.

Dress Code: Tropically casual

Weddings: Can be arranged. (The ceremony however, is not legally recognized in the United States.)

Rates/Packages: $520–$770 per couple per night. Total Experience Package for 4 days/3 nights, $3,200 per couple, includes accommodations in an over-water bungalow, American breakfast and lunch daily, dinner for two, shark-feeding excursion, 4-wheel drive excursion, parasailing, half-day rental in a FunCar, transfers, and use of tennis courts, fitness room, and nonmotorized watersports

Payment/Credit Cards: Most major

Deposit: Guarantee with credit card

Government Taxes: 11 percent

Service Charges: Included

Entry Requirements for U.S. Citizens: Passport and outbound ticket; if you're staying more than 1 month, you may need a visa.

HOTEL BORA BORA
French Polynesia

Remember those pictures of thatched huts perched on stilts over turquoise blue water? This is it. Bora Bora, the Grace Kelly of islands, flawlessly beautiful. Home to Hotel Bora Bora, a member of the prestigious Amanresorts group, this South Seas paradise appeals to sophisticates willing to go the extra mile to experience the exotic.

As your plane zooms in on this small island (only 4 miles long and 2½ miles wide), you'll spot palm-thatched bungalows half hidden in the greenery. Crystalline waters in blues, greens, and turquoise swirl around the white-fringed shoreline. Green volcanic peaks that run like a spine down the middle of the island soar toward the brilliant blue sky.

When you arrive, take off your watch, lie back, and soak in the scenery and seamless service. Many of those on the Polynesian staff have been working at the resort for over twenty years and truly know how to anticipate whatever it is you need.

Constructed of cedar, the individual bungalows and *farés* are spread over grounds that have had more than thirty years to grow lush and lovely. All have hand-tied, thatched pandanus (palm) roofs, private bars, radio/cassette players, and roomy tiled baths with freestanding, oval, wood-rimmed tubs and separate showers. Deluxe bungalows are located on the beach and have separate lounges and sundecks with steps leading to the water. Superior bungalows are also located on the beachfront and come with a small patio facing the sea and a hammock nearby. Bungalows have patios and are set in the gardens.

For the most fun opt for one of the bungalows over the water. Some are in the shallow lagoon waters; others are situated on a coral reef in a deeper section of the lagoon. Each of the over-water bungalows features an enormous room more than 750 square feet; a king-size, four-poster bed swathed in mosquito netting; sliding glass doors leading out to a deck with a pandanus shade overhang; and steps to a small platform, where you can sit on the edge and dangle your feet in the water. Floor-to-ceiling louvered panels allow the sea breezes to slide in, and you have a generous-size sitting area and dressing area with loads of storage space.

Farés, which are located on the beach and in the gardens, are very roomy and come with a living room; a bedroom with a king-size, four-poster bed; an en suite sitting room; a bathroom; and a large sundeck. Eight *farés*—very spacious, with 1,200 square feet—have private swimming pools enclosed in courtyards furnished with cedar lounges and comfortable cotton cushions; three have outdoor Jacuzzis set into sundecks.

You can eat at the Matira Terrace restaurant overlooking the lagoon or at the Pofai Beach Bar. Both have lofty thatched roofs and are open on all sides to great views and cooling sea breezes. By the time you realize that your dinner and drink tab is heading skyward like the volcanoes, you really won't care much; but be prepared. Meals are not included in the rates (unless you get the Honeymoon package, which gives you some breaks). Entrees can range from $15 upward; a reasonable bottle of wine, $35 and up.

You are entertained nightly by local musicians; a Tahitian dance show is held twice a week.

Many of the activities center on the water: picnics to deserted islands, outrigger canoe rides, sunset cruises, and sailing. You'll find the snorkeling very good just off-shore—the fish will eat bread right out of your hand. If you want to explore the colorful underwater world farther out, you can take one of the reef trips.

There is a scuba diving program for all levels of divers. Beginners can take a resort course or go all the way to certification. There are also catamaran sails, fishing excursions, deep-sea and saltwater fly-fishing, moonlight horseback riding, helicopter tours, island tours, jeep excursions, shark-feeding expeditions, and a library with enough books to fill any extra hours you may have.

A special package combines three nights in a *faré* at Hotel Bora Bora and a private yacht charter for three nights with full crew service aboard *Tara Vana,* a 50-foot cata-maran.

If you want to experience something really wild, for about $300 you can take part in the Polynesian Ceremony, a senti-mental marriage ceremony performed by a Polynesian group leader at sunset. At the lagoon's edge on the main beach, the site is decorated in the Polynesian style and the ritual accompanied by dancers and musicians. Flower crowns and leis crafted from native gardenias are offered and the couple is presented with a *tapa* cloth certificate at the end of the ceremony.

Hotel Bora Bora is restrained, in harmony with its graceful surroundings and the gentle, graceful people who live and work here. It will take you very little time to shrug off the jet lag, sink your toes in the sand, and get into the rhythm of a world that moves at a pace you can absorb.

Hotel Bora Bora

Location: On the southwestern coast of the island of Bora Bora, 160 miles northwest of Tahiti in the Leeward Society Islands

Romantic Highlights: Over-water thatched bungalows; king-size beds covered with clouds of gauzy net

Address/Phone: Point Raititi, Bora Bora, French Polynesia; 689–60–44–60; fax 689–60–44–66

E-mail: hotelborabora@amanresorts.com

Web Site: www.amanresorts.com

U.S. Reservations: Toll free (800) 477–9180; reservations@amanresorts.com

Owner/Manager: Amanresorts International Pte. Ltd; owner; Martial Thevenaz, manager

Arrival/Departure: Transfers from Bora Bora Airport are complimentary; VIP airport express services available on request

Distance from Bora Bora Airport: / minutes; flying time between Tahiti and Bora Bora is 45 minutes

Distance from Vaitape: 3⁷⁄₁₀ miles

Accommodations: 54 Polynesian-style bungalows and *farés* set amid the gardens, on the beach, or over the lagoon

Most Romantic Room/Suite: Over-water bungalows numbers 118 to 128 or a *faré* with in-deck Jacuzzi or private pool

Amenities: Ceiling fans, hair dryer, minibar, safe, telephone (optional), bathrobes, and slippers

Electricity: 110/220 volts

Sports and Facilities: 2 tennis courts, snorkeling, outrigger paddles and sailing, canoes, billiards, table tennis, basketball, and volleyball; optional activities include jeep excursions, glass-bottom boat tours, sunset cruises, reef trips, deep-sea fishing, scuba diving, shark feeding, and sailing and hiking excursions

Dress Code: Casually chic

Weddings: Can be arranged, but the marriage may not be legally recognized in the United States

Rates/Packages: From $700–$1,000 per couple, per night; Honeymoon package for approximately $2,900 per couple includes 3 nights' accommodations transfers, special in-room bed-of-flowers decoration, fruit and French champagne, 3 a la carte breakfasts, 1 candlelight dinner with wine served on the terrace of your *fare* or bungalow, sunset cruise, and an hour body treatment for two

Payment/Credit Cards: Most major

Deposit: Guarantee with credit card; 14 days notice (30 days in high season) must be given for any cancellations.

Government Taxes: 11 percent; tourist tax $1.50 per person, per day

Service Charges: Not included; not encouraged

Entry Requirements for U.S. Citizens: Passport and outbound ticket; if you're staying more than 1 month, you may need a visa.

AMANWANA
Indonesia

Ever thought of spending your honeymoon in a tent on some exotic, almost deserted South Pacific island? If so, then Amanwana, on the island of Moyo in Indonesia, may be your ticket to romance. There are only about 2,000 inhabitants on the entire 120-square-mile bit of land, and it's not exactly easy to reach. You need to get to Bali, take a plane and then a boat, and after about two hours you should finally be pulling up to the jetty of the Amanwana resort. You'll have to look hard to see anything, for this little spot of heaven has been carefully placed in this dense, junglelike forest—no trees were cut down during its construction, and all the work was done by hand.

Amanwana, which means "peaceful forest," is part of the upscale Amanresorts group, which has created unique, very special small vacation places in harmony with nature. Amanwana, in the resort company's hideaway category, is like going camping and having your cake, too. Its clever design combines the sense of camping in the wild with the luxuries of modern-day conveniences such as air-conditioning, king-size beds, and double tile vanities.

Set on an island that is a wildlife reserve, the spacious tented rooms are more luxurious than many resort hotel accommodations. The canvas ceiling swoops to a peak in the center of the room over the bed, which is enveloped in an umbrella of filmy netting falling from a high round crown. The canvas, which extends over an outside veranda, is actually roped and pegged to the ground. Here the similarity between this accommodation and the tent you slept in at summer camp ends. The floor of your room is polished teak; there is a generous sitting area with two corner sofas covered in a natural, off-white fabric, and there are practical, well-designed, but simple tables and chairs as well as a desk.

Three sides of the tent are windows with off-white, cotton accordion shades, and there are beautiful straw mats on the floors. Original native sculpture, tapestries, and paintings decorate the off-white walls. The bathrooms are really an unexpected pleasure, boasting double vanities, beautiful twin mirrors in teakwood frames, teak louvered windows, a shower and toilet, plus baskets containing toiletries on the shelf. And the rooms are air-conditioned as well as cooled by ceiling fans.

The tents are randomly linked by paths that lead to the beach, the reception area, and the dining pavilion. Located in a bungalow, the reception area has a library stocked with lots of books, and the decor is pure Indonesian, with hand-hewn wooden tables and stools and original wall hangings, carvings, and paintings.

The open-air pavilion, where you find the bar, restaurant, and lounge, is located under a soaring ceiling of woven bamboo. Views are of the sea; food is basic, fresh, and good with choices from both Western and Asian cultures; and dinner is by candlelight. In fact, since the lighting tends to be less than bright even in your rooms, you'll find the mood can readily be called seductive anywhere you are in camp after the sun goes down.

There is a teak sundeck perched on the edge of the shoreline with coral steps leading to the water. Lounges, which are sturdy and constructed of wood and have upholstered cushions, provide a great inducement for those who want to lie back and relax in the sun. You can also have a private dinner on the deck or on the beach.

Activities are centered on the crystal-clear turquoise sea and the land. A guided trek into the tropical forest takes you to a beautiful inland waterfall, where you can swim in the pools created by the cascading waters. Walk under the wide tamarind, banyan, and native teak trees; catch a glimpse of monkeys, deer, and wild boar.

Or head out to sea for a late-afternoon sail and see the sun go down over the Flores Sea. Amanwana also has a fleet of nine vessels, including an outrigger canoe that can take you on a cruise of the area, stopping for a picnic on the beach along the way.

Scuba enthusiasts will love it here. The island is ringed with a wonderful coral reef, and a number of interesting dive sites are accessible right from the front of the camp as well as by boat. A Scuba Diving Certificate course is $295, excluding tax. Other instruction is also available.

Keep in mind that the rainy season is from December to March; the rest of the year is pretty dry.

For a real South Pacific experience, you might try combining a stay at Amanwana with two or three nights at one or more of the other Amanresorts. (Please see description of Amanpuri in this chapter.)

Amanwana

Location: On island of Moyo, east of Lombok and Bali

Romantic Highlights: A hideaway close to nature; luxury tented "villas"

Address/Phone: Moyo Island, West Sumbawa Regency, Indonesia; 62–371–22233; fax 62–371–22288

E-mail: amanwana@amanresorts.com

Web Site: www.amanresorts.com

U.S. Reservations: Toll free (800) 477–9180; reservations@amanresorts.com

Owner/Manager: Amanresorts International Pte. Ltd.

Arrival/Departure: Most transfers to Amanwana from Bali are in a Cessna Caravan amphibian. The state-of-the-art 8-passenger floatplane lands on the bay directly in front of the resort. Flying time is 65 minutes and guests need to arrive at the airport in Denpasar just 30 minutes before the flight. Round-trip transfers are $550 per person.

Distance from Denpasar Airport: About 3 hours total travel time from door to door

Accommodations: 20 luxury tents with king-size beds and en suite bathrooms

Most Romantic Room/Suite: Open-front tents closest to the shoreline

Amenities: Hair dryer, toiletries, air-conditioning, ceiling fans, mosquito netting, twin vanities, minibar, veranda

Electricity: 220 volts

Sports and Facilities: Trekking excursions, boating, snorkeling, cruise excursions, sports fishing, jungle cove massage; freshwater dipping pool; scuba diving can be arranged

Dress Code: Casually smart

Weddings: Can be arranged

Rates/Packages: $650–$750 per tent, per couple includes all meals, water sports, and nonalcoholic beverages. Supplement of $75 per person, per night includes all meals, non-motorized water sports, non-alcoholic beverages, and laundry.

Payment/Credit Cards: Most major

Deposit: Guarantee with credit card deposit within 7 days of acknowledgment from the Bali Central Reservations Office; should a reservation be canceled within 7 days of arrival date or in the event of a no-show, the first night's charge along with transfer costs will be charged to the credit card or deducted from the prepayment.

Government Taxes: 11 percent room tax

Service Charges: 10 percent

Entry Requirements for U.S. Citizens: Passport or round-trip airline tickets.

Closed: January 15–March 15

Note: It is recommended that you start taking antimalaria medication (e.g., doxycycline) before you arrive.

AMANPURI
Thailand

In Sanskrit *Amanpuri* means "place of peace." It is. No discos, no slot machines, no traffic noise. Amanpuri, the first of twelve intimate Amanresorts, is a haven from the fast-paced world many of us live in. Once here you'll have plenty of time to unwind and soak in the tranquillity and beauty of Amanpuri. In fact, doing nothing in an exotic place is exactly what many come here for.

One thing for sure: You'll know you're in Thailand when you arrive in Amanpuri. Most of what has been built here has been created out of local materials made by local craftspeople.

The main roof of the Grand Sala, the centerpiece of Amanpuri, soars to 40 feet. Its multiple, pitched roofs and columns are reflected in the rectangular pool, which is filled to the brim with the clearest of water. The Grand Sala, simply yet elegantly decorated with live orchids and antique furniture, is where you are greeted when you arrive at Amanpuri. At that time a manager is assigned to look after you for the duration of your stay.

Built on three levels into the trees and tropical foliage of a former coconut plantation, forty pavilions are spread out over twenty acres. They stand on stilts linked by elevated walkways. The design of the resort is refined, with guest pavilions and the Grand Sala integrated into a harmonious whole. Steep-pitched roofs curve to a sharp peak—like Buddhist temples—and buildings are constructed of wood accented by earthy, red-hued trim.

You'll find a well-equipped gym with treatment rooms where you can be pampered with massages, facials, and other soothing delights. The Grand Sala, a huge open-air reception area with a lounge and pool, is on the second level.

A lot of natural materials such as bamboo, stone, and teak are used throughout the resort. You'll find caned chairs, baskets, stone walls, and teak floors.

Pavilions are very spacious, containing 1,200 square feet including the bedroom, dressing area, bath and shower, outdoor sala (sitting area), and sundeck. Each bedroom is quietly elegant. Decor doesn't jump out and hit you with a resounding "wow!" Rather it seduces with creamy, white walls; floor-to-ceiling decorative wood panels; fiber rugs; carved furniture; soft, handwoven cottons and silks; pottery; plants; and Thai sculpture. Bathrooms are enormous, designed for two; closets have enough drawers to hold an entire winter wardrobe.

Although some rooms have good ocean views, most are located in the dense palm groves overlooking the gardens. When Amanpuri was built, the integrity of the land was respected.

The Terrace Restaurant features fresh seafood and Continental and Thai specialties daily; and surprise, there is also an Italian restaurant where you can dine by candlelight on the veranda overlooking the sea. Musicians will serenade you as the moon rises over the water. Service is seamless, gracious. If you prefer a quiet party for two in your pavilion, you can call on room service any hour.

You'll find a wide range of water sports activities on the beach, including sailing, sailboarding, Hobie-Cats, and snorkeling. Amanpuri has an excellent marina and maintains more than twenty yachts, available for charter. Pack a picnic, your snorkeling gear, and flippers, and explore some of the neighboring islands and bays close to the resort. Or climb aboard a restored classic Chinese junk for a sunset cruise.

Want to see some of the wonderful life beneath the sea? Check out the H2O Sportz operation, a full-service PADI facility geared to scuba divers of all abilities. The resort course will give you a basic introduction to diving; for the more advanced and certified divers, there are trips to a number of world-class dive sites for exploring underwater caves and crevices as well as coral reefs and walls.

The resort has a library with a collection of more than 1,000 books and a gift shop where you can purchase a variety of Asian artifacts, including jewelry, textiles, pottery, and small sculptures.

It's a long way to this part of the world, so consider seeing both Thailand and Indonesia. Stay at Amanpuri in Thailand and Amanwana in Indonesia, a luxury "tented" island resort on the tiny island of Moyo, near Bali. Both are members of the Amanresorts group.

Amanpuri

Location: On the island of Phuket, off the southern coast of Thailand

Romantic Highlights: Private treetop pavilions; serene island retreat

Address/Phone: Pansea Beach, Phuket

Island, Thailand; 66–76–324–333; fax
66–76–324–100

E-mail: amanpuri@amanresorts.com

Web Site: www.amanresorts.com

U.S. Reservations: Toll free (800)
477–9180; reservations@amanresorts.com

Owner/Manager: Amanresorts International
Pte. Ltd.

Arrival/Departure: Complimentary transfers
provided from Phuket Airport; frequent air
service from Bangkok daily (1-hour flight)

Distance from Phuket Airport: 12 miles (20
minutes)

Distance from Phuket Town: 10 miles

Accommodations: 40 pavilions, each with
its own outdoor *sala* (sitting area); also 30
guest villa homes, with two-, three, or four-
bedrooms, each with a black-tiled pool and
separate dining room and living room. A
live-in maid and cook attend to all guest
needs.

Most Romantic Room/Suite: Numbers 103
and 105, with ocean views

Amenities: Hair dryer, toiletries, air-conditioning, ceiling fans, mosquito netting, twin
vanities, minibar/refrigerator, sundeck, in-
room safe, stereo cassette system, 24-hour
room service

Electricity: 220 volts

Sports and Facilities: 2 lighted tennis
courts, pool, gym, Aman Spa, beach club,
sailing, sailboarding, snorkeling, waterskiing, deep-sea fishing, scuba diving; golf
nearby; island cruises

Dress Code: Casually smart

Weddings: Can be arranged

Rates/Packages: Pavilions, $675–$1,550
per room, per night; villa homes,
$1,800–$7,350 per couple per night,
including transfers

Payment/Credit Cards: Most major

Deposit: Guarantee with credit card at time
of reservation; for refund, 14 days' notice
(30 days in high season) must be given; in
the event of a no-show; the first 2 nights'
charge along with transfer costs will be
charged to the credit card or deducted from
the prepayment.

Government Taxes: Approximately 18.75
percent

Entry Requirements for U.S. Citizens: Passport that is valid for duration of stay and
ongoing or round-trip airline tickets.

Note: It is recommended that you start taking antimalaria medication (e.g., doxycycline) before you arrive.

AFRICA

LA MAMOUNIA
Morocco

Wide, palm-lined boulevards lead into the blush-pink city of Marrakech, one of Morocco's romantic, seductive cities. Known as the garden city, several acres of land are planted with flowers, trees, and shrubs. Snake charmers, jugglers, acrobats, and vendors perform for change in the sprawling Place Djemaa el-Fna, the central square located adjacent to the twisting alleyways of the souks. Several camels stay cool in groves of olive trees on the edge of town.

Those looking for an exotic, luxurious, private oasis amidst all the hubbub can check into the legendary Moroccan palace, La Mamounia, where guests lounge around lovely pools and fountains, lush landscaping, and garden courtyards.

You will experience an explosion of bounty for the senses: Lie back in your teak pool chair and soak up the fragrance of rosemary, highly scented rose bushes, herbs, and night-blooming jasmine while the sound of water soothes the soul. Gently waving palms and brilliant hibiscus and bougainvillea tumbling over the walls please the eye.

La Mamounia, which opened in 1922, derives its name from the gardens, known three centuries ago as "Arset el Mamoun" and named for Prince Moulay Mamoun, son of Sultan Sidi Mohamed Ben Abdellah, ruler of Marrakech in the eighteenth century.

The gardens, covering nearly twenty acres, are filled with lush foliage and flowering plants, including lemon trees, jacarandas, palms, roses, mimosas, acanthus, bamboo, guava, yucca, and banana trees. There are many interesting birds here as well: storks, turtledoves, goldfinch, chaffinch, yellowhammers, warblers, spotted flycatchers, nightingales, wagtails, and bulbuls. Thirty-four full-time gardeners maintain this remarkable landscape, transferring 140,000 new plants into the soil each year.

Inside, polished marble floors, flowers floating in pools, large urns, arches, pierced metal lighting fixtures, intricate Moorish-style artwork, and exquisite mosaics all lend elegance. Le Patio Andalou is defined by arches and ornate columns and a covered arcade.

There are five places to eat and drink. Le Marocain, with sunny banquettes, mosaic floors, Moroccan chandeliers, and a profusion of mosaic decorations, offers traditional cuisine: a colorful kaleidoscope of exotic foods flavored with pungent spices, tagines (food cooked in tent-like clay dishes), and mint tea. Typical dishes include tagine of pigeon with almonds; couscous with beef, chickpeas, and raisins; pigeon pastilla (a mixture of pigeon, sugar, almonds, and spices topped by a light flaky pastry); lamb mechoui; and a kebab of marinated lamb with onions and tomatoes. Popular fish items include sea bream, monkfish, and John Dory. Moroccan pastries, often made with almonds, and honey, are very sweet. There is a nightly show featuring an Andalusian band and belly dancers.

With a decor that evokes the famous ocean liner the *Normandie,* the Marrakech l'Imperiale is the resort's gourmet restaurant, and it features creative Continental cuisine leaning toward French. L'Orangerie provides "bourgeoise" cooking (unpretentious French dishes) in an informal setting on the large terrace near the gardens and pool. Located in the nightclub, l'Italien features Venetian-inspired dishes, and Les Trois Palmiers serves grilled meats and fish, salads, and desserts by the pool, buffet-style.

When you want to toast your love, you have five bars to choose from: the Churchill Piano Bar, a seductively dark hideaway illuminated by dramatic stained-glass panels and set with comfortable leather seating that feels a bit like an English Club; Le Bar du Soleil, recalling the 1930s with views of the gardens and pool; Le Bar des Trois Palmiers, the poolside bar; Le Bar du Squash; and Le Bar du Club de la Mamounia, a disco and bar. There is also Le Grand Casino with 129 slot machines and eighteen game tables. The lovely pool is surrounded by tall palms including a couple planted in a small "island" in the corner of the pool. Chaises surround the pool.

Massages, sauna, and a Turkish bath are available in the Beauty Center.

Think Arabian Nights in your elaborate bedroom, which reflects the mystery of Morocco with Moroccan-designed fabrics, tassels, sweeping drapery, and French doors opening to balconies. La Suite Marocaine with its columns, mosaics, and arches is indeed elaborate and alluring. Baths are decorated with beautiful patterned tiles. Especially intriguing are the seven themed suites including the Orient Expres, the Menzeh, and the Baldaquin.

Part of the fun in Morocco is shopping in the souks (markets). Although aggressive, the merchants are not, for the most part, obtrusive and even if you walk away buying nothing, they will say goodbye with a smile. But they do love to bargain and if you have plenty of time, you can obtain dramatic discounts from the original price.

You can spend hours shopping for woodware, leather products, brass, lamps, jewelry, carpets, spices, dates, slippers (both the pointy Arabic shoes and the round-toed Berber shoes), clothing, fabric, and other goods.

While Morocco is a land with an intact culture dating back thousands of years, you will still see incursions of the twenty-first century. Those wearing the traditional burnouses (cloaks) or hajibs (head coverings) are seen side-by-side with others smartly dressed in Armani suits and designer shoes. Streets are swept by people using brooms handmade from grasses as well as modern cleaning equipment.

Well worth visiting is the Dar Si Said Museum palace, which is filled with Moroccan art, jewelry, artifacts, furniture, carpets, fashions, and magnificent ornamentation.

La Mamounia

Location: Set amidst idyllic gardens that are almost three hundred years old and surrounded by the city's twelfth-century ochre-colored ramparts

Romantic Highlights: Exotic gardens; seductive rooms decorated with a mixture of traditional Moroccan and Art Deco decor; dinner on your private balcony

Address/Phone: Avenue Bab Jdid, Marrakech, Morocco; 212–44–44–44–09; fax 212–444–4940/44 46 60 or 212–44–44–49–40

E-mail: resa@mamounia.com

Web Site: www.lhw.com

U.S. Reservations: (800) 223–6800

Owner/Manager: The Moroccan National Railroad Company, Société La Mamounia, owners; Robert Jean Berge, managing director

Arrival/Departure: The hotel sends a car/van to pick guests up from the airport

Distance from Marrakech Menara Airport: 2.4 miles

Distance from Casablanca: 2½ hours

Accommodations: 171 rooms, 57 suites, 7 theme rooms, 3 villas

Most Romantic Room/Suite: Themed suites

Amenities: Direct-dial phones, television, minibar, air-conditioning, terry robes, turn-down service, full-length mirror, hair dryer, fine toiletries, in-room safe; 24-hour room service

Electricity: 220 volts

Sports and Facilities: Pool, tennis, squash, fitness center, whirlpool, boule games area, Ping-Pong, French billiards, the Mamounia Club Casino. Nearby is an 18-hole golf course.

Dress Code: Coat and tie required for dinner in Marrakech l'Imperiale. Casually elegant in other restaurants.

Weddings: Yes

Rates/Packages: From about $255 (converted from Moroccan dirham); honeymoon packages and other packages available

Payment/Credit Cards: Most major

Deposit: By credit card

Government Taxes: Included

Service Charges: Included

CAPE GRACE
South Africa

You couldn't ask for a better location. Overlooking the international yacht basin on Cape Town's Victoria and Alfred Waterfront, Cape Grace is within walking distance of the aquarium and all the shops, craft stalls, restaurants, and other attractions.

After only three years, Cape Grace was voted "Best Hotel in the World" by *Condé Nast Traveler* Readers' Choice 2000 and was the hotel of choice when President Clinton came to Cape Town during his presidency. Its rooms may not be the largest I have ever experienced, its appointments the most spectacular, or the facilities over the top, still the overall package is one of perfection.

From the seamless service to the terry slippers placed on a white cloth on the floor in the perfect position for you to slip into

them while sitting on your bed, Cape Grace doesn't miss a beat. The reception/guest liaison people speak several languages including Axhosa, Norwegian, and Swedish; the scones are set out for afternoon tea; and you are even offered complimentary shoeshines. (The only remotely nitpickable thing I could find was that the elevators were a tad slow.)

Rooms are quietly yet elegantly appointed. Traditional furniture, floral prints along with rich tapestry fabrics, Oriental carpets, upholstered stools and benches, Cape art, and fresh flowers create a soothing yet uplifting haven after a day of sight-seeing. Some rooms have balconies and all have French doors overlooking either the harbor or Table Mountain, which looms in the background. From my room, I got a close-up view of the marina, the yachts, fishing boats, and the complex of attractive waterfront buildings.

The baths are spacious with enclosed toilet areas, double vanities, and walk-in closets. Each room has a sitting area and there is a desk with a strip of converter plugs that accommodates most countries' personal appliances.

Tea is served throughout the afternoon in the library on the waterfront terrace at a cost of about $5.00. You'll agree it's the bargain of the century when you see the full table of goodies such as salmon sandwiches, fresh fruit, jams, pastries, tarts and other tasty items. Forget your book? The library shelves are well stocked with a variety of interesting reading materials.

Bascule, a cozy, intimate bar with the air of a private yacht with its brass-rimmed round "porthole" wall designs, is carved into the man-made quay around the pool. Come here often and you can have your own wine bin with an engraved name plaque.

Here you can relax in large comfortable chairs accented with piles of pillows, and sip a cocktail. The bar stocks more than 420 whiskies and the wine cellar is filled with top South African selections as well as wines from other parts of the world. Each evening at six guests are invited to come to hear about the history and local viniculture of the Western Cape and to sample South African wines.

One Waterfront Restaurant, with its high windows opening onto the gardens and pool and natural color palette, is effectively decorated in a clean minimalist style. Large contemporary urns sit on top of a divider between the bar area and the dining room, which is furnished with smart upholstered chairs, contemporary art, and graceful iron chandeliers. A glass conservatory overlooks the pool and gardens. In

the evening this unpretentious restaurant turns divinely elegant with candles and soft lights. At breakfast fresh fruits of all kinds, hot dishes, rolls, breads, meats, cheeses, cereals, yogurts, jams, jellies, and fresh-squeezed juices create a feast for the eyes as well as appetite.

The Spa at Cape Grace offers a variety of spa services including aromatherapy massage, deep-tissue sports massage, reflexology, and Swedish massage as well as manicures and pedicures. The Spa is located on the top floor with a sauna, steam room, and mineral spa bath. There is also an outdoor heated pool surrounded by a tiled terrace furnished with cushioned chaises.

Cape Town is a wonderful place to start a romantic trip in South Africa and with the U.S. dollar so strong against the Rand, South Africa is a good value. Dinner with drinks at Cape Grace or one of the best restaurants in town can cost less than $25 per person.

Nestled at the base of Table Mountain on a peninsula on the southwestern coast of the country, Cape Town has gardens, tree-shaded streets with Victorian houses, museums, a seventeenth-century castle, and a newly renovated waterfront with a two-story shopping mall, the Two Oceans Aquarium, craft markets, and more than seventy eateries including outdoor cafes and entertainment areas.

Running through the historic center of the city, the wide pedestrian walkway known as Company Gardens is banked by African flame trees, agapanthus, cycads, palms, birds-of-paradise, and huge beds of other flowering plants that create a long green oasis.

Highlights of a Cape Town trip include the Jewish Museum, a ride to the top of Table Mountain for sweeping views of the city and the Atlantic, a tour of Robben

Island and the prison where Nelson Mandela was incarcerated for more than eighteen years, and excursions into the wine country.

You can drive south along the coast to Cape Peninsula National Park, a natural reserve containing a rich variety of flora and fauna dotted by cushions of white everlasting, more than 270 species of ericas (heathers), and hundreds of proteas that thrive in this open windswept land.

If you want to push the envelope, you can go base jumping—skydiving off a cliff or other fixed object; kite-surfing (the steady Cape winds can lift you 30 feet into the air off the waves at Blouberg Strand); hiking into Suicide Gorge; and rock climbing.

Farther south on the Boulders Beach in Simons Town, more than 3,000 tidy penguins play in the waves and line up on the beach often standing in pairs.

Cape Grace

Location: On Cape Town's Victoria and Alfred Waterfront surrounded by water on three sides

Romantic Highlights: Views of the waterfront and Table Mountain; in-room bubbly treatment; massages for two

Address/Phone: West Quay Road, Victoria and Alfred Waterfront, Cape Town, South Africa; 27–21–410–7100; fax 27–21–419–7622

E-mail: reservations@capegrace.com

Web Site: www.capegrace.com

U.S. Reservations: Leading Hotels of the World (800) 223–6800

Owner/Manager: Meikles Africa, owner; Tony Romer-Lee, general manager

Arrival/Departure: Most arrive by air at Cape Town International Airport. Transfers can be arranged.

Distance from Cape Town International Airport: About 20 minutes

Distance from Cape Town: In town

Accommodations: 81 king/twin bed luxury rooms; 10 superior rooms with balconies; 18 loft rooms; 10 suites; 2 penthouses

Most Romantic Room/Suite: #420 with views of the harbor as well as Table Mountain from the side patio. The loft suites also provide excellent views of the mountains and water.

Amenities: Satellite TV with Internet facilities, hair dryer, air-conditioning, minibar, in-room safe, tea/coffee service, radio, robes and slippers, free shoeshines, Charlotte Rhys toiletries, fax/Internet modem lines, stocked mini-delis, high-speed Internet in suites, 24-hour room service, transfer service, and wine tastings

Electricity: 220 volts

Sports and Facilities: Pool, Spa at Cape Grace, gym equipment in room on request, access to nearby Virgin Active health club

Dress Code: Resort casual

Weddings: Can be arranged

Rates/Packages: Approximately $563–$1,375 per room including breakfast and VAT; penthouse suite, $1,487–$1,858

Payment/Credit Cards: Most major

Deposit: By credit card

Government Taxes: Included 14 percent

Service Charges: About $4.00 per room per night.

Entry Requirements for U.S. Citizens: Passport and return or onward ticket required

GRANDE ROCHE
South Africa

Your first view of the Grande Roche is the long terrace that runs along the front of this immaculate, white-washed, Dutch Cape manor house. Sitting here in the fresh air for breakfast or a glass of a splendid Cape wine, you can drink in the magnificent vistas of the vineyards spreading over the gardens out to the mountains. This beautifully restored eighteenth-century manor house is not only the centerpiece of a thriving vineyard, but an intimate hotel and fine restaurant.

As in many buildings in the region, Grande Roche, a member of the prestigious Relais & Châteaux group, with its distinctive scalloped gables and design, showcases the influence of the early French Huguenot settlers. Inside, drapes, crystal chandeliers, mirrors, and black marble columns reflect a French influence. Leading out from the main house in the back, two historic, long, thatched buildings, the former wine cellars and the slave quarters, frame either side of a central courtyard. There are five two-story suites in the Wine Cellar, five in the Slave Quarter.

Other rooms are located in three separate one-story buildings containing the Terrace Suites. These have vine-covered terraces that overlook the valley or vineyards. Because of the exuberant growth of the flowers and shrubs, many of the terraces are very private.

Each suite is different. In most cases there are sitting rooms downstairs; upstairs there are bedrooms and baths, some with high, pitched thatched ceilings. If you open your window when morning breaks, you may hear the gentle cooing of doves.

I loved the thatch: Lying in bed you could look up to the reeds and grasses that were bound to the ridge poles in the traditional way. It smelled good, too. Other rooms have ceilings of hand-hewn timbers. Floors are white tile or wood covered with area carpets. Some rooms are decorated in themes such as the Bonsai Terrace suite, which has Oriental-style furniture and a large wall mural of bamboo.

Baths connect to rooms with frosted glass doors. Double vanities, separate bathtubs and showers, heated towel racks, radio, and telephone bump up the luxury level.

Dining in the elegant Bosman's Restaurant in the main house, is a superb experience. A Relais Gourmand restaurant, Bosman's specializes in gourmet cuisine using local fish, game, produce, and herbs. The manager, Horst W. Frehse, a wine connoisseur, takes great pride in his wine cellar, which contains more than 300 wines.

Bosman's international cuisine includes items such as breast of quail with celeriac and truffle jus, marsala-flavored crayfish with black tagliatelle, feta cheese-encrusted karoo lamb loin with tomato couscous, grilled vegetables and rosemary jus, and ice apricot parfait with baked blueberry samosa. Wines might include Fairview Viognier 2000, Landau du Val Semillon Reserve 2000, or Bellingham Spitz Pinotage 1997. An intimate dining venue seating sixteen is located in the former manor house kitchen. There is also the Tarantella Bar open for drinks and pub meals. Light meals and drinks are served on the sunny patio.

Tucked into the courtyard gardens, the pool and terrace are perfect for a late afternoon drink and swim. The Kraal pool adjacent to the fitness area offers another heated swimming and lounging venue and is more private.

The Grande Roche is ideally situated for exploring the many vineyards and small villages found in the valley. For a special adventure, I'd suggest you take an early morning hot air balloon and drift over the countryside. It is really quite beautiful.

Grande Roche

Location: Amidst a vineyard in fertile Paarl Valley just 45 minutes from Cape Town.

Romantic Highlights: Cooing doves; terraces overlooking vineyards and valleys; cottages with thatched roofs

Address/Phone: PO Box 6038, Plantasie Street, 7622 Paarl, South Africa; 27–21–863–2727; fax 27–21–863–2220

E-mail: reserve@granderoche.co.za

Web Site: www.granderoche.com

U.S. Reservations: Contact the hotel directly or Relais & Château (800) 735–2478. For a complete tour of the wine country and Southern Africa, contact Karell's African Dream Vacations (800) 327–0373; Web site: www.karell.com; or Tim Farell: safaritim@aol.com

Owner/Manager: Horst W. Frehse, general manager

Arrival/Departure: Most arrive by car; transfers available

Distance from Cape Town International Airport: 30 minutes

Distance from Cape Town: 45 minutes

Accommodations: 34 rooms and suites

Most Romantic Room/Suite: Honeymoon "Stable" Suite located in a separate building at the end of the rear courtyard. It has a private roof terrace, king-size bed, double shower, and Jacuzzi. Also the 1-story

thatched suites: "Dauphine" at the end of a block of terrace suites, with a view of the vineyards; and "Bamboo," furnished with Oriental accents.

Amenities: Air-conditioning, minibar, radio, TV, DVD/CD players, telephone, heated towel rails, double vanities, robes, radio in the bathroom, tea and coffee service, fax facility (optional), 24-hour room service, valet service, gift shop, e-center

Electricity: 210/220 volts

Sports and Facilities: 2 pools (one heated), 2 floodlit tennis courts, hiking trails, fitness center with sauna, steambath and fitness equipment, massage therapist, bicycles, horseback riding, and on-site chapel. Hot air ballooning, fishing, squash, and golf nearby (Paarl Golf Club and Paarl Valley Golf Club—a Jack Nicklaus course)

Dress Code: Casually smart

Weddings: Weddings can be held in the historic "Slave Chapel," which seats just 8 people. A Wedding Package priced at Rand 10,730 (US$1,021) includes 2 nights' accommodations in the Honeymoon "Stable" Suite, a champagne breakfast, buffet breakfast, massages, services of a hairdresser, organist, flowers, cake, and dinner.

Rates/Packages: Per room rates from Rand 1,300–2,630 (US$216–$438) low season; Rand 1,800–3,680 (US$300–$613) high season; 3-night Romance Package from Rand 7,221 (US$1,203) per person

Payment/Credit Cards: Most major

Deposit: By credit card

Government Taxes: Included (except 1 percent tourism levy)

Service Charges: Not included

Entry Requirements for U.S. Citizens: Passport

Closed: Mid-May–July

MALAMALA
South Africa

Rattray Reserves, which owns MalaMala, a vast game reserve, operates two camps. Where you stay depends on your budget and what you are looking for in the way of a safari experience. You can't really go wrong whichever place you stay.

On a knoll overlooking the Sand River, MalaMala features spacious thatched-roof cottages overlooking the Sand River. Rooms are beautifully furnished with king-size beds or side-by-side twins, soft carpets, African art, rattan chairs and headboards, and spacious bathrooms. Large French doors open onto terraces and most rooms have two baths, dressing areas, and closets.

Guests at MalaMala enjoy flexibility when it comes to how long the game drives last and when the drives take off. The lodge, a spacious airy room with high-beamed ceilings, extends out to a large deck, a perfect place to watch the wildlife below.

The Sable Camp is an efficiently run operation with an excellent staff. The difference in price is reflected in the size of the rooms and appointments as well as the range of flexibility and services.

But this does not mean that quality is compromised. All camps have infinity pools, *bomas,* a viewing terrace, bar, and lounge and share the MalaMala game-viewing ground, and all rangers are superbly trained and highly competent. Perhaps Norman Pieters of Karell's Africa Dream Vacations summed it up best when he said, "The animals don't know what you're paying when they decide to show up."

At MalaMala it's all about game. Your wake-up call comes about 5:30 A.M. After a cup of tea or coffee in the lodge, you climb into an open Land Rover and, with a ranger-driver and armed tracker aboard, head into the bush for a magic morning of game viewing. You may see a mother cheetah sitting under a tree with her four cubs, or you may pick up the trail of a lioness loping along, her tail swaying back and forth. You'll get close to giraffes and elephants, warthogs, kudu, and waterbucks. Later, back at the lodge, you'll feast on a lavish breakfast.

Afternoons at camp are spent as the animals spend them: leisurely. You can take a nap, swim in the pool, or sip a cool drink under the shade of a tree.

Night drives begin in late afternoon after tea while the sun is still hot, but beware: Once the sun goes down, it may cool off rapidly. Bring a jacket.

Often it's a matter of tracking animals wherever they go. Each drive brings new discoveries. On my recent visit, in order to keep abreast of a mother leopard as she led her two cubs to dinner (a baby impala she had killed earlier and hidden under a tree), our amazingly skillful driver/ranger kept the cats always in sight. We plunged through the bushes, crossed a sand-bedded stream, and ducked under thorn acacias.

As evening turned into night, our ranger kept up with the determined cats who seemed totally oblivious to the sound of our vehicle. We were told that the leopards were so used to the noises of the vehicles, we were for now part of their world and fortunately not a member of their food chain.

Our tracker played a spotlight on the trio as they silently walked through the bush. Finally the mother sat down as her son prowled around looking for the hidden catch. When he found it, he dragged it into a thicket and began his meal.

Back at the lodge the meals are served in an air-conditioned dining room or outside in the *boma,* a traditional South African open-air gathering spot. You sit in a large circle with everyone facing a log fire blazing in the center of the area. Your meal includes beautifully prepared fresh local fruits and vegetables and game meats such as venison and impala.

Each MalaMala camp has a cozy bar where people gather in the evenings after the game drives to compare their sightings. It's always a challenge to see if you qualify for the prestigious "Big Five Club"—spotting lion, leopard, rhino, elephant, and buffalo.

MalaMala's rangers are highly trained and qualified; all have university degrees in areas like ecology or zoology; and all have an intimate understanding of animals and their relationship to their environment.

During a two-night, three-day safari trip, you'll have time for four game drives and one or two game walks. For a more leisurely pace, stay three nights.

I would suggest you roll your safari experience into a two-week South Africa trip visiting Cape Town, the wine and garden regions, and Bushman's Kloof, an area where you can see 10,000-year-old Bushman rock drawings. You can also combine a safari in South Africa with game viewing in a Botswana tented camp. Karell's African Dream Vacations, specialists in this part of the world, can arrange travel to South Africa as well as Botswana, Zimbabwe, Namibia, and Zambia.

The romance of MalaMala is a heady concoction of exotic safari experiences; warm, knowledgeable people; exceptional accommodations; and brilliant African skies.

MalaMala

Location: MalaMala Game Reserve, a private, 33,000-acre game reserve adjacent to Kruger National Park, in the northeastern part of the country

Romantic Highlights: Moonlight safaris; thatched rondavels overlooking Sand River

Address/Phone: MalaMala Game Reserve, P.O. Box 55514, Northlands 2116, South Africa; 27–11–442–2267; fax 27–11–442–2318; fax to camp 27–13–735–9300

E-mail: reservations@malamala.com

Web Site: www.malamala.com

U.S. Reservations: Tim Farrell & Associates, P.O. Box 3029, Westport, CT 06880; (203) 762–8050; safaritim@aol.com. For a full southern Africa program including a safari to MalaMala, contact: Karell's African Dream Vacations, (800) 327–0373; Web site: www.karell.com.

Owner/Manager: Michael Rattray, C.E.O./managing director; Tom Bloy, camp manager

Arrival/Departure: MalaMala offers daily direct flights on SA Airline (a division of SAA) from Johannesburg into the MalaMala airfield where you will be met by rangers from MalaMala Camp.

Distance from MalaMala Airfield: 5 minutes

Accommodations: MalaMala Camp, 18 luxury rooms (including suites); a disabled unit, and family rooms; Sable Camp, 7 luxury suites

Most Romantic Room/Suite: Suites, #12, #17, and #19

Amenities: Air-conditioning, ceiling fans, and electric shaver plug, *New York Times* fax daily, laundry service, hair dryer

Electricity: 220 volts

Sports and Facilities: Wild game viewing, swimming pool, guided bush walks, walking safaris

Dress Code: Bushveld casual; during winter (May to September) very warm clothes, including a windbreaker, are essential.

Weddings: Can be arranged

Rates/Packages: MalaMala Camp from about $500 per person; Sable Camp from $750. Includes accommodations, meals, game drives, walking safaris, laundry, transfers, and VAT.

Payment/Credit Cards: Most major

Deposit: 50 percent deposit required to secure accommodations; balance due 30 days prior to arrival.

Government Taxes: Room tax, Rand 5.70 (US 54 cents) per person per night

Service Charges: Included in daily rate

Entry Requirements for U.S. Citizens: Passport and return or onward ticket required. Check whether visa is necessary.

SHAMWARI
South Africa

For the ultimate African adventure, head to Shamwari Game Reserve, a 49,000-acre private game reserve located near Cape Town. Here you'll have your choice of six luxury lodges, some thatched, some former manor houses. Shamwari's guests have no doubt about being in the African bush yet have all the luxuries you can imagine. Sunrooms, private plunge pools, wellness spas, luxury linens, air-conditioning—you get the picture.

It is at Lobengula Lodge that Tiger Woods popped the question to Swedish beauty Elin Nordegren, while Brad Pitt and John Travolta unpacked their safari gear and cameras at Eagles Crag Lodge. I stayed at Riverdene, where from the pool deck I could look out on a landscape dotted by acacia trees spreading out to the horizon and the hills. Ranch-style rooms were decorated with African artwork, print fabrics, and natural sands, browns, and chocolate hues, which reinforced the African beat. We dined outside on the covered patio near the pool, enjoying delicious traditional foods like bobotie (a sort of savory bread custard with lots of ground lamb, curry, fruit, and nuts), baked yams, and freshly baked breads.

Shamwari, which means "friend" in the Shona (African) language, encompasses a rich landscape of plant and animal life. A hundred years ago this area was one of the richest games areas on the Continent, yet over the years most of the animal life had been exterminated by hunters and encroaching civilization. It is only since 1990 that a huge effort was launched by Mantis' founder Adrian Gardiner to bring back these animals and birds. Gardiner and his partner, Dr. Gaston Savoi, bought the land from nineteen farmers, rejuvenated the region, reintroduced pairs and groups of animals, and built the safari camps. Highly committed to conservation, several hundred acres have been declared a true wilderness and are thus protected. Although walking safaris are allowed, vehicles are not.

With sweeping vistas from hilltops and endless plains reaching to the horizon, Shamwari is a wonderful place to discover the wild side of Africa. And since it is in a malaria-free zone, there is no need to take medication. Where you stay will depend on your tastes and budget. Long Lee Manor, built in 1910, is a splendid Edwardian Manor House with sixteen rooms and two suites, two pools, a columned patio, and colonial, somewhat formal-style furnishings. Meals are served in the main dining room or around the open fire in the restored barn.

Set in a secluded valley, the ethnically decorated Lobengula Lodge affords a more traditional experience with five thatched rooms and the Chief suite, which comes with a spacious private lounge with fireplace. From your king bed, you look up at the high-peaked timbers and thatch of your ceiling. Baths are very large with double vanities, and there is a pool and pool bar, wellness center/spa, and a magnificent wooden deck overlooking the bush.

The intimate Bushmans River Lodge has just four deluxe rooms, a thatched game viewing deck, pool, and thatched *boma* (outdoor enclosed area). Riverdene Lodge is a restored settlers lodge with nine lovely suites, a stunning infinity pool, outdoor barbecue area, and African-inspired decor.

For the tented experience stay at Bayethe, where nine permanent luxury tents on stilts are set along the river. But these sturdy accommodations are no ordinary tents. Each is air-conditioned and has an outdoor shower, private plunge pool, and viewing deck. Meals, cocktails, and social gatherings take place in the stone-walled and thatch-roofed lodge.

Eagles Crag Lodge, nestled in a valley, is at the top of the luxury scale with nine rooms with private decks and pools, indoor and outdoor showers, wall-to-wall glass doors on two sides, and a spa. The decor is light, contemporary with four-poster beds and uninterrupted views of the bushveld. There is a dining area, library lounge, and cocktail bar, all with high sweeping thatched roofs.

The highlight of a stay in a safari lodge is, of course, the game drives and safari walks, which take place when the animals are most active: the early morning, late afternoon, and sometimes at night. You'll track game in rugged open Land Rover safari vehicles which run over brush like World War II tanks. The rest of the day, you can chill out at the lodge pool or in the gardens. At Shamwari the game rangers are superb: personable, knowledgeable, amazing drivers.

It is still dark when you are awakened. You quickly throw on your khakis and walking boots, mist up with Backwoods Cutter, and grab your cameras. The sun is just rising as you meet your guide to begin your game drive. In the next two hours, you'll see a variety of birds and animals, perhaps even catch a glimpse of the elusive wild dogs or eland. You'll see impala grazing under acacia trees and perky warthogs scurrying into the underbrush. Giraffes gaze intently in your direction before loping away, followed by herds of zebra.

Land Rovers take you off road, giving you a close-up view of the animals. You sit motionless as a herd of elephants, mostly females, some with youngsters, start across your path. You hardly breathe as a bull elephant brushes his trunk on the front of your Rover's grill, flapping his ears before turning to continue on his way.

A mother elephant silently glides into the bushes, trailed by her baby as cute as a

Teletubby. Antelopes, waterbucks, buffalo, and wildebeests dash across the landscape. You come upon a pride of lions, full and lazy from having just finished eating their most recent catch. One of the females rolls over on her back and goes to sleep, legs straight up in the air; a male with a full mane lolls nearby.

At night, you snuggle up a bit closer as sounds invade your territory: the steady chomp, chomp of hippos munching their way to a nearby lake; the cacophony of tree frogs; the occasional cry of an animal, perhaps a lion or elephant. You feel vulnerable, but you have been assured by rangers that you are safe. Finally you both drift off to sleep.

When to go: Since South Africa's climate is the reverse of ours, expect midsummer in December and January but in Cape Town and the southernmost part of the Western Cape, winters are quite mild and Durban and KwaZulu-natal coastal areas enjoy a sub-tropical climate with sunshine year-round.

Shamwari

Location: In the Eastern Cape, a malaria-free zone along Bushmanos River

Romantic Highlights: Sundowners in the bush; African-themed rooms with king beds; the thrill of getting up close to lions, giraffes, and other game; dining under the stars

Address/Phone: P.O. Box 113, Swartkops, Port Elizabeth, 6210, South Africa; 042–203–1111; fax 042–235–1224

E-mail: reservations@shamwari.com

Web Site: www.shamwari.com; www.mantis collection.com

U.S. Reservations: (877) 354–2213

Owner/Manager: Adrian Gardiner and Dr.

Gaston Savoi, Mantis Collection

Arrival/Departure: Transfers can be arranged from Port Elizabeth Airport or you can drive. There is also a private landing strip at Long Lee.

Distance from Port Elizabeth Airport: 50 minutes drive

Distance from Port Elizabeth: About 40 miles

Accommodations: Six lodges: Long Lee Manor, 16 rooms, 2 suites; Lobengula Lodge, 5 suites, 1 Chief suite; Bushmans River Lodge, 4 rooms; Riverdene Lodge, 9 suites; Bayethe, 9 luxury tents; Eagles Crag, 9 rooms

Most Romantic Room/Suite: This depends on what you are looking for. Thatched, tented, luxury lodge, manor house?

Amenities: Air-conditioning, hair dryer, robes and slippers, designer toiletries, luxury linens, international direct dial from all rooms, wine cellar at I ogenbula and Eagles Crag and gift shops at all lodges

Sports/Facilities: Fitness center, sauna, massages, steam room

Dress Code: Casual

Weddings: Can be arranged

Rates/Packages: Including accommodations, meals, most activities, and alcoholic beverages: $370–$870 per person, per night; Long Lee Manor $390–$735; Lobengula Lodge $800–$870; Bushmans River Lodge $390–$655; Riverdene Lodge $390–$655; Bayethe $370–$655; Eagles Crag $800

Credit Cards: Most major

Deposit: Guaranteed with credit card

Government Taxes: Most included

Service Charges: Not included

Entry Requirements for U.S. Citizens: Passport

INDEXES

Alphabetical Index

Resorts with Golf on Premises
(Many other resorts offer golf nearby)

Sea/Lakeside Resorts

Resorts with Fireplaces

Le Manoir aux Quat' Saisons, 179
Longueville House, 195
Manor on Golden Pond, The, 62
Mirbeau Inn & Spa, 71
Post Ranch Inn, 20
Snake River Lodge & Spa, 91
Sonnenalp Resort of Vail, 24
Woodstock Inn & Resort, 83

Resorts with Horseback Riding

Ahwahnee, The, 9
Amangani, 88
Auberge du Soleil, 11
Boulders, The, 2
Fairmont Banff Springs, The, 94
Fairmont Jasper Park Lodge, The, 98
Gleneagles, 204
Grand Roche, 231
Greenbrier, The, 86
Hotel Hana-Maui and Honua Spa, 41
Hyatt Regency Scottsdale Resort, 6
Hyatt Regency Tamaya Resort and Spa, 64
La Casa Que Canta, 166
Maroma Resort & Spa, 160
Sandals, 113, 132–33, 146–47
Snake River Lodge & Spa, 91
Westin Turnberry Resort & Spa, The, 106
Woodstock Inn & Resort, 83

Resorts with Tennis

Amanpuri, 222
Anse Chastanet, 141
Auberge du Soleil, 11
Beau-Rivage Palace, 208
Bedarra Island, 212
Bora Bora Lagoon Resort & Spa, 216
Boulders, The, 2
Cambridge Beaches, 115
Camelback Inn, 4
Caneel Bay, 155
Cap Juluca, 104
Chatham Bars Inn, 52
Curtain Bluff, 106

Disney's Grand Floridian Resort & Spa, 28
Equinox Resort & Spa, The, 79
Fairmont Banff Springs, The, 94
Fairmont Jasper Park Lodge, The, 98
Four Seasons Biltmore, 16
Four Seasons Resort Maui at Wailea, 36
Four Seasons Resort Nevis, 135
Grande Roche, 231
Gleneagles, 204
Greenbrier, The, 86
Grove, The, 174
Grove Park Inn Resort & Spa, The, 77
Half Moon, 129
Hayman, 213
Hartwell House, 176
Hotel Bora Bora, 218
Hotel de Mougins, 187
Hotel Guanahani & Spa, 139
Hotel Hana-Maui and Honua Spa, 41
Hotel Schloss Fuschl, 171
Hotel Villa del Sol, 164
Hyatt Regency Scottsdale Resort, 6
Hyatt Regency Tamaya Resort and Spa, 64
Jumby Bay Resort, 108
Laluna, 128
La Mamounia, 226
Kona Village Resort, 44
Little Dix Bay, 123
Manele Bay Hotel, The, 46
Le Manoir aux Quat' Saisons, 179
Mauna Lani Bay Hotel and Bungalows, 48
One&Only Ocean Club, 111
Peter Island Resort and Yacht Harbour, 125
Rancho Valencia, 22
Reefs, The, 118
Ritz-Carlton, Cancun, The, 162
Sandals, 113, 132–33, 146–47
Villa d'Este, 199
Wauwinet, The, 54
Westin Turnberry Resort & Spa, The, 206
Windjammer Landing Villa Beach Resort &
    Spa, 148
Winnetu Inn & Resort, The, 57
Woodstock Inn & Resort, 83

Resorts with Area Skiing

In-City Hotels

Adventure/Safari Lodges & Resorts

Resorts with Private Pools

ABOUT THE AUTHOR

KATHARINE D. DYSON is a freelance travel writer who specializes in romantic getaways. For this book her work has taken her around the world. Her articles have appeared in many print and online publications, including *Bride & Groom, Endless Vacations, Robb Report,* AmericasBride.com, *Cooking Light, Altitudes, GolfStyles, Links, Divot,* the *Boston Herald,* and others. She is a member of the Society of American Travel Writers and Golf Writers Association of America, and a romantic travel advisor for *Redbook* magazine and Match.com.

For further information log onto the author's Web site at www.honeymoonsaway.com.